Journeys Towards Progress

Journeys Towards Progress

Essays of a Geographer
on Development and Change
in Oceania

Ray Watters

Editor: Ginny Sullivan

Victoria University Press

VICTORIA UNIVERSITY PRESS
Victoria University of Wellington
PO Box 600 Wellington
victoria.ac.nz/vup

National Library of New Zealand Cataloguing-in-Publication Data

Watters, R. F. (Raymond Frederick)
Journeys towards progress : essays of a geographer on
development and change in Oceania / Ray Watters.
Includes bibliographical references and index.
ISBN 978-0-86473-596-6
1. Oceania—Economic conditions. 2. Oceania—Social
conditions. I. Title.
330.995—dc 22

Printed by Printlink, Wellington

Contents

Maps

Tables

Figures

Photographs

Cover: The village of Atuo near Ablingi on the south coast, West New Britain, PNG, 1982. (Chris Tyrell)

Between pages 96 and 97

1. Nalotawa, a relatively traditional village in the Dry Zone, Ba Province, Western Viti Levu, Fiji, c.1960. (R.F. Watters)

2. Jone Lotawa and his wife Rebeka and other members of his extended family in Nalotawa, Viti Levu, Fiji, 1958. (R.F. Watters)

3. A Fiji Indian tenant farmer with his working bullock, western Dry Zone, Viti Levu, c.1960. (Rob Wright)

4. A typical Fiji Indian general store, western Viti Levu, Fiji, c.1960. (R.F. Watters)

5. A view from the air of shifting cultivation – trees recently felled to make a new garden. West Guadalcanal, Solomon Islands, 1969. (R.F. Watters)

6. Kariatebike, the Government Station, Abemama, Kiribati. Petrol drums and fish drying on a pandanus mat to the left, a pandanus tree to the right, 1972. (R.F. Watters)

7. A house on Abemama, Kiribati. In the foreground, fish is drying in the sun, middle distance right a pig forages for scraps. In the house a woman uses a hand-powered sewing machine. (R.F. Watters)

8. The traditional ceremonial starchy root *babai* (*cyrtosperma chamissonis*) growing in a *babai* pit. Pandanus baskets packed with the best leaf litter float in the fresh water lens above the lower salt water. North Tarawa, 1982. (Ginny Sullivan)

9. Left: A man with his tobacco makes a point in recounting traditional stories, Tarawa, 1982. Right: A woman telling traditional stories, Tarawa, 1982. (Ginny Sullivan)

10. A man and his wife return in their outrigger canoe after fishing in the lagoon, Abemama, Kiribati, 1972. (R.F. Watters)

11. A typical bridge crossing a reef channel in North Tarawa, 1982. (Ginny Sullivan)

12. A villager puts out his copra to dry in the sun near his house. Small breadfruit tree right centre. Tamana, southern Kiribati, 1972. (Roger Lawrence)

Between pages 192 and 193

13. Erosion resulting from deforestation in the hilly interior of western Viti Levu, Fiji, 1983. (D. Leslie)

14. Somalani from the sea, showing typical overcrowding of small islands, Kove society, north coast of West New Britain, PNG. (Ann Chowning)

15. A relatively large, missionised village on the coast, Arawe, south-west West New Britain, PNG, 1982. (R.F. Watters)

16. A typical small hamlet in the great forest, Gimi Rauto, southern West New Britain, PNG, 1982. (R.F. Watters)

17. Taro growing in a new garden: shifting cultivation in Gimi Rauto. Note fence on left to keep out wild pigs. West New Britain, PNG, 1982. (R.F. Watters)

18. Men making holes to plant taro in a new garden, Dulago, Sengseng society of Passismanua, West New Britain, PNG. (Ann Chowning)

19. View from the gardens. Taro growing in an area of limestone, Seuk, Sengseng, Passismanua, West New Britain, PNG. (Ann Chowning)

20. Burning after felling. A garden of shifting cultivators. Gimi Rauto, near Kandrian, West New Britain, PNG, 1982. (R.F. Watters)

21. Girl playing bamboo flute, Dulago, Sengseng society, Passismanua, West New Britain, PNG. (Ann Chowning)

22. Trying to persuade man in the middle to accept pearl shells, Dulago, Sengseng society, Passismanua, West New Britain, PNG. (Ann Chowning)

23. Woman attending ceremony draped with wealth in shell money, Somalani, Kove society, north coast of West New Britain, PNG. (Ann Chowning)

24. Trader in full traditional regalia, Dulago, Sengseng society, Passismanua, West New Britain, PNG. (Ann Chowning)

Preface

As Ray Watters' first PhD student I am honoured by this opportunity to write the preface to this collection of his essays on Oceania. The collection is an extended reflection on a large section of his life's work but certainly not all the work he produced in a career that includes a marvellous collection of historical geography essays *Land and Society in New Zealand* (1965), a widely quoted and respected book on Latin America entitled *Poverty and Peasantry in Peru's Southern Andes, 1963–90* (1994) and an edited collection on *Asia-Pacific: New Geographies of the Pacific Rim* (1997) in which he shared editing responsibilities with Terry McGee and Ginny Sullivan. This is only a half of it; there are the reports too numerous to list here on such diverse topics as shifting cultivation in the Amazon (FAO), a World Food Programme project in Guizhou, P.R. China, the challenges to rural development in what was then the British Solomon Islands Protectorate, and so the list could go on.

The omissions are as worthy as what is presented in this book and their presence off stage attests to both the wide-ranging interests and energy Ray brought to his pursuit of understanding the emerging world of twentieth-century Oceania and the Pacific Rim. As a leading light in the Wellington School of Geography, where scholars could choose to focus on issues of political economy, Ray forged a distinct intellectual and disciplinary path in which cultural geography, his training as an historian and fascination with sociology and anthropology played equal parts. As a thesis supervisor, the expectations he imposed on graduate students to have thoroughly read and understood all the classical and recent literature on a topic were no less than what he expected of himself. It was not enough to have ideas, command of a regional literature; not enough to have a synchronistic account to argue, information had to be empirically triangulated and referenced to the latest theories and observations. Closure was an ephemeral pursuit. It was always disturbing, but right up to the delivery deadline on any work there was always something else to read, another work to reference and another point of view to consider.

In this collection we are privileged to read what commitment can achieve in the quest for a better understanding of the world. Childhood memories of intolerance on the part of those around him, the lessons implicit in the exercise of personal freedom, the privilege of being able to physically explore the world at his door step with a minimum of adult interference remained an enduring attitude of the scholar: 'I can find out, and I will!'. The allotted lifetime of three score and ten years may have passed but its passing has not diminished Ray's willingness to revisit and update his work, embrace contemporary writers like Escobar, review old puzzles, and to update and refine his most enduring legacy, the MIRAB model that is still widely used to characterise the economies of the Pacific's island microstates.

What I have found most rewarding in *Journeys Towards Progress* is the enlightenment optimism that Ray brings to his work, the determination to make sense of the world in a way that is true to his upbringing, and the era in which the first drafts of these works were prepared. Ray has written a series of essays which are at one and the same time commentary and contemporary history. The underlying philosophy is remarkably consistent with the thinking of R.G. Collingwood, the English historian in his posthumously published *The Idea of History* (1948), a text Ray made mandatory reading for his masters class in historical geography. Because it encapsulates both Ray's view of history and the way he (re)presents his writing as part of a formal and personal exploration, it is worth quoting at length:

> . . . history is 'for' human self-knowledge. It is generally thought to be of importance to man that he should know himself: Where knowing himself means knowing not his merely personal peculiarities, the things that distinguish him from other men, but his nature as man. Knowing yourself means knowing, first, what it is to be a man; secondly, knowing what it is to be the kind of man you are and nobody else is. Knowing yourself means knowing what you can do; and since nobody knows what he can do until he tries, the only clue to what man can do is what man has done. The value of history, then, is that it teaches us what man has done and thus what man is.
> (R.G. Collingwood, *The Idea of History*, 1948, p. 10)

The provenance of each essay is provided, and these brief introductions build a personal profile of a life's work that tell us a lot not only about the Pacific and Ray as researcher, but also about the nature of twentieth century scholarship: the confidence to subordinate details to overarching generalisations and work within broad structural paradigms. In a world now less tolerant of terms such as 'primitive', 'tribal' and 'peasant', sensitive to what 'traditionalism', 'neo-Victorianism' and 'modernisation' might mean, it is still possible to appreciate his distinct voice, the voice of a scholar who both reads and travels widely, someone who believes that the often uncomfortable challenge of going to see for yourself is the most important part of learning. Ray provides us with genuine, carefully researched and thoughtful observations that are true to the discourse of his era, and thus to this extent tell us much about twentieth century 'man'.

The singular value of *Journeys Towards Progress* is that it is an exemplary record of the Pacific in the second half of the twentieth century as interpreted by a person who had the capacity to work at both village and government level and report what he found in the context of the social science theories of his time.

John McKinnon
Development Studies
Victoria University of Wellington

Dedicated to the villagers who live
in the mosaic of islands of the Pacific

Acknowledgements

It is impossible to thank all the people who have assisted me over the course of the last 50 years in the South Pacific. I will not repeat acknowledgements already made in my book *Koro*, the island and team reports, and in various research papers, as those people have already been thanked and some of them, sadly, are now dead. My greatest thanks are due to the villagers I met throughout the islands of the South Pacific as they are the real heroes of the whole region.

In Fiji, in addition to the villagers, I was and remain greatly indebted to my interpreters, field assistants and friends, to Ratu Epeli Kanaimawi and Ratu Epi Seru, and to my old friend the chief of Nalotawa village, Ratu Jone Lotawa who is probably now deceased.

In Kiribati and especially on the island of Abemama, I am grateful for the support and interest of Bauro Tokatake, Te Uea and president of the Island Council in 1972, and the friendship and assistance of Teratabu Tira and his wife Rebeka and members of the Island Council. Frank Smith and his wife Tonamaina were especially helpful as was Kamatie Johnson, Ientumoa Kauriri and his wife Tate. The Sisters at Manoku mission and the late Father Kirieta were most interested in the study and it was a great pleasure for our family to visit them occasionally. The hardworking agricultural officers Neil McNaughton and Perry Langston greatly assisted my work. The greatest debt of gratitude is owed to the members of the 16 households whom I intensively studied and to Kabiritaake Banibati, my field assistant. They put up with my constant detailed questions and enquiries with unfailing patience and good humour: I remain in awe at how they get on with their lives with fortitude, often in conditions of considerable hardship.

On Tarawa many government officers assisted project members. The staff of the Department of Agriculture under Director Ray Harberd were most helpful. Special thanks are due to Bob Bryden and Dave Wimblett who assisted the project in many ways; Tony Hughes and Mike Walsh of the Planning Office helped in the early stages, supplying information and keeping abreast of our findings.

I am grateful too for having been associated with team members involved in the two large rural socio-economic surveys. We all benefited from the interaction of our interpretations and insights: John McKinnon, Ian Frazer and Murray Bathgate in the Solomon Islands;

and Roger Lawrence, Betsy Sewell, Anne Chambers and Bill Geddes in the islands that later became Kiribati and Tuvalu.

In the intensive three-volume Kandrian-Gloucester study, we acknowledge the assistance and information provided by 144 people: academics, scholars, scientists, consultants, planners, managers, public servants, politicians, plantation managers, farmers, missionaries, diplomats, teachers, aid post orderlies, engineers, foresters, agronomists, Big Men and last but by no means least ordinary villagers. Others to thank include Nat Sigiala, Provincial Secretary; Wellington Belawa, Departmental Administrative Secretary; and our counterparts Herman Talingapua, Peter Dau and our interpreter Peter Ulelio. We acknowledge assistance from Ron Brew, Otto Mark and Dave Edwards at the National Planning Office; Geoff Bastin, David Freyne and Graham Tyrie at the Department of Primary Industry; the Director of the Office of Forests, A.M.D. Yauieb.

In Chapter 11, I record the names of our team for the Kandrian-Gloucester study. I thank them all for their expertise and efforts in a demanding but stimulating exercise. I am especially grateful to Chris Tyrrell, Team Manager, for his expertise and friendship.

I thank the staff of Crown Agents and the Land Resources Development Centre, London. I owe a debt to Gordon Bridger, Senior Economist of the Overseas Development Administration who retained a keen and critical interest in our Rural Socio-Economic Surveys in the Pacific as well as in many aspects of the development process; and also to George Porter, formerly Deputy Director of ODA.

Much of my critical understanding of Melanesian societies in Papua New Guinea is indebted to Ann Chowning, formerly Professor of Anthropology at Victoria University who worked with Lakalai, Sengseng and Kove peoples of West New Britain for lengthy periods between 1952 to 1992. I am grateful to her for her comments on Chapter 11 and for discussions on Melanesia and Papua New Guinea in general. Her deep and broad scholarship, generous sharing of her knowledge and warnings of the dangers of generalising were of inestimable value. I am grateful too for valuable descriptions and analysis of changes in Kandrian-Gloucester in recent years by Dr Mike Bourke, geographer at Australia National University and formerly agronomist in WNB; and Dr Jim Specht, Archaeologist of the Australian Museum in Sydney. For our work in the Solomon Islands I am grateful for corrections and comments made by Rhys Richards, former New Zealand High Commissioner to that country; and to Dr Murray Bathgate, former team member.

On Vanuatu I was assisted by Rick Woodham, a senior economist at New Zealand Aid; and Chris Davidson, educational consultant.

The interesting task of updating my knowledge about conditions in the islands today relied heavily on information supplied by the Programme Officers of New Zealand's international aid and development agency, NZAid. I am grateful for comments and information supplied by Jacquie Dean (Vanuatu), Mat Halsey (Kiribati), Margie Lowe (Papua New Guinea), Don Will (Fiji), Matthew Howell (Solomons), and Dominic Walton-France and Vicki Plater (Economic Advisers). Dr Teresia Teaiwa of Pacific Studies kindly checked the manuscript, especially on Fijian and Kiribati words. I also appreciated discussions with them on a range of Pacific issues.

Over the course of working at Victoria University for nearly four decades, I have been lucky to be part of a community of scholars and I am grateful to them for their collaboration and shared interests: in the early years the historian Dr J.C. Beaglehole and Professor Ernest Beaglehole who worked in Tonga and the Cook Islands; and geographers of my own department, the late Professor Keith Buchanan, Terry McGee (now Professor Emeritus of UBC, Vancouver), John McKinnon and Roger Lawrence. I also enjoyed collaboration with Mary Boyd (Pacific History), Rod Alley (Fiji politics), Professor Jan Pouwer and Hal Levine (anthropology of PNG), and the sociologists Professor Jim Robb and the late Professor John McCreary. I have enjoyed collaboration over a number of years with Geoff Bertram (economist as well as geographer) on the economies of Pacific microstates, as well as Peru. To hundreds of students over the years (whom, I fear, I too often lectured *at* rather than *to*) I am also grateful.

My final thanks are due to Ann Carroll of Keyline Secretarial for her great accuracy and speed in typing lengthy drafts as well as her unfailing patience in coping with heavy workloads over the last four years; throughout she has showed great interest in the issues. My editor Ginny Sullivan has also coped with lengthy scripts and unfailingly reduced, reorganised and shaped my jottings, curbing my worst excesses and producing coherence from incoherence. Her own experience of living in Kiribati brought an added bonus on top of her already formidable editorial skills. Finally, I want to thank Fergus Barrowman, publisher for VUP, who made various suggestions about reducing an over-lengthy script to its present format. I am sure these changes have enhanced the book. Thanks are due to Ann Chowning, David Leslie, Rob Wright, Ginny Sullivan and Roger Lawrence for permission to use some of their photographs and to Chris Tyrrell for the photo on the cover.

I would like also to thank my partner, Helen Stokes, for her understanding and forbearance over the last four years.

Ray Watters

Foreword

Growing Up in Hawkes Bay

This book reflects part of my intellectual journey over the last 55 years, and in parallel these essays present my interpretations of the journeys of a number of Oceanic societies in which I worked. Clearly, my views are affected by the great events and tumultuous changes of the second half of the twentieth century.

Equally, they were influenced by my family and the place where I grew up. I discovered early that my dearly beloved maternal grandfather had had to leave school in Oxford, Canterbury, somewhat precipitately at the age of 12: his school master was beating a pupil mercilessly. After about six strokes of the cane, my grandfather asked the master to stop. When told sternly to shut up, he knocked the teacher down, jumped out the window and ran home. Needless to say, this was the end of his schooling, and for the rest of his working life he had to accept unskilled labouring jobs when they became available. He went to work in the 'Forty Mile Bush' but was frequently unemployed. The importance of achieving an education was not lost on me.

The terrible events of 1917 reverberated in my family for decades. In that year, my mother gained very high marks in matriculation and planned to go to Victoria University College (where she would have been one of very few women students), but late that year her beloved brother Syd was killed in the Battle of Passchendaele after only three weeks on the Western Front, and her uncle was gassed (and later died). At home, her father became suddenly unemployed and the family was traumatised by Syd's death. Mum had to give up the idea of university and get a job in the Audit Office to bring in money for the family. Later, when I gained some success in my studies, I felt I was doing it for her.

I grew up in Napier in the Hawkes Bay in the 1930s and 1940s, starting school in 1934, the last year of the Great Depression. My family was not poor but I sensed that hardship was widespread. When I got to school, I realised that I was the only pupil in my class who was wearing shoes. Mum refused my request to go barefoot, but after I got round the first corner I removed my shoes and put them in my bag, performing the reverse process on my way home.

We lived 'on the flat' of Napier South on the edge of town. Running beside Georges Drive was the Tutaekuri River, and the uplift from the great Napier earthquake of 1931 meant that the river gradually ran dry. It was a wonderful playground for small urchins living a kind of Huckleberry Finn life, catching eels, flying home-made kites and making hockey sticks from the plane tree branches. On the other side of the river, the raupo bullrushes were taller than we were – we called this area the 'Amazon jungle' and we ventured into it a little way with some trepidation only occasionally. Each street had its own gang and we ambushed and wrestled with rival gangs and pelted them with mud. As this was the era before washing machines, our mother was long-suffering indeed.

My brother Syd, two years older, was very practical and could make almost anything with his pocket knife. Later, he scrounged at the town dump material from which he built his first lathe; with a hacksaw we cut through a section of discarded railway line which we managed to bring home on the old bike. We were inseparable companions and he was my closest friend for life (he ended up as a successful builder in Hawkes Bay). Our sister Christine was born 18 years after me.

Soon I discovered the Public Library which was even more entrancing than the 'Amazon jungle', and thereafter I always had my head buried in a book. A little later Syd and I both became Cubs, progressing to Boy Scouts. Even then, in the 1930s, it seemed a rather old-fashioned movement, but we enjoyed the games, and the emphasis on both team work and individualism. The discipline imposed was worthwhile as well as the ethics of the movement and its toleration of all races, creeds and classes. Learning new skills when we passed different badges encouraged us constantly to set new goals to achieve, a useful preparation for later life. Best of all was camping, when we set off on our bikes to cycle the 16 miles to Weka Flat, the Scout camp at Rissington, each Easter or Labour Day. By the time I was 12, the three men whom I admired most in the world were Grandpa, Uncle John and Baden Powell.

Unfortunately, I saw Grandpa only once a year for Christmas holidays when we made the exciting journey in Dad's car from Napier to Wellington where my grandparents lived in Miramar. When I was about 10, my Grandfather remarked casually that his grandfather "had been at the Battle of Peterloo". I had no idea what this meant, but about six years later when doing School Certificate History, Max Campbell, our history teacher, explained that the Battle of Peterloo in 1819 was the first great working class rally in the world. On the edge of Manchester, at St Peters Field (or Peterloo), tens of thousands of working class people gathered to hear 'Orator' Hunt and other well-known leaders of the growing labour movement speak to the workers about their rights, conditions of work, and the refusal of the governments of the day to allow working men to meet together or 'combine' and to form trade unions. I found out later that my grandfather's grandfather was John Parsons, a boy of 16 who walked with his parents for many miles like thousands of other workers to St Peters Field for the great meeting. Just after Orator Hunt had begun speaking, however, the Yeomanry hidden in the neighbouring streets suddenly rode into the huge crowd to beat them with the flats of their sabres and ride down the fleeing, panicking workers. Several people died and hundreds were wounded from sabre cuts or trampling by the horses. The Parsons family fortunately escaped but the story made an impression on me for two reasons. My grandfather's grandfather and his family had been at an important historical event at a time when the working classes were struggling to improve their working conditions and human rights (the Cotton Mills Act of 1819 fixed the working age of children at nine, and their working week at 72 hours). And secondly, I realised with wonder that family history or genealogy could take me back to the time of Napoleon, the Duke of Wellington and Waterloo. Today, as a man who has just turned 80, I am still in awe at how these events of previous generations reverberate in the lives of the living.

As a teenager, I attended Napier Boys' High School where 'Potty' Foster was Headmaster. He was a fine Classics scholar who had graduated from Oxford, a stern disciplinarian who seemed to most boys to be too strict and repressive. On reflection, however, I am grateful that he ran such a 'tight ship'. These were the war years, and undoubtedly he was under great pressure of staff shortages. Later, in my last year at school, I ran the Scout Troop – all the Scout masters had gone to war and I was appalled at the thought of the Troop collapsing. Fortunately, I managed to keep it going until the beginning of 1947 when I left Napier to begin university.

A major event happened around 1944 when I was about 16. We frequently went to Uncle John's house which was nearby, and Dad, Syd and I joined Uncle John in playing bowls or putting on his carefully manicured back lawn while the women chatted. One day at tea, however, Uncle John made the comment that Adolf Hitler was indeed a dreadful man who had caused much death and misery in many of the countries affected by the War. But he did agree with him on one thing: "He dealt with the Jews as they deserved". I was shocked at his comment and that it came from the mouth of my dear Uncle John. After a stunned silence, I could not leave the remark unchallenged. "How can you say that?", I blurted out. My family was silent and the conversation changed and moved to safer topics. Of course, I did not stop liking Uncle John but he ceased to be one of my heroes. I was learning painfully that ordinary people whom we loved and admired often had feet of clay. The incident also reminds me of how reticent people were then about their thoughts and feelings – I never heard whether Mum or Dad agreed with my views or, on the contrary, the anti-Semitic views of Uncle John. In a 'stiff upper lip' society, communication and truthfulness, even on important issues, left much to be desired.

Living in New Zealand

Locked away comfortably at the bottom of the South Pacific, my country New Zealand was a remote little nation, a complacent, innocent, rather unquestioning and conservative society, very ignorant of the world. The Second World War changed that, however. For a short time we feared the possibility of Japanese invasion, and I, along with most New Zealanders, listened to the BBC News on the 'wireless' and read the press each day avidly following the terrible events of the war and seeking to understand our times.

At Victoria University College in Wellington from 1947-50, I was awakened with many others by the stimulus of my teachers and the excitement of learning, the great ideas contained in scholarly books, and their analyses of the world and its historical development. I was introduced to the crisis within medieval feudalism by Peter Munz, the birth of modernism by Freddie Wood's lectures on the Renaissance, and imperialism and colonial policy by J.C. Beaglehole. I was attracted to the study of history and geography and would certainly have taken anthropology if it had been taught in New Zealand in those years. I had been given as a school prize *Vikings of the Sunrise* by Peter Buck (Te Rangi Hiroa) and this aroused my interest in other cultures as well as in one of the widest diasporas the world has seen – the migration of Polynesian people to occupy eight island groups throughout the vast Pacific Ocean, the last occupation of any part of the world by humankind.

In my last year as a geography undergraduate at the University of Auckland, I experienced fieldwork for the first time. We were sent to visit a sample of farms flanking the eastern side of Lake Rotorua, and were introduced to ethnographic techniques and social science methodologies such as interviewing, the use of questionnaires, and the setting up and testing of hypotheses. Moreover, I discovered that 'Maori land' was regarded as synonymous with idle, uncultivated land in the hidebound primary-producing consciousness of New Zealand's agrarianism. My interest was aroused not only in fieldwork but also in social-cultural factors affecting land use. In my last year at the university, I did an MA thesis on early Western impact on Hawaii.

New Zealand in the 1950s was a small and very remote country. Although the fall of Singapore in 1942 made us suddenly aware that we were dependent on the United States for our defence, McCarthyism after World War II led New Zealand to follow other countries as well as the US in fighting communism. We were still very Eurocentric, almost automatically aligning ourselves with Britain 'The Mother Country' and Australia in world affairs.

I was shocked at the severity of the waterfront strike of 1951 which lasted 151 days, and was opposed to the draconian tactics of both the Holland government and the Federation of Labour, led by the sinister authoritarian figure, Finton Patrick Walsh. The more militant unions grouped in the Trade Union Congress supported the strike. One of the leaders of the strike was Toby Hill, whom I remember as a mild, friendly man, a neighbour of my grandfather in Miramar who regularly joined him to play putting on the back lawn in a 'Last of the Summer Wine' group of old men. The government prohibited advertising the watersiders' case and imposed penalties on those who paid, fed or assisted their families. The armed forces were sent to the wharves to maintain exports and imports. For the first time I caught a glimpse of ugly factional hatred in my beloved New Zealand, which was to be repeated later in the 1960s over the Vietnam War (which I, with others, saw as a local civil war rather than as symptomatic of the 'domino effect' of expanding communism) and in the 1981 Springbok Tour when I took part in the peaceful protests.

This glimpse was reinforced by the Mazengarb Report in 1954 on adolescent sexual activity in the Hutt Valley, Wellington, which found that there was a decline in social and moral values, a situation of "depravity" and "laxity" due to the fact that mothers were working outside the home, and to "over-sexed or morally degraded" young women who allowed young men full licence with them. However, as juvenile offending was no worse that year than in previous years, the Report was more significant for what it revealed about middle class fears and insecurity in changing times than anything else.

At the university, attitudes were illustrated by the narrow horizons of the University Council in 1956 when, at the height of the Cold War, it refused permission to Keith Buchanan, the newly appointed first Professor of Geography, to visit China with a group of people which included James Bertram. Bertram was highly regarded internationally as he, together with the American Edgar Snow, had been the first

Western journalists in China in the 1930s at the time of the Japanese invasion and the early stages of the Maoist revolution.

The European Experience

After two rewarding years teaching at Wellington College and serving as a housemaster at Firth House to save for overseas study, I worked my passage on board ship to England with the intention of studying for a higher degree at either Oxford or Cambridge. However, I learned that I would have to pass the Responsians entrance examination in either Latin or Greek before being admitted. As this would involve at least several months study to upgrade my third-form Latin (now largely forgotten), I settled on the London School of Economics (LSE), reputed to be the next best university. After reading my Masters thesis, my supervisors admitted me to the PhD degree programme. I was a part-time student while teaching history and physical education (and even woodwork!) at a number of schools in Greater London.

Being immersed in a large-scale urban-industrial society with a heavily Eurocentric world view was an interesting and humbling experience. The distant South Pacific including New Zealand never entered people's ken, let alone appeared in the news. I did, however, quickly discover the worth of some of the better newspapers, reading *The Observer* (and subscribing to it for 40 years), the *Manchester Guardian* and occasionally the *New Statesman* and the *Economist*.

One day while having 'high tea' at an English school, we heard on the BBC that the French had suffered a massive defeat in what was then called French Indo-China at Dien Bien Phu by a nationalist Vietnamese army; the French would shortly be pulling out of the country and ceding independence to the Vietnamese. The enormity of the news slowly sank in: a major European power had been decisively defeated by a little known insurgent force. The established order of things was being fundamentally challenged, Western empires were on the retreat, and the shape of a new world order was beginning to emerge that was very different from the perspectives from London, Paris, Washington or even Wellington.

At LSE, I was aware of the earlier influence of Harold Laski and the importance of the social sciences. Many interesting students had passed through: Jomo Kenyatta, father of Kenyan independence and author of *Facing Mt Kenya*, had recently studied there. While I enjoyed the Geography Department and had R.O. Buchanan (the Professor and an economic geographer who hailed from Tapanui, Southland) as my supervisor, the great influence for me was Raymond Firth, a

New Zealander who was one of the leading anthropologists of the day. He was then completing *Social Change in Tikopia*, the sequel to *We the Tikopia*, and I was intrigued by his concepts of social structure, social function, and social alignment and realignment for describing and analysing tribal societies that were changing. Later in Fiji, a small-scale descent-based society similar to Tikopia, I found some of his methodology to be very useful.

After a year, my fiancée Bethlyn joined me, we were married at Oxford (on the day an elderly, ill Churchill resigned as Prime Minister) and lived in a small apartment in Pinner, north-west London. Twice a week and later full time we commuted to the LSE or the British Museum Reading Room. Occasionally, I would walk down the Strand to the Visitors Gallery of the House of Commons to listen to Eden, the aging Churchill, Gaitskill, Harold Wilson, Macmillan and others, debate the issues of the time such as the crisis in Iran with the nationalisation of Anglo-Iranian oil, and the uneasy tensions associated with the founding of Israel. We managed two trips to west and southern Europe as well as driving around most of Britain, visiting landscapes and towns saturated with history. After two and a half years, my dissertation on the impact of the West on Samoa was completed and was accepted for the degree. I was offered a lectureship at the Australian National University, Canberra, which was just initiating its research programme in the School of Pacific Studies. But we both wanted to live in New Zealand and so returned to Wellington to a temporary junior lectureship (a full lectureship became available six months later). Our passage back to New Zealand was to pass through the Suez Canal but had to be diverted to the Cape Town route because of the Suez Crisis.

The Political Landscape

The 1950s was an interesting and exciting period in which to begin one's lifetime career. The twin tyrannies of Fascism and Stalinism had been defeated or buried, the horror of the holocaust exposed and old empires were in steady decline. The great Marshall Plan assisted the rapid rebuilding of a devastated Europe, for although the tip of the iceberg had been destroyed, as E.F. Schumacher remarked (1973), the underlying structures of modern industrial economies and society were still intact, providing a solid basis for modernisation. The United Nations had been founded and its agencies such as the FAO, WHO and UNESCO worked energetically in Africa, Asia and Latin America in the areas of rural development; health, sanitation and the elimination of disease; and literacy and education. Commodity prices boomed, restoring confidence for widespread economic growth in New Zealand and worldwide, including developing countries. Although Churchill warned that an 'Iron Curtain' had descended over Europe dividing it into two hostile alliances and the Cold War had begun, reconstruction promoted a mood of optimism. After the liberation of conquered societies in World War II and the resettlement of millions of refugees, it was a short step to freeing societies from colonialism or economic exploitation.

Ideals of liberty, political democracy and social justice were in the ascendant and, following the independence of India, Pakistan, Nigeria and Indonesia (all large countries), scores of new nations were born. When a dynamic and charismatic John F. Kennedy became American President in 1960 and launched the New Frontiers policy initiating the Alliance for Progress aid programme and founding the Peace Corps, the mood of unrestrained optimism continued. New Zealand launched its own Volunteer Service Abroad in 1962 and I was a founding member and served on the Council for some years.

I too was infected by this rose-coloured view of the times. While views of early nationalist leaders such as Sukano, Nasser, Nkrumah and Nyrere were imbued with hope, over time they offered a sobering message. All too often, representative or responsible governments collapsed, to be followed by venal and corrupt elites at the mercy of international forces or by brutal dictatorships. And overseas aid at that time involved little more than the massive, simple transfer of Western technology to developing countries, with little if any regard to scale or appropriateness. As former colonies became independent nations and United Nations members with voting rights, the pace of decolonisation accelerated. Yet there was a world of difference in the conditions of tiny Pacific microstates compared to the large Asian and African former colonies. Were they ready for independence, for fending for themselves in stormy seas when cut adrift from their former colonising power?

Next to the Cold War, nationalism was one of the greatest issues of the day. Former colonies rushed to throw off the yoke of colonialism. Xenophobia was rife, and it was widely believed that with independence, autonomous development and modernisation would naturally follow. Whereas nationalism especially flowered in Europe in the nineteenth century after great secular changes, in East, South and Southeast Asia and the Pacific none of the same pre-conditions existed. As Gunnar Myrdal wrote (1968), in Asia the middle class was small, ancient religions still held sway and industrialism had barely begun.

Nationalism is by definition a popular and mass movement although it invariably begins as a movement espoused by intellectuals or a modernising elite. It tends to arouse strong emotions and to satisfy a deep-felt public need such as the attainment of independence and the overthrow of a foreign, occupying power or a tyrannical or corrupt ruling class. Only a few charismatic figures manage to 'ride the tiger' or divert the direction of nationalism for a short time. History is strewn with moderate leaders replaced by more extreme ones whose stance satisfies public emotions better. Whereas in the West nationalism was associated with a movement for liberalism and emancipation, in Asia nationalism and modernisation have often been associated with authoritarian regimes, such as Marcos's 'New Society' of the Philippines, Suharto's Indonesia or later Mahathir's Malaysia.

The classic figures of Asian nationalism are still Gandhi and Nehru. Their brand of Indian nationalism is associated with the idea of equality, and with the raising of living standards and social justice. Gandhi, a great figure, was a true Westernised liberal, radical and revolutionary in his goals of social justice and the elimination of poverty. However, his ties with tradition and religion were necessary to give him a mass following and to turn him into a Pan-Indian national leader. This in fact tempered his modernism, and his realism and rejection of violence made him compromise his radical revolutionary ideals – the rich would be accepted if they acted as trustees for the underprivileged. Ultimately, his trusteeship idea is consistent with a paternalistic, feudal, pre-democratic society.

Nehru, on the other hand (riding on the nationalistic tide that Gandhi had largely created and partly guided), was less fettered by tradition. He criticised Gandhi's support for a system which he saw as obviously decaying, and creating misery and waste. As a socialist, a moderniser and a centralist he condemned a way out that looked to the past that blessed all the relics of the old order – the feudal states, big zamindaris, the capitalist system. But the important point is that India needed both Gandhi and Nehru, for the complementary roles of the two great men provided outstanding leadership and stability to India in turbulent times, enabling development and modernisation to get under way.

Chaos in Ceylon in the 1950s and 1960s ensued when the fires of nationalism got out of control with the social mobilisation of the Tamils, fearful of Sinhalese domination. In other plural societies, the slaughter of tens of thousands of Chinese residents in Indonesia in 1965 and 1966; the terrible tragedies of Croatia, Bosnia and the Basque region; and genocide in Uganda, Ruanda and other African countries illustrate how situations of rapid social change and growing disorder require the outstanding leadership of the complementary Gandhi-Nehru type, backed by a fully working constitutional structure and system of law and order. The withdrawal of the great colonial powers all too often has left a political vacuum in plural societies to be exploited by venal elites. Only when the dislocating effects of change are dealt with by returning to primordial loyalties and recognising the ancient rights of kinship, common language and custom in institutional ways that recognise minority rights and help to unify different ethnic groups within the new nation has a basis been laid to achieve stability. However, from the perspective of several decades later, it can be seen that the integrative revolution was more apparent and symbolic than real: Indonesia today seems to hang together only tenuously.

In Oceania, the worst excesses of nationalism have on the whole been avoided. However, in New Caledonia the Kanak struggle for independence against the French has been protracted, and in Bougainville tribes rose first against the great copper mine and then sought secession from Papua New Guinea. Civil war ensued with the Papua New Guinea government for years. In Polynesia, the more structured and stratified societies were less seriously affected than the looser unstructured societies of Melanesia, although the struggle for self-government in the Cook Islands in support of Albert Henry has been of huge local significance.[1] The most serious case of all, however, is that of Fiji where failure to establish a basis for the evolution of a multi-racial society by the early to mid-1960s has had tragic outcomes.

The Wellington School of Geography

I joined the infant Geography Department in Wellington in 1957, teaching Historical Geography and the South Pacific. The young department grew rapidly as student numbers (and staff appointments) rose.

The main figure in the fledgling department was the first Professor of Geography, Keith Buchanan, a Birmingham graduate who had come to Wellington after teaching in Natal, Nigeria and at the LSE. I have described him in his obituary as a "radical geographer, a socialist, a champion of the dispossessed and an unrelenting critic of orthodoxy, capitalist regimes and power elites".[2] Buchanan was always controversial and thus was often cursorily dismissed or rejected out of hand. But he was a brilliant, provocative lecturer who spoke with the moral fire of a Welsh preacher and who attracted large numbers of students to his classes. Although his judgement was not always sound, I believe that in sum his voluminous writing represents a powerful case directed against some of the great evils and dangerous traits shaping the later twentieth century world. Buchanan wrote a number of books of importance, with *The Transformation of the Chinese Earth* probably his greatest work, but it is as an essayist and polemicist that he will probably be remembered. A reviewer in the *Sydney Morning Herald* once likened his writing to that of Montaigne, the prolific French essayist and, like Montaigne, he wrote on the deepest issues affecting the world in his day.

One former geography student saw Keith Buchanan's legacy not only in his published work but also in a "generation of geography students who learnt about racism, ethnocentrism, capitalism, socialism, environmentalism and feminism taught through a medium of moral Marxism". So "It was Buchanan who introduced us to *Silent Spring* and *The Power Elite* and encouraged us to read the *American Monthly Review*. It was Buchanan whose name we associated with C. Wright Mills, A.G. Frank and F. Fanon; Cuba, Vietnam and the Red Dawn in the People's Republic of China. It is to his credit to remember that this was all before Edward Said and latter day radicals like David Harvey".[3] Another former student believed that what captured their fascination with the man was that Buchanan "was intellect, knowledge, humanism, passion, vision and charisma, all rolled into one: a man to look up to, to emulate and admire".[4]

Buchanan's approach to geography was primarily cultural, following the Belgian geographer Pierre Gourou. Thus, the links between the physical and human elements in any environment "come about through the medium of civilisation, that distorting prism which, in accordance with the laws peculiar to each civilisation, transmits the influence of the physical environment to the human elements of a landscape. If the nature of the prism is changed, if a people's civilisation undergoes a transformation (such as the Maoist revolution in China from 1949-76), then the character of the relationship between a society and its physical environment is changed too; the significance of the various elements in the environment may undergo a profound alteration".[5]

Other personalities too were important in the emerging Wellington School of Geography. Harvey Franklin, also a Birmingham graduate, emphasised the economic foundation in Human Geography. He produced original and rigorous analyses of the European peasantry following his fieldwork in France, Italy and Southern Germany, and also taught and published on European capitalism and the New Zealand mixed economy. His books on *The European Peasantry: The Final Phase* and *Trade Growth and Anxiety* on New Zealand, which won the Montana Book of the Year in 1978, were major works. Terry McGee, after doing an excellent thesis on the Indian community in

Newtown (a working class suburb in Wellington), embarked on the study of Asian urbanisation and Southeast Asian societies. His later book *The Southeast Asian City* was to become a classic of geographic literature, and he eventually became a major figure at the University of British Colombia as an Asianist and an urbanisation specialist. From 1958, I followed up my earlier work on Samoa by beginning fieldwork in Fiji, and from 1963, in response to an invitation to study shifting agriculture by the FAO, began working in agrarian societies in Latin America.

For us at Wellington, geography was not to be confined within the usual parameters of areal differentiation or mere regional description. We drew extensively on the related disciplines of history, sociology, anthropology and economics and concerned ourselves with the trends and forces that have shaped and are continuing to shape the turbulent and diverse nations of the world. Wellington geographers took an interdisciplinary or 'holistic' approach within regions or nations when other departments adopted the "paradigm of the decade".[6] In this sense, Wellington, a 'maverick department', was unfashionably consistent in finding its strength by concentrating on the geographic implications of social and economic change. In contrast to 'what-places-are-like geography', we studied process as an essential means of explaining pattern, and regarded Marxism purely as a tool of analysis. Our emphasis was on the political economy of development and the comparative economic study of countries over time.

The important point about geography at Wellington was that the ideas, political viewpoints and personalities were often very different but nevertheless complementary, stimulating fresh thinking among both staff and students. And many other staff and students contributed valuably to the intellectual debate: Warwick Armstrong, John Bedkober, Iain Buchanan, Margaret Carr, Anne Magee, John McKinnon, Ewan McQueen, Phil Morrison, Christine Rowlands, Andy Trlin, Cros Walsh, Sue White, Richard Willis and others. There was a magic chemistry in the air: it was a good time to be alive and to be a student at Wellington. As a former student said, the staff was "… an incredible team of complementary opposites, each member with his own strongly held and well reasoned explanations of social reality. *This* is what made 'Vic' geography in the later 1950s and early 1960s so exciting".[7]

Of course, this kind of geography also had its defects and limitations; the use of quantitative techniques and the testing of more conventional models were neglected somewhat, and emphasis on the Third World was so great the developed countries received less attention. In general, however, the benefits far out-weighed the defects.

In 1953, before Buchanan's arrival, a third-year course in Asian geography was introduced. It pioneered Asian studies in the University and became popular with students, dealing with major issues and trends such as the Maoist Revolution in China.

In 1959, at a staff meeting, Terry McGee and I proposed that the department should found a new journal. The motion was passed unanimously, the journal, named *Pacific Viewpoint* (now *Asia Pacific Viewpoint*), was to present an interpretation *of* and *from* the Asia-Pacific, and Buchanan was appointed first editor. I later acted as editor for 20 years and Phil Morrison for even longer. The journal brought international recognition to the department. Many well-known scholars such as the French agrarian writer René Dumont, the French economist Charles Bettelheim, the Cambridge Sinologist Joseph Needham and leading Asian scholars Ooi Jin Bee and Robert Ho wrote in the journal in the early years. In the first five years, its ten issues contained 24 major articles on Asia. Buchanan, Franklin, McGee and I contributed several articles in the early years.

Certainly the 1960s was an exciting period when the world's political landscape was being rapidly refashioned. At the same time, the apogee of the import-substituting model of the New Zealand economy had passed, with its full employment, rapid growth and relatively high per capita income (fourth highest in the world). By the mid- to late 1960s, there were increasing signs of inefficiency and inadequacies of the New Zealand mixed economy with its 'borrow-and-hope' policies of politicians, lack of competition and dynamism, and plethora of regulations and government controls. New Zealand too was entering a new and uncertain stage.

While New Zealand society had some defects, it also had some strengths: unfettered by tradition and class barriers that inhibited people in the Old World of Europe, Kiwis often possessed initiative and a readiness to test new ideas and new approaches. We may have been naïve and still affected by colonialism, but we did have energy, and a Kiwi 'can-do' attitude. The world was indeed our oyster!

1

Introduction

The chapters in this book traverse the varying experiences of a number of countries in Oceania over the last half-century while they have responded to the intense impact of Western capitalism and its ideologies, and the complex process of decolonisation. It also traverses my own journey of working in some of them, studying them, and grappling with the discrete complexities of each one of them as they emerged into the modern world and confronted the assumptions and inroads of globalisation.

My method has been fieldwork, observation and an awareness of the great movements of our time; my task has been revealing the inter-relationships between empiricism and theory, and the synthesis of valid hypotheses and interpretations. Throughout the book, I use the inductive method to test hypotheses on trends shaping a region or nation, while the study of historical background often provides a good basis for research on modern problems and situations. In my role as geographer, I have become increasingly aware that geography as it is taught and studied today must by necessity contain a strong anthropological, sociological and economic component as well as its traditional environmental and physical perspectives. It must link not only crops and climate but also economic development with social change and political advancement so that cultures are looked at in context, both local and global.

The South Pacific since the early visits of European explorers, and the subsequent rapaciousness of slavers, whalers, and sandalwood and other traders, has been seen through the eyes of those outsiders as a potential source of riches, of a free-an-easy way of life, of plentitude and fertile abundance. It was characterised generally as a storehouse and garden for Europeans, and while its beauty and variety were appreciated and rhapsodised over, and its peoples regarded as variously conforming to or differing from their ideas of the 'noble savage', it was scarcely ever seen in its own context. Its otherness was a contrast to Europe, not an expression of full and rich traditional cultures. The colonialism that inevitably followed continued the ethnocentrism of most early contact and dug it in deeper, as religious beliefs, political structures, social organisation and economic management were eroded, annihilated or transformed.

The Pacific which I began to study in the late 1950s was sitting on the fulcrum of colonialism and development, with the impacts of incursions into every aspect of life being visible, the neo-traditional structures teetering. What those in the West heard about, if they heard anything at all, was either a version of Margaret Mead's since-disputed picture of people unassailable in their freedom and innate psychological health, robustly withstanding the onslaught of missionaries and colonial government officers; or a disaster story of the impacts of European disease and alcohol, and their unhappy relationship with a happy-go-lucky, vaguely directionless philosophy of life. Of course, the various invasions into the Pacific region during the Second World War had other impacts, bringing both devastation of a new physical kind as well as millenarian cults that speak volumes about the disparities between not only Western goods and their availability but also concepts of ownership, wealth and entitlement. These World War II invasions were also expressions of the forces behind the early invasions, regarding the vast ocean and the small islands it surrounded as a theatre for activities that had nothing to do with the region and everything to do with aspirations, conflicts and power disputes from far, far away.

The essays in this book represent my work as a geographer over the last 50 years, encompassing the periods of later colonialism, decolonisation and independence, and the increasing impacts of globalisation, mounting resource extraction by external powers, and the decline or closing of traditional markets for Oceanic exports with the emergence of major protectionist economic blocs such as the European Union. They identify problems that emerged from the particular sets of circumstances I found myself confronting through my fieldwork or reading. By portraying each of these societies at a point in time – usually the point at which I began fieldwork – the essays show us snapshots of these microstates as they grappled with particular histories, issues and dynamics, and thus enable us to make analyses that were relevant at the time of research and writing, but that also remain relevant today. And it is this continuing relevance that underlines the fact that while change is by definition dynamic, tradition is also dynamic, and carries the seeds of the past into the present and the future. Although the facts and situations have changed greatly, the essential problem remains the same: it has not gone away and, in fact, has often worsened.

It is commonplace for Westerners to believe that if there is a problem there must be a solution. While various 'solutions' have sometimes been tried in Oceania, it is perhaps one of the enduring characteristics of Third World countries that difficult or recalcitrant problems such as poverty, racism, under-development, inequality, environmental crisis and political instability remain and persist in intractable forms, often crippling or endangering nations or large sections of their populations. The problems exist at all those points where traditional ways of life are touched hard enough by outside influences to lose their salience. The 'solutions', which usually also come from outside, are therefore clearly likely to exacerbate the stability or viability of the endemic status quo. However, contact has been established and now the touch cannot be lifted. These small countries are therefore inexorably involved in the global economy, and need and want the advantages of material goods, technology and spending power, and a share in the equality, justice, safety and health that those in the developed world assume are theirs by right.

The book therefore presents a catholic, wide-ranging set of essays on rural development and change in some of the diverse young nation states of Oceania as they have made their often faltering, sometimes failing, journeys towards progress – towards attaining at least an acceptable or decent standard of living; the eradication of poverty, hunger and the scourge of disease; the achievement of at least a measure of national unity, peace and harmony; the banishment of racism (particularly in Fiji); the expansion of modern systems of education and health; the marrying of traditional with modern land-use systems; and the evolution of an efficient and sustaining system of democratic government.

This collection illustrates the use of the micro-level (village) approach to study tribal and post-tribal societies, complemented in some cases by meso- (regional) and macro-level (national) analysis. Some chapters show a geographer at work, addressing the interaction of environmental, socio-economic and cultural factors (for example, Chapter 7, Sorolevu: A Sugar Cane Village); while others are avowedly inter-disciplinary and illustrate the links of human geography with anthropology, sociology, economics and politics (for example, Chapter 13, The MIRAB Economy). Several chapters are concerned with social change and the transition from colonial status to nationhood (for example, Chapter 12 on Vanuatu). Whereas some reveal how nationalism can be a force for good, encouraging unity, others focus on places or times when rabid nationalism has stoked the fires of racism (see Chapter 5 on Fiji, for example).

The book attempts to show that there is no substitute for understanding the nature of countries on their own terms: the particular, distinctive kinds of society we are dealing with, and the structures, systems and processes that exist or are at work. The key questions to emerge from these essays are: how do relatively traditional village people in a tribal society adapt to change, maintain their subsistence and reciprocity systems but gradually introduce new crops for market sale or capitalise on opportunities for wage labour? How do they maintain their cultural integrity without bowing to the pressures of the cultural imperative? And how can their viability and distinctiveness survive best while also allowing them to embrace the advantages of communication, education, health, equity and choice that are central to Western notions of development and are arguably the outcomes and rewards of globalisation?

Consequently, the book revolves around several themes and returns to them from various angles and in several contexts. The one underpinning them all is development, but development both as abstract and concrete, notion and practice, can exist only in relation to what was there before. And this, the pre-existing state, the neo-traditional way of life as it was known and as it was manifest through fieldwork, is fundamental to the essays in this book.

The Tradition-to-Development Continuum

Productivity of the Village Sector

Europeans commonly underestimate the productivity of the traditional sector. While the level of productivity varies greatly, we should remember, as M.J. Ormsby pointed out in the case of Samoa, that it "has been producing surpluses for hundreds of years: surpluses to finance wars, ceremonial journeys (*malaga*), ceremonial feasts (*fa'alavelave*), the erection of buildings and houses (*fale*), and the manufacture of canoes and longboats. In recent years, surpluses have been produced to build huge churches of extravagant, often amazing design, as well as to keep them and the pastor in good repair. Of course, all these projects are community or family based, rather than individually based. Rivalry of a friendly and productive nature also exists between families and villages rather than between individuals".[1]

The village sector can also produce large surpluses if labour is harnessed in traditionally meaningful ways rather than in typical European ways:

> As a simple example, individualistic-based paid employment might not be the most satisfactory way of unleashing productivity. This was found to be the case in the early days in New Zealand, and we have evolved some rather unique institutions, like contracting gangs and share milking, which have built-in incentives and avoid some of the disagreeable aspects of paid employment. It has been suggested that the young men of the village ... who traditionally do much of the heavy labouring and

cooking, would make a natural unit for training as contracting gangs for fencing, forestry work and so on.

The Manager of a large estate here gets much of his heavy labouring done by employing an entire village. A village will clear acres of scrub in a short time to raise money for, say, a new roof for their church or for a *faalavelave*. There are other objectives of a communal nature, schools, clinics, cinemas, water reticulation, electric lighting and so on. However, the only attempts to tap customary practices that I have come across have been made by the Samoans themselves, and as mentioned before, their confidence in this approach is continually being undermined by the professional advice they are receiving from outside experts and economists.[2]

Pacific islanders now have a choice. They can choose to live in the village sector or to make various incursions into and commitments to the development sector. But the fact is that whereas the village sector used to sustain them, now it does so less efficiently. And its structures and understandings are not often drawn in to activities that could, from an outsider's point of view, be regarded as progressive or innovative. If adhering to the village sector sustains them within the paradigm of subsistence affluence, villagers will inevitably be poor in comparison with compatriots who are positioned to take part in the formal economic sector, or with migrants who have left the village and gone beyond it to the cities within the nation-state or in the countries far away with which the nation has a migrant-remittance relationship.

However, while it is possible to arrive at a reasonable understanding of the village sector in its earlier condition, it is arguable whether it was ever unsullied or ever, by implication, static. Oral histories, genetic analysis and archaeological evidence point to pre-European exploration, migration and colonisation; to the mix afforded by juxtaposition of cultures and dynamism of life on small islands reliant on sea-faring and the great voyages undertaken by accident or deliberation. These small societies, while comparatively unitary, were unitary only by degree, not by any absolute standard. Mobility was slower and more haphazard, but nevertheless was still a fact of life, and indeed an essential element. Tribal societies could and did expand or contract over time (due to population growth or decline and political ambitions), with clans or sub-clans splitting off from other kin groups to move to other residential locations. And incursions by various Westerners had their own impacts, small and particular in some cases, such as the very sighting of these different pale people and the introduction of some of their goods, and bigger and more resonant in others, such as the inadvertent introduction of disease or the more thoroughgoing effects of settlement, involving genetic colonisation, missionisation and economic exploitation.

It could be argued, therefore, that at no time is tradition ever contained, immobile and impervious to change; it can be so only by degree. Thus, as Ward has noted, it is better not to view the region of the Pacific as it often is by Europeans, as Earth's empty quarter, vast and empty. Rather, it should be viewed as the islanders view it, as a mosaic of islands and connections between those living on the periphery and those in the centre, between those in the homeland and those in rim countries. This model recognises sufficiently the initiative and mobility of Pacific island people and their readiness to find new forms of adaptation; it also recognises what may be viewed as a permanent state of transition between tradition and development that in fact epitomises the historical mobility of the Pacific peoples.

In the conditions of the new political economy that has evolved in Oceania, it is clear that such mobility plays a crucial role in development. Murray Chapman analysed Melanesian mobility in these terms:

> As John Waiko once observed in a private conversation: 'We Melanesians are all engaged in a tapestry of life, where the threads of movement hold everything together.' Consequently the essence and meaning of a people's mobility becomes far more comprehensible when conceived as an active dialogue between different places, some urban, some rural, some both and some neither, as incorporating a range of times simultaneously ancient and modern, and as the most visible manifestation of a dialectic between people, communities and institutions. Persons involved in such a dynamic and open-ended process do not see themselves as belonging exclusively to a city residence or to a village birthplace, as being explicitly modern or explicitly traditional in their individual behaviours or collective orientations. ... As White has observed (1992: 100), when considering an entirely different topic for Melanesia, 'it would be a mistake to assign conceptual priority to either the indigenous, or to the exogenous in this encounter'.[3]

The Invention of Developmentalism

In recent years, a number of important studies have shed light on developmentalism, which covers issues of economic development, the Third World and mass poverty as they have been conceptualised, presented and packaged since 1945. Such writers as Escobar (1995), Rahnema (1992), Scott (1998) and, earlier, Polanyi (1957) have reminded us, if we needed reminding, that the evolution of advanced capitalism in North America and Europe in the post-war years, allied to the rivalry for world hegemony of the two superpowers during the Cold War, was a culturally specific process that had enormous impact on the world and how we thought of it.

Of course, the beginning of this process pre-dates 1945. As Marx pointed out in his theory of alienation, the evolution of industrial capitalism in the nineteenth century severed the connection between the craftsman and the products of his labour; as machine production became dominant, the role of labour was dehumanised. The vestiges of the manorial system, with attitudes of *noblesse oblige* or caring for tenants in return for lifelong work and service, rapidly disappeared in the nineteenth century and were replaced by the bleak, impersonal workhouse. This led to the loss of any status the poor may have had.

At the same time, powerful forces of modernisation were at work: the expansion of the market economy, the spread of education and the introduction of political changes such as the Western notion of democracy. The evolution of welfare-state thinking following the Great Depression of 1929-34, including the New Deal in the United States and the Beveridge Report in Britain, suggested a particular approach to alleviating poverty. Traditional societies had always dealt with its reality through their concepts of community, kinship and frugality, but the spread of the market economy led to an undermining of community and kinship mechanisms for dealing with poverty.

Poverty as what Rahnema calls a "pauperising myth" arrived after World War II just as poverty on a global scale was discovered and recognised. When hunger is defined in terms of an identifiable nutritional disease or a quantifiable lack of calories, poverty, squalor and misery become objectified and measurable and may be analysed causally. The annual per capita income of US$100 was chosen by the World Bank in 1948 as a measure to calibrate poverty, and people who lived below this income were defined as 'poor'. It then became known that these 'poor' comprised about two-thirds of the world's population. The reason for this problem was seen to be an insufficiency of income, and its solution clearly was to institute economic growth.

When the other new concept, the 'Third World', appeared in distinction to the capitalist 'First World' and socialist 'Second World', its most essential characteristic was identified as poverty. Development was thus not merely the result of this combination, a slow elaboration of these elements or the result of the introduction of new ideas. It was not even the effect of the establishment of the new financial institutions or international organisations such as the International Bank for Reconstruction and Development (World Bank) and the International Monetary Fund (IMF) at the Bretton Woods Conference in 1944, the UN and its specialised agencies in 1945, and much later the General Agreement on Tariffs and Trade (GATT). Development, therefore, was rather the result of the establishment of a set of relations among these elements, institutions and practices and of the systemisation of these relations to form a whole.

The concept of welfarism also helped to create a great new domain of knowledge and a panoply of interventions that several researchers have termed "the social".[4] The transformation of the poor into 'the assisted' reinforced the break-down of vernacular relations and also helped set in place new mechanisms of control. The 'poor' were now seen as a 'social problem' that required new social strategies. The consolidation of the welfare state and the ensemble of techniques in the twentieth century under the heading of 'social work' (including the concepts of poverty, health, hygiene, employment and education, and recognition of the stress of living in towns and cities) constructed a vast new arena of knowledge about human populations and appropriate modes of social planning.

In his Inaugural Address in 1949, as fears of Communism were growing, President Harry Truman announced a new plan of action. In Point Four of his speech he said:

> ... we must embark on a bold new program ... for the improvement and growth of the underdeveloped areas ... we should foster capital investment in areas needing development ... Greater production is the key to prosperity and peace. And the key to a greater production is a wider and more vigorous application of modern scientific and technical knowledge.[5]

Truman advocated that American business, private capital, agriculture and labour should work together with other rich nations to raise the industrial activity, economic development and standards of living in "under-developed" countries. There was no place in this new age of development for the previous exploitative international relations under imperialism; instead, the emphasis was to be on "democratic fair-dealing".

It is argued by Rist (1997), Escobar (1995), Kindon (1999) and others that the language and ideas inherent in Point Four of Truman's speech launched what is variously called the 'Development Age' or the age of developmentalism. The world was reconceptualised so that previously colonised nations were to be incorporated through the development discourse to become members of a single family, helped or assisted by more developed or advanced nations. Developmentalism was presented as a set of measures that were neutral and outside the realm of politics – the use of scientific knowledge and technology, increase in economic growth and the expansion of trade.

This development model discredited colonialism and justified decolonisation, effectively dismantling old colonial empires like the British and the Dutch and enabling access to new emerging markets. By launching the 'Development Age' and the terms 'developed' and 'under-developed', it established a new language with some new definitions that fixed countries' positions in the world order. This put into practice a new anti-colonial imperialism and charted a new global strategy for different regions of the world.

The scene was well and truly set for the later initiation of the Alliance for Progress, the world's greatest aid programme in the Third World, and for the particular forms it took. The type of development promoted conformed to the ideas and expectations of the affluent West, to what Western countries deemed to be a normal course of evolution and progress. And by conceptualising progress in such terms, the development strategy became a powerful instrument for normalising the world.[6] It was rationalised, standardised, generalised, stereotyped and routinised to enable bureaucrats to simplify development and apply normative 'rules of the game' to Third World problems. The precise nature and geographic and cultural distinctiveness of these Third World realities were thus glossed over and distorted. Further criticisms of these concepts include the invisibility of women and the gross under-representation of their major role in development, and the emphasis on scientific surveys and study of the resource base of countries which ignored the internal ascription of meaning and accessibility to these resources and supposedly provided guidelines for rational planning and development.

The region of Oceania was of very little importance internationally because of the absence of major resources, but the critical battles that were in fact turning points in World War II – the bitter Guadalcanal campaign, and the Battles of the Coral Sea and Midway – gave it a strategic importance out of all proportion to the size of its populations, resources or markets. Its militarisation during the Second World War, the benefits of infrastructure development and wartime prosperity, and the growth of a sense of collective identity of the South Pacific led to the founding of the South Pacific Commission in Noumea in 1947. Its purpose was to strengthen Pacific island social and economic development and the ties of Pacific countries with Australia and New Zealand. Underpinning this new arrangement was the new military alliance between Australia, New Zealand and the United States (ANZUS) under which Australia and New Zealand accepted strategic responsibility for the island nations in the South Pacific.

'Development' in Action

When I started fieldwork in Fiji, I largely believed, like most of my contemporaries in the fields of geography, development studies and economics, that underdevelopment could be reduced to a set of obstacles to be overcome. Such beliefs were founded on the theories of circular causation and stage theories of development that were, in themselves, circular, closed and inflexible. I also believed that the shortage of investment capital (which would help to overcome these obstacles) was of primary importance. By the end of the 1960s, however, economists began to revise their theories because although many Third World countries had managed to raise their savings and investment rates to well above target levels, take-off into sustained growth was proving elusive.

Dependency theory went beyond economics in attempting to provide a general explanation of underdevelopment. A good and popular example was Gunder Frank's 1969 paper, *The Sociology of Development and the Underdevelopment of Sociology*. The policy implication of those who supported the dependency school was for countries to dissociate themselves from the world market which doomed them to underdevelopment because linkage to the centre involved chains of surplus extraction. Only when this was done to a considerable extent by adopting an independent stance of national self-reliance would real autonomous development begin. There would need to be a more or less revolutionary transformation.

By the late 1970s, my own economic views had changed to what has been called by Todaro a modern "neo-structural position":

> This approach ... views underdevelopment in terms of international and domestic power relationships, institutional and structural econom-
> ic rigidities, and the resulting proliferation of dual economies and dual societies both within and among the nations of the world.[7]

Since the 1970s we need to add on to Todaro's statement the various new schools of thinking that are moving steadily to a more comprehensive, indigenous-oriented, geographically-oriented, green-oriented form of development.

At the start of *Koro*, my book that gives a full account of my fieldwork in Fiji, I quote the words of my friend, the Fijian anthropologist Dr R. Nayacakalou, who expressed the hope that Western influences would not strangle the village:

> ... this is only a hope; a hope for the sake of the things which make

village life in its own way as satisfying as town life – its simplicity, its security and peace, its shared work and the excitement and laughter of living in a group.[8]

I also fully shared this hope, as I too admired these things and also realised that the *koro* (village) was the primary focus of Fijian culture. But as a geographer, I felt I had to find, on the ground, examples of enterprises and activities that worked, that not only provided an income and employment but which also contributed to the national economy. The most impressive examples of these were various *galala*, independent farmers living outside the village (and so less inhibited by the demands of their kin), and some entrepreneurs. I devoted two chapters to case studies of Fijians in those two roles, and also examined the partial success of cooperative societies.

It was apparent to me that any solution to the Fijian problem of under-production in the national economy had to be home-grown. But I did agonise over this, pointing out that if Fiji were like Western Samoa, it could afford the luxury, if it liked, of remaining 'traditional' and indulging in the money economy at a rather low level or in desultory ways – if hospitals or schools had to be closed, so be it, it was their choice. But since Fiji was also the home of a large immigrant ethnic group, Indo-Fijians, this choice was not available. Given the situation in Fiji which was very much a plural society, Fijians who already had political dominion had to perform substantially in the cash economy. Indeed, it was very much in their interest to do so.

Was my recommended path trapped by the circular understanding of development that was current then, prescriptive and external? Perhaps so, but one can lean over backwards too far – development is a Western concept, but if a country wants to achieve it, certain actions have to happen for it to occur. It is interesting that my recommendations were the same as those of the Burns Commission, the Spate Report, Belshaw (1964b) and Ward (1965). (Like me, Spate and Ward were geographers.) It was certainly not a matter of ideological conviction on my part but, as a scholar of my time, it was the inescapable conclusion that arose from the evidence of my case studies, from the intellectual and political climate in which I began my career as an academic and as a geographer in the field.

I was undoubtedly influenced by Raymond Firth's approach which was a latter day structural-functionalist updating of Malinowski's pioneering functionalism of the 1920s. I read other major writers on Fiji: Hocart (for example, 1952), Buell Quain's *Fijian Village* (1948) and W.R. Geddes (1959). A major book emerged when Marshall

Sahlins completed his *Moala: Culture and Nature on a Fijian Island* on an island in the Lau Group. When I arrived in Suva, I studied primary sources in the Archives and also went through the papers of the Legislative Council.

At the core of the economic study were key factors of production – land, labour and capital. These needed not only precise measurement but also the indigenous forms in which they occurred identified for Fiji. Thus, lagoon area (and even perhaps some of the open sea outside the reef) needed to be added to the land area and classified into its various types of use (see also Chapter 10 on Abemama, Kiribati). And 'capital' not only involved in the Western sense cash funds held, savings and access to credit, but also fishing hooks and spears, forks and spades, machete and bullocks used for ploughing, since they all produced goods, and also root stock used in this environment where planting was cultigen rather than seed-based. (Thus, after a disastrous flood at Lutu, I noticed that many banana trees had been uprooted and washed away, but when the fallen trunks were chopped up into pieces they became planting stock for many new banana trees.)

I found, however, that land, labour and capital were themselves not enough to understand development in village Fiji, even allowing for the various important ways of mobilising labour under village conditions which illustrated the importance of local initiative aimed at larger attempts at cash cropping or building new European-type houses. I was considerably influenced by the economist Joseph Schumpeter who emphasised the role of entrepreneurs, and came to believe that Third World societies as well as those of the capitalist First World or socialist Second World also needed entrepreneurs, innovators and leaders.

As there was no good overview of the system of shifting cultivation (or rotating land under bush fallowing), I resolved in 1959 to make a study of some of its characteristic forms in Fijian conditions. I tramped up and down many forested hills in various villages, describing, examining, counting and measuring the numerous crops involved, and covered in particular a large number of the gardens possessed by the sample households that were part of my ethnographic study. Sometimes soil samples were taken for analysis to estimate soil nutrient changes throughout the cycle of fallowing. At the same time, I undertook extensive research in Wellington on the literature on shifting agriculture, comparing and evaluating the systems in a wide range of countries in the hot wet tropics. Out of this emerged 'The Nature of Shifting Cultivation', published in the opening issue of *Pacific Viewpoint*.[9]

From the beginning, it became apparent that economic development that involved Fijian society was very much associated with the processes of social change. As villagers moved away from some traditional lifestyles to adopt new transitional or more modern roles, they confronted alternative and often competing or conflicting choices. And where new roles were adopted, social consequences followed. Social change as well as economic development thus involved a movement from colonial situations (attitudes, policies and institutions) to new, more independent patterns of life. Consequently, the process of decolonisation, often assisted by European and other foreign agents, was also involved. Thus, my work in Fiji crystallized many concepts to do with tradition and development that remained central throughout my career.

As I continued in my academic work, my commitment to fieldwork as my main methodological approach to study and scholarship anchored me to what I could call cultural holism – an appreciation of a viable integrated cultural system that in all cases contained the mechanisms for its survival, even when they were eroded by the incursions of colonialism, developmentalism or globalisation. This approach also shored up my commitment to the notion that development cannot be imposed but must be embraced from within, that the indigenous people may not know what they can have or even what questions to ask, but they will know what has congruence with their values and aspirations. I grew to understand that development imposed from the outside with no heed paid to local conditions, beliefs or desires, i.e. ignoring the environment and ignoring the values of the people, will sit like a sore until it scars over or erupts. It will never become part of the whole. But I still believe in 'development' as long as it is the community's own choice, and is sustainable environmentally, economically and culturally. Indeed, all societies need development to pay for their schools, health systems and the entire infrastructure of social efficacy and functionality.

The Structure of the Book

Chapter 2, 'The Economic Response', refers to the people of the South Pacific loosely as half peasants, long since emerged from that cultural, social and economic state usually described as 'primitive' or 'tribal', but still painfully groping towards an uncertain future. Study of this condition and the various processes of change led me to wonder, like Geertz, whether some of these developing nations or emergent societies really were emerging or developing; or whether they were reeling from the intensity, forms and impact of Western capitalism and colonialism. This chapter therefore examines structural economic change in these island societies. While they have been monetised, with new cash crops fitted into the village mode of production for over a century, there has been virtually no change in production technology. With the growth of towns or cities and areas of modern capitalist production, a dual economic situation and system emerged. Over time, there has been a centralising process under way in both the larger countries and especially the island archipelagos. This involved migration of both a short-term temporary nature, and longer-term circular, then semi-permanent and permanent migration from the village peripheries to the main places of employment, and especially the cities and towns. As the small port-of-trade enclaves and colonial towns grew into more complex and sophisticated towns and cities with a wider range of functions, institutions and attractions, urbanisation became a greater force in social change.

Chapter 3 reminds readers that the region of Oceania possesses none of the characteristics of the major continents of Europe, America and Asia. In many parts of Asia until recently, most rural people usually lived in conditions of grinding poverty because of over-population, where the average small farmer could barely scrape together a living because of lack of land and capital though using his meagre resources to the full. The situation is very different in Oceania. Here the reverse is true, for the production unit, the household, could produce as much as it could consume with the use of only part of the land and labour resources available to it. The Australian economist E.K. Fisk, returning from Asia to work in Papua New Guinea around 1960, reached conclusions that were similar to those I reached while working in Fijian villages, and which were confirmed by the Victoria University of Wellington Solomons team project a few years later. As Fisk (1962, 1964) concluded, the subsistent, self-sufficient type of farmer in the Pacific had a considerably higher standard of consumption than hundreds of millions of poorer peasants of Asia at the time, and could achieve this with relatively little work (about 10-25 hours per week per household) and with virtually no money income. Thus was born the concept of subsistence affluence, a factor that has not been widely recognised by administrators, scholars, and even economists studying or planning development in Oceania.

Chapter 4 sets out a generalised model of the village mode of production (or the mixed subsistence-cash cropping mode). Of course, the detailed characteristics and crop combinations vary from country to country in Oceania, depending on micro-environmental differences, the varying response rate of villagers to adopting new crops to introduce into the system and many other factors. It is important to note that its very success as a system relies on its sound ecological basis, exploiting a complementary association of plants with a variety of growth habits. Its diversity minimises losses to pests, disease and climatic factors and usually ensures security in food supplies to meet family nutritional needs. These are all important strengths in supporting a *subsistence* system and limiting the dangers. The problem occurs, of course, when it is adapted to achieve ends for which it was never designed: the production of cash crops destined for *market sale*.

It is the response to planting permanent crops (such as coconut palms), and competition for land, population pressure and the desire to earn money that have led to modifications in the traditional gardening system. Thus, in Vanuatu crops of yam which were of paramount ceremonial importance (and time consuming to grow) have been confined to reduced areas in favour of more easily cultivated taro, manioc, sweet potatoes and bananas.[10] Where the length of fallowing has been reduced due to land shortage, the grower has resorted to root crops that will out-yield yams in a situation of declining fertility. These modifications have largely maintained food production and in constrained space and time but are not maintaining soil fertility in the shortened bush fallow. Moreover, the introduction of a crop like manioc means the nutritive value of food crops produced is declining.

One can tinker with the system to an extent by modifying the crops planted, but once the sound ecological basis of restoring soil fertility by an adequate bush fallow period is jeopardised, the grower will have to move to a new and costly system requiring regular inputs of fertiliser, and disease and pest control. Specialisation of production resulting in bigger harvests of crops with good market prices may bring monetary gain, but lowered botanical diversity might bring lowered soil fertility, erosion, the danger of crop failures, or increased pest and disease problems. We should remember that the village mode of production underpins not only subsistence but also provides the economic basis of the village social security system in these countries where the governments are too poor to be able to afford national social security systems.

The succeeding chapters discuss development and change in several Oceanic countries: Fiji (Chapters 5, 6, 7 and 8), Kiribati (Chapters 9 and 10), Papua New Guinea (Chapter 11) and Vanuatu (Chapter 12) and their varying journeys to what they hope will be progress.

Much of my approach to Fiji grew out of my understanding of the Polynesian societies I had already studied – Hawaii and Samoa. And although Fiji is classed as Melanesian in ethnic type, this is rather misleading, for after the Tongans occupied the southern and eastern areas of the Fiji group in the eighteenth century, the socio-political structure was largely reshaped. The extensive social stratification of Fiji reflected the Tongan pattern. When a great chief who held several of the highest-ranking titles such as Ratu Sir Lala Sukuna emerged and also achieved outstanding prominence and acceptance in the European world, I realised that such a man could wield enormous influence, whether for good or ill. I resolved to examine his role as a leader in Fiji in the period of the 1930s-1950s to estimate whether he prepared the country to cope with the undoubted vicissitudes that would be found in the years of independence ahead (see Chapter 5).

There were a small number of turning points in the history of Fiji when fateful decisions were taken, or not taken, that made it more difficult for Fijians to adopt economic roles as independent farmers or to take on other commercial roles outside the traditional village structure where they might work in competition or alongside Indians. One turning point was the decision of Ratu Sir Lala Sukuna not to join the European-type company set up by the cult leader Apolosi Nawai in the 1930s or support his aims, but instead to repress the movement and banish Apolosi. The failure of any British Governor and his government in the 1930s or 1940s to make a sustained effort to encourage exemption of independent farmers made it less likely that this would happen, since little economic development of significance occurred within the village structure.

In Chapter 6, I give a case study of a Fijian village where I conducted fieldwork in 1959, Nalotawa. It was a small village I discovered as I undertook surveys in Viti Levu, and in many ways it seemed isolated and even protected from the influences of urban Fiji and the disparities in living standards between Fijians and Fiji Indians. Social cohesion was strong and the traditional clan-based organisation was evident. People related through their status and ascribed roles, and much of this degree of social organisation was based on access to land and land use. Village agriculture was of the shifting agriculture type, and the people were involved in the cash economy only peripherally, selling surplus goods at local markets, but basically operating in a traditional subsistence and reciprocal fashion. I characterised Nalotawa as a traditional village where people were generally happy with what they had and did not show aspirations to work harder, to find out about ways to improve production or to move away. But I was also aware of the forces of change surrounding Nalotawa and concerned about whether these forces could be accommodated or made room for; these ponderings were brought to a head for me when the cautiously progressive village chief, Ratu Jone Lotawa, showed that he was open to the idea of some of the village lands being used for a pine plantation project.

In Sorolevu, by contrast (Chapter 7), I found a Fijian village where traditionalism appeared to be having detrimental effects, and disparities in production levels between Fijians and Fiji Indians were pronounced and seemed to threaten survival and viability. In this chapter, I give an account of the sugar-cane industry in Fiji; levels of production; differing agricultural practices; and the interaction between environmental, social and economic factors. I also discuss what I identified as cultural impediments to economic progress in the village. It appeared that several of the traditional structures had broken down, and that there was a partial involvement in the wider economy, a malaise that meant that neither traditionalism nor enterprise was working, and therefore the village was suffering.

Fiji in Retrospect, Chapter 8, looks back with hindsight to the Fiji where I did my fieldwork 50 years ago, and brings to bear the intervening years on the dynamic forms of social organisation exemplified in Nalotawa and Sorolevu. This essay describes some of the huge political upheavals that have impacted on traditional Fijian society, including the growing involvement of villagers in the formal sector, the rise of racism, increasing land disputes and shortages, and the narrowing of the Fijian economic base. It shows that the production gap between Indo-Fijians and Fijians is the same as it was 40 years ago, and that such disparities underlie and feed the incipient racism of Fijian society. Paradoxically, Fijians are still economically inferior to the Indo-Fijians, though they remain, along with Europeans, dominant politically. This chapter addresses the essential character of traditionalism and the incursions of the formal sector and globalisation into it in a way that gives a useful linear and chronological approach to fundamental social change and economic pressures.

Chapters 9 and 10 are derived from the Victoria University of Wellington Rural Socio-economic Survey of the Gilbert and Ellice Islands of which I was director. Fieldwork was carried out in the early 1970s by a team of geographers and anthropologists in several islands of what is now the Republic of Kiribati, and one island of the Ellice group, now Tuvalu. The project included a study of the meaning of development. This was a major topic and was explored carefully with islanders by each team member. Our purpose was to find a way to identify an internal view of development, rather than to do what so many development projects had done: impose it from the outside. Essentially, the project showed an awareness of the fact that economic growth is not necessarily a sufficient or adequate process to ensure economic health or sustainability. Nor does it necessarily translate into better education, health and living standards. An internal view is likely to have different ways of assessing wealth, or even in deciding what it is. Notions of subsistence and capital are also likely to have local meanings. Internal and external views of development can be complementary in positive ways, rather than merely conflicting.

Chapter 10 focuses on Abemama, the Gilbertese atoll where I lived for a year with my family while I took part in this project. It provides a close examination of the island, the people and the culture, and the issues and problems it faced during this time. The chapter is thus a careful and stringent account of developmentalism in the field, of how people live their lives, create safety and security for their families, and ride the waves of outside influences and the demands of the cash economy. It presents details about the subsistence way of life and the cash economy, the pattern of daily life and the problems that are endemic in Kiribati as it has moved into independence: migration, urbanisation, high population density, the spread of disease, the breakdown of social order, poverty and pressure on social organisation.

Chapter 11, by contrast, gives the results of a multi-disciplinary team who set out to look at development options in Kandrian-Gloucester, West New Britain, Papua New Guinea. While the project seemed well-devised and supported, in fact it is an example of the more typical form of development project that prescribes and recommends rather than listens to internal ideas and values. Nevertheless, its conclusions have validity, both for the region and country, but await local acceptance. The chapter emphasises the huge challenge that the escalation of transport costs posed to rural dwellers. In fact, it identifies a 'vicious circle' operating in the region which unravels development and brings it to a complete standstill. While the team did not know about the particular factors and their precise interaction, it became clear through the comments of a visiting Australian scientist some years after our study that practically all produce or cash crops that had formerly been produced and shipped out to market had ceased, although traditional canoes might take very small quantities to local points of sale.

Chapter 12, A Tale of Two Leaders, is an account of national politics in Vanuatu. While there, I met and observed the wily and engaging Jimmy Stevens, leader of the Nagriamel politico-cult which momentarily offered the appealing vision of a future of working together with other cultures in peace and friendliness (the Nagriamel flag showed a white hand grasping a black hand). Sadly, Stevens' vaulting ambitions proved to be his undoing: he could not resist dealing with unscrupulous American adventurers and frustrated French settlers who used him to oppose the democratically-elected government of Walter Lini, and his secessionist rebellion was defeated. At the same time, I witnessed the emergence to national prominence of Lini who built up the Vanuaku Party, one of the most impressive nationalistic, modernising political parties in the South Pacific. Lini, in my view, has been the outstanding political leader in the whole of Oceania (despite being infected by the unrealistic idealism of the post-Vietnam War 1970s), but the difficulties he faced in his newly independent country and the onset of both ill-health and the re-emergence of the underlying social structure – the classic Big Man-style pattern of personalism, opportunism and self-aggrandisement – eventually undid and destroyed his leadership.

Chapter 13 presents the case of the small MIRAB economies (Niue, Tokelau, the Cook Islands, Kiribati and Tuvalu), which in sharp contrast to the much larger and resource-rich countries of Melanesia (Solomons, Vanuatu and Papua New Guinea) are poor in a monetary sense but have ingeniously discovered, with the assistance of metropolitan parties such as the United States, France, New Zealand or Australia, a novel combination of factors to provide a moderate level of income and considerable economic, social and political stability over time. These are migration, remittances, overseas aid, and the forms and functions of bureaucracy (which make up the acronym MIRAB). As a descriptive device, the acronym captures the four main elements and drivers of these economies, and as an analytical tool it has gone a good way to explaining the real dynamics sustaining and shaping the economies of these small nations.

These essays are merely my attempt, as a working journeyman, to identify the major problems and issues affecting some Pacific countries. I invite you to make up your own mind about them and to enquire further.

2

The Economic Response of South Pacific Societies

'The Economic Response to South Pacific Societies' was first published in Pacific Viewpoint, *in 1970. This paper was deliberately speculative, focusing on questions not usually addressed in South Pacific studies, and provided a broader framework within which changes in individual island societies could be more adequately assessed. I looked at a variety of hypotheses that could be used to illustrate the characteristics of these countries in a global context, and postulated how future research may well revise a number of them and suggest more accurate alternatives.*

It is obvious that any schema applied to such a heterogeneous region, embracing as it does such a multitude of different cultures that have all been subjected to different forms and intensities of Western impact, and have developed their own patterns of socio-economic response, must be very generalised. Since most concepts which form part of the schema are especially fruitful in only a small number of island groups, I attempt to relate most generalisations to one or two specific groups.

The people of the South Pacific may be broadly referred to as 'half peasants', long since emerged from that cultural, social and economic state usually described as 'primitive' or 'tribal', yet painfully groping their way towards an uncertain future.[1] Study of this condition and of the processes of change leads one to ponder, like Geertz, whether some of these "emergent societies" really are "emerging" or "developing".

And while it may be clear what are they emerging from, it is not as clear what are they developing into. Their emergence is arguably dependent on extrinsic factors such as the force of the world economy, the pull of migration and the attraction of 'progress' and consumerism. Such pondering also arrives at an important question: if, ultimately, the solution of emigration is denied to South Pacific societies, will some remain semi-modern, 'permanently transitional' societies (cf. Geertz, 1965), committed increasingly to the modern world, yet possessing such minuscule natural resources and inadequately modernised economies that their aspirations cannot be fulfilled? 'Modernisation' is here used in a limited sense to encompass all those structural and organisational changes of societies and their economies, but omitting mainly 'behavioural change' and 'normative' and 'ethical change' except where these are related to economic response.[2] I use the term especially to refer to clearly discernible economic and social changes.[3]

Structural Economic Change

Intensity of Western Impact

The greatest force of change in the South Pacific has been the impact of Western capitalism and colonialism and the incorporation of the region and its societies into the world market system in varying ways. While the first task in historical research is clearly to document the occurrence of the main events in the intrusion of the West, it is unfortunate that studies of sociological history have barely begun in the region. The major effects of Western penetration were the alienation of land, which was extensive in the Solomons, the New Hebrides and New Caledonia, moderate in Fiji and minimal in most other groups; the effects of introduced diseases, alcohol and firearms; the beginnings of coconut oil and later copra trade (following the earlier supply of fresh food to whalers and the trepang and sandalwood trades); the 'missionisation' of island societies; the foundation of plantations by expatriates; the labour trade; the opening up of wage employment following the foundation and growth of towns; and the evolution of the colonial administrative structures, and new commercial and service occupations. The general result of Western economic impact has been the dominance of the modern economic sector in most island groups by Europeans, while the middleman's role has often been monopolised by immigrant Asians.

Western enterprise involves both the monetisation of island societies as their land, labour and produce acquired market values, and also the progressive introduction of the market economy with its radically different principles of integration. The tiny, fragmented economies of the Pacific, while predominantly of a subsistence or self-sufficient nature, can usefully be described as 'reciprocity' and 'redistributive' economies, since integration was partly achieved and goods and services moved according to principles of reciprocity or at the behest of the redistributive appropriatory role of chiefs.[4]

In considering the region as a whole, it is clear that the form of Western impact was highly variable. The ravages of introduced diseases and the effects of alcohol and of blackbirding took an especially heavy toll in Melanesia; and resettlement from inland to coastal locations, forced by the missionaries, led to more rapid depopulation in some islands[5] than occurred, for instance, in Samoa.

Western penetration can be assessed too by the size of investments, the number of job opportunities available on the new plantations and the extent of capitalisation that occurred in previously non-monetised societies. Here, the force of American and French impact in Hawaii and Tahiti, and the relatively heavy investments by expatriates in Fiji[6] contrasted, for example, with the less intense impact and lower level of investment in Western Samoa, and minimal investment in Tonga and the Cook Islands. Island groups such as Samoa and Tonga, which lacked mineral resources, offered little land and very small markets, and enjoyed a measure of protection from missionary or government authorities (or, frequently, from the effects of international rivalry), have thus experienced less far-reaching changes than those parts of Melanesia which have experienced blackbirding, large-scale land alienation and government policies that have provided fewer obstacles to capitalists in their search for profits. Whether changes have been traumatic in their effects depends on how they are perceived by indigenes and whether they believe the control they feel they have over the circumstances governing their lives is seriously threatened.[7] Variations in the severity of Western impact and in indigenous perceptions may be closely related to patterns of response to new opportunities and indigenous self-assertions of independence, but it would seem largely to account for the strength of traditionalism in Western Samoa, where a neo-traditional form of the social structure has appeared to survive substantially intact and is only now beginning to undergo structural change.

In socio-cultural terms, Western penetration has been characterised by Valentine (1963) as being relatively tolerant and mild in Polynesia and Micronesia, working often through indirect rule, with somewhat variable and often flexible systems of ethnic stratification introduced into societies whose high degree of stratification made them not incompatible with the social exclusiveness of the colonial system.

In addition to their well-developed stratification system, Polynesian societies were characterised by a centralisation of political authority to a greater degree than in the stateless and highly segmented societies of Melanesia. Accordingly, Polynesian responses were predominantly secular, and mediated principally through indigenous institutions or chiefly councils. Valentine notes that they were strongly acculturative and largely non-millenarian, often at least passively accepting ethnic stratification and oriented towards either assimilation or nationalism. In Melanesia, however, egalitarian, highly segmented societies could claim only limited sovereignty since the loci of power were fluid and political systems were even less centralised. Western socio-cultural impact here was severe and relatively rigid, and static ethnic hierarchies were introduced along with forms of direct rule in Melanesia (excluding Fiji) and French Polynesia. Melanesian responses were thus supernaturalistic, expressed through religious forms, apocalyptic and syncretistically acculturative. Often they have been violently anti-European, strongly opposed to ethnic stratification and have become politically innovative.

Forms of Western Impact

Associated with the severity of Western impact are the forms of syncretism and reintegration that island societies have been able to achieve primarily through the process of 'missionisation'. The reintegration of village society under the protective guidance of the missionaries or local pastor is a major feature of the whole region in which church and mission school continue to play vital roles. Although there is a large literature on the activities of missionaries and their rivalry in the Pacific, there are few good studies of the complex sociological changes involved in the evolution of societies toward a theocratic traditionalism and pastoral neo-Victorianism which in the form of the reorganised village social structures served to insulate islanders from the painful external world.[8] That missionisation causes a pronounced 'cultural bias' to a society, creating in fact a new culture (though one fraught with internal inconsistencies) as well as new patterns of response can be seen in recent studies comparing the responses of 'Christian' and 'pagan' sub-cultures within the one culture.[9] For example, Keesing's work (1967) on Malaita in the Lau Lagoon describes the heathen Lau as the most progressive people in technological and economic terms, consciously maintaining their own cultural identity. Michael R. Allen (1964 and 1968), in contrast, shows the Christians of Aoba, Vanuatu, to be the champions of change in opposition to the more traditional pagans. The commercially-minded Christians became richer as they planted coconuts at the expense of pig breeding, while the pagans who clung to the graded society ritual and associated pig feasts became impoverished as they grew fewer coconuts. Moreover, as pigs became scarce, the prestige of pagans declined accordingly. The slogan for the first two decades of the twentieth century could well have been 'Christ and Coconuts'.

Variations in styles of colonial rule have also been important, and ideas of trusteeship and benevolent rule expressed in the concept of 'Indirect Rule' in Fiji, for example, provide a major contrast to more direct forms of colonial rule such as practised in Melanesia and French Polynesia, and in the Cook Islands under Colonel Gudgeon in 1901-11.[10] In Fiji, society which had been greatly weakened by internecine war, the ravages of disease, liquor and the labour requirements of the new plantations, was able to achieve a new, stable reintegration in the village 'communal system' where a new cultural amalgam, or 'traditionalism', could flourish. In the Cook Islands, Gudgeon attacked the institutions of a social system which he believed produced "slothful" people by cutting away the authority of the chiefs in land tenure, the judicial system and political administration.[11] In spite of relatively mild forms of economic exploitation, longer periods of more direct rule in the Cook Islands would appear to be a reason for the greater degree of change that has undoubtedly occurred in comparison to Fiji.

In addition to patterns of missionisation and styles of colonialism, other significant issues in the sociological history of the South Pacific over the last century result from the distinctive forms in which islanders participated in the market economy. While some of these result from the nature of the traditional economic system and social structure which will be discussed below, colonial policies in some parts and periods enabled islanders to pay taxes in kind. In general, they were encouraged to grow cash crops within the village setting, which involved little social dislocation. An additional way in which islanders became incorporated in the market economy was to rent their land to Europeans, Indians or other expatriates. Such a passive 'rentier' role leads to minimal change, and the Spate Report (1959) provides evidence of the structural changes in Fijian society occurring in communities actively engaged in marketing and cash cropping compared to those which live 'mindlessly' off rent incomes. Above all, islanders were fortunate (or unfortunate, depending on one's point of view) in that an indigenous crop, the coconut palm, acquired a market value. All that was needed was an extension of the planted area and little social change has been required. Yet the quality of South Sea copra is amongst the poorest in the world and yields per acre are also very low by world standards. Other cash crops, such as the banana, have been 'contextualised' by being incorporated in the traditional crop assemblage of the shifting gardens, causing on the whole little structural change to the agricultural system.

Thus, in Western Samoa, the main changes appear to be merely an expansion of the cultivated area up until recent times and the introduction of cocoa and bananas (sometimes inter-planted) into cropping systems which, on the whole, are little changed although growing population pressure has led to such a reduction in the fallow period of the system of rotational bush fallowing that "degenerative change" might occur.[12] This could force changes not only in crop combinations but also ultimately in the type of land use system and the possible evolution of a new type with different ecological and sometimes different economic and social consequences (cf. Boserup, 1965). And despite a great expansion in the needs and aspirations of Samoans and their experience of cash cropping for nearly a century, Lockwood has stressed that there has been virtually no change in production technology.[13] In Apter's terms (1965), innovation has been "traditionalized". Similar examples of the lack of substantial structural change in land use systems are provided by Johnston (1967) for Aitutaki, Cook Islands, and Watters (1969 a, b and c) for Fiji.

Few examples of maladjustment and poor articulation of sectors of the economy in the course of modernisation could be more significant or serious; as we will see below, Pacific islanders are rushing into the modern world insofar as their expectations and needs are concerned. Yet the agricultural systems on which their economies so largely depend remain traditional and undeveloped.

Plantations

The most important institution of Western capitalism in the region has probably been the plantation. While detailed studies are needed of the sociological role of expatriate coconut plantations comparable to the work of Steward and associates (1956, 1959, 1967) on plantations in Latin America,[14] it would appear that the plantation has been a poor way-station on the road to modernity. Thus in Fiji, the Solomons and New Hebrides, European plantations form an enclave set somewhat apart from the indigenous economy, and there seems to be little 'spin-off' of socio-cultural influences and little economic linkage, except with other expatriate enterprises. Rarely do islanders attempt to copy the superior agronomic methods of nearby European coconut plantations. Islanders work on plantations for only short periods for 'target income' and then return to their villages, which are usually economically autonomous.

In the Solomons, Bellam (1964, 1969) argues that the less acculturated work on plantations while the more acculturated seek earnings in the town. This also seems to occur generally in Papua New Guinea. The cultural distance separating European employers from Melanesian labourers insulated in their labour lines could hardly be greater; even semi-skilled foremen in the New Hebrides are mainly recruited from Micronesians or Polynesians rather than from New Hebrideans. Indeed, it can probably be argued that the role of the plantation has been primarily anti-developmental, dampening rather than enhancing development, for plantation earnings subsidise the continued existence of some largely subsistence villages which might otherwise cease to exist (when land is in short supply), and more favourable trends set in train. The colonial plantation seems to play a role somewhat like the Dutch sugar mills and colonial policy in Modjokuto, Central Java in the 1920s-30s,[15] encouraging the emergence of a partial-proletariat who are neither wholly capitalist nor precapitalist, but who move uneasily between the two sides of the dual economy.

The integration of islanders is only partial, never complete, and few opportunities exist in the plantation system for upward social mobility, for evolution from 'tribesmen' to 'peasant' or, more likely, to 'rural proletarian' (cf. Bassett, 1969). Like the people of Modjokuto who have "one foot on the rice terrace and one foot in the sugar mill", many South Pacific societies remain predominantly 'tribal' or 'part-tribal' yet partly 'peasant', partly 'rural proletarian'. Such are the rigidities and inadequacies of the plantation system (and so inflexible are immigration barriers in metropolitan countries surrounding the region) that there is a real danger of societies remaining 'permanently transitional'. However, the new job opportunities in the rapidly growing towns may offer a partial solution in the larger economies.

Changing Markets

The characteristics of the European plantation are not unnaturally related to the characteristics of the international capitalistic economy. And frequent and massive fluctuations in the world copra price have left their indelible mark not only on the expatriate plantation but also on native copra producers. Unfortunately, the number of variables to be evaluated in analysing the causes of the rise or fall of indigenous copra production are so many that it is extremely difficult to determine the extent to which price fluctuation motivates native response. There is, however, much fragmentary evidence on short-term trends indicating increased native plantings (and harvesting) when the cash return is favourable. And it would be useful to test the hypothesis that when prices fall drastically, the village adopts the typical peasant response of retreating into his 'capsule community' with its subsistence economy, substituting perhaps primarily subsistence root crops (surplus sold on the local market) for cash crops which now bring in such a low return. For example, Lockwood (1968) notes that the village of Utuali'i in Western Samoa, the most commercialised of those he studied and one in which land had become scarce, went out of banana production rather than accept lower returns to labour or change to permanent cropping methods. In spite of Western emphasis on the 'limited needs' and unsustained motivation inherent in island cultures, these characteristics may not be endemic to those cultures but result rather from limited demand[16] and serve as useful defence mechanisms for societies whose progress to modernity is repeatedly nipped in the bud by uncertain market prospects.[17]

Social Structures of Melanesia and Polynesia

The profound difference between the social structures of Melanesia and Polynesia underlies almost all comparisons of indigenous economic response throughout the region, since all forms of economic response should be studied in their special historical and socio-economic contexts. The model of a New Guinea type of society (applicable to much of West Melanesia) has been clearly depicted by Barnes (1962): the structure of social relationships is largely determined by unique networks built up by self-made leaders ('big men'), it is flexible, readily adjusts to new circumstances and incorporates foreign culture traits. While there is local variability, strong individualism and residential mobility are characteristic. Bilateral or quasi-unilineal descent and inheritance occur, local group membership is determined by multiple criteria, and there is little or no emphasis on seniority, specialisation of labour or hierarchy of any sort. The implications of this type of structure for promoting rapid economic development are well known: factors of production are relatively variable, the 'Big Man' pattern is conducive to the emergence of entrepreneurs, the absence of solidary institutions with fixed status means that sociological barriers are few, and the accent on individualism and achievement is congruent with the requirements of capitalism. In these societies, the main barriers to economic growth may well be the shortage of capital, skill, technology, poor infrastructure and market access, and constraints imposed by external factors such as colonialism and poor market prospects; however, the need for would-be entrepreneurs to distribute much of their savings to display their generosity is a serious obstacle to economic growth.

It will suffice here to allude briefly to one example of the enterprising response of a society which broadly conforms to the 'New Guinea' model: the Nduindui of West Aoba, New Hebrides.[18] Allen estimated that between a quarter and a third of all adult males made at least one trip to the Queensland plantations in the period of the labour trade:

> The songs and tales of the Queensland era tell of many hardships and cruelties, but they also convey a sense of excitement, curiosity and an eagerness to acquire both the knowledge and the material possessions of Europeans.[19]

Amongst other examples of such Melanesian societies are the Gorokans who value wealth highly, seek the prestige that comes from accumulating and managing wealth, and when acting as members of a group, often pool their wealth for specific purposes.[20]

In contrast to those west Melanesian patterns of response that appear to be strongly conditioned by their distinctive social structure, Polynesian societies are much more inflexible, hierarchical and cohesive. Solidary social groups comprise a fixed hierarchy of segments, whose status is determined largely by descent. Ascription is much more important than achievement and elaborate ceremonial, and prescribed patterns of decision-making make the whole structure more hierarchical and less flexible than the west Melanesian pattern (excluding Fiji, whose social structure is closer to the Polynesian type). The narrow scope for individual enterprise in a Samoan-type society has been criticised by economists[21] and geographers[22] who note that the *matai* system inhibited social deviancy, discouraging innovation or the accumulation of individual savings.

Does the apparently less favourable 'Samoan' type of social structure provide a greater barrier to social change and economic development than the west Melanesian system?[23] No clear answer can be given at this point, although I believe the social obstacles facing the commoner are more formidable than in Melanesia. Thus Mead (1928) has shown the small scope for social deviants or would-be entrepreneurs that exist in Samoa.[24]

To some extent, the attainment of a rapid rate of economic growth in Samoa requires changes in traditional norms or an increase in the number of enterprising social deviants rather than an extension of traditional achievement motivation into modern activities. However, the disadvantages of Polynesian systems are in reality less great than they appear to be.[25] In fact, Samoa has incorporated much more change within the apparently unchanged structure of *fa'a Samoa* than is generally recognised.[26] While the main institutions appear to be reasonably intact and the symbols of tradition continue to be important, the growing tide of emigration from Western Samoa and accumulating evidence of substantial organisational change and social realignment (to use Firth's terms, 1959b) suggest that a process of massive transformation might well be under way. The traditional structure has been manipulated to capitalise on new advantages of wage earning. Thus, although the segmentation of the ambilineal descent group (*aiga*) and of *matai* titles are traditional processes,[27] it appears that increased economic (and political) incentives in modern times have induced Samoans to make frequent use of these mechanisms. Lockwood (1968) notices, for example, that the desire of untitled men (*taulele'a*) to acquire banana licences which can only be granted to *matai* has led to splitting of *matai* titles or the creation of new titles. Boyd[28] has noted the great increase in the number of titles necessary for acquiring the franchise that preceded the 1968 election, and recently that the applications of 600 would-be *matai* were turned down prior to the 1970 election. And in the 1950s, the desire to acquire control (*pule*) over land lying along a new road route coupled with the declining authority of *matai* led to segmentation and re-settlement of some *aiga* in the village of Taga.[29]

Such social realignment or the readjustment of institutions to new circumstances by more extensive use of traditional mechanisms are everywhere characteristic of the modernisation process. But in the last two decades there is mounting evidence to suggest that 'organisational' and even possibly some 'structural changes' are in themselves not adequate to meet the new rapidly expanding needs and aspirations of Samoans. For even if we did accept the dubious view that the pattern of change is relatively evenly paced and harmonious, we cannot ignore the fact that over the period 1955-66 the net emigration total reached over 10,000: by 1966, 8 percent of the Samoan population was living abroad.[30] (In the 1966 NZ Census, 26,271 Polynesians from the Pacific were in New Zealand, including nearly 12,000 Samoans.) By 1965, moreover, as much as £255,000 had entered the Western Samoa economy unofficially in the form of remittances, which represents nearly 10 percent of cash income earned from copra, cocoa and bananas. The even greater magnitude of emigration from the Cook Islands and its enormous dependence on remittances shows the same trend even more clearly, emphasising the position of the islands as backward regions in a total South Pacific economy in which the metropolitan countries are the advanced poles of development.

Changing Ecotype and Cultural Ecological Change

Study of the variable intensity and forms of Western impact on the South Pacific should deepen our knowledge of the pattern of change, but most insight might be gained from case studies of positive and effective indigenous response.

Recent studies in this field include Scarlett Epstein (1968) for the Tolai of New Britain; Lasaqa (1968) on the Tasimboko, Guadalcanal; Michael R. Allen (1964) on the Nduindui, Aoba, New Hebrides; Spate (1959), Belshaw (1964b), Ward (1965) and Watters (1969a) on Fiji; Johnston (1967) and B.J. Allen (1969) on the Cook Islands; and Lockwood (1968) and Pitt (1970) on Western Samoa.

In a field in which the evaluation of so many variables is difficult, the use of models is particularly useful in rigorously directing attention to correlations of strategic importance. Thus, Fisk (1962, 1964) has formulated a model of a primitive economy based on the proposition that production in a situation of "primitive affluence" is limited by the ceiling that exists to demand rather than any shortage of factors of production (e.g. labour or land). When regular contact is made with the advanced market sector, however, he suggests that the degree of participation in the market will vary with the strength of the incentive to do so, which will largely depend on the effectiveness of linkage to the market. The findings of Lockwood above give general support to this model, though the complexity of the response factor (generalised in the model) must not be overlooked.

The importance of linkage with the market, including the crippling cost of transporting goods from isolated regions, has been demonstrated for Guadalcanal by Lasaqa (1969). Thus, in his analysis of produce sold in the Honiara market, Lasaqa found that the region of Tasimboko West contributed up to two-thirds of all goods sold. The dominance of this region was attributed to its productive alluvial soils, proximity to Honiara, and the ease of arranging both sea and land transport. In contrast, Paripao District which is about 40 miles from Honiara and is served in the main only by difficult foot tracks contributed less than 2 percent of all produce sold in the market.

Without disputing in any way the validity of Epstein's subtle analysis of Tolai economic development in which she stresses the suitability of indigenous institutions as vehicles for modern development, she does not overlook the existence of the sizeable nearby urban market of Rabaul, the excellent roading systems of the Gazelle Peninsula nor the productive soil base. These are, perhaps, some of the necessary, though not sufficient, conditions to explain economic 'take off'. Indeed, Finney has noted that rapid economic development in New Guinea, in spite of the Melanesian penchant for achievement, is largely limited to only a few areas, notably the Gazelle Peninsula, Goroka and other accessible areas of the Highlands.[31] This indicates the vital importance of exogenous factors, including suitable crops and soils, good communication and marketing facilities, and an attitude that is at least permissive on the part of the administration and European private enterprise.

In general, patterns of response in Fiji confirm Fisk's proposition but in addition exemplify how the domestication of an alien crop may radically alter social structure. Thus, in contrast to the usual dependence on the indigenous coconut palm, the cultivation of a field crop – sugar cane – has in a few parts of Fiji acted as an engine of change that might ultimately transform local society. Former subsistence shifting cultivators are now becoming accustomed to new field routines and in pursuit of high cash returns are using artificial fertilisers and other technical innovations. With growing individual investments in clan land, quasi-freehold and capitalistic attitudes are emerging, and a chain reaction process of change is underway.[32] It must be stressed, however, that these trends are occurring in only some villages in the highly capital-intensive cane zone of western Viti Levu, Fiji, where the combined impact of the highly efficient South Pacific Sugar Mills Ltd, and the existence of high prices, excellent infrastructure, quasi-urban conditions and the economic challenge posed by Indians provide a unique economic environment, encouraging change that is unrivalled throughout the entire region. Indeed, it is perhaps surprising that Fijian villages of the cane zone, encapsulated in their 'traditionalised' communal system by the over-protective policies of indirect rule, and enjoying the cushion provided by subsistence affluence, have resisted the opportunities of modernisation for so long.

In terms of a more general model of modernisation (though one which necessarily loses usefulness, as an analytical tool, compared to Fisk's more precise formulation), individual choice at Sorolevu has been strongly influenced by the revolution in economic environment or 'ecotype' that has occurred with the development of the cane zone which is part of the advanced or capitalistic sector of the dual economy. In Wolf's terms (1955), Sorolevu is becoming part of a "neotechnic" ecotype in contrast to the relatively stagnant 'paleotechnic' ecotype of villages in the traditional sector. Erasmus (1967), Geertz (1965) and Potter (1968) have recently documented the chain reaction process of change that substantial alterations to infrastructure, including greatly improved linkage to the market in Fisk's sense and other increases in capitalisation, induce in a society leading to a destruction of 'peasant' or 'tribal' systems of production and culture, and the evolution of 'farmer' or other rural capitalist socio-economic types characterised by appropriate cultural conditions.

Urbanisation and Social Change

Most forms of change discussed so far come under the broad category of what J.C. Mitchell[33] terms "processive" or historical change, since they embrace overall changes in the social system, including the norms of in-migrants. But it is apparent that in the few genuine cities of the region (Suva, Rabaul, Noumea, Port Moresby, Papeete), the urban structure and institutions have evolved sufficiently to require 'situational change' on the part of new in-migrants, in that their behaviour necessarily changes when they participate in the different social system of the town. New action patterns appropriate to the new situation are called for. Indeed, without using these terms, Nayacakalou[34] describes situational change when he refers to Fijian conformity to trade unions in Suva in spite of their non-Fijian ideology and ethos. Whitelaw (1966) and McTaggart (1963) have described respectively the urban geography of Suva and Noumea, and the character of industrial and administrative structures and of demographic factors within the city. These structures may act as powerful agents of social transformation, or situational change, as A.L. Epstein (1967) argues for Central Africa, and there may be 'towns within the town' or differences between suburbs in the influence of urban structure on the migrant. Indeed, in 1969 there were 28 officially recorded, unproclaimed Fijian villages in Suva, and Harré and McGrath (1970) have recently noted the wide variation in forms of adaptation to the urban milieu which they represent. As nearby housing estates develop, some (like Raiwai) gradually dissolve and lose much of their identity. But as a geographer, I am conscious of the danger of reifying the importance of situational change and overstressing the importance of urban structures. The most pertinent question is not what is Suva like, but what is it thought to be? Studies on urban institutions are important, but more important is the character of Fijians living in Suva (cf. Kay, 1963, for Papeete). We must look through the institutional structure as if it is transparent to the people that it contains and see Suva as the confluence of the life histories of many individuals who came there and who will come there for private reasons.

Critical questions in elaborating an adequate model of urbanisation relate to labour commitment and the level of consumption. Are Pacific islanders like the Mambwe of Zambia, whose visits to the urban copper belt have been described as "peasants robbing the cash economy" of goods?[35] (The term "rob" is unfortunate as presumably the Mambwe earn through their labour the goods they acquire in the city.) Thus, the employment of New Hebrideans as stevedores at Santo does not imply any alteration in their labour commitment, for although only one person in 20 in the New Hebrides is still engaged solely in subsistence agriculture, urban employment is still primarily for "target income".[36]

Similarly, I found in Fiji that only a small number of villages and a small number of people in most villages had reached a level of commitment to the money economy that was sufficiently complete or sustained to put them beyond the "modified target worker" category. Most notable among these were permanent migrants to Suva and the most progressive cane farmers of the Dry Zone. But Whitelaw found quite different patterns of labour commitment in comparing two peri-urban villages near Suva.[37] One, Suvavou, had only 12 out of 66 males over 18 in permanent employment in the city, most men gardening on their own land and engaging in casual work at the Suva wharf. In Tasivua, in contrast, which is made up of migrants from almost every province of Fiji, 64 men out of 65 households are in permanent employment in Suva, presumably because they do not own land and, in contrast to Suvavou, the extent of land holding is limited. This conforms to Kunkel's hypothesis that where sufficient land (or lagoon) area is not available and local cash earnings and cash relations are scanty, villagers are forced to participate in external economic activities by exporting a cash crop or labour.[38] As their local economic autonomy declines and their participation in the economic system of the nation becomes greater, so their social organisation becomes increasingly consistent with that of the nation.

Centralisation

The importance of money as a means of achieving the goals of migrants moving in to Pacific island towns or to metropolitan countries has now been at least tentatively established.[39] Money is needed to buy the cultural symbols of social importance sought by islanders. This suggests that islanders increasingly prefer the job opportunities of the towns to continuing in village agriculture, supplemented by occasional forays into the wage economy. Typically, employment in towns provides an annual income that is rather higher than most villagers derive from cash cropping at current levels of labour input (though below the incomes of leading rural entrepreneurs), and it appears that a wage dualism between town and country might develop.[40] Moreover, the low status of agriculture compared to collar-and-tie employment may be significant factors in Samoa[41] and the Cook Islands.[42] The decisions of migrants are, of course, dependent on their cognition of the town, and the significant distinction that Tahitians make between the preferred "fast money" (received in weekly pay-packets in urban-type employment) and the less popular "slow money" (gained in less regular payments of cash crops grown in the country)[43] might help our understanding of patterns of urbanisation.[44]

The increasing urbanisation of South Pacific societies is part of the process of social change accompanying or associated with the growing centralisation of island economies. This trend, described in Tonga by Walsh (1964), appears to occur in almost all South Pacific groups. Thus, in the Cook Islands the population of Rarotonga comprised only

25.1 percent of the total population in 1902, but by 1956 it had reached 43.2 percent and by 1966 nearly 52 percent. Increasing concentration of population distribution and economic activity might perhaps lead to greater interest and involvement by more people in the affairs of the city, the nation and national politics.

The consequences of centralisation are many: in the political field, the concentration of power at Apia is certain to introduce major changes to a traditional polity in which, apart from the occasional concentration of paramount titles in one person, the traditional basis for a stable, centralised system of political authority was weak. In the absence of a strong traditional, centralised form of government, the problems of creating a bureaucracy that can meet the insistent demands of the external world create internal dissension and conflict, and difficulties of reconciliation become acute. Associated with this are the varying degrees in which islanders become 'politicised', or members of the 'participant society', who are sufficiently aware of and involved in nationalistic or universalistic goals, rather than purely parochial and traditional goals. Boyd (1968) documents the problems faced by government in such a situation, including problems arising from the strained relationships between "the fast runners" near the capital and their "slow brothers" in outer districts. Although one-party states are characteristic of the region, social mobilisation and politicisation are likely to be increasingly affected by the centralisation process with its sociological consequences.

But centralisation of island economies and migration to towns within the region might merely presage historically a more significant migratory movement outside the region to metropolitan countries. If recent trends are continued and immigration restrictions in New Zealand do not become completely prohibitive, a classic movement of peoples would appear to be under way, with the village-town migration in the islands representing merely the first step of a much larger movement ultimately to the main pole of development in the entire South Pacific region.[45] Seen in this light, migration reflects a growing awareness by islanders of the relative economic backwardness or inadequacy of their island homes.

Migration to New Zealand needs to be studied in its full perspective, including not only its negative features (the loss of the most skilled and most enterprising people) but also assessing its positive role in recent change. Clearly, the isolation of closed communities has gone forever. Although the degree of exposure to mass media varies greatly throughout the region,[46] in the age of the transistor and other modern forms of communication many Pacific islanders appear to be more and more discontented with their life situation and increasingly anxious to attain a living standard or acquire the symbols of social importance that can only be gained from New Zealand wage levels.

Thus, Salter shows the rising level of demand in the region, which led to an increase in imports per capita of about 21 percent in the period 1955-1962. The case studies of Douglas (1965) and findings of McCreary (1969) and Boardman (1969) on islanders in New Zealand support this view. It remains for the consequences of migration to be explored more fully. Does the demonstration effect of life in New Zealand, fostered by chain migration, lead to an idealisation of life in New Zealand and, conversely, a psychocultural rejection of their own particular environment? Do emigrants become symbols of a new style of life? What role does the returned emigrant play in society? Does emigration increase social opportunities in the islands, leading to greater upward social mobility and causing structural changes in society (cf. Lopreato, 1967)?

With the communication revolution, increasing numbers of islanders are acquiring a new perspective of the world and of their insignificant place in it.[47] It would seem that processive change, including the effects of a Western education that often seems singularly inappropriate for local conditions,[48] has brought would-be migrants or emigrants into the mainstream of the 'Great Tradition' of the West without providing them with the economic base that goes with it. In this sense, island societies are societies in search of urbanism – an urbanism that can never be developed in small-scale island economies.[49]

An Overview of Change

Modernisation has been described "as a confused, usually vulgar, rarely successful, but yet poignantly serious struggle to become part of the modern world and yet remain oneself".[50] This chapter has considered some economic and social responses of island societies in their groping toward modernity. A rather complex conceptual schema has been outlined employing a series of generalisations about the patterns and trends of change in the region, generalisations that are supported by much evidence from the Pacific region.

The dynamic impetus to change, whether in a progressive or degenerative fashion, results from Western intrusion into closed island eco-systems. The intensity of impact varied considerably throughout the region both in respect to the severity of warfare (sometimes stimulated by the introduction of firearms), catastrophic epidemics of European diseases, the effects of alcohol, the depredation of labour recruiters, and in the extent to which land was alienated and sizeable European investments established. Perceptions of the effects of change also differ. Similarly, variations occur in patterns of 'missionisation' which caused various further social dislocations and enabled cultural reintegrations to occur within a neo-Christian framework. Varied styles of colonial rule, whether of a 'direct' or 'indirect rule' type, played their part in breaking up neo-traditional institutions, solidifying them, or revamping 'cultural codes' that served to reconcile the old and the new.

The accidents of history and the peculiarities of place are not unimportant in influencing economic response. Thus, the imposition of taxes in kind, the opportunity to earn cash painlessly through a passive rentier role, or the ease with which an indigenous crop, the coconut palm (rather than a strange new crop with different ecological requirements) could be grown within the village setting, eased the process of change. Some of the most promising regions in the South Pacific today are those which possessed comparative economic advantages that were capitalised upon early by local villagers.[51] But, in general, traditional agricultural systems can be thought of as somewhat inert, responding only sluggishly to the opportunities of change because of the resilience of neo-traditional social structure. Although the area of cultivated crops has expanded and 'organisational change' has occurred in land use systems, structural changes have been few. Above all, little real technological change has occurred in village agriculture (e.g. in Western Samoa), and economic development usually involves widening economic disparities between the town and the areas of modern capitalistic agriculture on the one hand and the under-capitalised neo-traditional village on the other, which is increasingly affected by out-migration.

Village communities thus seem to comprise sub-systems of the market economy which recognisably interlock economically with the larger system through the medium of the plantation, the trade store and the import-export firm (or Asian middlemen). But because these institutions are but weak agencies for modernisation, the integration of island communities into the larger system is incomplete, not generally requiring participation in a common culture or the evolution of a viable economic base. Larger-scale enterprise is almost exclusively owned by expatriates, as Salter has described, and the expansion of the "open" or "outward looking" type of economy[52] has been facilitated especially by the shortage of local capital and skill, but also to a degree by local unwillingness to adjust indigenous institutions radically to new requirements.

The role of the plantation and the effect of uncertain, fluctuating markets have not generally aided modernisation, encouraging the evolution of only a 'partial peasantry' or 'partial proletariat'. Islanders become dependent to some extent on the plantation or the export firm to hire their labour or buy their produce, yet they have not in general induced changes leading to economic 'take off'. While the existence of an assured market for local cash crops which could lead to agricultural development after the Western model offers opportunities for the Tasimboko in Guadalcanal and communities like Utuali'i in Western Samoa, this market is usually not large and the middleman's role is often dominated by non-indigenes.[53] When markets melt away or government replanting subsidies terminate, labour inputs drop with villagers retreating into their 'capsule communities' and the subsistence system.

Major distinctions between the social structures and cultures of west Melanesia and Polynesia appear to influence indigenous response, and the structural flexibility of Melanesian societies manifested in their capacity to adapt existing institutions to radical changes in the external environment (exemplified by Michael R. Allen's work on Aoba, New Hebrides, 1964, 1968) contrast markedly with the less flexible, more hierarchical, institutions of central Polynesia, illustrated by Lockwood's research in Western Samoa (1971). Fisk's propositions and the fieldwork testing of his model underline the importance of limitation of demand in the primitive economy, the existence of a potential labour surplus, the importance of the incentive factor and the effectiveness of linkage to the market. Lasaqa and Lockwood in particular have documented the effect poor linkage (especially high freight costs) has on local cash cropping, and other studies on exposure to mass media are needed to examine the effects of other forms of linkage. Inspection of some of the most progressive regions in the South Pacific (Gazelle Peninsula of New Britain, Goroka, Aoba) gives tentative support to the importance stressed by Fisk of good infrastructure and nearness to market, although, of course, complex socio-cultural changes are also relevant. The role of introduced crops in altering social structures illustrates the value of cultural ecological studies and suggests a broadening of the concept of a changing infrastructure to one of a changing ecotype, illustrated by a dry zone village of Fiji.[54]

A complex set of cultural ecological changes is making society more capitalistic, and where local economic autonomy breaks down (for whatever reasons) the community is enmeshed more fully in the wider social and economic system. Studies of labour commitment are needed and the transition from 'target' work to semi-permanent and permanent wage labour clearly plays a crucial part in the urbanisation process, which varies from labour migration in New Guinea (often circular or 'pendular' migration), temporary short- to medium-term urban residence in the Solomons,[55] to semi-permanent and permanent urban migration in Tonga, Western Samoa and Fiji, and migration to a metropolitan area from the Cook Islands. These migration movements are indicative not only of the stage of change reached and the local 'mix' of factors in processive change, but also of the strength of the urban influence. Studies of urban structure (civic, industrial, commercial and demographic) are needed in the larger towns to determine the role of 'situational' change or whether the urban migrant is merely playing a role appropriate for the new milieu. The cognitive views that islanders have of the town and of Western wage work vis-à-vis traditional agriculture are greatly needed, as a certain degree of empathy must be attained before a migrant can sustain a new and demanding role in the town.

Finally, migration out of the region to New Zealand is now at such a scale as to suggest that the closed island world has long since ceased to exist. A new perspective is being fostered among islanders and research is needed into many aspects of the effects of migration on social change, for it would appear to act as a dynamic factor which might cause structural change in island societies. While undoubtedly retaining much of their neo-traditional culture, some who adjust successfully and live permanently in New Zealand appear to share the 'great tradition' of the West. Detailed study is needed of the process of adaptation, but some evidence appears to confirm the view of Dalton (1969) that societies can become culturally 'peasant' (or 'townsmen') while remaining before migration economically at a 'pre-peasant' or 'tribal' level.

In general, the evidence and concepts presented here suggest that social change involves an extension of the range of options between which individuals are able to choose. But in some parts the range may be narrowed somewhat by the constraints of an emerging class structure. Thus, Finney (1965) notes that although until the 1950s most Tahitians were "peasant" or "tribal" producers and fisherman, by 1965 over three-quarters of all able-bodied Tahitians were wage labourers. Depopulation of the smaller islands is both inevitable and desirable and, increasingly, with tourism the islander can be expected to lay down the copra knife to pick up the guitar. But ultimately the internal changes analysed in this chapter must be seen in broad perspective, for overall constraints on the direction and pace of change are imposed by external decisions made in metropolitan countries: decisions concerning the size and conditions attached to aid and capital investments, marketing, trade policies and immigration. For these reasons, it is to be deplored that ultimately the course of change will be determined by the choice not of Pacific islanders but of European citizens in metropolitan countries.

3

Subsistence Affluence in the Pacific

This paper was written specifically for this book. Its point is to identify and characterise the nature of endemic economic organisation in the Pacific, and to show how 'subsistence affluence' in this setting has functioned (through the case studies of early Samoa and Tahiti). It also examines the effects and consequences of contact with the West and the encroachment of trade on subsistence economies, focusing particularly on the example of Fiji.

The Theory

Prevailing theories and paradigms of economic development over the last six or seven decades have arisen essentially out of study of the major continents of Europe, the Americas, Asia and other regions which, while differing greatly in economic, social, religious and political backgrounds and resource endowments, have developed relatively complex or sophisticated economic organisations, where there has been specialisation and division of labour in the economy, where money has long been in use, where markets exist with internal and external trade occurring, and where market towns and large cities have developed.

This experience has, in general, led to greater knowledge and understanding of the economies of under-developed areas. But as further study of areas in Africa, and in our case, Oceania (or the South Pacific as it is often called) occurred, it was realised that these new economies possessed none of the characteristics listed above. In this extremely remote world region, the last area of the globe to be settled by humankind, probably about 2,000 years ago, economic organisation was based on sustenance of the basic economic units. The term "primitive affluence" or later "subsistence affluence" was first coined by the Australian economist E.K. Fisk who had studied grinding poverty in Asian regions of over-population. There, the average small farmer could barely scrape a living because of lack of land and capital though using his meagre resources to the full. When Fisk returned from Southeast Asia and visited the non-peasant societies of Papua New Guinea, he found a very different situation. Here the reverse was the case, for the production unit, the household, could produce as much as it could consume with the use of only part of the land and labour resources available to it. Thus, in this non-monetary system, the productivity of labour was very high. As Fisk concluded:

> The result is that the subsistent, self-sufficient type of farmer in the Pacific can have a considerably higher standard of consumption than hundreds of millions of the poorer peasants of Asia, and can obtain this with relatively little work and with virtually no money income.[1]

This "primitive economy" as it was termed (we will call it "subsistence economy") has been described by Lockwood, following Fisk, as having the following characteristics:

> ... a number of relatively small independent subsistence units each of which controls its own means of production such as labour, land, useful trees and livestock, and tools and equipment.
> Technology is simple, although the producer may exploit the natural resources available to him with great skill.
> The subsistence community is small so that there is little opportunity for specialisation and division of labour.
> Within each subsistence community, most production is planned for the use of the producers and to discharge kinship and other social and ceremonial obligations.
> The exchange of goods and services is regulated through the social system and has an underlying basis in reciprocity.
> There is no all-purpose medium of exchange such as relates all goods and services to each other in a market exchange system, although there may be commodities which have special social value and act as a medium of exchange in some circumstances.[2]

Furthermore, although stratified chiefly systems of rank had evolved in some areas, no elite or class-based structure existed, hence there was no large-scale extraction of the 'surplus' or amassing it in the centre. Consequently, no evolution of a state system of political control, administration and domination occurred. The various small archipelagic societies in the vast ocean have been studied only by explorers, missionaries and, latterly, mainly by geographers and anthropologists. Economists have only come much later, perhaps because they customarily deal with exchange economies and societies with the usual array of financial institutions, and have generally less understanding of 'primitive' or subsistence economies.

Of course, with Western contact and trade with an outside market economy, change occurs: the market, money, modern economic organisation, and financial and government institutions are introduced, and so it is soon evident that dualism now exists, consisting of a modern or market sector and the traditional subsistence sector. But the basic structure still persists as well as the newly introduced economic organisation.

The fundamental issue affecting economic development and agriculture in Oceania has thus always been the transition from the subsistence state to the market and the innumerable difficulties that occur along the way. Yet, unhappily, the visiting economists (usually coming to Western Samoa, Papua New Guinea or Fiji for just a few weeks while escaping from the European or American winter) often miss this point and instead complicate and falsify the development issues.

The Case of Early Samoa

La Perouse (1798), the first European known to have landed in the Samoan Islands, left little doubt that the people of one community that he visited lived in a state of 'subsistence affluence'. He visited –

> ... a charming village situated in the middle of a wood, or rather of an orchard, all of the trees of which are loaded with fruit. The houses were placed on the circumference of a circle, of about a hundred and fifty *toises* [300 yards] in diameter, the interior forming a vast open space, covered with the most beautiful verdure, and shaded by trees, which kept the air delightfully cool. Women, children, and old men, accompanied me, and invited me into their houses. They spread the finest and freshest mats upon a floor formed of little chosen pebbles, and raised about two feet above the ground, in order to guard against the humidity .... The best architect could not have given a more elegant curve to the extremities of the ellipses that terminated the buildings ...
> The trees that produce the breadfruit, the cocoa-nut [sic], the banana, the guava, ... hold out to these fortunate people an abundance of wholesome food; while fowls, hogs, and dogs, which live upon the surplus of these fruits, afford an agreeable variety of viands ...
> They were so rich, and in want of so little, that they disdained our instruments of iron and stuffs and would only have beads ... These Islanders, were we incessantly repeating, are undoubtedly the most happy inhabitants of the earth.[3]

In my doctoral thesis, I reconstructed the geography of old Samoa around the year 1840. The main features of the Samoan environment and economy at this period provide a description of the state of subsistence affluence that existed:

In Samoa the physical and social environments modified slightly a system of primitive cultivation from its intrinsically Polynesian form. Aims and practices were a little different and revealed themselves in a subsistence system that was rather more extensive, more static, and socially less important. Agricultural methods of the Polynesian heritage appear to have been gradually sublimated, for the wealth of resources in the Islands seems to have resulted in a narrowing rather than a broadening of agricultural practices. The practice of irrigation, common in Fiji and various Polynesian islands, was absent. Slopes were not terraced. Methods of cultivation were casual and weeding desultory. In the larger islands, the pressure of population on the land was only light and prodigal use of the land could be made.

In spite of the depredations of wild pigs, flying foxes (*Pteropus ruficollis, pe'a*), birds, rats, the dreaded rhinoceros beetle (after white settlement), or destruction caused through gales, tropical cyclones, or human agency in wartime, the loss of the entire taro or yam crop did not produce much hardship. Storms, droughts and pests were regarded as ministers of the wrathful god *O le Sa*, to whom propitiatory offerings were made before vigorous efforts by the gardener were begun to redeem his losses. The fact that planting could be done all the year round in most parts meant that losses would soon be recovered, and in the meantime the bounteous natural environment provided fish from the sea, wild yams and roots from the forest, and coconuts along the seashore.

Although supplementary food resources could be found in profuse and varied quantities, the fact that the Samoan neglected to utilise many of them, or did so only intermittently, is striking testimony to the productivity of his natural environment in relation to population pressure. Thus, wild fruits were rarely eaten, and wild dogs and rats – food relished in other parts of the Pacific – were generally scorned as food. Insects were rarely eaten. The deification of various birds and fish as family gods made them taboo to the villagers, but this was no great loss to the food supply. The absence of any method of drying fish was a disadvantage of little moment. So liberal was the Samoan natural environment that a subsistence system was supported more easily than in most other groups of the Pacific, and little effort was required to maintain comfortable living standards. The challenge of the natural environment was on the whole only slight, and the response of the Samoan culture was accordingly small.[4]

Thus, the literature suggests that before foreign influences developed a market and market exchange in Samoa, Samoan villages approached the Fisk ideal of a subsistence unit in all essential respects.

The Case of Early Tahiti

We might also note the case of Tahiti. Although the various Polynesian and Melanesian groups varied greatly in wealth of edible plants, the early explorers were rapturous in their praise of the abundance of Tahiti which Forster called "the queen of the tropical islands".[5] Europeans stressed the riotous growth of "native" food plants. About 30 plants were cultivated (mostly Asian plants but including the South American sweet potato). The Polynesian triad of pig, dog and fowl was to be found and amongst the tuber crops some 30 to 40 varieties of taro were utilised. More conspicuous was Tahitian aboraculture for, as Lewthwaite describes, there was a wealth of fruit trees. The peripheral lowlands were covered with various kinds of fruit trees remarkable mainly for their abundance. Most important was the breadfruit of which the missionaries collected the names of 40 to 50 varieties. Almost every household had its own tree which had three crops a year. So heavy was its yield that Cook affirmed that a man who planted but one in his lifetime had served his own and succeeding generations as fully as a husbandman of cooler latitudes could do in a lifespan of seed time and harvest. While most breadfruit were eaten at once, great quantities were preserved for a month or more in huge district ovens.[6]

A great many other useful plants were available, as well as the ubiquitous coconut palm of which there were at least 16 varieties. Bananas (*Musa paradisiaca*), at least 18 varieties of plantains, the *vi* or 'golden apple' (*Spondias dulcis*), the juicy *ahia* (*Eugenia malaccensis*), the Tahitian chestnut *mape* (*Inocarpus edulis*) and sugar cane are also worthy of mention. Although one should not become swept away with the idea that Tahiti exemplified the concepts of Jean Jacques Rousseau or that of Bougainville who felt himself "transported into the Garden of Eden", it is scarcely surprising that Cook and especially Bligh were driven to stern measures to restrain their crews, for after weary months of hardship at sea, the sailors were welcomed by a bounteous nature as well as the obliging local women. The Society Islands was clearly a core region and culture hearth inheriting ancient and widespread culture traits and plants from Asia and South America as well as providing a foundation for much of twentieth century Polynesia. Tahiti in the late eighteenth century was almost certainly the most outstanding example of subsistence affluence.

The Economic Significance of Subsistence Affluence

Experience in Fiji in the early plantation period had suggested that the ordinary Fijian villager was not attracted to long hours of hard work for small money wages. This was not laziness on his part but merely the result of a situation in which the normal household could acquire all the food it needed for adequate nutrition from a total of about three man-hours per day or 15-25 hours per week from all members, which would also cover a small surplus for reciprocity and social insurance against natural hazards. With the addition of a cash crop or two such as copra, bananas or kava, only a few more hours per week were required. I discovered this from my fieldwork in my first village study, Nalotawa in 1958, and similar fieldwork results were obtained in the other villages studied and also in the Solomons and Gilbert and Ellice Islands socio-economic studies which Wellington geographers and anthropologists produced in the 1969-75 period (see chapters 9 and 10).

Cash cropping in the Pacific has usually been grafted on to the subsistence system in a supplementary way, and other sources of income outside agriculture are also usually available, but the level of subsistence affluence is such that village producers will give up production of a cash crop (such as banana growing at Utuali'i in Western Samoa)[7] if the market price falls below a level deemed to be the minimum acceptable. Even though no other cash crop or money-earning option might be available as an alternative, villagers frequently choose to give up production at such an uneconomic level, preferring to spend the time saved in other meaningful village activities. Thus, motivation and alternative choices of action arise from the socio-economic and cultural environment that we term the 'village mode of production'.

In this situation of subsistence affluence, the development problem essentially boils down to how incentives can be provided to enable the surplus labour and land to be mobilised for production. In some of his later refinements to his model, Fisk added "incentive factors" (such as the provision of a feeder road, or other improved infrastructure or marketing or distribution services), and compared the strength of these incentives transmitted to the subsistence group by market forces with the resistance or inertia of the subsistence group to changes required for supplementary cash production (which he termed the "response factor").[8]

In the case of Fiji, the strength of this subsistence affluence factor was supported not only by the expressed preferences for village living rather than external wage labour (see chapter 6, for example), but also by census data. In spite of accelerated social change in the two decades after World War II, the 1966 Census showed that less than 21 percent of the Fijian population still lived in urban areas.

In a macro sense, the contrast between the two ethnic groups in Fiji could not be more obvious in the 1960s: Fijians owned over 83 percent of the land and with 40 percent of the population controlled the political system (since the Deed of Cession, most Europeans backed the Fijians politically) and contributed only about 5-10 percent of the GNP; the Indians with 46 percent of the population owned only about 2 percent of the land (and had only insecure access by short- to medium-term leases to sugar cane land) and produced over 50 percent of GNP. The blatant inequities of these facts were political dynamite, even as early as the 1960s.

Other consequences of subsistence affluence in Oceania are also highly significant. The reluctance of Fijians to work as labourers on early cotton and later sugar plantations, whether due partly to cultural and social unfamiliarity with the hard conditions and regularity of work on plantations or also to subsistence affluence in the village sector, led Sir Arthur Gordon to introduce Indian indentured labour into Fiji. Indians not only became overwhelmingly the labour for plantations and major growers of sugar cane, but also the main traders and shopkeepers in towns.

The effect of these factors is also shown in the economic roles played by the various ethnic groups in Fiji in the years leading up to independence in 1970. The 1966 census showed that 45 percent of the economically-active Fijian population were engaged wholly or mainly in subsistence agriculture and thus were only marginally in contact with the modern monetary sector of the economy. A further 20 percent were engaged wholly or mainly in commercial agriculture or other primary industry (such as mining). In the other main ethnic groups, Indians, Europeans, part-Europeans, Chinese and part-Chinese, less than 1.5 percent were involved in subsistence agriculture: almost all were involved in the monetary sector, with 51.3 percent of Indians engaged in commercial farming (mostly sugar cane).[9]

With respect to the statistics of the four most buoyant groups of industries into which most foreign and new private investment was being directed – secondary industry, construction, commerce and the group serving the tourist industry (transport, hotels, entertainment) – it is clear that over 56 percent of the economically active European and Chinese groups were engaged in these industries in 1966, and over 32 percent of Indians but less than 15 percent of Fijians. Moreover, a much larger proportion of Fijian participation in these most outstanding growth industries was confined to the least skilled and lowest categories of employment.[10]

As Fisk has convincingly argued, prior to independence in Fiji a picture emerges of a three-tier society. At the top, "the European/ Chinese group manage and operate the large corporations and institutions, often on behalf of foreign owners, the Indians own and operate most of the medium to small-scale enterprises, including most of the commercial farming land, whilst the Fijians own most of it and are still heavily engaged in a non-monetary, but affluent subsistence sector. All are well off by comparison with many similar groups in other lands of the less-developed world".[11]

Plantation agriculture was often marginal in Oceania because labourers demanded relatively high wages, well above the level in countries like the Philippines where poverty, land shortage and class stratification emphasised choices dependent on the economics of scarcity. Similarly, smallholder agriculture in Oceania outside the village sector which I term the village mode of production is relatively unimportant as wage rates would have to be high to attract labour from the village sector.

The existence of subsistence affluence in the village sector provides a 'floor' below which real incomes in the islands will not fall unless the village mode is destroyed; and there is little likelihood of this happening. Of course, the subsistence economy is closely related to and inter-penetrated by the modern sector.

4

The Village Mode of Production and Agricultural Development in the South Pacific

'The Village Mode of Production and Agricultural Development in the South Pacific' is partly based on an article called 'The Village Mode of Production in MIRAB Societies' that was originally published in Pacific Viewpoint *in 1984. It continues the analysis begun in chapter 3 of agricultural development in Oceania which is characterised by smallholder production. It looks also at the introduced modes of production such as the plantation, and the necessary requirements of any effective economic organisation: the presence of a market; the necessity of an infrastructure to support the market; the presence of physical, psychological and cultural resources; and an institutional structure that combines and organises these factors. It examines the work of scholars such as Hardaker, Fleming and Harris on agricultural development in the South Pacific.*

In their review of smallholder modes of agricultural development in the South Pacific, Hardaker, Fleming and Harris (1984) make a number of useful points on factors inhibiting agricultural development. The actual performance of agriculture in the South Pacific in the last two decades is gloomy indeed: per capita agricultural exports for most countries have been stagnating or even declining, while the range of products produced has narrowed rather than diversified. There are, of course, many reasons for this, some referred to by the authors: the great fluctuation and frequently low level of prices for crops produced in the region, the tiny land areas of the island states, and their fragmented and dispersed location which in turn makes the problems of transport and marketing exceedingly difficult and very expensive.

The authors identify both extrinsic and intrinsic disadvantages that affect smallholders as well as plantation production. However, as they admit, they do not adequately pursue the point that other factors besides organisational structure determine performance. As Fisk and Honeybone (1972) have noted, the success of any rural enterprise (including a smallholder or plantation production unit) depends on a number of necessary elements.

A modified set of factors is as follows:

1 a market for the goods or services produced;
2 the motivation to succeed;
3 the presence of physical resources, such as land for agriculture, minerals for mining or a special skill;
4 labour;
5 capital;
6 leadership;
7 an institutional framework in which elements 2 to 6 inclusive can be effectively combined to provide goods and services to element 1.

The Village Mode of Production

A major reason for the stagnation of agriculture must be attributed to the 'village mode of production' – a term I prefer to the South Pacific Agricultural Survey (SPAS) term, 'mixed subsistence-cash cropping mode', and the authors' vague 'smallholder' terminology. The term 'village mode of production' is appropriate because the vast majority of smallholdings in the South Pacific are part of a village or hamlet settlement and socio-economic system, and because fieldwork has shown that the environment of the village (social, cultural, economic, political as well as physical) greatly affects the production process. Thus, the *galala* in Fiji in the 1960s who lived a mile or two outside the village environment consistently achieved yields higher than villagers.[1]

I do not fully agree with the authors' contention that specification of the appropriate organisational modes requires more investigation, though it is true that policy-makers do not appear to base their approaches on an understanding of the case studies already documented. With the partial exception of the diverse cultures and environments of Papua New Guinea, there are now a considerable number of fieldwork studies which show quite clearly how the village mode of production actually operates, and they examine in some depth how various matters intrinsic to village life actually impinge upon production. Thus, Lockwood (1971) and Fairbairn (1970) for Western Samoa; Bathgate, Frazer and McKinnon for the Solomons (1973); Geddes et al (1982), Roger Lawrence (1983), Sewell (1983), and Watters and Banibati (1984) for Kiribati; Chambers (1984) for Tuvalu; and Belshaw (1964b), Rutz (1978), Ward (1965), Watters (1969a) and the Spate Report (1959) for Fiji, shed a good deal of light on the village smallholding systems in these countries. Brookfield and Hart (1971), Connell (1978), Lea

(1964), D.D. Mitchell (1976), Oliver (1955), Rappaport (1967) and Mike Bourke (current) and Bryant Allen (various dates) have made major contributions to the study of the village mode of production in Papua New Guinea.

Apart from some densely populated atolls or parts of the Central Highlands of Papua New Guinea, it is generally true that there is an abundance of land and often marine resources, allowing most societies of the South Pacific to live at a level of subsistence affluence while only a relatively small part of the total potential resources of land and labour available is used. Studies such as those named above have supported the Fisk model, and show that villagers sustain a level of consumption for a small labour input, varying from about 15 to 25 man hours per week usually for both subsistence and cash crop production. Lam (1982) reviews the relevant data from Papua New Guinea. An excellent illustration of how the social organisation and important institutions such as reciprocity can affect work input or lead to a conflict of goals has been provided for Western Samoa by Ala'ilima and Ala'ilima (1964). Except in areas of pronounced out-migration, labour surplus has existed and only modest amounts of labour input have occurred in the village mode of production. This obviously indicates the relatively low, variable or unsustained motivation of smallholders with respect to crops that are destined for market sale; a conclusion that is confirmed by daily time allocation studies of sample households.

The Case of Vanuatu

The traditional sector based on the village mode of production is often regarded as backward and unproductive, but it should not be underestimated, and also needs support. The largely non-monetised rural economy in Vanuatu has successfully supported a 90 percent increase in the rural population since independence (from about 95,000 in 1980 to an estimated 180,000 now).

The dominant agricultural system in the village sector is of course shifting cultivation, or bush fallowing. With population increasing over time, the average garden size per household has declined and, according to the 1983 agricultural census, was about 0.1 to 0.15 hectares or only about half or two-thirds the size of earlier times. A table covering 15 islands or island groups drawn from the Internal Planning Office's Island Resource Survey (partly based on the ORSTOM Soils Atlas) gave the following totals or average areas of garden land per island and family in 1985:[2]

Table 4.1. Garden Size per Island and Family, Vanuatu 1985

	Rural population	Rural families	Hectares arable land	Less Hectares coconuts* & plantations	Balance garden land	Ha Garden land avail. per family	Ha per year with 10-yr rotation
Total	117,800	23,500	548,220	78,300	469,700	Av. 20	Av. 2.0

Includes smallholder cocoa and cattle grazing which is mostly under coconuts.

Weightman (1989) calculated that if we allow for a fallow of seven years to succeed three years of cropping, the rotation cycle is 10 years. The agricultural census revealed that 19 percent of gardens were fallowed for less than five years and some for as little as two. A later survey by Weightman gave similar figures and identified a number of problem areas suffering from fallow periods that were too short – west Ambae, Paama, north Pentecost, Atchin, Nguna, South Efate, Middle Bush, and east and west Tanna.[3]

Population pressure and increasing competition with foodcrops posed by cash cropping has led to a shortened fallow period and, as the gardening cycle has accelerated, to progressive degradation of the bush fallow from forest to bush; to scrub; to an association of broad-leaved weeds, sedges and grasses; and finally to grasses favoured by frequent burning, such as the curse of the Tropics, *Imperata*, and those that can be seen in the degraded 'white grass' areas of Vanuatu, such as Tanna.

The best way to deal with this degeneration process and to restore the quality of the short bush fallow period is to plant kasis (*Leucaena leucocephela*), which is a fast-growing, deep-rooted woody legume that will dominate the fallow and improve soil fertility. This valuable plant, said to have been introduced from Rarotonga in blackbirding times, has already proven its value in enriching the bush fallow in north Efate, its off-shore islands and in parts of Northeast Malekula.

'Farm' Tenure, 'Land' Tenure and Other Changes

As Sir Henry Maine noted long ago, in a community based on kinship, land is an aspect of the group, but not the basis for grouping. Spatial extension and the resultant rights to exploit the environment are mere aspects of the social group. To Western powers, however, property and its contractual relationships as well as the market provide the fundamental basis of grouping and organisation in Western-type national states. Historically, ideas of 'indirect rule' pioneered by Sir Arthur Gordon in Fiji and Lord Lugard in Nigeria led colonial governments to grapple with the problem of how to preserve valued kinship groups in colonial frontier situations in which immigrant Western planters had already introduced the market and established plantations. This dynamic led to a tendency to turn kinship groups into corporations aggregate before the law. For example, in Fiji, land was registered and surveyed in the name of *mataqali* (sub-lineages), and boundaries were set and land laws were codified. This meant that some valued qualities of kinship were retained with the *mataqali* unit and at the same time they were made legally into corporations, the units of modern society based on contract and market. Whereas before, the Fijians had 'farm tenure' in the sense of a traditional area which they traditionally farmed, after registration they had 'land tenure' and a man had land rights only in so far as he was part of a lineage. These systems were superimposed on the traditional one, and the *mataqali* now became a legal entity[4] as well as a social group. Fijians recognised that this change preserved the practice of 'communal land' ownership, altering its configuration but strengthening the concept of social insurance while at the same time enhancing the institution of private property in the Fijian countryside.

Rational ecology and utilisation of the traditional shifting cultivation (swidden) system led to a desirable flexibility in land use. Once a garden was fully harvested and left to bush fallow, the planter would return less and less frequently to gather bananas or other fruit from useful trees amidst the regenerating fallow vegetation. His rights to the land would wane, and while he might reclaim and clear the plot again later when soil fertility was judged to have been restored, it was equally likely that a planter from another household would claim and reclear it. Fixing of land boundaries by colonial governments brought rigidities into this flexible system, and changes in population size between descent groups brought incongruous results. Some lineages might have abundant land, others found they were now short of land and long-time absentees still retained rights.

It has been noted by Ward (1986) that in recent decades the encouragement of cattle grazing in several countries has led to a certain irrationality of land use. Thus, in Viti Levu, Fiji, fertile river flats formerly used for intensive root crop gardens were converted to intensive cattle grazing at a much lower level of productivity in terms of food production. I saw this happen also at Lutu. The reason for this incongruous land use is the application of criteria for land use from the commercial and subsistence sectors, and the lack of any form of common 'currency' for equating the two sectors.[5] Where indigenous groups can establish use over large areas by traditional mechanisms, they may not feel any pressing need to use prime areas in intensive ways.

Modernising the Production System

In Table 4.2, a number of factors that characterise the village mode of production and lead, in part, to this low or unsustained market production, are summarised. Hardaker, Fleming and Harris (1984) do not address these important issues, nor the fundamental ecological problem of how policy-makers increase output from a smallholder system when it relies for regeneration on rotational bush fallowing. Is it feasible or economic to convert the shifting gardens into permanently cropped land? Again, the rationale (point 3) which obviates the need for artificial fertiliser (when regenerating growth restores soil nutrient status) or for herbicides (when weeds are crowded out by bush fallow) changes completely if the system of agriculture is totally reformed. How do you bring plant disease control to 50 or more scattered gardens when the affected crop is only one of a number in an intricate inter-crop assemblage? How can government planners or extension officers ensure that the appropriate tasks are done, and at the right time, especially since planting is by cultigen[6] rather than by seed and is often done all through the year at the same time as harvesting? There are many other demands on people's time: maximising security or maintaining good social relations may be goals that are just as important as maximising market production.[7]

Over the last four decades, there has been growing evidence of the greater emphasis on cash cropping leading to further changes in the traditional village mode of production, altered and reinforced as it was by the colonial registration and legalisation process we have described. Ideas of private ownership began to intrude into the customary system of usufruct. This was especially evident where long-term tree crops could be planted in some density. For example, coconuts which bear after seven years lasted at least 60 and sometimes up to 100 years, so that some individuals or families held the same plot of land through continued use for several generations. In these situations, the planter, his family and others came to regard such land as no longer community land but the planter's own land.

While in the past a group or family with little land could readily gain access to the unused land of others, in recent decades this accommodation has been harder to achieve. For example, people from the relatively poor and highly populated island of Malaita in the Solomon Islands could migrate to the larger main island of Guadalcanal and, if they went through a customary series of prestations and showed deference and gratitude to the local hosts, land would be granted to them to plant food crops. However, with rapid population growth and

Table 4.2. Problems of Modernising the Village Mode of Production

1. The goals of production are diverse and competitive.
    Maximising output is not usually important.
    Goals are
    - subsistence for the household (usually the main consumption unit)
    - reciprocity (gift exchanges)
    - redistribution (in 'big man' or chiefly systems)
    - market sale.

2. Social insurance against natural hazards such as hurricanes. Security and community well-being are the prime concerns, achieved through
    - sharing and reciprocity.
    (These are admirable principles but conflict with maximising production.)

3. Land use system consists of
    - groves of tree crops
    - shifting gardens
    - gathering, hunting.
    Under rotational bush fallow, perhaps 50 or 100 scattered gardens in a village.
    Characteristics:
    - inter-cropping
    - difficult and costly to achieve a transition to permanent cropping
    - impossible to achieve scale economies
    - difficult to apply modern techniques and not greatly needed with bush
    - fallowing, e.g. artificial fertilisers
    - disease control
    - weed control.

4. Adapted to a demand ceiling
    - subsistence affluence and 'limited needs'
    - labour input 15-25 hours per week sufficient to obtain requirements
    - agricultural tasks merely part of whole socio-economic field of activity.

5. Production techniques adapted to non-monetary capital inputs.

6. Customary land tenure system a disincentive:
    - multiple or clan 'ownership'
    - 'land' not 'farm' tenure
    - fragmented small plots
    - absentee owners with out-migration
    - land or boundary disputes
    - often a poor basis for gaining a bank loan.

7. Innovations, new crops often 'contextualised' in crop assembly – very difficult to mechanise.

8. Alternative sources of income are often important (e.g. remittance income from migrant relatives, wage labour, fishing).

9. Sometimes traditional (rather than modernistic) leadership.

10. Absence (due to out-migration) of would-be entrepreneurs, most skilled and educated people, and a considerable proportion of the younger labour force.

increased focus on cash cropping rather than primary subsistence, the situation changed rapidly. Population growth over 3-4 percent, amongst the highest in the world in the 1970s, occurred, and amicable relations between Guadalcanal people and immigrant Malaitans were put under severe strain.[8] As Ward notes, often if land is lent, a specific ban may be placed on its use for cash and particularly tree crops. "Land, instead of resembling a common good to which all have access, is becoming a private good through which money can be earned, accumulated and directed to personal use."[9]

After World War II, Tonga appeared to be a model for other Oceanic countries to emulate in land tenure as their nineteenth century constitution granted each adult male the right to a lifetime lease of 3.2 ha. of agricultural land (api). However, many Tongans today have no such leases as population growth has occurred and some nobles have not subdivided all their estates into api. In some countries, such as Fiji, legislation has tended to keep pace with changing requirements for leasing land. In other cases, the modified systems of the post-colonial period have allowed land accumulation by individuals under the mask of "tradition".[10]

The various factors bearing on the village sector, including cash cropping, wage labour, out-migration and emigration, remittances, foreign aid and changes in land tenure have increased inequality within rural communities. While this sometimes capitalises on traditional status or rank, it often runs counter to it. In Koro, I gave case studies of emergent farmers and a number of rural entrepreneurs. Education was, of course, an important factor, and those trained in modern agriculture were sometimes seen as undermining the traditional base for authority in the village. Agricultural extension officers could also be seen negatively as their approaches bypassed traditional ways of doing things.

In all Pacific countries, there have been for some time people who Ward calls "big peasants" who use a mixture of "traditional" and "modern" mechanisms to control significant areas of land for commercial production. Even on a small atoll such as Abemama in Kiribati, where population density was relatively high, people such as Kamatie Johnson and Frank Smith held large plantations of over 30 acres of relatively superior coconut palms; much of this land had been bought from the nobility (banuea) in the 1920s-30s.[11] At the other extreme is a growing number of people who no longer have access under traditional mechanisms to a sufficient area of land to provide for more than a meagre subsistence. Even Fiji has a system of payment of destitute allowances, and although the scheme was designed for elderly

Indians, by the late 1970s over half the claimants were Fijians who mostly lived in rural areas.[12] Clearly, agriculture and the village mode of production no longer provided a safety net for all rural Fijians.

Throughout the South Pacific, peace, and law and order brought by colonial governments and the missions, as well as the introduction of steel tools, have meant that labour demands of subsistence cropping have lessened and the level of subsistence has increased, with the opportunity cost of the additional labour time spent on cash crops being relatively low. The village mode of production (mixed subsistence-cash crop system) was successful up to the close of the 1960s as it provided the majority of the people with access to a new range of consumer goods and an increased material level of living. Even in Western Samoa as late as 1970, villagers at Utuali'i were not too disappointed at giving up the marketing of bananas when the price fell even though the time saved was not invested in other economic activities.[13]

The South Pacific Agricultural Survey of 1979 estimated that, in Papua New Guinea, the contribution of the village mode of production to the cash economy was 40, 41 and 70 percent respectively to cacao, copra and coffee exports in 1975/76, and 61 percent of Solomon Islands copra in 1976/77. In Fiji, approximately 40 percent of copra comes from the estates but virtually all other cash crops come from the village mode of production and other smallholders. In Western Samoa, the estates of the Western Samoa Trust Estates Corporation (WESTEC) accounted for 16 percent of copra and 14 percent of cacao production; and about 28 percent of Kiribati copra is from plantations in the Line Islands. Otherwise, the village mode of production is responsible for virtually all other cash cropping in the remaining countries of Oceania.[14]

Commercial Production

Exports produced by the village mode of production were copra from the Solomons, Vanuatu, Kiribati and Tuvalu; cocoa, coffee and copra from Papua New Guinea; copra and coffee from New Caledonia; copra and bananas from Fiji, Tonga, Western Samoa and the Cook Islands; cocoa from Western Samoa; copra, vanilla and oranges from French Polynesia; and oranges from the Cook Islands. The best chance of commercial success for Western Samoa was the production of bananas, and for Niue the production of passionfruit.

Commercial production has faced many difficulties, however. While the Samoan Agricultural Department carefully organised and coordinated the pickup of bananas at the roadside with the arrival of ships at Apia, as well as spraying for disease control, by the early 1960s, plant diseases and storm damage seriously affected banana production in Fiji and Western Samoa. At the same time, the passenger trade on the boats carrying bananas to New Zealand was increasingly being lost to air transport, and shipping services fell below the fortnightly schedule required to maintain a steady flow of exports to New Zealand. As a consequence, New Zealand turned to Ecuadorean plantation-produced bananas as a more reliable source. While these fruit perhaps lack the flavour of island bananas, they have better presentation and superior and more dependable quality. These factors in combination virtually destroyed the Western Samoan, as well as the Fijian, Tongan and Cook Islands banana export industries, and attempts in the 1980s to revive them have not achieved much success.[15]

Other attempts to optimise the commercial value of indigenous crops or to graft cash crops on to the traditional agricultural system have had only modest success (e.g. cocoa in the Solomons). Oranges established in groves by New Zealand agronomists in the Cook Islands in the 1950s and 1960s declined in production after a number of years because growers did not tend the trees adequately. Instead, they increasingly gained income from non-agricultural sources. In the case of the pineapple industry, the costs to government of supporting the industry in the late 1970s exceeded the total income gained. Moreover, on the main pineapple island of Mangaia, planting the crop on sloping land led to accelerated erosion.[16]

Many areas in the Pacific have long relied on copra as the main cash crop, but after World War II extreme price fluctuation and declining yields from increasingly senile palms added to the problem of rising costs and unreliable inter-island shipping. Long-established and formerly affluent areas such as the copra-growing regions of the eastern Fijian provinces of Lau and Lomaiviti suffered especially from these problems, only partly offset by the expansion of the local cash crop kava. Eastern Fiji was also severely damaged by hurricanes in the 1970s and 1980s leading to government disaster relief. While future returns from copra produced from the village mode of production probably did not justify the level of government services and subsidy of inter-island shipping, the area's social and political importance (Ratu Mara also came from Lau) may have led to such support being sustained.

Plantations

The other major mode of agricultural development in the Pacific is the plantation. While some of these were established before colonisation (for example, in some of the larger Oceanic countries such as Western

Samoa, New Britain and Vanuatu, and in the small islands of Kiribati where George Murdoch planted a plantation of coconuts on the island of Kenna), new colonial governments welcomed and supported such ventures. The benefits were mutual: governments were able to raise internal revenue, and plantation owners gained regular and cheap supplies of labour and security of their land.

Since the late 1910s, however, the plantation system has not been particularly secure in the Pacific islands. At this time, Indian indentured labour to the cane zone in Fiji ended, leading to the collapse of sugar plantations; thereafter the plantation company became millers and overall managers of cane operations, with the cane being grown partly on plantation land but mainly on small tenanted farms leased by Indians from Fijian owners. Coconut plantations were able to persist for a longer period with their less perishable product, lower labour needs and less exacting requirements for labour. In the 1960s, however, erratic fluctuations occurred in the world market price, partly due to the increased competition from other vegetable oil substitutes from both tropical and temperate regions. As plantations had overwhelmingly delayed replanting aging groves with more productive new hybrid stock, copra plantations either stagnated or declined.

In Western Samoa, the formerly successful German-owned plantations were merged into a government-owned corporation, WESTEC, but poor, inexperienced management, labour supply problems and aging palms led to serious decline. The cocoa part of WESTEC production was severely affected when a major mistake was made in choosing a particular clone (LAFI7) for replanting cocoa bushes. Large-scale planting of rice on a plantation basis in the Solomons in the 1960s was a disaster for many participants. However, the most successful copra plantations were in the Solomons where, despite war damage, the large British company Lever Brothers continued a major research programme. A lack of other alternatives for wage labour meant that labour supply was more dependable.[17]

Independence led to political uncertainties for plantation owners. Indigenous landowners in Vanuatu received through the constitution leasehold lands that plantations had used; and with uncertainty prevailing, some plantations were abandoned. The enormous spread geographically of plantations posed great ongoing transport costs. In Papua New Guinea as well, a good number of plantations were abandoned while others continued in a precarious way (see Chapter 11 on West New Britain). While changes were less serious in the Solomons, productivity of plantations has also fallen.[18]

Many countries in Oceania experienced labour shortages because of low wages. Such factors show the continuing effect of subsistence affluence. Ward (1986) has noted, however, that these wage rates are considerably higher than those ruling in competing countries such as the Philippines, where land shortage and widespread poverty appear to provide classic conditions which help to sustain the plantation. The plantation may survive in larger islands where a labour reservoir exists of traditional villagers who are in the early phases of entering into the wage economy. Thus, in parts of New Guinea some labour may come from such people who work on the plantations for a few years before growing experience and confidence leads them to seek higher wages in unskilled labouring jobs in towns and cities.

Sources of Income

In many parts of the South Pacific, agricultural production is not viewed as the principal source of income. Many small island groups are now closely integrated in the economies of the large metropolitan countries of Australia and New Zealand, and significant flows of capital, overseas aid, remittances, labour, skills and enterprise indicate that agricultural development schemes or programmes of *autonomous* development conceived in isolation of these trends at the macro-economy level are often futile. In these societies which I have termed 'MIRAB societies' (MI = migrant societies, R = remittance incomes, A= aid dependent, B = bureaucratic organisation, with a virtual absence of an indigenous private sector), remittance and aid flows provide the basis for local incomes, and therefore the motivation for agricultural production for market sale is becoming progressively weaker (see Chapter 13).

At the national level, government revenue is provided by aid, philatelic sales, taxation and duties rather than from agricultural exports. Indeed, the demise of agriculture in the Pacific is occurring not because it does not make agronomic sense, but because it is making less and less *economic* sense. Such conditions apply in the Cook Islands, Niue, Tokelau and almost certainly Western and American Samoa and Tonga. They probably apply to a degree in Fiji as they also do in Kiribati and Tuvalu, though these societies lack normal migration outlets. Under such conditions, if hopes of substantial agricultural development are to be realistic, they must be based on an organisational mode in which good quality of management and the *dependability* of regular labour can go a long way towards ensuring a substantial output. Samoa illustrates the point: if high quality management can be found for the large WESTEC copra estates, production could be increased, given appropriate investments and inputs. It is far more difficult to ensure similar production increases from the village mode of production which dominates in the rest of the rural sector.

Extrinsic Factors

Finally, Hardaker et al are correct in emphasising the importance of extrinsic factors, such as shipping and marketing facilities. A sufficient number of plantation-type enterprises have to survive in remote areas to maintain an optimal level of land-based and shipping services so that smallholders in the villages can survive. When I worked in the Kandrian-Gloucester area of West New Britain, Papua New Guinea, in 1982, I noticed that the *regularity* and size of plantation output had in the past enabled surrounding villages also to market their copra. With the collapse of the plantation system, coastal ships on the Rabaul-Lae run would only visit one or two locations infrequently to deliver merchandise; villages were no longer visited as, by themselves, they could not guarantee a minimum pick-up cargo of 10 tonnes.[19]

Since the great bulk of the rural population lives in villages, the village mode of production is too important to be ignored. It fulfils major basic needs, such as security, community wellbeing and continuity with the past quite admirably. But it does not, regrettably, provide an encouraging environment for agricultural market production in the future. Alternatives are few, for settler smallholder schemes are notoriously expensive; the projects best served by infrastructure and easy access to required inputs and to the market are likely to be the most successful in the long run.

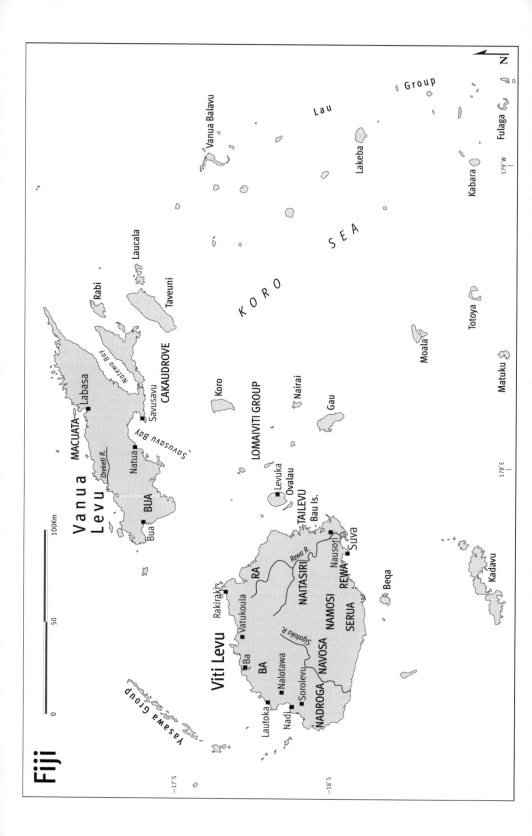

5

Fiji: The Development of Traditionalism

*This essay was first published as chapter 2 of my study of Fiji,
Koro (1969). It argues that the traditional qualities of Fijian
society have in part been created and strengthened by the early
British rulers in an attempt to protect Fijians from the modern
world. It looks at the village economy as a source of stability
rather than growth, but also as a source of entropy in a context of
the impacts of the international economy; and at the leadership
of Ratu Sir Lala Sukuna.*

Gordon and Colonial Government

The impact of the West was shattering on Fijian society. By 1874, after
70 years of contact with itinerant whalers, adventurers, missionaries,
and traders in sandalwood, bêche-de-mer, coconut oil and copra, island
society was already greatly altered and disorganised. The ravages of
liquor, firearms and European diseases were considerable, followed by
a measles epidemic in 1875 that killed an estimated 30,000 to 40,000
people, or over one-fifth of the entire population. The two rival native
governments under the paramount chiefs Cakobau and Ma'afu were
powerless to avert chaos, and events moved inexorably towards cession
of the group to Great Britain in 1874.

The Deed of Cession of 1874 was the first recognition of the allegiance
of the Fijian people to the British Crown. The second was the occasion
in 1875 when the Governor, Sir Arthur Gordon, was, at Cakobau's
suggestion, inaugurated Vunivalu or paramount chief of all Fiji. As
Gordon said, "The significance in the eyes of the native population of
the public act of homage rendered, not only ... by Cakobau himself,
on behalf of others, but by all the assembled chiefs, can hardly be
overrated".[1]

The traditional qualities that Fijians have often been enjoined to
practise in modern times, "loyalty, obedience and reverence", coupled
with the tribal emphasis on descent and hierarchy, have tended to prolong
the colonial status of Fijians. Indeed, colonialism involved merely the
projection by the Fijians of their own rank and status systems into the
colonial situation, so that all Europeans automatically became chiefs

and the Queen the greatest chief of all.

The period of Sir Arthur Gordon's governorship proved decisive for the modern history of Fiji, for his policy established lasting institutions that have guided the development of the Fijian people to the present day. Gordon was one of the first to formulate a system of 'Indirect Rule', or administration through native authorities, that later under Lord Lugard in Nigeria became the model for British colonial practice. Gordon decided that the "good government, prosperity and advance in civilisation" of the Fijians was as important as the commercial success of European settlers; preference for the latter, he believed, would be at variance with the understandings and objectives of the time of cession. Thus, for reasons of justice and sagacity but also because of financial stringency, Gordon put the native interest first, and determined to rule through native institutions.[2]

From the outset, he made it known that he intended to uphold Fijian custom and the authority of the chiefs. He recognised the importance of seizing "if possible, the spirit in which native institutions have been framed, and endeavour so to work them as to develop to the utmost possible extent the latent capacities of the people for the management of their own affairs".[3] Accordingly, he elaborated and modified the existing skeleton of the first Fijian administration, consisting of 12 *roko* or provincial chiefs for the 12 provinces, with Fijian stipendiary magistrates to assist them, and 82 *buli* of first, second or third class rank to supervise the affairs of the *tikina* or districts. To this structure, Gordon added at the top a council of chiefs (*bose vaka turaga*), an institution he developed from an earlier informal gathering, and which, up to the present, has been the mouthpiece of Fijian opinion.

Gordon's codification of traditional custom led, however, to problems of interpretation. The chiefs did not always agree about custom, and there appeared to be some regional variations (e.g. in Western Viti Levu) as to whether *mataqali* or *i tokatoka* were landowning entities or whether, traditionally, chiefs had alienated land. Where the chiefs' views differed from Gordon's, he considered them corruptions of tradition due to European influences. Thus, one 'custom' was imposed on the whole of Fiji. Accordingly, France (1968 and 1969) has argued:

The tenets of the orthodoxy, conceived and propagated by a protectionist administration, have become ineradicably absorbed into the Fijian national consciousness.[4]

At the time of rapid expansion of plantations by European settlers, Gordon foresaw the danger to village society that extensive and lengthy

1. Nalotawa, a relatively traditional village in the Dry Zone, Ba Province, Western Viti Levu, Fiji, c.1960. (R.F. Watters)

2. Jone Lotawa and his wife Rebeka and other members of his extended family in Nalotawa, Viti Levu, Fiji, 1958. (R.F. Watters)

3. A Fiji Indian tenant farmer with his working bullock, western Dry Zone, Viti Levu, c.1960. (Rob Wright)

4. A typical Fiji Indian general store, western Viti Levu, Fiji, c.1960. (R.F. Watters)

5. A view from the air of shifting cultivation – trees recently felled to make a new garden. West Guadalcanal, Solomon Islands, 1969. (R.F. Watters)

6. Kariatebike, the Government Station, Abemama, Kiribati. Petrol drums and fish drying on a pandanus mat to the left, a pandanus tree to the right, 1972. (R.F. Watters)

7. A house on Abemama, Kiribati. In the foreground, fish is drying in the sun, middle distance right a pig forages for scraps. In the house a woman uses a hand-powered sewing machine. (R.F. Watters)

8. The traditional ceremonial starchy root *babai* (*cyrtosperma chamissonis*) growing in a *babai* pit. Pandanus baskets packed with the best leaf litter float in the fresh water lens above the lower salt water. North Tarawa, 1982. (Ginny Sullivan)

9. Left: A man with his tobacco makes a point in recounting traditional stories, Tarawa, 1982. Right: A woman telling traditional stories, Tarawa, 1982. (Ginny Sullivan)

10. A man and his wife return in their outrigger canoe after fishing in the lagoon, Abemama, Kiribati, 1972. (R.F. Watters)

11. A typical bridge crossing a reef channel in North Tarawa, 1982. (Ginny Sullivan)

12. A villager puts out his copra to dry in the sun near his house. Small breadfruit tree right centre. Tamana, southern Kiribati, 1972. (Roger Lawrence)

labour indenture schemes posed. Abuses associated with *kanaka* or 'blackbird' labour were widespread throughout the South Pacific, and Gordon decided that every labour contract of over a month was to be entered into in the presence of the local magistrate and no contract was to be longer than 12 months. Chiefs regarded this policy for labour recruitment as posing a threat to their authority and to the communal system:

> It interferes seriously with the supply of food and is prejudicial ... to the increase of the population, prolific of all kinds of trouble, breaking up homes and families and creating a wandering and vagabond class ... who are notorious for little else than setting at defiance all authority and every domestic tie and bond.[5]

To enable Fijians to earn money, a tax in the form of produce which could be grown on village lands was instituted. This freed Fijians from the pressure of having to work on plantations and encouraged cash cropping in the villages.

To solve the labour problem for the plantation sector, Gordon argued as early as 1875 that cheap indentured labour be sought in India. In 1879, the first 'coolies' arrived, the vanguard of a total 60,500 Indian indentured labourers who were brought to Fiji to work in the sugar cane sector. While undoubtedly protecting Fijian society from exploitation, this policy laid the basis for ethnic strife and crises in the second half of the twentieth century.

In support of his constitutional and political arrangements and labour policy, Gordon's land policy enabled Fijian society to preserve intact that base necessary to ensure its future livelihood, economic independence and much of its associated culture. A Lands Commission upheld only 414,615 acres claimed by Europeans, or half the area sought out of a total of 4,514,000 acres in the colony. This was a triumph for Gordon's policy and was due in no small measure perhaps to the instructions of the Earl of Carnarvon, Secretary of State, to the Lands Commission, that Fijian lands "should be held by the Crown in trust for, and left for the present in occupation of the tribes, families, or chiefs who at present possessed them".[6] An Ordinance issued in 1880 declared that Fijian land was to be inalienable to any non-Fijian except through the Crown and under restrictions.

In this age of traumatic culture-contact, when traditional sanctions, beliefs and authority systems were being seriously challenged, Gordon ably served the needs of nineteenth-century Fijian society for reintegration and consolidation. As Morrell (1960) has stated, by an act of creative statesmanship Gordon cemented their unity and "welded a collection of sometimes discordant tribes into a people".[7] Just as Hawaiian society under King Kamehameha at the beginning of the century, Tongan society under King George Tupou in the second half of the century or Maori society in New Zealand in the 1860s felt the need for reintegration under strong leadership after an era of rapid cultural loss, so Fijian society (or at least the chiefs who were its spokespeople) welcomed policies that enabled its culture to remain viable.[8]

If it can be conceded that Gordon's policies were highly desirable for the conditions at the time, the consequences of these policies when they were continued into the mid-twentieth century[9] have been little short of disastrous. Internal disparities in income levels between the different ethnic groups have widened, and although it might have been thought that the consolidation of Fijian society could provide a solid base for economic development within the traditional 'communal system', only slight development, as we shall see, has in fact occurred. Moreover, institutions often have a rigidity of their own that makes them inflexible in the face of new influences, especially when they involve the creation or consolidation in power of a new elite, in this case the *roko* whose authority was backed by the power of the colonial government. The indigenous institutions utilised by the English rulers were given dangerous permanence and inflexibility once they were incorporated into the colonial administrative framework. Furthermore, the new colonial relationship put Fijians in a position of dependency upon the English rulers that was at once a consequence of colonialism itself, and a natural projection of their own rank and status systems into the contact situation. The foundations of a particularly intractable form of dualism had been laid: although Gordon did not believe that the interests of Fijians and settlers were always irreconcilable, his policy of parallel development was later to widen the gulf between the two, and especially between the Fijians and the Indians.

In the decades following Gordon's departure from Fiji in 1880, the Fijian population experienced serious depopulation and growing demoralisation. Colonial policy became more paternalistic, ethnocentric and autocratic, especially when the commission studying Fijian depopulation reported in 1896 not only on the deplorable conditions of hygiene and sanitation existing in villages but also on the inadequacy of the traditional communal system to cope. For two decades, there was a clamour for the replacement of indirect rule by direct rule, the opening of Fijian lands to European settlement and the individualisation of Fijian land tenure with the view often expressed that the Fijian 'needs to be led' by European enterprise.

Several new trends emerged, however, in the 1920s to arrest these policies. After 1921, the gradual increase in the Fijian population led to a resurgence of confidence in the communal system. At the same time, the rapid growth in the Indian community marked the beginnings of Indian political pressure and the evolution of modern land problems as Indians completing their indenture period took up leases of Fijian land at a rate of about 3,000-5,000 acres a year. Just as significant was the emergence after 1920 of an outstanding Fijian leader, Ratu Sir Lala Sukuna.

Ratu Sir Lala Sukuna and Fijian Leadership

As his nephew, Ratu Sir Kamisese Mara has said, Ratu Sukuna was the "best equipped Fijian leader in the twentieth century".[10] He was also Fiji's most famous and influential leader, for three reasons: his great rank and status, his ability and education, and his work experience.

He was born a chief of the Royal House of Bau, a little island off the east coast of Viti Levu, the seat of the most powerful chiefs in all Fiji, the Cakobaus. His grandfather was a cousin of Ratu Seru Cakobau, the Tui Viti who with several other chiefs ceded Fiji to Great Britain in 1874. His mother was the eldest child of Tui Nayau, the paramount chief and the highest title in eastern Fiji. Moreover, as Vasu Levu of Lau, his chiefly status was greatly enhanced. His education at Wanganui Collegiate in New Zealand, followed by graduation from Wadham College, Oxford, and induction as a barrister-at-law of the Middle Temple in London, happened at a time when only half a dozen Fijians had entered an overseas secondary school and none had gone on to university. His main life's work over several decades was the Native Land Commission, which gave him unrivalled knowledge and insight into the *mataqali* and *yavusa* so that he became the acknowledged authority on all matters Fijian. Two other significant factors should also be mentioned. In the First World War, he joined the French Foreign Legion; such was his bravery that he was cited for the award of *Médaille Militaire*. He lived in an era of great transition when the British colonial rulers needed an important local leader to move the Fijian people towards greater development and self-government under the Westminster system, and also in return to translate and explain Fijian custom and viewpoints to the British. In short, he became the key cultural broker between two vastly different worlds.

Sukuna felt that he was not like a man *chosen* to captain a ship in European terms – he was rather *born* to captain. He used to say, "his life was dominated by ritual … the ritual of the *yaqona* ceremony with its invocation of gods and deference to senior men, linking present with past, epitomising the legitimacy of authority by descent".[11] It is perhaps ironic that Sukuna who possessed enormous traditional authority became the first in the Empire to become head of district administration, ruling *for* the colonial administration from 1932.

His experience as a soldier in World War I taught him that democracy and freedom were concepts that were relevant only to modern large-scale societies, and when as a young man he read J.G. Frazer's famous study, *The Golden Bough*, he agreed with the view that belief in the divine nature of chiefs was common and appropriate to 'savage' societies such as Fiji. Steeped in the hierarchical traditional system, it is hardly surprising that Sukuna's friend, the anthropologist A.M. Hocart (1952), wrote that "the true religion of the Fijian is the service to the chief, if reverence, devotion and belief in the supernatural are required to make up religion".[12] Sukuna could not have put it better.

An early test for the young Sukuna as he gained experience in administration was posed by the radical syncretist movement launched by the prophet Apolosi Nawai. Apolosi preached economic development and personal responsibility and sought legitimacy by setting up a European-type commercial company (although he was inept at running it) and also a rival Fijian administration. He taught that Fijians were being exploited by Europeans and their native supporters. Apolosi blamed the chiefs for selling too much land to the Europeans, for leasing more to the Indians and pressuring ordinary men to sign on as labourers. A good many disappointed chiefs especially from the West supported him and he planned to make the Tui Vuda (the highest title of the West) King of Fiji; on other occasions, he appeared to seek that title for himself. Apolosi appealed to Sukuna as the only educated Fijian to support him but Sukuna rejected him as a charlatan. Although Apolosi's goals were very similar to the vision of many Europeans of the day for a future Fiji, Sukuna could not brook this challenge to authority and to the legacy of trust between Fijians and Europeans. He accused Apolosi of fomenting racial hatred and had him banished. The Apolosi affair illustrated how deeply conservative Sukuna was, in spite of his overseas experience and outstanding education. As Scarr (1967) notes, his view of his own society's future was amazingly static.[13]

Sukuna believed that Fijian society was quasi-feudal in nature, and particularly oppressive and barbaric. For generations, people had lived in a rigid oligarchic autocracy characterised by a type of communalism in which people owned no property and were absolutely controlled in every sphere of life. Inter-racial warfare was commonplace. He saw that this way of life created the positive qualities of docility and suspicion, with fear and respect for constituted authority being indelibly stamped on people's minds; while on the negative side, he saw that independent thinking was suppressed and over the centuries the native population became dependent on the will and guidance of the rulers.

Moreover, as Scarr has noted, education had done little to broaden the ordinary Fijian's outlook. Mission schools led to dependence on the Bible as a textbook. The Bible dealt with patriarchal societies and the divine right of kings. In a Fijian, it "tends rather to create profound reverence for his political institutions and provide sanctions for his former barbarities than to broaden and re-edify his primitive mind".[14] Moreover, arithmetic, the other staple of mission schools, so fixed the value of things as to harden the narrow perspective of the Fijian people.

Sukuna could see no evidence for any desire for development. Villagers would work for any special purpose they understood, such as the erection of a village church, the construction of a village or building a district vessel – or 'target work', as this can be termed. For the ordinary purposes of daily life,

> ... there is no need for any more work than they already do and there never is unless the mind becomes more developed, the development bringing with it tastes that demand satisfaction. For the present, however, the native appears to have reached the height of prosperity commensurate with his degree of development. Any call for the modification of a social system, if it is to be of any lasting advantage, must come from within, from those whose lives are likely to be affected by it. And ... there would appear to be no very strong reason why the people should not be allowed to live the life they desire and understand.[15]

Maintenance of the village system was ensured by the communal work enforced by government. A programme of work was decided annually at provincial councils: the villagers were required to build and repair houses, weed the village, maintain roads and tracks, carry messages, entertain strangers and generally be available for such 'communal work' for some 80 days a year.

When exemption from the burden of communal work became a goal favoured by the Director of Agriculture and others in the 1930s, Sukuna pointed out that only a few "exceptional" Fijians were suited to the new individualised lifestyle (and the monetary cost of exemption was not cheap), moving from centralised villages into nuclear households which settled in the countryside on a share of *mataqali* land. When it was pointed out that the village system had failed to produce income for Fijians, he argued that the reason was not co-residence but the socio-cultural factors mentioned above and a simple lack of markets.

By the 1950s, therefore, the unique, all-powerful and pervasive role that Ratu Sir Lala Sukuna had played for the last 40 years in government had worked to the same effect and contributed substantially to the earlier factors we have mentioned: the fashioning of a form of indirect rule that incorporated Fijian institutions within the government structures, and the bond of trust forged at the Deed of Cession which placed Fijians in a position of depending upon the English rulers. When the anthropologist C.S. Belshaw arrived in Fiji in the 1950s, he aptly summed up the position of Fijian society in the title of his book *Under the Ivi Tree*. Outsiders might be tempted to think that the fine tall *ivi* trees would provide good shelter under their branches when it rains. If they were to seek shelter, however, they would be surprised to find that raindrops readily flow off the shiny leaves to fall below. In the same way, the Fijian people can be seen to have been protected and sheltered by the Fijian administration and its special powers and privileges within the national government as a whole; but the shelter was not effective in the long run. Rather, it can be argued they should have been exposed to the robust conditions of the open market economy in which Indians and others have to earn their livelihoods.

6

Nalotawa: A Late Colonial Village

This essay on Nalotawa was first published as chapter 3 of Koro *in 1969 and presents a case study of a Fijian village based on fieldwork I conducted in the late 1950s and early 1960s. Nalotawa was a village that adhered mainly to the traditional subsistence model but that was also influenced by the market. In some ways it straddled both worlds, and the essay is indicative of views about developmentalism – what may be called the developmental imperative – that were and remain prevalent in the literature.*

In the tawny brown hills of the dry zone lies the village of Nalotawa, nestling in a valley bottom at the junction of two streams. One's first impression on approaching the village down the slopes of the Mount Evans Range is one of peace and quiet. This impression is deepened by closer acquaintance with the life that goes on beneath the traditional thatched roofs of the village and on the village lands around it. For Nalotawa, if greatly changed since pre-European times, is still a 'traditional' type of village; it has retained most of the old patterns of life by integrating them with elements of the new into a revitalising complex that is satisfying and stable for the community. If tiny cracks can be detected in the foundations that support this way of life, few amongst the villagers are aware of them or even see the need to come to terms with the modern world and the Indian half of Fiji. It is almost as if the Western world and Indian Fiji end at the divide that is known as Mount Evans Range. While it is true that the influence of each does to some extent overlap into the hills beyond, the feeling persists with Fijian villagers that their lives, comfortable and secure as they have known them, will continue to survive substantially unaltered.

The People: Social Organisation

In 1959, 72 people lived at Nalotawa. They were the conscious heirs of a long and rich local tradition. Local history says that the village was originally sited at Tore, a defensible ridge near the Mount Evans Range. Later, the village moved to Vunitoleke in the present Ba closed area, then to Naquaqi above the neighbouring village of Navilawa, and then during the Church wars to Karewa, a hilly site a few miles to the south. Then Ratu Tevita, the current chief's great grandfather, moved to the present site of Nalotawa and made his temporary home there near his gardens (*teitei*). After one more change of site, to Navituasolaki, near Mota, the chief and his people settled permanently at Nalotawa about 80 years ago.

Such frequent changes of site were typical in Viti Levu during the nineteenth century.[1] Fierce internecine warfare rose to a new frenzy with the coming of Western values and the spread of firearms. The fear of conquest, local power shifts and possible fluctuations in population underlay the frequent segmentation of clans from the social units with which they lived; these clans migrated to other areas where they formed new alliances with other clans for defence, so that new villages and new confederations (*vanua*) embracing several villages resulted. The

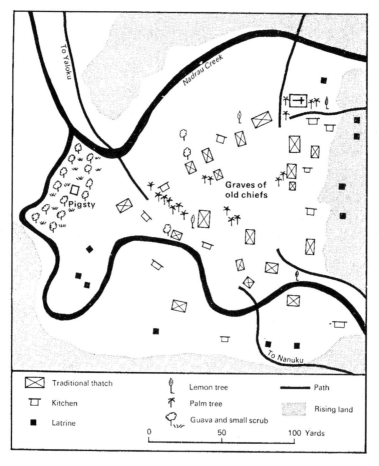

Figure 6.1. Nalotawa Village

changes of site of Nalotawa express this movement. This fluid process was checked to some extent with the coming of the Pax Britannica, when the people of Nalotawa lived at nearby Tore. King Cakobau of Bau Island, who had established his hegemony over most of Viti Levu, instructed his subjects to accept peace and adopt Christianity. He sent a messenger to the area with gifts of a piece of cloth, a knife and a dog, symbolising the changes of the new era. Ratu Tevita accepted the gifts on behalf of his people and within a few years all villages in the Ba hills were pacified and converted to Christianity.

The people of Nalotawa are conscious of close ties that connect them to other villages in the Ba hills. The villages of Navilawa, Yaloku, Nanuku and Tukuraki, together with the daughter settlement of Rara, seem to have been allied politically with Nalotawa in the past. Three villages – Yaloku, Rara and Tabataba – are linked to Viyagonivalu of Nalotawa. In this *vanua*, no villager would regard another as a stranger (*vulagi*) and a sense of common purpose seems to be still shared. The regional cohesion of these villages was reinforced by the government's decision to establish administrative districts (*tikina*) conforming to *vanua* areas: the five villages were linked in the same *tikina*. Although in 1947 the old *tikina* of Nalotawa was amalgamated with others into the larger district of Magodro, incorporating about 15 villages, this feeling of regional solidarity persists to the present.

Within the village can be found a typical association of social divisions (see Table 6.1). We must be careful not to ascribe too much importance to groupings which, although formerly important in the traditional structure, have now lost many of their earlier functions. Thus we shall see below that some major aspects of cultural organisation are no longer based on the *mataqali* or *i tokatoka* and that Fijians often cooperate regularly with people who are not members of these groups. Hence the less functional term 'social division' is preferable to 'social unit' since, in several important respects, the *mataqali* and *i tokatoka* no longer appear to be part of the social structure. Indeed, the work of Nayacakalou, Geddes and others has recently shown that patrilineal descent is not the only important organising principle governing patterns of social relations, and our data below confirm the importance of affinal ties.

Until 1943, two *yavusa* lived together in the village. Each *yavusa* comprises a group of members descended in the male line from a common founding ancestor. Ideally, *yavusa* are segmented into smaller sections of *mataqali*, which are regarded as groups founded by the sons of the founder of the *yavusa*. In turn, the smallest groups, *i tokatoka*, may sometimes be considered as descended from the sons of the founder of the *mataqali*. The actual pattern does not always conform to the ideal, and in many villages of Fiji *yavusa* comprise *mataqali* that are not genealogically related. More commonly, *i tokatoka* are enlarged extended families or groups of families linked by common descent for only the last few generations.[2]

In identifying the social divisions of Nalotawa, I discovered many different opinions as to what constituted a *yavusa, mataqali* or *i tokatoka*. When asked for the name of his *tokatoka*, a man would often answer with the name of his *mataqali* or even *yavusa*. As Belshaw has explained:

> ... whether such and such a unit was a *mataqali* or a *tokatoka* or a *ya-vusa* is not really clear-cut at all. A *tokatoka* enlarging could become a *yavusa*; a *yavusa* enlarging could become a *vanua* (and in effect the converse could also take place); the system was one of bifurcation and amalgamation in response to pressures of population, and ambitions of powerful or weakening men. If I go into any village of this area today and ask a man his *mataqali* he might just as easily reply with the unit officially recorded as his *tokatoka* or *yavusa*. This is not muddle-head-edness on his part; it is an essential ingredient of the traditional system. Only those who have need to watch the legalities of the administration give the correct answers assuredly ...[3]

Thus, the variation in concepts as to what constitutes a social division probably reflects, in Nalotawa as elsewhere, the flexible nature of these units; as Spate has said, society was "very adaptable organisationally to local variables".[4]

The segmentation and migration of the past, as recorded in local tradition, seems to be reflected in current relationships between the exogamous *mataqali*. I was not able to establish, however, whether the two surviving *mataqali* – Navunidamanu and Yalomarawa – are genealogically related or not. If they are not so related, their amalgamation last century under *yavusa* Viyagonivalu probably occurred for reasons of defence. At any rate, relationships between the two *mataqali* were close and strong and the cohesion of the whole *yavusa* was most evident.

The most significant feature of the village's social structure is that only one *yavusa* is now resident there. That segmentation is a continuing process in Fijian social organisation was illustrated in 1943 by the migration of *yavusa* Wabu to Rara, five miles south of Nalotawa. Four years earlier, Noa Botitu, head of the *yavusa*, had gone to Rara to farm the clan lands as an exempted man. After he had pressed his clan to join him there, his kinsfolk followed, since they "wanted to grow crops for the market on their empty clan land". Thus a small, incipient *koro* began. Nalotawa was left with only one *yavusa* (Viyagonivalu): we shall see that Spate was right when he notes that "one-*yavusa* villages generally have a more united approach to their problems than those with two or more, and even when these do cooperate, this often rests on elaborate and perhaps precarious protocol".[5]

Two *mataqali* and three *i tokatoka* in the village represent sub-groups of *yavusa* Viyagonivalu. In economic activities, distinctions between these groups are blurred, for in all forms of cooperative activities members of each group cooperated with members of other groups.

Although *tokatoka Tawatawadi* embraced 44 people living in nine separate households and *tokatoka* Navuta and Naqilovatu each comprised only eight people living in two and one households respectively (see Table 6.1), the larger *tokatoka* did not dominate the smaller, for all groups were joined in the same *yavusa*. An analysis of inter-household social relations showed that affinal ties underlay much of the unity between *mataqali*. Affinal ties joined 12 out of the 14 households in the village, so that the scope for mutual cooperation and assistance based on kinship was very great indeed, compensating for the relative lack of importance of the household, which had an average of only 5.1 members. Also, the chief's authority was strong and ensured the mobilisation of labour for communal purposes.

Marriage ties reinforce this pronounced social solidarity for very few people marry outside the local area. Of the 12 wives in the *koro* in 1959, nine came from villages nearby, including seven from villages in the old *tikina* of Nalotawa.

The type of social organisation that exists at Nalotawa and in the surrounding area has important implications for economic development in the area. Individuals felt themselves to be an integral part of their clan, and social units were linked in continuing patterns of relationship. The effect of this local cohesion is such that no substantial change is likely to occur unless the local area as a whole is prepared to accept it. And

Table 6.1. Social Divisions, Population and Land Tenure of Nalotawa Village, Vanua Yakete, Old Tikina of Nalotawa, Magodro District, Ba Province

Yavusa	Viyagonivalu				Wabu			Yavusa not resident at Nalotawa
Mataqali	1. Navunidamanu		2. Yalamarawa		1. Vatawai	2. Naiyalavatu		
Tokatoka	1. Delavatu	2. Tawatawadi	1. Naqilovatu	2. Navuti	1. Qolou	1. Nabasau	2. Naloqi	
Number of Households	0	9	1	2	0	0	0	2
Population	0	44	8	8	0	0	0	10
Area of Land (Acres)	682	2,276	1,444	2,145	820	271	243	0

as we shall see, the prevailing outlook is one of staunch conservatism –
a placid parochialism untroubled by the inexorable developments that
will ultimately involve Nalotawa and its neighbourhood in the life of a
wider society and a wider economy.

The Land

Fijian social organisation is rooted in the land; the apportionment and
utilisation of land express the functioning of social units and their
adjustment to it by means of a system of shifting cultivation. Unlike
most parts of Fiji where the *mataqali* was the land-owning kinship
group, in Ba Province the *bita* (i.e. the *i tokatoka*) seems to have been
the unit in which land ownership was traditionally vested.

Table 6.1 and Figure 6.2 show that the social divisions of Nalotawa
hold 5,865 acres, an average of 81 acres per head. The apportionment
of land per head really varies according to the amount of land held
by each *tokatoka* and the number of people in each – i.e., from 52
acres per head in Tawatawadi to 180 in Naqilovalu and 268 in Navuti.
Moreover, there are 1,916 acres formerly owned by social units that are
now extinct; this land is now legally Crown Land ('Schedule A lands')
but in practice it is available, along with other areas of the *veikau*,
or village common lands, for use by villagers. In effect, then, 7,781
acres or 108 acres per head are available. This is greatly in excess of
the amount of land needed per head. Mapping of garden sites showed
that a total of only about 21 acres is cropped, or 1.75 acres per 'garden
family' (the number of people in a household dependent on the gardens
cultivated by its head and by other members), or about 0.3 acres per
head.[6] At the present rate of stocking, only two or three acres per head
are needed for grazing, leaving a large excess of land available.

The utilisation of land by an individual is not strictly confined to the
land owned by the *tokatoka* of which he is a member. Thus, in contrast
to many other villagers, there is no land problem at Nalotawa, and no
trend is under way toward individualisation of land rights or toward
the development of quasi-freehold rights. Although the holding of land
on a clan basis does present obstacles to development, as we shall see
later in this work, there are, except for the exempted men, no local
forces at Nalotawa working for change in the system.

Land Use and Social Organisation

The people of these social groups get their sustenance from typical
dry zone hill country. Rolling slopes of basaltic agglomerate and
andesitic flows give rise to moderate-to-poor latosol soils that have

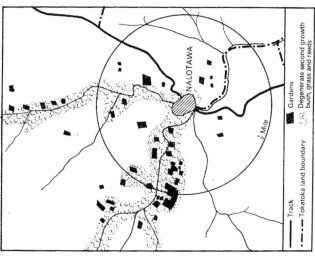

Figure 6.3. The pattern of shifting cultivation at Nalotawa Most gardens are found on the relatively fertile and moist alluvial soils of river valleys where second growth survives in part

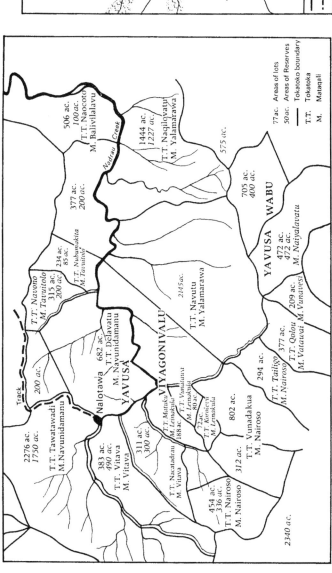

Figure 6.2. Land Tenure at Nalotawa

been considerably eroded in recent years. The village itself lies in a small valley and most *teitei* are scattered along its gentle slopes, where colluvial soils ensure higher crop yields. Here a struggling stand of second-growth bush contrasts with the bare slopes of the surrounding hill country, in which only an occasional mango tree relieves the monotony. High above the village, dominating the whole area, rises the Mount Evans Range; on its wet, steep flanks can be seen the only surviving bush of any great extent. Elsewhere the hillsides are covered with *gasau*, a tall, cane-like reed (*Miscanthus floridulus*), and the ridge tops with the coarse brown mission grass (*Pennisetum polystachyon*).

The visitor can see immediately that the people of the area no longer live in harmony with much of their habitat. Flourishing reeds and bracken fern indicate depleted soil fertility and greatly reduce the value of the land as a potential stock-grazing area. Pockets of rich guinea grass in the valleys are now almost non-existent, and even good-looking pastures of mission grass show on inspection much bare ground between the tall stems. Sheet erosion has removed much of the top soil from the steeper and more exposed slopes.

Yet the land of Nalotawa has not always been like this. The present chief, Ratu Tevita, recalls that 50 years ago more bush grew in the area, and all the streams were lined with dense tree growth. The evidence of soil scientists indicates that much earlier at least large parts of the dry zone were probably wooded.[7] We must assume that before the Europeans arrived local population pressure may have led to a deflection in the natural vegetation in areas that experienced long droughts and that grasses and reeds gradually became dominant. After contact, it seems that traditional conservation practices were less used,[8] and repeated uncontrolled burning became common.[9] Fires intended to clear land for cultivation frequently got out of hand and large areas were ravaged; perhaps local population pressure resulted in inadequate fallowing of land before it was again cropped. Thus, a revolution in environment has occurred, transforming forested areas into the grass and reed-covered landscapes of today.

What evidence is there at Nalotawa of a breakdown in traditional methods of conservation? On the *teitei* themselves, many excellent traditional practices remain, but on the *veikau*, stretching out over the hillsides, the reverse is the case. I was at first informed that burning rarely occurred, but it soon became obvious that this illegal practice happens very frequently in an area with an annual rainfall of under 70 inches. The people say that the cattle will not eat the old tough stems of mission grass and that burning is necessary to induce the growth of succulent young shoots. Yet, in spite of repeated burning, only 20 cattle were grazed by the men of Nalotawa on the 7,781 acres available. Most of this land could become reasonable grazing country if grass growth were controlled by careful stocking and rotational grazing in fenced fields. In 1959, the only 'paddock' in which to confine the cattle was an area of 50 acres bordered by steep gullies. Nobody realised the great value that barbed wire fencing would give to such country. It is indeed abundantly clear that cattle are entirely alien to the Fijian agricultural economy, and the half-hearted attempts to raise cattle at Nalotawa show that even the most elementary principles of stock farming have not yet been generally assimilated.

The Agricultural System

Village agriculture is, however, essentially based on cropping and here the traditional adjustment of humans to the environment has been largely preserved. At Nalotawa, as in most parts of the humid tropics, a form of shifting cultivation is practised,[10] in which the land is rotated rather than crops, and short periods of cropping are followed by longer periods of bush fallowing in which the depleted soil fertility is gradually restored.

Each gardener has three or four different *teitei* on which he grows, usually in mixed crop combinations, sufficient *dalo* (taro), cassava, yams, *kumala*, *yaqona* and bananas to meet the needs of his own household, and to furnish a surplus for sale at the market. Many minor crops such as maize, *kawai* (a type of yam), pawpaws, chilli and leafy vegetables such as *bele* and *mau*, are also grown between the staple crops. Most *teitei* can be cultivated for three to five years before declining fertility and increasing weeds force abandonment and the selection of new sites.

Since relatively dry climatic conditions at Nalotawa lead to a lower rate of leaching and slower destruction of organic matter than in the higher rainfall areas of the wet zone, the period of cropping is longer than in many other parts of Fiji. Declining yields and increasing weeds, however, enforce a resting period which varies at Nalotawa from eight to 10 years on favourite sites on colluvial or alluvial soils, to 20 to 30 years on little used land. A rough average appeared to be about 15 years. No systemic rotation of the land is practised, as abundant land is available for all households.

Shifting Cultivation and Soil Fertility

How effective is this system of shifting cultivation for the requirements of development at Nalotawa? Is it in harmony with normal ecological relationships and does it therefore conserve soil fertility? It is clear that there is nothing in the system itself that violates nature since its essential feature is the resting or fallow period in which natural fertility gradually builds up again after being depleted by cropping. The analysis of soil samples, averaging several at different stages in the system of shifting cultivation, showed a steady depletion in most nutrients with each successive year of cropping. However, nitrogen still remained at a reasonably high level after two years of cropping and high carbon-to-nitrogen ratios suggest a relatively slow mineralisation of the humus. In general, the chemical fertility of the soils is reasonably satisfactory for three years of cropping, after which many gardeners leave their land to fallow. Although a few favoured sites in a river valley near the village are over-cropped or rested for an inadequate fallow period, the soil analyses suggested that on the whole the length of fallowing was adequate.

Although shifting cultivation is much more wasteful of land than permanent cultivation, it does not impose serious restrictions to production at Nalotawa. Land is abundant, and even though much of it is of poor or moderate quality, there are as yet no real incentives to purchase fertilisers, grow tree crops or adopt such measures as might enable permanent use of any piece of land. Moreover, cash crops can easily be grown within the system, enabling and indeed sustaining the perpetuation of the traditional economy. While this is not a bad thing in itself, it may well foster the continuance of many related traditional features (such as land tenure) that are themselves obstacles to increased production.

The Penetration of a Cash Economy

For many years, the people of Nalotawa have been incorporated into the cash economy by selling surplus produce at the weekly markets at Ba or Lautoka townships, even though this entails transport of their produce by packhorse and truck and an overnight stay at another village before reaching the market. But this cash cropping represents merely an *extension* of the *traditional* system in which crops were produced for subsistence and reciprocity (exchange for social and ceremonial purposes). Thus, no real alteration occurred in its practice or the productive methods employed, and it involves only indigenous crops, not the adoption of new exotic crops (see Table 6.2).

One of the two chief cash crops is *yaqona*, used to make kava. The cultivation of *yaqona* for the market simply means that more cuttings are planted than in former times. Bananas,[11] the other main cash crop, have fitted easily into the intercropping pattern, being planted in *dalo* and yam gardens or along the contour at the bottom of a hillside garden

Table 6.2. Crops Planted by Average Gardener at Nalotawa in 1958 (Mean of eight households)

Yaqona[a]	380 plants	Yams	280 plants
Tapioca	410 plants	Banana[a]	92 plants
Dalo	370 plants	*Kumala*	12 plants

[a] *Primarily cash crops. Minor quantities of the subsistence crops are also occasionally sold at the market.*

where deeper, moister soil accumulates. Their cultivation merely entails the planting of a portion of stock and thereafter an occasional slashing of weeds. Other minor cash crops comprise traditional subsistence crops (*dalo*, *dalo-ni-tana*, pawpaw) or chilli, a crop of only minor importance adopted as a result of contact with Indians. It is clear that no fundamentally new attitudes towards the land or to crops have, as yet, resulted from the penetration of a cash economy.

The use of the one plough in the village illustrates the way in which a major agricultural innovation has been incorporated into the traditional framework of agriculture. In 1947, Jone Lotawa bought a plough and a pair of working bullocks thinking that their use would lead to greater production. However, only three small 'fields' were ploughed each year, and (with one exception) each was scarcely any bigger than a large garden. These were planted with traditional crops, and often interplanted in the same way as an ordinary *teitei*. Also, ploughed 'fields' were abandoned after three or four years of cultivation just like any garden. While the plough enabled the cultivator to control weed growth and improve the friability and texture of his soil to a greater depth than with hand tools, it has not led to permanent field cultivation, as it was not accompanied by the use of fertilisers or any of the usual techniques of permanent ploughland cultivation. One attempt was made to utilise the plough for a new departure in cash cropping. Rice was grown for three years running, but yields were low, producing only £30 in the best year; transport to the market was difficult and pests were very severe in the last year. The attempt has not been repeated. Thus the value of the plough for increasing production has not by any means been fully realised, even though the villagers recognised its superior technical qualities and its owner no doubt gained added status by its possession.

Yet the very existence of cash cropping in Nalotawa, however inadequate, does demonstrate the people's commitment to certain Western goods and the values they represent. Indeed, certain European goods are now as fundamental in their lives as many of their cherished traditional values. Cash cropping is to some extent undertaken by all (see Tables 6.3 and 6.4), in order to purchase such goods as cigarettes, tea, tinned fish, brightly coloured print dresses, shirts and secondhand sewing machines.

The degree of Nalotawa's involvement in the cash economy can be demonstrated in four ways: by an analysis of income and expenditure accounts in the village, by the numbers of people who have ever been engaged in regular wage labour, by a record of the diet of typical families and by an estimate of the amount of time spent by a typical villager in economically productive work. Conclusions drawn from diet charts and work patterns alone should be treated as highly tentative, as the period of study was too brief to give a good picture of the true patterns, but these data do complement the fuller findings of the survey of income and expenditure patterns.

Table 6.3. Incomes of Eight Households at Nalotawa (1958)

Household	£	s.	d.
1	76	6	0
2	39	3	0
3	52	3	0
4	106	2	0
5	107	12	0
6	198	10	0
7	48	14	0
8	123	10	0
Mean	94	0	0
Median	91	0	0

Table 6.4. Sources of Income at Nalotawa (1958) (Average of items of income of eight households)

	£	s.	d.
Bananas	31	0	0
Yaqona	22	8	0
Dalo, dalo-ni-tana	11	13	0
Chilli	8	4	0
Pawpaw	2	10	0
Roro (leaves of dalo)	2	7	0
Oranges	2	1	0
Tapioca, yams, kavika	1	6	0
Wage labour[a] (cutting cane and bamboo)	1	5	0
Curry	1	0	0
Sale of pigs, cows, horses, goats	10	0	0
Repayment of loans		12	0
Total	94	6	0

[a] *Wage labour involved only one person.*

An analysis of the annual incomes of eight out of the 14 households in Nalotawa gave a mean income of £94.[12] Incomes in the village vary widely – from £39.3s. to £198.10s. per household. This variation is probably indicative of the uneven penetration of Western values that motivate cash cropping. Thus, while the expenditure chart (Table 6.5) and the diet chart (Table 6.6) show that a fair range of Western goods and foods have become necessities rather than luxuries in the life of all people at Nalotawa, not all people possessed equally, or alternatively could sustain with equal force, the attitudes and work patterns that would enable them to earn sufficient money to satisfy these wants. This conclusion is also borne out by a consideration of the nature of cash cropping: it is significant that only just over half of the average total income (56 percent) results from a deliberate planting of crops that are destined in the main for cash sales. Almost as much money is gained by the sale of surplus subsistence crops and surplus livestock. While there may be some market motivation involved in the planting of these crops, it is almost as reasonable to regard large plantings as a safeguard against drought, hurricanes or other natural hazards. Nor is the cropped area significantly larger than the area used by almost pure subsistence cultivators in other parts of Melanesia. Moreover, a large item of income which points towards the possible development of a livestock industry is derived from the wholly casual, unplanned sales of pigs, cattle, goats and horses to Indian dealers. The influence of the market is important at Nalotawa, but its influence should not be exaggerated since it has not yet succeeded in drastically altering the agricultural system from its essentially subsistence and reciprocity basis. It has not altered methods of work and it has not led to any significant technological advances. Cash cropping, though essential, is merely an adjunct to the traditional pattern of subsistence and exchange.[13]

Aspects of Social Change

What signs are there of change in the village? Certain obvious criteria of Westernisation throw some light on the stage of social change reached in 1958. Thus, the villager's fortnightly visits to the market in Ba or Lautoka denote an attraction to the life of the town that cannot be explained purely in economic terms. This is, of course, to be found throughout Fiji today and is shown in the pronounced urban drift characteristic of almost all the interior or isolated provinces in the colony.

Nine people left Nalotawa in the three years after the 1956 Census. Although this indicates the definite 'pull' of the town, a much greater

Table 6.5. Expenditure Pattern at Nalotawa (Average of items of income of eight households)

	£	s.	d.
Stores in Ba, Lautoka	33	0	0
Local store	5	1	0
Clothes	19	8	0
Household items, tools	7	3	0
Fares	6	16	0
District tax	3	16	0
Socials, amusements	2	19	0
Cigarettes, tobacco[a]	2	16	0
Church	2	6	0
Payment of debts	1	2	0
School	1	5	0
Gifts		10	0
Miscellaneous	9	6	0
Total	95	8	0

[a] *A small proportion of money spent at the stores also includes cigarettes and tobacco.*

Table 6.6. Summary of the Diet of Typical Households of Nalotawa (81 meals)

Items of Food	Units[a]	Percentage of total
Fijian	142	70
Indian	27.5	13
European	34.5	17
Total	204	100
Bought foods[b]	44	21

NOTES: *(a) Most items of food (e.g. dalo, meat) were allotted one point. Minor items of food, such as curry or onions, were given only half a point. Tea, sugar, condensed milk, cocoa and salt were not included as they were consumed in all villages.*

(b) Rice and curry were bought but the great majority of bought foods were 'European foods'.

Table 6.7. People of Nalotawa Who have Been Engaged in Wage Labour

Number of People	Type of Work	Period Worked
1	Morris Hedstrom, CSR Stores, Copra Schooner	2 years
1	Morris Hedstrom Store, Lautoka	Under 1 year
1	CSR factory	5 years
1	Teacher	3 years
1	Planted cane	6 months
1	Housework for CSR overseer, Ba	3 years and current
1	Housework for European in Ba	2 years and current
2	Manganese mines	3 months
1	Gold mines, Vatukoula	6 months

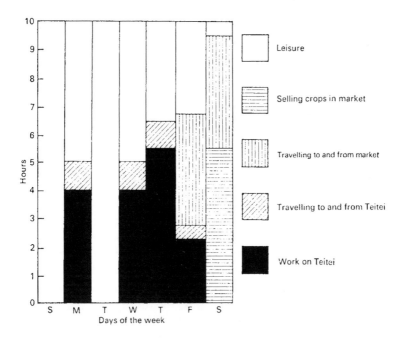

Figure 6.4. The Amount of Time Spent on Economic Activities at Nalotawa, Based on a Study of Three Typical Villagers. The importance of leisure is apparent

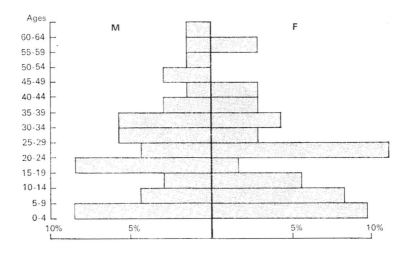

Figure 6.5. Age Structure

number have left many interior villages of Viti Levu during this period. Examination of the various age groups reveals certain unexpected deficiencies: we may perhaps note few boys in the 5-14 age groups because they are away at school (mostly at Nanuku, 4 miles away), practically no girls between 15-19 (this includes young brides now living in other villages and one or two working in the town) and a few men in the 20-24 age group who are now working outside the area. Most of the age groups up to the age of 40, however, are approximately normal, and in a village of only 72 people a male labour force of 19 can be mobilised for communal tasks.

Not all adults have visited Suva, but most have been once or twice. It is significant that a few frequently travel the 120 miles to spend Christmas with kinsfolk or friends living in the city.

More precise data on the effects of urbanisation on Nalotawa were gained by a survey of the numbers of people who had ever been employed as wage labour. Ten people of the 72 resident in the village had worked at some period for wages, excluding the occasional jobs done for Indians that lasted for only a few days or a week or two (see Table 6.7). Only four can be considered to have made the adjustment to the conditions of Western-type work with any degree of permanency: a man who worked in the Colonial Sugar Refining Factory (CSR), two girls doing housework and an ex-teacher.

Throughout Fiji, there is a strong desire to improve children's educational standards. At Nalotawa, only five people have been educated to a level beyond that reached by the local village schools (including three still at school), and only two speak English with any degree of competence. However, the people of the area worked hard for several years to raise money for a new concrete-block district school. The chief's son "felt it was God's Will for him to return" to the village after the War to lead the fund-raising campaign instead of going to New Zealand for further training as a Navy signalman. The men of the village earned £200 by cane-cutting, promoting an illegal race meeting and other activities; £200 was contributed by the government. Later, they earned £180 by cane-cutting to enable a promising boy to attend secondary school. However, such enthusiasm for what is considered to be a worthwhile *community* project is not sustained in any aspect of economic development in the area.

Yet the desire for economic development is strongly held, as one other major fund-raising drive showed. The expectations and aspirations of the villagers concerning it provide an eloquent commentary on their attitudes toward economic development as a whole. This project was the extension of the road from Mota over the hills to Nanuku, only four miles from Nalotawa. A few years ago, the six villages of the area raised £300 for the road and engaged a bulldozer driver: a tortuous, badly graded 'road' was built. Although the road was really fit only for Land Rover traffic, for a time a truck managed to navigate it every Friday to take the villagers and their produce to market. However, the unsurfaced road rapidly deteriorated and by 1958 was impassable, so that the villagers had to travel right down to Mota on foot or by horseback. It is significant, however, that the improvement of this road was one of the most commonly expressed 'felt needs' of the area, as was another feeder road from Sabeto in the south that might alternatively open up the entire area by connecting with the Nanuku road. In short, the people of Nalotawa, along with others in the area, regarded the road as a panacea for all their economic ills, a device that would almost magically transform their countryside and bring riches to all. Although there can be no doubt of the very real economic advantages that feeder roads do bring, and the stimulus that often accompanies their construction, the villagers had practically no specific ideas about how to capitalise on the construction of a road. On the whole, the men of Nalotawa are happy with their present lot, content merely to dream of a bright future created by such 'handouts' provided by the government of Suva.

The Galala: Individualism and Traditionalism

In this area, and throughout Fiji, some of the richest men are galala who have been granted exemption from communal duties and the right to reside outside the koro, living to some extent apart from the enmeshing ties of custom that bind the ordinary villager. An understanding of the part these men play as leaders in agricultural achievement is crucial in any study of the issues involved in the economic development of the area.

In 1958, to gain exemption a galala had:

1 to maintain at least three acres of land;
2 to provide not less than two acres of pasture land for each beast where cattle are kept;
3 to manage his holding so as to make a gross income of not less than £100 per year;
4 to have at all times growing and properly-cared-for crops sufficient for the requirements and welfare of himself and those dependent on him;
5 to pay, in addition to Provincial Rates, the Commutation Rate of £1 per year.

In return, they were exempted from the regular communal services that involved all villagers. Exemption could be revoked by the *roko* subject to appeal. Annually, the *roko* and a provincial committee reviewed the cases of commutation and sometimes cancelled an individual exemption, without compensation, for failing to meet one or more of the conditions.

It can be seen from these latter stringent conditions that the policy of the administration in 1958-9 was biased against the independent farmer and directed at maintaining the cohesion of the village 'communal' unit. Moreover, a monetary income of £100 is, as we have seen, above the sum earned by the average villager at Nalotawa. The attitudes of the *galala* and the conditions under which they live in comparison with villagers are revealing; most exempted men worked harder, had larger gardens and earned well over £100 a year. The following record of a discussion with one exempted man, who lived near Nanuku, three miles from Nalotawa, is typical:

Q: Why did you want to become a *galala*?
A: In the village I couldn't keep any money with traditional obligations to observe and many children to feed. I tried for two whole years to gain exemption. On the third application to the Tikina Council, I saw the head of Yavusa Quwalinabulu as well and he put forward the application and it was granted.
Q: What did the people in the village think when you left to live as a *galala*?
A: Most of the people were indifferent.
Q: Are you lonely here?
A: I don't want to go back to the village as I am much happier here. I am saving to build a European-style house so the children can benefit. I only go to Yaloku to see my brother about the village store which we jointly own. I may sometimes stop in the village for the night on returning from town.
Q: What crops do you grow for the market?
A: *Yaqona*, *dalo*, banana, chilli, *dalo-ni-tana*, pawpaw, *roro*, *mau*, cassava, maize, curry. I get over £100 a year from *yaqona*. I also take to market once a fortnight one or sometimes two packhorses of other crops [i.e. about £60 at £2 to £2.10s. per load].
Q: How much land do you have for your crops?
A: I have six *teitei* with over 6,000 *yaqona* plants on two of them. I plant just over 1,000 *yaqona* plants a year [cf. Table 6.2]. I could use more land if I could get it from my *mataqali*.
Q: Do you ever work with the villagers or have them working for you?

A: They came to help me build this house. I gave them £27 for their help and £8 for mending the roof. Six people were here for three weeks. I killed a cow, presented *yaqona* and gave them a *magiti* (feast). The kitchen was built for £12 and two latrines for £2.10s. each. In the case of the house, the people in the village needed £27. I have told them that if they are in trouble to come and work for me.

The facts that emerged from this interview were corroborated by discussions with most of the other *galala* of the area; they illustrate the relationship between some important aspects of the process of economic development and social change. In successfully living alone and farming independently, the *galala* is more of an individualist than his kinsfolk in the *koro*; his attitudes to farming, money and the land are more commercialised and his half-ownership of the store indicates his entrepreneurial instinct. In contrast to the rapid dissipation of money by villagers, he exhibited a keen desire to save[14] and his *bure* contained a new radio, a better-than-average sewing machine, new suitcases and a new clock. Further discussion suggested that he spent many more hours a week on his gardens than did the average villager (see Figure 6.4). And yet, in spite of his relative freedom from the yoke of custom, he is still to some extent bound by it: although he is primarily interested in capital accumulation he does not deny his kinsmen money, even though he requires them to do some work for it.

Thus, the position that the *galala* occupies in society is merely on the fringe, not outside, the normal patterns of behaviour; a position that has important implications for the future. If the *galala* were a revolutionary whose life and work were motivated by a completely different set of values, his own economic progress would admittedly be greater, but his influence on village society would be much less. But since he respects the local leadership pattern and does not completely repudiate tradition, he maintains rapport with society and serves as an effective agent of social change. Much of his influence is due to the fact that the differences between him and the villager are of degree, not of kind: he is not an innovator in the sense that his patterns of living are substantially different, he is merely more market-oriented and more individualistic. Moreover, exemption is a logical development of trends under way in village society, for as the use of labour has become more clearly an economic transaction rather than one involving reciprocal social relationships, so economic relationships have become depersonalised and much of the social content involved in traditional economic organisation has been steadily eroded away.

The rapport between the *galala* and village society is expressed in the generally favourable view held by most villagers toward exemption. While I suspect that the villagers felt that this attitude might accord more closely to a European viewpoint, it seemed to be genuinely held on the whole. Thus, it was asserted that the village "hasn't grown at all for the last 100 years" and that "if more people became exempted there would be much more progress". When I pointed out that one reason for the government's lack of encouragement to the exemption movement was the failure of many independent farmers during the 1930s and early 1940s, it was retorted that "Fijians were not so money-conscious in Sir Philip Mitchell's time as they are now"; and "three big *dalo* brought only one shilling then, now they may sell for up to seven and sixpence".

Yet, in spite of such cash-consciousness, there is a significant difference between a vague approval of *galala* and an earnest endeavour to become one: in Nalotawa itself there was only one *galala* and in the area of the six villages not more than a dozen. This small number is the result of several factors: the erroneous belief that a man must have £100 in the bank before his application will be favourably considered,[15] the attitude of disfavour with which the local *buli* regards exemption and the relative lack of promising opportunities for agriculture in the area. But the villagers also admitted, not entirely with dissatisfaction, that they are "bound by church matters, custom and government matters". And, with one or two exceptions, the men of Nalotawa are content with the round of life in the *koro* as they know it.

In some cases, their concept of exemption expressed no real trend towards individualism at all, but was merely a reassertion of the traditional tendency towards segmentation and migration of a social unit. Thus, when Jone Lotawa said he would like Nalotawa to break up and move up the slope of Mount Evans Range where he had his *yaqona teitei*, he was not recommending a radical individualisation of the settlement and production patterns, but the movement of the people of his own *tokatoka* (of which he was second in seniority) to a new site where they would form a new incipient *koro*, just as the people of another *yavusa* had done under Noa Botitu to form Rara several years ago.[16]

Thus, the exemption movement, which is a form of economic and social change that is essentially Western in character, can be reinterpreted locally in purely Fijian terms expressing the functioning of traditional social organisation.

Conclusion

This survey of economic and social aspects of life at Nalotawa has revealed a good deal of evidence of change. However, our analysis of the agricultural system, the penetration of a cash economy and the exemption movement disclose the persistence of a resilient traditionalism, a happy and unquestioning acquiescence in the status quo. Comparison of these patterns of life with those of other villages shows the various ways in which Nalotawa is, on the whole, a relatively conservative, traditional village in the Fiji of today. Some of the reasons for the relatively slow pace of change have already been touched upon. In brief, they hinge around opportunities for change available at Nalotawa and the real satisfactions of life that still exist in the village.

Economically, the opportunities for development in the area are considerable, given heavy capital outlays and the application of modern science and technology. It would seem that aerial top dressing and over-sowing with exotic grass seeds of some parts in the hilly dry zone, if economic, might ultimately transform some of the existing poor pastures into at least second-class grazing country.[17] Afforestation too has distinct possibilities. Moreover, the improvement of the Nanuku road and the construction of a road from Sabeto would undoubtedly stimulate cash cropping and grazing in the area.[18] Such developments, however desirable, remain remote however, since they would depend largely on government action, and because of the shortage of capital available for development, a higher priority will be given to other more fertile areas that produce export crops. But the villagers themselves could do much with little capital outlay, if they could be induced to fence their land, practise controlled rotational grazing, prevent burning and learn the fundamentals of cattle breeding.

Why has nothing been achieved so far towards this? In the first place, Fijian administrative policy has the effect of reinforcing the status quo, and traditional institutions such as land tenure provide formidable obstacles to development. These issues will be taken up more fully later. Secondly, the people of this isolated area receive no technical help; the people of Nalotawa had never been visited by an Extension Officer of the Agricultural Department or by an assistant of the Economic Development Officer (Western Region). I was in fact the first European to visit Nalotawa for 10 years. This deficiency, though serious, is not by any means a complete explanation for the lack of change, for many villagers know the efficient CSR cattle ranch of Yanqara and have some ideas of what should be done.

The fundamental reasons for the persistence of traditionalism stem from strong enduring satisfactions. Economically, the people can satisfy their needs by working in their gardens for only 15 to 20 hours each week (see Figure 6.4). Enough land was available for all, and a steady market for *yaqona*, bananas and *dalo* ensured a household income of about £90 that seemed to be satisfactory for most people. Although evidence over a period of years is lacking, it seemed that cash cropping had reached a plateau several years earlier, and output was not noticeably increasing. Moreover, isolation was an advantage as well as a disadvantage; it removed Nalotawa from the worries of economic competition with Indians living nearer the coast while at the same time the distance was not too great to prevent fortnightly visits to the market (12 miles away) and occasional participation in the interesting life of the town. If any large sum of money was required for some community project, the men of the village could easily raise the money by going as a group to cut cane for Indian farmers. Thus in many ways Nalotawa enjoys the best of both worlds.

Moreover, the persistence of custom hinders many cash-oriented activities. I was appalled to learn on arriving at Nalotawa on my second visit that the only surviving bull in the village had been killed for a *magiti*. Although some of the villagers wanted to build up the size of the herd, such considerations had to take second place when a man's status in the eyes of his relations was involved. Traditional work patterns persist in spite of the admitted economic advantages of specialisation of labour. The construction of the chief's new *bure* involved all men of the old *tikina* for five weeks, hindering gardeners from tending their crops at the right times and costing by *vaka vanua* methods about twice as much as the contract price (see Table 6.8).

Several tasks are still done communally, such as house building, clearing the village compound, tending the village garden and assisting any individual in major tasks on his *teitei* if help has been requested in the traditional manner. Moreover, much time is spent in life-cycle ceremonies. Funerals take five to 10 days, weddings a week and births one day. Undoubtedly, such traditional practices relieve the monotony of life in the village and provide deep satisfactions to a people who are still basically Fijian in culture. But from a purely economic standpoint, these practices and the values associated with them seriously hinder the expansion of commercial cropping and grazing.

Socially, the satisfactions of life at Nalotawa were even more pronounced. An individual felt secure because of the strength of enduring ties that linked him with his kinsfolk. On the one hand, he identified himself with his forefathers whose hallowed graves lined the

Table 6.8. Cost of the Chief's New House

Size: 6 fathoms by 3 fathoms
Labour force: About 60 men from the five villages of the old *tikina*
Time of construction: Five weeks

Total Cost	Consumed in 11 *magiti* held at certain stages of construction
10 cattle	1. When the wall posts arrived
1 pig	2. When the posts were in
4 large bags of sugar	3. When the foundation stones were laid
9 bags of flour	4. When all rafters and beams were on
11 pounds of tea	5. When all walls were thatched on the inside with reeds
5 40-lb tins of biscuits	
Large piles of *dalo* and other food	6. When the walls were thatched on the outside
10 *tabua* (whales' teeth)	
Roots of 10 big *yaqona* plants	7. For all the women of the other villages who provided food for their menfolk during the work
	8. For the people of Vakabuli village because they supplied food, and because the Chief is *vasu*[a] to Vakabuli
	9. When the house was completed
	10. When all the rubbish from the work was cleaned up
	11. For the people of Nalotawa

[a] *A relationship between a chief and his sister's son, under which the son had many privileges.*

rara (village green) and, on the other, he was united by ties of descent with other members of his *tokatoka*, *yavusa* and *vanua*, and by affinal ties, he was linked with Fijians in other areas. Moreover, the pattern of leadership in Nalotawa provided the link between the untroubled past and the present. Since Nalotawa is a one-*yavusa* village, no conflict existed between chiefs of equal rank. A good man, with a staunch belief in the values of the culture that nurtured him, the chief provided a firm but not unbending surveillance over all activities in the village. The heir-apparent, his son Jone Lotawa (the owner of the plough), will be a chief who will usefully combine qualities of moderate enterprise and initiative with adherence to traditional values. Since my initial fieldwork in 1959, Jone Lotawa has attempted several new enterprises, not all of which should prove abortive.[19]

The meaning of village life to the typical man, and its solid values in contrast to the uncertainties and anxieties that are to be found in the wider world outside, are expressed in the words of Ratu Tevita. He spoke of how, when he was young he worked for colonial firms in various parts of Fiji. But he worried about his work always and even his sleep was troubled. When he returned to Nalotawa to get married, he did not want to travel any more. Here he could do what he liked, needing to work only occasionally and sleeping all day if he wished: "There are no worries in the village".

This almost idyllic conception of life at Nalotawa, while admittedly that of the chief who is a member of the older generation, was substantially shared by the majority of the people who live in the village. But at the beginning of this chapter we referred to the tiny cracks that might ultimately destroy the foundations of this peaceful, slow-changing existence.

These cracks are the forces of social change, embodied in the processes of urbanisation and the exemption movement which represent a way of life substantially different from life in the *koro*. But equally important is likely to be the challenge of events happening elsewhere in Fiji which the men of Nalotawa can no longer afford to ignore and which may force them to reassess drastically the fundamental basis of their existence.

7

Sorolevu: A Sugar-growing Village

This study of Sorolevu was first published as chapter 6 of Koro *in 1969 and also draws on Watters, 1963. It was an attempt to explain the disparities in sugar production between Fijians and Indo-Fijians, based on a study of a sugar-producing village where I conducted fieldwork in the late 1950s. Three possible causes of low productivity were identified: poor or variable environmental conditions, unfavourable economic conditions or the character of Fijian culture. The chapter suggests that while social change was occurring in Sorolevu, and there were some attempts to improve agricultural management and systems, cultural impediments to economic progress were evident in many village practices.*

History of Fijian Cane Production

Although sugar cane is indigenous to the South Pacific, it was not grown commercially in Fiji until the latter part of the nineteenth century. By the 1880s, the Australian firm Colonial Sugar Refining Company had become dominant and later acquired a monopoly using indentured Indian labour. Around 1920 when indenture ended, most Indians on completion of their indentured period moved to either lease land from the CSR plantations or much more increasingly to lease from Fijian land-owning sub-clans.

Fijians did not begin to grow cane commercially until the early 1930s, 60 years after large-scale cane growing had begun in the Colony, and 20 years after Indian smallholder production became common. In 1933, some villagers refused to renew Indian leases as they wanted to begin cultivation themselves.[1] In the same year, the Legislative Council passed the Native Land Occupation Bill to encourage Fijians to go into individual planting. By 1936, 1,131 Fijians were growing sugar on about 3 percent of the colony's cane acreage, from which they earned £27,017.

In the period of high prices from 1953 to 1957, their percentage of the total area harvested varied from about 4 percent to a little over 5 percent and their percentage of the total tonnage from 3.2 to 4.8.[2]

Fijian tenants of the South Pacific Sugar Mills usually produce about 1.5 tons of cane less per acre compared to Indian tenants, while Fijian contractors harvest about four tons per acre less than their Indian counterparts. Fijian yields per acre have not improved since the 1930s. With rare exceptions, the only Fijians who consistently produce comparable or greater yields than Indians are *galala*, who mostly live outside the village. Moreover, the discrepancy between Indian and Fijian growers is much less among tenants of the CSR, who are relatively free from the social ties of the village and receive more technical assistance than do the village contractors.[3]

A striking illustration of variations in Fijian efficiency at cane farming is provided by a comparison of Navukai and Wagadrai, two CSR estates near Sorolevu, where Fijian tenants are settled on 7.5-acre blocks. The Wagadrai estate, which began in 1942, has a high average production which exceeds the Indian overall average for the Nadi district (27.2). Navukai, however, averaged only 15.3 tons per acre, in spite of the fact that 44 of the 57 tenants were also ex-Drasa trainees who had been thoroughly taught the techniques of efficient cane production at the Company's special training farm for Fijians. Indeed, Navukai in 1956 seemed to be at the stage Wagadrai had been at several years earlier. The reasons for low production were clear enough: communal obligations such as house-building interfered with the necessary routine work on the cane plots, the tenants could not raise money on their land since they did not possess title to it, and late planting was common, which often meant that some seed cane did not germinate or the crop was checked by drought. On the other hand, Wagadrai is an example of almost individualistic farming and there the tenants emphatically rejected the suggestion of returning to group forms of activity. Its success seems to have been due to the cultivators on that estate being free from the enmeshing bonds of traditional communalism, since they mostly came from distant villages and few social calls were made on their earnings.[4] In the opinion of one senior CSR officer, a comparison between Navukai and Wagadrai indicates that Fijian tenants on company estates should be allowed to employ traditional forms of group activity on the cane plots for the first five years, after which they should be encouraged to branch out individually.

Cane Growing at Sorolevu

The men of Sorolevu produce less cane per acre than most Indian farmers in the locality. In 1958, 1,996 tons were cut from 99 acres by 41 growers, giving an average of 20.2 tons per acre, compared to the average figure of 24.5 for the whole of the predominantly Indian-settled cane district of Qeleloa, in which Sorolevu lies. A survey in the cane zone in 1967 showed that average incomes among Indian growers ranged from £704-£900, while Fijian incomes averaged only £304. Why is Fijian production lower than that of the Indians? The answers to this question are of considerable significance to the country as a whole. It is clearly important that Fijians should steadily increase their share in total cane production in order to avoid complete Indian dominance in the colony's greatest industry. Also, since the contentious Reserves policy is steadily making more cane land available to Fijians, race relations will be further inflamed if cane land ceases to be utilised or produces lower yields when it passes from Indian to Fijian hands.

Low sugar production can be attributed to one or a combination of three possible causes: inferior environmental conditions, unfavourable economic conditions or the character of Fijian culture.

The Physical Environment

Sugar cane requires abundant and regular moisture, much sunlight and warm temperatures throughout the year. Sunlight and temperature conditions are ideal at Sorolevu.

The average annual total of rainfall is 70 inches. Monthly totals are low from May to October – in these months, potential evapo-transpiration exceeds rainfall. However, water contained in soil storage is available for growing plants until October when, usually, a month of deficiency occurs before rainfall again exceeds potential evapo-transpiration with the onset of the rainy season in November. Although the climate is thus too dry in one or two months for optimum unirrigated sugar production, if planting is not done too late (after May) the rainfall is entirely adequate and high yields can normally be obtained. Average figures, however, are a rather inadequate guide, as annual totals have varied by as much as 400 percent and monthly rainfall totals also vary greatly from year to year. In some years, a drought may check cane growth in several months.

The moisture balance data at Navo were gathered in 1958, the year in which the production methods of growers were studied in the field. In May, June, August and September, potential evapo-transpiration exceeded rainfall, but July and October were wetter than usual. Thus, growers who planted later than May might still obtain good yields (see Table 7.1) through these fortuitous showers

How fertile are the soils of Sorolevu for cane production? The soils, developed from alluvium or from volcanic material, are intermediate in age in terms of the length of the soil leaching process. Volcanic parent

Table 7.1. Cane Production per Acre and Correlation with Soil Fertility

Grower	Description of soil fertility	1959 tons per acre	1960 tons per acre	Extent to which production correlates with natural fertility (percent)
A.D. Naevo	Good	18.3	13.7	35
P. Naqari	Poor	20.0	27.6	60
M. Naurea	Poor	9.0	34.0	55
M. Driu	Medium	36.0	34.0	85
S. Donu	Poor-Fair	9.3	-	25
K. Aria	Medium	12.0	-	30
V. Lagilagi	Poor-Fair	28.0	26.5	70
T. Idro	Fair	13.0	16.0	35
V. Levi	Very Good	50.0	-	100
J. Natua	Medium	29.3	44.0	90
A. Duve	Good	36.3	38.7	85
T. Labalaba	Fair	19.0	-	50
R. Dresu	Fair-Poor	27.0	36.0	80
A. Naevo	Fair	22.7	42.0	80
K. Naqone	Fair-Poor	31.5	20.0	65
Average		24.1	22.2	63

material gives a reasonably fertile soil on the highest of the river terraces. The two lowest terraces are, on the whole, even more productive, as the silt deposited by occasional floods of the Nawaka River renews much of their fertility. Figure 7.1 shows the classes of land and topography of Sorolevu. The soil of the area has been termed the Sigatoka clay loam and may be described as a dark brown soil with a clear profile development and a friable to firm texture. With the exception of the Dobuilevu clays, the alluvial Sigatoka clay loams have the highest nutrient status of all Fijian cane soils. Though they appear to have a low humus content, only small dressings of sulphate of ammonia seem in general to be needed. In comparison with most cane soils, they are easy to cultivate and maintain good structure.

In order to check these known facts about soil fertility and to measure more precisely the current nutrient status, I took soil samples from 15 cane plots on a cross-section of all classes of land. These were analysed by the soil chemist of the CSR Company.

In Figure 7.2, the amounts of phosphorus and potash and the pH figures are shown in relation to optimum figures. It can be seen that the nutrient status of Sorolevu soils in 1959 thus varied from very good to poor; the location of some of the latter on the lower terraces suggests

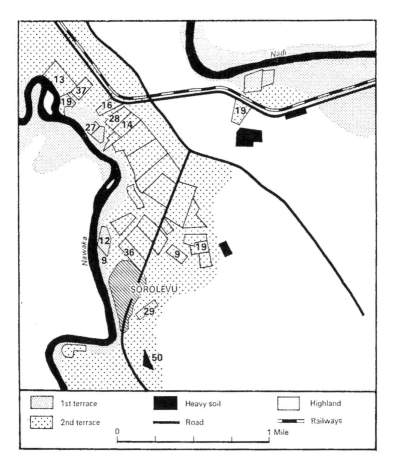

Figure 7.1. Classes of Land on Family Cane Plots at Sorolevu. Tonnages per Acre of Sample Growers are Shown

overcropping (probably in the form of inadequate fallowing or a lack of fertiliser) over many years. However, soil fertility does not depend merely on nutrient status, for other properties affecting fertility – the water-holding capacity and aeration – are good, as the Sigatoka clay loam possesses good structure. Thus, the soils are on the whole well-suited to sugar production and, in the opinion of the chief agronomist of the CSR Company, the lowest terrace should be producing 50 tons per acre under current forms of husbandry, while the higher terraces should be giving 45 tons per acre. In view of the rather lower nutrient status revealed by some analyses, this empirical estimate could be conservatively adjusted to 40 tons per acre on the poorest land.

The actual per-acre production of the owners of each plot sampled for soil analysis can now be compared with the estimated production

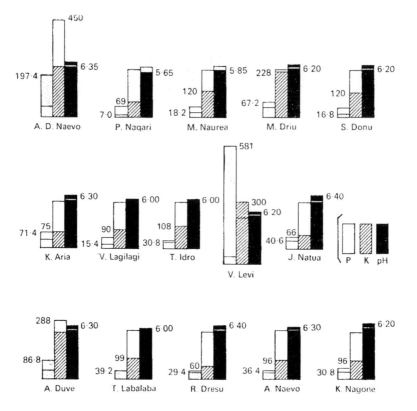

Figure 7.2. Some Criteria of Soil Fertility on a Sample of Growers' Cane Plots at Sorolevu The amounts of P and K and pH readings are given. Optimum readings are shown (P=44, K=228 and pH=6) so divergence from these readings can be measured for each grower. Compare with Table 7.1 showing yields per acre.

that could, not unreasonably, be expected from each soil type, and the performance of each grower then expressed as a very rough percentage of the potential (Table 7.1). These estimates vary from about 25 to 100 percent, the average being just over 60 percent. At most, only two out of the 15 growers obtained reasonable tonnages per acre. Also, growers were characteristically inconsistent. Thus, a very fertile plot that produced the highest yield in the village in 1959 was worked by the man who, on another plot, had the lowest yield.

Economic Conditions

We must turn to other factors to explain the failure to realise the production potential of Sorolevu soils. Some immediate causes of low production could, of course, be seen in an inspection of the cane fields, but I tried to isolate the main deficiencies of production by submitting a questionnaire informally to a stratified random sample of cane growers in the village. Twenty-one of the 41 growers in the village, with cane plots totalling 60.4 acres or 58 percent of the total area under cane in 1958,[5] answered it. Field inspection of the growers' plots provided a rough check on some of the answers. The questionnaire, and the results obtained, are given in Table 7.3. For purposes of comparison, optimum practices are also given. In order that the efficiency of Fijian cane growers may be roughly compared with a sample of Indian farmers, the result of a stratified random survey of 37 Indian farms, occupying a cross-section of soil types in the Nadi-Lautoka area, is also included (Figure 7.3).

Planting was the first field operation investigated. Insufficient data were collected on the type of seed cane used in planting, but it is clear that a good number used cane that was too old (i.e. over 12 months old) or alternatively did not take the trouble to use only the tops of old stalks. Only three growers out of 11 used fungicide when planting, while the practice of replacing stools that had failed to germinate was generally uncommon.

Fallowing of cane land was rare, only nine of the 60.4 acres, or an average of only 0.4 of an acre per grower, being currently spelled. Only two growers out of 21 claimed that they ever followed a regular rotation. However, in the opinion of the Chief Agronomist of the CSR, soils of the fertility and structure of the Sigatoka clay loams need not be fallowed or farmed in a rotation, provided adequate dressings of fertiliser are regularly applied, and a good standard of cultivation maintained. Twelve out of 21 informants, however, did not use fertiliser, six applied only one dressing and only three applied the optimum two dressings, although not all used adequate amounts. Nor was green manuring common as a method of restoring nitrogen to the soil, and only two growers had ever ploughed in the trash after the cane was cut, most burning it instead.

The village's response to innovation could be observed in connection with a new variety of cane (Ragnar) suited for flat land. Although by 1958 it was widely known that the new hybrid produced significantly higher yields than the older noble varieties, and was disease-resistant, the village lagged behind Indian farmers in adopting this new variety. In 1958, 84 percent of the cane area of the Qeleloa District as a whole and 42 percent of its total tonnage consisted of the new hybrids Ragnar and Pindar, but in Sorolevu the old varieties Ajax, Badilla, Galba and Pompey comprised over 80 percent. However, in 1959 the village swung over to Ragnar on the advice of the CSR Company.

These various deficiencies undoubtedly lowered yields considerably,

Figure 7.3. Data on Fijian Sugar Production, Sorolevu Village

Question	No. of Informants	Answer	Average per grower	Yes	No
1. Number of acres planted in sugar	21	60–5/12	3 acres		
2. Fallowing of sugar land	21	9/60½	·4 acres	2	19
3. Use of fallow land for another crop	21	Tapioca		1	20
4. Good planting material used (young cane tops)	5			1	4
5. Month of planting in favourable wet period	21			11[a]	10
6. Fungicide used when planting	11			3	8
7. Ever grow a green manure?	18			2[b]	16
8. Use of trash	21	All burn it[c]			
9. Number of tons per acre at last harvest	21		20·2		
10. Number of growers planting new, high-yielding strains	21				
11. Number of ratoon crops (one optimum)	21		1·1		
12. (a) No dressings of fertilizer per crop		12			
(b) One dressing of fertilizer		6			
(c) Two dressings of fertilizer		3[d]			
13. Number of years growing cane	21		7½ years		
14. Any rotation of land	21			4[e]	17
15. Number of inter-row cultivations per crop	15		2		
(a) 1 Inter-row cultivation		3			
(b) 2 Inter-row cultivations		10			
(c) 3 Inter-row cultivations		1			
(d) 4 Inter-row cultivations		1			
16. Number of hand weedings	21		2		
(a) 1 hand weeding		5			
(b) 2 hand weedings		12			
(c) 2–3 hand weedings		4			
17. Number of months from planting to harvest—Optimum over 15 months	21		15		
18. Equipment owned					
(a) Ploughs	20			12	8
(b) Harrows	20			2	18
(c) Scarifiers	20			6	14
(d) {Pair of bullocks	21			11	10
{Pair of working horses				10	11
19. Hire of tractor for first ploughing	20			20	
20. Method preferred in farming land	21				
(a) Individualism				21	
(b) Communalism					21
21. Do members of grower's clan ask for, or receive, a share of cane monies?	19			7[f]	12
22. Do other members of your clan or extended family question your right to the land you use?	22				22
23. Do social obligations interfere with cultivation of your cane?	19			18[g]	1
24. What do you consider to be the size of a minimum economic holding?	21	10 acres			

NOTES:

[a] Three of these growers planted in the marginal month of May.

[b] On one occasion each.

[c] One grower has sometimes left his trash to rot and one other has occasionally ploughed his trash in.

[d] Sometimes these dressings are inadequate in amount.

[e] Two of these have fallows, not a rotation.

[f] Five of these involved the giving of yaqona to clan members, two providing financial help to family members, and two, gifts of drums of kerosene.

[g] Thirteen said that house building and village cleaning interfered, four declared that the district programme of work caused interference, and one said that social obligations in general tended to clash with planting times.

Figure 7.4. Data on Indian Smallholder Sugar Production
(Summary of methods of 37 growers, selected on a cross-section of major soil types, Nadi-Lautoka and Sigatoka areas)

	Answers	Yes	No
Size of Farm	14½ acres average		
Tenure:			
C.S.R. Lease	21		
Native Lease	12		
Other[a]	4		
Class of Land			
First Class	12		
Second Class	13		
Third Class	12		
Method of Rotation:			
Short fallow with cow peas	28		
Short fallow with mainly rice	5		
Long fallow with mauritius bean	4		
Planting period Optimum (January–May)	All growers		
Planting Material:			
Under 10 months	31		
Over 10 months	6		
Fungicide used when planting if dry		2	14
Use of Trash:			
Burnt	25		
Ploughed in	12		
Tons per acre (average 1959–60)	36		
Use of Fertilizer:			
No dressings per crop	0		
One dressing	13		
Two dressings	18		
Three dressings	6		
Number of cwt. per acre each dressing:			
One	1		
Two	11		
Three	11		
Four	12		
Five	2		
Use of Coral sand as fertilizer		17	10
Use of mill mud as fertilizer		7	24
Number of inter-row cultivations per crop[b]:			
Two	1		
Three	6		
Four	14		
Five	9		
Six	5		
Seven	1		
Eight	1		
Number of Weedings per crop:			
One	1		
Two	17		
Three	12		
Four	4		
Five	2		
Six	1		
Use of Herbicide		9	28
Own a Tractor	6		
Hire a Tractor	28		
Own Working Bullocks	27		
Own Working Horse	16		
Other Source of Income	17		
No other Source of Income	20		
Ideas on future land use on land freed from cane		20	17
No. of years experience growing cane	22 years average		
No. of years of schooling	4 years average		
Attitude on ownership of sugar processing and marketing[c]:			
Favour continuation under Company	8		
Favour Indian co-operatives	3		
Favour Government nationalization	19		
No opinion	7		

NOTES:

[a] These include 2 freehold, 1 crown lease, and 1 sub-lease from an Indian lease-holder.

[b] To some extent the number of inter-row cultivations and weedings depends on the soil type.

[c] Of these, 3 favoured some Government control over the freedom of the Company in fixing the cane price. However these answers were affected by the 1961 dispute between growers and Company.

while other practices that were impossible to check statistically must also have had an effect, such as failure to prepare the land sufficiently well before planting and careless handling of seed cane during planting, which might result in the breaking of eyes. But perhaps the greatest single cause of low production was weed growth. Inspection of the cane fields showed that on many plots weeds grew profusely along the rows, in sharp contrast to the clean-weeded rows and taller, healthier cane of Indian farmers nearby. Of 15 informants from whom clear answers were obtained, only one man ploughed between his rows on four separate occasions. One man did three inter-row cultivations, 10 did two and three men did only one. The amount of hand weeding done was also inadequate. Instead of the optimum six to eight hand weedings, four growers did two to three, 12 did two (the average) and five did only one. Such inattention leads to thickly matted weeds between the rows and undersized stands of cane – sights all too common at Sorolevu.

An inadequate number of inter-row cultivations and poor preparation of the land prior to planting reflect to some extent a shortage of working animals and implements. This fact prohibits approximately 45 percent of Fijian contractors from doing the right thing at the right time according to the Economic Development Officer who made a survey of Fijian cane lands in the Nadi and Nawaka Districts in 1959.[6] He found that this forced the individual grower to wait until he could borrow the animals and implements, and when he eventually received them, conditions were often too dry to be ideal for planting. Similarly, by the time animals and implements were available for inter-row cultivation, the weeds were often so prolific that the crop was virtually ruined. He found in Sorolevu that, out of 40 registered cane growers, 27 had neither working animals nor implements. There was a total of eight pairs of working bullocks, two working horses, 11 ploughs, two harrows and two scarifiers.

I checked the correlation between late planting and the amount of rainfall – an interrelation between climate and agricultural practice that is of the utmost importance in cane growing. Of 21 growers, 10 planted later than May when rainfall is normally insufficient (nine of these were poorly equipped with animals and implements). The common explanation of late planting is that subsistence crops are planted about August and that the cultivator carries over this traditional planting time to cane. This may be partially true (as late planting is commonly done at this time), but the close correlation with a lack of implements suggests that enforced waiting is the main reason. Only one of those growers well equipped with animals and implements planted after May. It must be emphasised, however, that a shortage of animals and gear is not the only explanation, as infrequent hand weedings and other deficiencies marked the work patterns of even the well-equipped growers and clearly affected their production figures.

A common explanation of low production is that Fijians have had insufficient time to become adjusted to the requirements of cane growing. However, there were at least one or two Fijians growing cane at Sorolevu 25 years ago, and the number has grown steadily over the years. Six informants had been growing cane for less than five years, 10 between five and nine years, and five for 10 years or longer; the average was seven years. The number of years seems to be less significant than the amount of time each cultivator spent on his crop each season. Though data over a period of years are lacking, it would appear that there is rather more time spent on the cane fields today than hitherto.

The labour needed for cane growing cannot be adduced as a reason for low production in Sorolevu. The village population of 300 is typically young (Figure 7.5) and there are 89 males of working age. An estimate of the labour needed for an average-sized holding of three acres producing 30 tons per acre gives the low figure of 36 man-days or 50 man-days a year per acre, including cutting. District programmes of work (which are never observed) allow a fortnight a month for cane growing activities, which is more than adequate, even allowing for the fact that approximately 30 days a year are spent on weddings, funerals and other social gatherings.

Figure 7.5. The Age Structure of Sorolevu

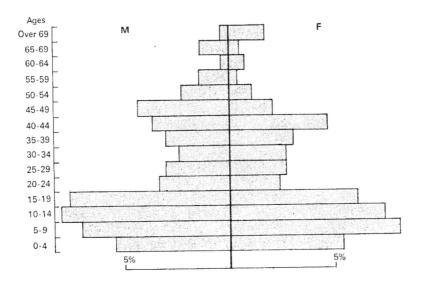

Thus, the results of the questionnaire, supported in part by field evidence and the survey of the Assistant Economic Development Officer, show that there are many deficiencies in cane production at Sorolevu. In particular, production suffers from a shortage of animals and implements, inadequate weedings, and various other shortcomings at various points between planting and harvesting. It is obvious, however, that these failings are only the *immediate* causes of low production, being merely symptoms of deeper-seated factors. Since in virtually every case the growers knew what they should do to obtain much greater yields, yet failed to do it, we must turn to the cultural level.

Cultural Impediments

The underlying reasons for the lower production of Fijians compared to Indians become apparent when we consider the persistence of traditional patterns of culture that directly conflict with the individualistic entrepreneurial qualities required for progressive cane farming.

Writing of Fijian sugar production in general, Spate attributes considerable importance to traditional and communal hindrances:

> Among the factors leading to the low Fijian output per acre are the interruptions due to communal demands and almost incredible care-lessness in the use of draught animals, while it is not uncommon for fertilizer, supplied by the Colonial Sugar Refining Company, to be sold at about half its price to Indians: £2 in spot cash against a future deduction of £4 from the cane proceeds ... this tendency to barter a small immediate gain against a larger future loss is recurrent.[7]

The Fijian leader, Ratu K.K.T. Mara, has himself stressed that economic activities must be pursued in an environment free from social encumbrances:

> The member of the *mataqali* who cultivates cane on *mataqali* land can only continue to do so if he shares the proceeds of his cane with the rest. There is a definite disincentive to produce more since it means more for other members of the *mataqali*.[8]

In fact, while this is undoubtedly a real problem in many villages in which social change has proceeded less far, social encumbrances are no longer greatly troublesome in Sorolevu, though they do have some effect. For example, 12 out of 19 growers said that their *mataqali* did not ask for (or receive) a share of their cane moneys. Two said that their *mataqali* expected money, while five gave drums of kerosene, *yaqona* or some other help to their *mataqali* or to their closest kinsman. This relative independence was reflected in the fact that there was only one *galala* in the village; few men wished to become exempted as they felt that life in the village offered sufficient independence, at least for the present. The weakness of village-wide cooperation was reflected in the absence of a cooperative society. But although the villager of Sorolevu does possess considerable independence of action, he is still part of a web of social relationships. Thus, about 20 men in the village have taken the precaution of obtaining 10-year leases from their *mataqali* to avoid eviction from the land in the event of a dispute. The trend away from group patterns of working and thinking is evident too in the large number of fines incurred each year (about 10) for failure to perform communal duties. Moreover, in the opinion of 18 out of 19 informants, communal obligations in the form of housebuilding and village clearing required by the District Programmes of Work do interfere with cane cultivation. While the men of the village unanimously expressed a decided preference for farming individually, in theory if not in practice, they still admired the communal principle and valued it more highly than individualism. Wistfully, one man opined, "The people of old did not use any method to keep all people's minds as one".

Cultural impediments to economic progress were also apparent in the expenditure patterns of the village. The propensity to save a portion of money earned was less developed than at Nacamaki, for old practices of immediate consumption led to the rapid dissipation of income. There was almost no desire to spend money on implements[9] or in ways that would ultimately benefit production. But wise leadership by the *Tui*'s son has mitigated the effect of traditional values where they directly conflict with farming activities. Thus, no working bullocks had been killed for feasts for the past two years,[10] and selling implements and bullocks to secure money for immediate use had become uncommon. Generosity still appeared to be generally admired in the village but no longer seemed to involve much prestige.

Criteria of Social Change

It is apparent from the evidence that the Fijians of Sorolevu have advanced much further than their fellows in other areas such as Nalotawa. Indeed, it may perhaps be argued that our study of the deficiencies of cane production at Sorolevu tends to ignore the very considerable progress that the village has in fact achieved. Our real interest, however, is in the Fiji of tomorrow rather than in the Fiji of the past; in the years ahead, it will be imperative that Fijians contribute a much greater share to the national income if they are to avoid becoming an economically insignificant and backward community in their own land, whose only claim to power resides in their native origin and entrenched legalities. The manner in which progress has been attained at Sorolevu illustrates the nature of the processes of change, processes likely to be repeated in other parts of Fiji in the future.

The degree of change that had occurred up to 1959 can be observed not only in the weakening of traditional social relations but also in the changing needs of the people, their income and expenditure patterns, their changing attitudes towards the land and to technological change.[11]

8

Fiji in Retrospect

This chapter looks back to the Fiji where I first did my fieldwork 50 years ago. In looking back, it is clear that the problems in sugar production that were apparent in the late 1950s are still present: the disparity in yields between Fijian and Indian sugar growers and the lack of security in land tenure. The impact of these factors of course falls on the entire Fijian economy, and this essay examines the progression of the sugar-cane industry and the economy in the context of current political and social trends.

The People and the Land

Fiji today is sadly the culmination of the structures, systems and processes that dominated the small colonial economy that existed 50 years ago when I first arrived there. The structures were composed of a 'traditionalised', overprotected, but increasingly fearful and insecure indigenous Fijian people who owned 83 percent of the land, and a numerically greater (for 30 years, until the coups of 1987 and 2000 led many to flee overseas) individualistic and insecure Indo-Fijian society who owned only 2 percent of the land. While the Indian population has had little political influence, it has contributed the greater part of the GDP of Fiji.

Over time, the Indians feared for their security: the 1959 riots in Suva and the 1961 cane strike in the Dry Zone brought the very real danger that the Fijians would attack them with their bush knives. The Indians needed a rapid expansion of secondary and tertiary industries to provide employment for their youth coming on to the labour market and they also needed access to more land. Without this, and especially when the economy could not expand, Indians faced falling standards of living, unemployment, poverty, hunger and malnutrition.

The third racial group, European-Chinese, though small in numbers, occupied positions of authority in government and possessed great economic power as they ran the largest businesses and controlled most dealings with the outside world. They respected the legal rights stemming from the Deed of Cession that fortified Fijian land ownership, and their pro-Fijian attitudes have enabled the latter, even when in a minority, to maintain political control and to resist repeated Indian claims for land reform. These three groups have been referred to by Fisk (1970) as the "Three Fijis".[1]

Another major feature of both colonial and independent Fiji has been the over-cautious, rather laissez-faire and generally inadequate government and public service. The wide-ranging recommendations of the Burns Commission and the differing economic roles of the three crucial groups required the formulation and implementation of many completely new government policies. Sadly, the government failed to provide a real lead for the country, both economically and socially.

The 1960s and 1970s saw a continuation of good prices. By 1979, however, the South Pacific Agricultural Survey (SPAS) carried out by the Asian Development Bank (ADB) warned of impending land shortages and the growing inadequacy of the village mode of production (see Chapter 4). Increasingly, subsistence affluence would be less widespread or less effective in influencing motivation and there was a growing need for major new policies and attitudes in the rural sector, a situation that was re-emphasised by R.G. Ward, the leader of the SPAS team a few years later.[2]

When the government's Fiji Sugar Corporation (FSC) took over from the CSR in 1973, it revitalised the industry, taking advantage of the current world sugar shortage and, following the prevailing conventional wisdom of such bodies as the World Bank, launched a programme of expansion. While the CSR had well-grounded fears of soil conservation problems on hill land, the FSC encouraged areal expansion. The area of cane harvested rose from 46,000 to 70,000 ha. between 1973 and 1982, the number of growers increased from 15,000 to 22,000, and sugar production grew from 300,000 to almost 500,000 tonnes.[3]

In line with the current belief of the unions that the proportion of gross income going to the miller was too high (42 percent in 1960) under the FSC in the 1970s, the proportion dropped to under 35 percent, with the growers' share of income rising from 58 percent to 71.4 percent (or 68 percent of gross income).[4] With the benefit of hindsight, this appears to have been an over-payment that encouraged reckless expansion and lower quality cane growing, doing considerable damage both to land conservation and the financial health of the government sugar corporation.

The buoyant agriculture sector of the 1970s came to an end as unimproved land that could easily be brought into permanent cultivation was finally used up. In fact, most of Class I and II lands, comprising 29.9 percent of the country's area, were fully utilised under the prevailing technological methods by this date.

The intense competition between people, and especially between Indian tenants and Fijian landowners, increased by the late 1970s, and this pressure resulted, especially on marginal land, in substantial land degradation and erosion. Leslie and Ratukalou (2002a) point out that at this time issues of land availability and quality, land tenure, labour mobilisation, depopulation in some outer islands and sugar cane areas, and a changing balance between subsistence and commercial agriculture within the Fijian village sector all contributed to the fact that fewer people were now dependent directly on agricultural production.

It is hardly surprising, in view of the structures and systems we have identified, that the tensions and fears of each racial group became unbearable and, after a period of less favourable economic conditions, the Sitiveni Rabuka coups of 1987 occurred. (Commonly in the Third World, coups occur after periods of rapid modernisation when gloomy conditions ensue.) In May 2000, there was a third coup led by George Speight that overthrew the first democratically elected Indian-led government of Mahendra Chaudhry.

It can be noted that at the close of the twentieth century, the Fiji economy still had a very narrow base. Essentially, it still depended on the success of the tourist and sugar industries. The big improver over the last 40 years has been forestry, while traditional commodities such as *dalo*, kava and coconut oil are grown for niche markets, and there has been some expansion in cocoa and the new crop, ginger. Agriculture remains the main pillar of the economy and accounts for nearly 50 percent of total employment, 19 percent of GDP and almost 43 percent of foreign exchange.[5]

Total population over the 40-year period 1956-1996 increased by over 427,000 or 124 percent, while the amount of land used for agriculture increased from 215,013 ha. to 393,272 ha., an increase of 178,259 ha. or nearly 83 percent. Between 1986 and 1996, the total rural population declined by 23,826 (about 6 percent),[6] a trend that can be attributed overwhelmingly to the two coups of 1987 which led Fiji Indians to move to cities, or in many cases to emigrate to another country. Over the period 1990-2000, the urban population increased by 10 percent.[7]

The benefits of development have been very unevenly spread, and there are wider disparities than ever before in Fiji. While cities have generally prospered, mushrooming squatter settlements on their outskirts reveal the expansion of the informal sector or the plight of low income or unemployed people. Compared to the urban sector, rural areas have increasing levels of unemployment, low literacy rates and inferior living conditions. In some rural areas, poverty is now common and it is estimated that about 25 percent of the population is now living below the poverty line.[8]

Leslie and Ratukalou (2002a and b) identify many deficiencies and inadequacies with land use practices, issues and impacts:

- Because of the expansion of cash cropping and grazing on flatter land, subsistence gardens are increasingly being forced onto steeper slopes.
- With greater poverty and greater competition for land and between cash and subsistence crops, growers are increasingly shortening the length of bush fallows, which leads often to deflection in the vegetation to grasses and weeds, declining soil fertility and increasing danger of accelerated erosion.
- Because of the predominantly poor adoption and application of land husbandry practices and resultant degradation of land and water resources, the impacts from natural disasters are becoming more acute, especially vulnerability to droughts and flooding.
- There is serious under-resourcing for line ministries responsible for agriculture, forestry and land use in general as well as in the public service areas which need to undertake environmental planning, management and enforcement.
- The Land Conservation Board did not utilise the powers vested in it and there was minimal government support for the board to use its powers fully. It has not effectively tried to address causes of environmental degradation.
- There is a "poor awareness of the interdependence of conservation and development".[9]
- The majority of government and corporate (e.g. Native Land Trust Board [NLTB] and FSC) field officers are not conversant with the law. There have been no public awareness programmes to inform people about land husbandry provisions in the law and how they can be written into rural leases. Indeed, for "30 years there has been in essence no enforcement or policing of these provisions; thus, a whole generation has been kept in the dark since land conservation laws were last seriously regarded and enforced".[10]
- It is asserted that "poverty can be seen in all communities".[11] Indeed, the recent droughts and subsequent floods probably have exacerbated and increased the incidence of poverty through their effect on land use.

Accordingly, Leslie and Ratukalou follow their indictment of recent and current land use practices by formulating a Rural Land Use Policy for Fiji.[12] It is sadly ironic that one of the main recommendations of the major commission of enquiry in 1960 into the natural resources and population trends (known as the Burns Report) was at last accepted and adopted in 2002, over 40 years later!

The Sugar Industry

Cane and beet sugar is produced in 110 countries in the world, but Fiji and Papua New Guinea are the only producers in Oceania. Sugar has always been at the core of Fiji's economy, usually contributing 40-65 percent of total exports, around 10-12 percent of GDP, and providing the livelihood directly or indirectly of about 20 percent of the population.

In 1950, Fiji gained from Britain guaranteed preferential purchase of specified volumes of sugar for a negotiated price under the Commonwealth Sugar Agreement (CSA). In 1975, under the Lomé Convention (Article 25) and later under the Cotonou Agreement, the European Community undertook to purchase imported cane sugar from the relatively disadvantaged ACP (Africa, Caribbean and Pacific) states. In 2003, Fiji had a quota from the European Union (EU) of 165,348 tons of sugar, or approximately 40 percent of its total production,[13] with the balance having to be sold at the much reduced world price. (The EU preferential price is 2-3 times higher than the world price.)

After a World Trade Organisation ruling in favour of richer sugar-producing countries such as Brazil and Australia that subsidies to former European colonies violated global trade rules, the EU decided that the ACP Sugar Protocol would end in July 2006, and the EU would begin to cut ACP subsidies by 36 percent during the next four years. The subsidies dropped 5 percent in 2006, 17 percent in 2007.

The grim marketing decision has appalled Fijians, with about 200,000 people, or nearly one-fifth of the population, directly or indirectly relying on the industry for their livelihood. Although the EU will pay compensation, it is clear that the bleak marketing prospects have thrown the industry into a state of crisis.

In a vertically integrated industry, with cane harvesting, cane transport and sugar cane milling (sugar manufacture) all succeeding the farming phase and preceding marketing, it is unfortunate to note that considerable difficulties also occur at these phases. In the 1950s, when cane growing was largely confined to the narrow strip of fertile flat land in Western Viti Levu, a small, light railway line was established by the CSR and supplemented by portable branch lines. Today, about 50 percent of the cane is transported to the mills on this system which is owned, operated and paid for by the miller at a cost of about F$12 million. The balance of the cane which comes mainly from sloping or hilly land is transported by a fleet of about 2,000 seven- to 10-ton capacity trucks, many of which are very old and only operate because the Land Transport Authority of the country exempts them from complying with axle loading requirements (this exemption may not continue in the future). The cost of running these antiquated trucks also reaches about F$12 million per year and is borne by the grower, not the miller.

At the crushing level, the state of the four surviving mills is another reason for anxiety. The mills are very old (described as 'Dickensian'), over-manned, inefficient and expensive to operate. Penang Mill (F$340 per tonne of sugar produced), Lautoka Mill ($320 per tonne), Labasa on Vanua Levu (F$230 per tonne) and Rarawai (F$160 per tonne) are all well above the cost of production in most mills in India – F$70 per tonne. Over the past two decades, the FSC has invested around F$300M in mill upgrades yet there is little evidence of improved capacity.[14]

Our central issue is, however, performance of farmers in growing sugar cane. In 1970, 15,542 farms operated and by 1993 the number peaked at 23,454. In 1994, production reached 517,000 tonnes of cane. The data for the 21-year period of 1981-2001 assembled by Mahendra Reddy (2003), however, shows that production fluctuates widely, partly due of course to variable weather, but also reflecting a long-term downward trend due to both low productivity and the gradual decrease in the area under sugar cane cultivation.[15] In the 1950s, Fijian productivity appeared moderate and reasonably sound when compared with other competing sugar cane countries.[16] Fifty years later, however, the industry is much less efficient. In the year 2000, cane production fell by 9 percent and by a further 12 percent in 2002. Of 20 sugar producers from the ACP countries, Fiji now has the second-lowest cane yield per harvested hectare and the lowest sugar yield per harvested hectare.[17]

It was expected over the last two decades that increased productivity would occur as numerous high yielding, disease resistant cane varieties specific to particular soil types have been introduced. Yet, in spite of this technical advance, productivity has stagnated or declined.

The 51 percent increase in the number of cane farms from 1970 to 1993 can be attributed largely to the World Bank-funded Seaqaqa sugar project, in which most soils were of lower fertility than those in the old cane zone. Moreover, with the higher prices paid by the FSC after their takeover from CSR, farmers began to use progressively more marginal land for cane plantings.

Sugar is a crop that is vegetatively propagated by planting sections of the stalk (seed cane). The first crop, called plant cane, in general has the highest yield, and if portions of the stalk are left underground (known as ratoon crops) and subsequently harvested, the crop yield is generally lower. Reddy has used FSC research centre annual data to show that over the last 25 years the percentage of total area under new crop has been declining. Whereas the new crop was 24 percent of the total in 1966/70 (the remainder being ratoon), by 1991/95 the percent of new crop had declined to only 15 percent of the total and in 2001 to only 5 percent.[18]

Cane harvesting and burning also contribute additional problems affecting production. During the harvesting season, there is invariably a shortage of cane cutters which increases harvesting costs. In recent years, there has been a decline in unskilled agricultural labourers seeking cane-cutting jobs as more students are continuing their education in pursuit of white and blue collar jobs. As it is a seasonal job, cane cutting is less attractive than permanent work, and is poorly paid, averaging only F$1,500 per season.

Harvesting deadlines set by sugar mills send panic signals to individual growers, leading to a rush to harvest their crop. Ideally, farmers hope to get their whole crop harvested before the end of the season in November to avoid losses and wet weather. The only way to meet the deadline is to jump the queue and the main way this is done is to burn their cane. The high proportion of burnt cane has become an issue of great concern to the industry. Whereas in the 1970s only about 10 percent of total cane crushed was burnt cane, the practice increased gradually and by 1990 the record level of 58 percent of the total was burnt. The FSC strongly opposed the practice, arguing that burnt cane of this level could result in losses of millions of dollars due to reduction in crushing rates, increase in season length extending to the wet season (incurring additional harvesting and transportation costs), and loss of sugar in the burning process.[19] Farmers also lose by extension of the crushing period into the wet season, and loss of sugar content from burning. Farmers say that the reasons for burning are shortages of cane trucks and/or cane harvesting quotas, limited capacity of the mill to crush cane during peak weather periods and harvesting deadlines which alarm growers who fear their crop might be left on the farm to rot. As Reddy (2003) argues, the solution to the problem is better milling capacity and a more professional organisation of the industry which would result in a decline in cane burning.

During my study of Sorolevu in the late 1950s, we identified a relatively progressive Fijian village in which most households grew sugar cane, with average yields of 20.2 tons per acre. In the predominantly Indian-settled cane district of Qeleloa in which it was located, yields were 24.5, a difference in production of 4.3 tons per acre.

Forty years later, evidence from a variety of sources shows that the production gap between Indo-Fijians and Fijians has not changed but is almost identical with that figure. Data based on sample sizes of over 2,500 growers by the FSC research centre from 1985-89, and Reddy's own survey of 397 growers in 1996, show Indian harvests average 22.01 tonnes per acre compared to the average Fijian harvests of 17.90 tonnes – a gap of 4.11 tonnes.[20] Not only have average yields per unit area of all growers of both ethnic groups not increased over the 50-year period, but also the Fijians have not closed the gap of about 4 tonnes per acre below Indians.

Furthermore, Reddy's explanation was the same as mine 50 years ago: "Ethnic Fijian farmers, relative to the Indo-Fijian farmers have demonstrated significantly lower input use, in particular labour, fertiliser, weedicides and machines".[21] Especially since the rapid expansion of the area planted in the 1970s after the FSC took over, a considerable number of Fijians have become sugar growers for the first time and, since then, more and more Fijian landowners on reserve lands have opted not to renew leases to Indian tenants but to plant the crop themselves. Around the year 2000, the sugar industry comprised about 25 percent Fijian farmers compared to 75 percent Indian. As the percentage of Fijians grows, it can be expected therefore that total productivity will continue to fall since Fijian farmers on average produce lower harvests than their Indian counterparts.

Factors to do with Land Tenure

It is abundantly clear that one of the greatest problems afflicting the sugar industry is the lack of security of land tenure arising from the absence of well-defined property rights. About 70-73 percent of sugar cane farmers are cultivating land leased from landowners through the Native Land Trust Board. While many growers farmed only 3-4 ha., there has been a tendency for the NLTB to relet for periods of 30 years and to combine many of the smaller holdings. Over the period of 1997-2002, a total of 3,323 sugar cane leases expired, 883 were renewed to existing tenants, 1,132 were issued to new tenants and 1,308 were not renewed.[22] It seems that by 2009, 95 percent of the total cane leases will have expired and, if current trends continue, it is likely that 27 percent of the land will be taken away from tenants. As sugar prices rose, it is not surprising that Fijians showed greater interest in their land reverting back to them; increasingly, they were less inclined to renew leases to Indian tenants.

The critical factor is to have a tenure system which provides security and stimulates investment by means of using land as collateral so credit can be obtained cheaply to make farm improvements that will increase production. The Agricultural Landlords and Tenants Act (ALTA) of

1976 is reasonably successful in achieving this[23] and enabling tenants to reap the benefit of their investment without fear of losing it, but Fijian owners believe they paid the cost of making their land available for the benefit of others. They see the Native Land Trust Act (NLTA) as an alternative to ALTA. The two acts have substantial differences in security for tenants and landowners. The failure of the two sides to come to some agreement on this contentious issue has had a very negative effect on cane production, on Indian tenants, the rental income of landowners, foreign reserve and national income. The non-renewal of leases occurs to small farmers who have few options. Skilled cane farmers and workers are lost to the industry, often ending up in poverty in urban squatter settlements, to be replaced by people of lesser skill and experience, many of whom appear to be less committed to the industry. Understandably, Indian tenants who, like their parents and grandparents, have spent their lives in sugar growing feel desperate and dispirited and their children hold no hope of carrying on, looking for education and other forms of employment which are in scarce supply as an alternative. Embittered tenants who are evicted sometimes demolish their houses and illegally burn down their crops;[24] and other Fijian Indians leave their embattled existence and start new lives overseas.[25]

The uncertainty, insecurity and risk associated with leasing cane land have led to a great lack of confidence in the industry. This has naturally lessened farm investments which in turn has had a negative affect on farm productivity. When the other inefficiencies by growers are added in together with poorer transport, crushing problems at the mill, inferior organisation and planning,[26] and among the highest freight rates in the world to markets in distant Europe, it is clear that several factors interact in a form of circular causation to produce lower output of raw sugar or poorer quality. The end result is a lower income for the grower, company and country. Reddy in earlier research estimated that, while technical efficiency was quite high, allocative efficiency of Fiji's cane farms was only just over 48 percent.[27]

Factors to do with Profitability

Fiji's sugar farmers make only a very small marginal profit. Based on 1995-2002 data, Reddy has calculated that for a typical 10-acre farm with a total production of 22 tonnes per acre, the total net income of an average farmer is only F$2,891, which is well below the poverty line income of $7,000.[28] Fiji's low productivity falls far short of that of many other sugar producers.

While the Fiji sugar industry is often criticised for its lack of mechanisation, this is not a significant factor. On the one hand, there is an abundance of family household labour, and on the other, labour requirements are not high. For example, in 1958, I calculated that for an average 10-acre (4 ha.) holding with 6.5 acres of cane each year, only approximately 140 man-days of labour would be required, including cutting. As profit margins have progressively shrunk, the challenge to farmers has been to utilise unpaid family members as fully as possible and in the most efficient ways to cut costs. This is, of course, a classic 'peasantising' process. Where cane can be fully or partly cut by family labour including women and children,[29] the cost of employing external (commonly Fijian) labourers is reduced. This, of course, reduces the expected income received by migrating Fijian cane cutters.

The FSC is in deep trouble. It overpaid growers in the 1970s to its own detriment, and in recent years its financial position has deteriorated. In 2003, it was only able to mill sugar due to a government write-off of a major loan, with a guarantee of further loans.[30] In 2005, it was reported that the FSC was technically insolvent.

Fiji Now: An Economy in Dire Straits

After years of delay and steady decline, and with the agricultural sector's contribution to GDP falling from 22 percent in 1990 to only 16 percent in 2000, it is clear that urgent and widespread changes are needed. It is abundantly clear, as Leslie and Ratukalou and Reddy's analyses have shown, that comprehensive changes need to be made in land and soil conservation practices to develop sustainable production, and that new and better technologies and efficiencies need to be introduced at all levels of sugar production.

Several plans involving a strong emphasis on privatisation failed to gain widespread acceptance, and a government-appointed Sugar Steering Committee was unable to find a consensus among stakeholders on the way forward. At this point, the government requested the government of India carry out an independent study. The report of a team of Indian experts on the industry is thorough and wide-ranging, outlining a detailed plan for investment and reform. Investment totalling F$86m would be required for the reform plan to be implemented over a two- to three-year period. The Indian government has generously provided a loan of this amount at an interest rate of only 1.7 percent for a term of 15 years, including a three-year grace period.[31] The Fijian cabinet has accepted the funding in principle. After dialogue with the Fiji Labour Party, an agreement was reached to accept the report. A constructive and significant step forward was thus achieved involving the main opposition party working with government in forming a Parliamentary

Select Committee to oversee the reform of the industry.

Recently, two other options have appeared that may be valuable innovations for the sugar industry: extensive bagasse[32] generation for electricity (which is in very short supply) and fuel ethanol development. While Fiji should plan carefully before reducing the volume of sugar cane available for market sale, currently feasibility studies are underway on these options as the energy crisis increases. The success of using sugar cane for ethanol production has been shown recently in Brazil, which leads the world in biodiesel production.

Since 2000, national security has been threatened several times by political uncertainty and coups, the first led by George Speight, and the last being the overthrow of Laisenia Qarase's government by Army Commander Voreqe Bainimarama. Bainimarama took charge of the country to prevent the government passing its National Reconciliation and Unity Bill, which was designed to pardon or to drop charges against many of the leaders of Speight's coup. Clearly, not only the underlying ongoing racial problem, but also the economic crisis and desperate state of the sugar industry require a government of national unity at this time. If sugar fails, Fiji will have to rely very largely on its tourism industry (with about 62 percent of expenditure immediately leaking out of the economy), and the earnings and remittances of hundreds of Fijian ex-soldiers who work as mercenaries in the Iraq War.[33]

By mid-2006, more than 2,000 Fijians had served with the British Army in Iraq and another 1,000, mostly ex-Fiji Army soldiers, worked as mercenaries for security firms. While this is dangerous and unenviable work and some Fijians have returned home in body bags, the demand for Fijians is a positive indication of their reputation as soldiers. It is argued that in the last few years mercenary work overseas has transformed Fiji into a remittance economy, rather similar to Tonga and Samoa. Money sent home exceeds NZ$272m a year according to the Reserve Bank of Fiji, which is 7 percent of the GDP. It now surpasses sugar earnings and is second only to tourism.[34]

When I worked in Fiji, I believed, along with almost all other observers, that to break down the 'three-tier' society and achieve greater racial harmony, and also to contribute more fully to economic development, Fijians needed to expand into commercial production and especially cash cropping. By the end of the 1960s, however, I realised that I had been wrong. I began to appreciate that when tribal societies exist in a plural society situation, the transition process throws up various opportunities and options that are harder to predict. At that time, the major studies by Scarlett Epstein (1968) and Salisbury (1970) of the Tolai of East New Britain took account of their outstanding entrepreneurial abilities and cast them in the role of 'primitive capitalists', as compared to other nearby tribes. It seemed likely if laissez-faire conditions continued to operate that Tolai would secure nearly all the key jobs in the newly emergent independent country of Papua New Guinea. No government could afford to let this happen. In the case of Fiji, the country's political economy evolved in such a way that a similar outcome could be expected: Indians had a clear advantage in most commercial jobs, in small retail businesses and in smallholder agriculture, just as they did in cane growing. Over time, however, Fijians realised their services were valued and in great demand in other jobs – in tourism, hotel services, *meke* (dance) bands, the police, army and gold-mining. They were natural soldiers and hence performed well as mercenaries in various hot spots around the world. And on a per capita basis they are amongst the best rugby union players in the world (rivalling New Zealand as the best Rugby Sevens team in the world). It is only appropriate that Fijians also seek their fortune in these other novel, non-traditional roles.

A Reflection: Sugar and the Politics of Race

When he was Prime Minister, Laisenia Qarase, with some truth, accused Indian leaders involved with the sugar cane industry of the birth of party politics in Fiji. (He goaded his opponent, Mahendra Chaudhry, with his role as a leader of the growers' trade union.) Nevertheless, the history of sugar cane production in Central and South America and other Third World countries shows clearly that this was inevitable, for expatriate and class interests associated with either plantations or sugar-milling companies on the one hand, and smallholding native 'peasant' (or, more correctly, 'rural proletarian') growers and cane cutters on the other, inevitably seem to collide. It has been said with much truth that "cane is the favourite child of capitalism". Of all crops, perhaps only cotton has a worse history of ruthless exploitation of labour. Since cane must be crushed within 48 hours of cutting or the sucrose content will fall, and mature cane can only last in the fields uncut for a limited period, bargaining over the proportion of gross income retained by the miller and that paid to the grower is always intense and keenly fought. Over time, as large sugar companies with huge crushing mills have evolved, they usually possess considerable financial weight and can often rely on strong political support. Cane growers and cutters, on the other hand, can only rely on collective support, their trade union, and sometimes political backing from labour or left wing political parties.

The 1960 Fijian cane dispute reflected many years of smouldering discontent that erupted into a serious argument over the terms of a new contract on the sale and purchase of cane. I reviewed this in Watters (1963). The cane strike caused much damage to the industry: a 26 percent reduction in the amount of cane normally crushed and huge financial losses to the growers, millers and the country. The loss of trust and confidence of stakeholders working together was even worse. The dispute also marked the emergence of an incipient Indian nationalism led by the lawyer-politician A.D. Patel, who believed the expulsion of the CSR Company would be the essential first step in the advancement of his people's interests. After visiting cane farms in the Nadi-Lautoka area in 1961, it seemed clear to me that a large majority of Indian tenants favoured nationalisation of the industry.

The 1961 Commission of Enquiry steered a middle course, apportioning blame equally among the protagonists, the Company and the growers and also reproving the British and Fijian governments.

During the hearing, the CSR published the dividends of its Fijian operations. These proved to be extremely low, varying from 5.8 percent in 1955-56 to 2 percent in 1958-59, while in 1959-60 the Company declared it earned only 0.6 on its capital of £13 million invested in Fiji. In 1960-61, the Company expected a heavy loss.[35] In 1957, company assets in Fiji were valued at F£12,788,842.

The Commission recommended that the Sydney-based company be handed over to a locally-owned subsidiary with shares issued for local sale. It recommended maintenance of the smallholding system on a tenant rather than a freehold basis to avoid land falling into the hands of moneylenders or ultimately being concentrated into large estates. The minimum size should be 10 acres and the suggestion that sugar lands should be planned, graded and licensed was excellent in a colony already suffering from overproduction of cane and in urgent need of land use planning for major soil types. Financially, the Commission believed that the net proceeds of £5,750,000 was a very large sum to originate from only 125,000 acres of land; this should be sufficient to ensure a fair price to growers, mill workers, millers and shareholders.[36]

While there were faults on both sides, with the benefit of hindsight it is clear that the CSR became a scapegoat for most of the cane growers' ills, blinding them to the excellent services and generally liberal treatment that the company provided. While cane was confined to the fertile *bila* soils of the lowlands, the portable rail system worked well and the Company provided extension advice on cane growing and supplied mill sand and organic debris for ploughing in to improve the soil structure as well as artificial fertilisers. Fijians could attend the Drasa Training School to be trained in the techniques of cane growing. The Company also undertook research which produced new higher yielding varieties more suited to some of Fiji's soil types, while its Agronomy Division undertook soil surveys and fertiliser trials to increase the knowledge of basic factors of cane soils. Nevertheless, it is clear that the returns on the CSR's investment were very low in the late 1950s and falling, and in view of the political problems, especially from 1960, it is clear that the CSR began to lose interest in its Fiji operation. Most important was the fact that it was predominantly an Australian company, very conscious that its operating costs were much higher in Fiji than in Queensland and the output per man on the farm and in the mill in Queensland was much greater than in Fiji. Thus, its withdrawal from Fiji became inevitable. Nationalisation was no real solution, as the FSC lacked the expertise and experience of the CSR. As a small, weak country, Fiji was always going to struggle in a harsh economic world in which there was considerable over-production of sugar, and from which Third World cane-growing countries were unfairly shut out by fortress Europe which subsidised its own sugar beet producers.

From the perspective of the whole South Pacific region, however, it is apparent that the particular mode of production practised over many decades was very successful in providing incomes considerably higher than most smallholders in the region acquired. And while it was a smallholder system of small tenants and contractors who were free of the harsh labour regime that applied to workers on a plantation, they also had ready access at low cost to co-ordinated services by the miller to cover marketing, technical services, training, credit and the supplies of inputs. As such this type of nucleus estate model was an interesting compromise between the separate models of smallholder outliers and central plantation production that worked – a marriage of aspects of the two. Since it has stood the test of time and proven its survival value, Fiji should not lightly throw this hybrid model aside.

9

What is Economic Development? A Study of the Gilbert and Ellice Islands[1]

'What is Economic Development' is based on the Team Report, Islands on the Line, published in 1982. It presents what was, at the time, part of a radical revisiting of the notion of development, removing it from its Eurocentric perspectives and setting it instead within particular contexts of indigenous social organisation and subsistence economies.

The essay arose out of the Victoria University of Wellington Rural Socio-economic Survey of the Gilbert and Ellice Islands of which I was director, and is founded on fieldwork conducted on Tamana, North Tabiteuea, Butaritari, Abemama and Nanumea.

After running the Solomons Socio-economic Project for three years, in 1971 I received an invitation from the Ministry of Overseas Development to plan and initiate a rural socio-economic study for the Gilbert and Ellice Islands Colony (GEIC) which it was planned would also become independent within a few years. The Ellice Islands separated from the Gilberts to become a separate country, Tuvalu, in 1978, and in 1979, the same year as the phosphate on Ocean (Banaba) Island finally ran out, the Gilbert Islands became the new independent country of Kiribati.

The Solomons project was judged to have worked well, as a reflective and consultative unit and as a multi-disciplinary team. The same approach of employing PhD students was thus adopted with various refinements. As a result of discussions with the GEIC government, four islands within the 16-island Gilbert group were chosen for intensive study and one from the Ellice group. The team members were Betsy Sewell, an anthropologist recruited from Otago University who worked on Butaritari, an island with abundant rainfall in the northern Gilberts; Bill Geddes, an anthropologist from Victoria University, Wellington, who studied North Tabiteuea, a large, relatively poor traditional atoll of the southern Gilberts; and Roger Lawrence, a lecturer in Geography from our Department who studied the small, *remote, drought-prone reef island of Tamana in the extreme south which had high population density. Anne Chambers, an anthropologist from California, studied the atoll of Nanumea, one of the nine islands in the Ellice Islands group. I worked on Abemama, a rather richer and unusually socially stratified atoll of only medium population density in the central Gilberts. As I had not studied coral atoll societies in any depth, I invited Dr Nancy Pollock, an anthropology lecturer at Victoria University who had done her PhD on an atoll in the Marshall Islands, to join the project as co-director.*

All members spent a year in Wellington reading and preparing for their fieldwork. This was followed by either a full year of fieldwork (continuous in my case from December 1971 to December 1972) or two-to-three fieldwork periods by other team members totalling 12 to 18 months. A final year of discussion, comparative analysis and evaluation was held by the team back at Victoria University.

The year-long experience of living as a family at the little government station of Kariatebike on Abemama was of course unusual, memorable and perhaps unique (although in the 1890s, Robert Louis Stevenson and his wife spent two or three months on the island). It was a rich experience indeed and a great privilege to get to know many Gilbertese people and learn about their way of life. But it was much easier for me as I worked each day in the seven villages, measured lands and babai pits, counted coconut palms and their nuts, and talked about custom with unimane; it was much harder for Bethlyn who supervised Jane (14) and Carla (12) doing their correspondence school lessons each day, and fetched Andrew (5) to and from the Kauma Seventh Day Adventist primary school six miles away on the back of her motorbike. Late in the afternoon she would go with the children to swim in the reef channel and on Sundays we would go with the girls on their bikes and Bethlyn and I and Andrew on our motor bikes to have a picnic in the 'bush' on the ocean side of the island, or perhaps visit the Australian nuns and Sister Agnes at the Catholic mission at Manoku. The girls joined the local Girl Guides and made many friends and Andrew made tree houses with Gilbertese friends. The children had bantams and cats as pets but it was a long, lonely year for Bethlyn away from home.

The Meaning of Development

'Development' means different things to different people. The European view of economic development is quite different from that held by many non-Europeans and it is important that the actual goals sought, whether by local people or by European planners, be identified and that everyone's understanding of the development process be clarified. Unless a major dialogue ensues to produce agreement and reconciliation, serious contradictions evident before development are likely to persist.

In the context of the Gilbert and Ellice Islands, the contradictions arise from several factors:

1 different goals and different types of development are often envisaged by Gilbertese and Ellice villagers on the one hand, and by European government officers or advisers on the other;
2 different aspects of the same reality are emphasised by different groups, while other aspects are either under-emphasised or ignored;
3 the kinds of social and economic benefits and costs that accrue from the type of development not only vary considerably, but are perceived quite differently;
4 it logically follows that the order and set of priorities aimed at and the consequent development strategy adopted also diverge to a marked extent.

The European or 'Outside' View

Essentially, the notions and goals of Europeans spring from assumptions and principles originating from outside, the result of a European approach to economics that evolved in a monetised, urban industrial setting. This viewpoint stresses increasing monetary income by growth in goods and services and especially of exports which earn overseas exchange. Only by achieving economic growth can economic development occur, with the resulting improvement in health, education and other social services. 'Growth in goods and services' or 'increasing the stock of wealth' are seen, however, largely in monetary terms, implying an expansion of the monetary and commercial sector.

Fisk (1974) has explained European planning in the South Pacific in the colonial era in these terms:

> Historically the planning of economic development has tended to be in the hands of the people who are specialists in finance, or in modern technology, or in modern business or production methods, or in modern

methods of Western agriculture. Most of these people have been sincere, able, professionally competent, and dedicated to enhancing the welfare of the countries they have chosen to serve. They have however, been people with knowledge about an exotic type of rural economy and situation which they have sought to reproduce in the Pacific in the course of development, rather than people who have made a special study and gained special understanding of the indigenous social, economic and agricultural processes which they proposed to change. There was a perfectly natural tendency for them to see the latter as an inferior set of factors to be abolished and changed in favour of the exotic system as quickly as possible.[2]

Before World War II, as Fisk points out:

... the less developed countries were expected to be financially responsible for their own development, and to finance it from their own productivity or the prospects of it. To do this, especially in a country whose economic activity was largely non-monetary and whose international earnings were minimal, required the inflow of foreign capital and skills and the monetisation of a major sector of the economy. Only thus could the resources be made available to establish a flow of income in foreign currencies to pay for teachers, administrators, and technical specialists, and to establish markets .... The quickest, and often the only immediate way in which to get development started was thus to introduce the foreign system which the developers, and those that could be induced to bring in the necessary capital and know-how, understood and knew to be productively effective.[3]

In many instances, this strategy worked, but it had serious disadvantages that have since become apparent to many observers:

It was effective in getting development started by providing the internal resources on which the basic steps depended, but it also led to dualism, elitism and other forms of inequality that tended to be cumulative, or at least self-sustaining, and which were incompatible with the rapid development of a workable form of democratically based self-government and political independence ...[4]

This essay goes on to give a more detailed account and explanation of the consequences of this 'Western mode of development'.

In its own terms, the Western mode of development could seem a "perfectly natural and understandable process in the context of pre-World War II political economy", but, as Fisk argues, "it is clearly far from an ideal course of development from the point of view of the indigenous peoples concerned".[5] Of course, if one considers an economy purely in *monetary* terms, one cannot fault the impeccable logic of the European view that genuine economic development can only derive from economic growth, for how else can improvements be paid for? Seen in this light, the task in the Gilbert and Ellice Islands is to lift copra (the main export apart from phosphate) and other forms of production, and since lack of motivation appears to be a major obstacle preventing this, the "crux of the problem ... was to change the character and custom of the people", as a District Commissioner stated at the Colonial Conference of 1956.[6] The record of many dedicated, determined Englishmen who struggled throughout the colonial era in lonely outposts to achieve this result makes interesting reading in the Western Pacific Archives, for it is the story of Englishmen battling often against great odds and almost impossible physical constraints to implant the Protestant Ethic and to graft the Western way of life on to local society. Many changes were introduced by such men but, prisoners of their own time and culture, they were blithely unconscious of their Eurocentric approach and the cultural imperialism of their message. Instead of starting with the indigenous social organisation and agricultural system as the foundation upon which the building was to be constructed, it was often considered in many South Pacific countries to be "rubble to be cleared away before the construction can start".[7]

It has become increasingly obvious to many students of developing countries over the last decade that the European approach is not only inadequate but also positively harmful. It either ignores, bypasses or undercuts (usually indirectly rather than deliberately) the traditional socio-political system and the subsistence agricultural system, without usually achieving great gains in per capita output. H.C. Brookfield, E.K. Fisk, K. Hart, W.C. Clarke and a number of others have criticised the alarming deficiencies and dubious goals of such policies in several countries and called for a basic change of both goals and tactical objectives in development. One should be trying not to introduce some new and foreign productive system but rather to improve and adapt the agricultural system and resources that are already there. A policy of making this the basis of development will inevitably lead to a slower growth in the national income and in internal government revenues, "but it will almost certainly be a faster process in the development of a viable and self-dependent indigenous controlled economy which in the absence of extreme poverty, is the more important objective".[8]

Clearly, different goals requiring different approaches are needed with respect to government policy, and also a greater awareness of the indigenous or 'inside view' of development. However, insofar as these islands are intrinsically part of an interdependent system and are committed to a monetary economy, there are aspects of this 'outside view' that are completely sound and must be learnt and understood by the villagers.

The 'Inside' View: The Attitudes of Villagers

The greatest difference in the meaning of development and the nature of the actual process is probably illustrated in the *Tamana Report*, although all the islands in the Kiribati group illustrate marked divergences from the European understanding.

Tamana

To some extent, there is a tendency – especially on Tamana and North Tabiteuea – to treat the subsistence and cash sectors as separate entities. People who are well-endowed with resources in the traditional sector often do not participate very much in the cash sector and vice versa. Thus, one could be rich in money (*kaumane*) or rich in things (*kaubai*), although riches in land could lead through the copra trade to money and possession of many imported items.

Since the potential for economic growth on Tamana is obviously very limited, even by Gilbertese standards, things are seen as being essentially controlled from the outside. *Tibanga* (luck or fate) is a concept of critical importance, indicating something over which people have no control, but which defines their lot in life. It may well reflect the lack of any substantial economic enterprise on the island and the legacy of paternalism from mission and government, a situation in which all major decisions are made from above and outside. Since improvements in living standards depend essentially on outside factors (success in gaining entry into one of the colony's two high schools, or success in being given a job by the phosphate company on either Ocean Island or Nauru), the concept of *tibanga* accurately sums up the real life chances of an inhabitant of Tamana. Intense jealousy is felt against people who are believed to have amassed an excessive number of *babai* pits, pigs or other forms of wealth. The emphasis on equality or conformity (*boraoi*) is perhaps the paramount feature of economic life throughout all the island studies, and it is believed that no one should attempt to rise above their normal station or living standard for to attempt to do so might prejudice another's ability to obtain a livelihood.

Islanders' understanding of economic development has naturally changed as the potential for cash earning has grown with the copra trade, and as money has acquired greater utility over recent decades with the establishment of cooperative societies, larger and more efficiently run stores, and an improved shipping service enabling stocks to be more regularly supplied. The differences between people in money-earning experience are reflected in the way in which money is treated as belonging to distinct 'funds' depending on the method of earning, size of sums and goals sought. Thus, on Tamana, *kabirongorongo* (money that you spend) denotes small sums of money that can be earnt at any time from the sale of copra or handicrafts and which is spent on everyday needs. *Karinimane*, on the other hand, is money that you keep, not productive capital but a form of nest egg. It involves larger sums of money which are banked or held for the future to pay taxes, school fees or other major expenses. Significantly, *karinimane* is associated with work off the island and is not to be had on Tamana.

It is interesting to note that the distinction between the two types of money is not recognised by many households which operate entirely within a *kabirongorongo* context and have no prospects of *karinimane*. While households receiving remittances may well regard them as *karinimane*, this is not necessarily so, and they may be used for everyday expenses including purchases of food. Thus, when the development plan calls for an increase in savings in the community, it should be realised that the form of those savings and how they are used depend very much on local perceptions and categorisation of money and different sources of income for different purposes.

On all islands studied, there appear to be two basic conceptions of development: innovations that come from government, and a greater opportunity to pursue particular local activities. Since an expectation of economic growth is not inherent in traditional society, the question of innovation does not arise. The idea of development is thus wholly associated with 'Tarawa' (synonymous with government) – what government does and institutes from outside. Most directly, it is seen in visible results in the form of airfields, roads, shipping services, medical dispensaries and services, Island Council schools, coconut replanting and improvement subsidies and the like. Since such infrastructure clearly leads to economic or social development, this view of development is sound enough. But it also sees development as a response to lobbying or manipulation of government where this is feasible. The greatest goal in politics to be sought by the Island Council and members of the Legislative Council is to induce government to start projects involving government expenditure on the island, and to find out 'what can be got out of Tarawa'.

But the other goal, of enabling people to pursue particular local ends, becomes easier to achieve if new opportunities arise to make money. In a very real sense, this is associated with the idea of security and of freedom (in the northern class-stratified islands *inaomata*, and on Tamana *oinibai*, being self-sufficient or free to control one's own activities). In spite of a well-established system of redistribution and reciprocity, people prefer to be *oinibai* or *inoamata*, for with adequate resources they do not have to worry about the future. Then they would also be above the need to *bubuti* (borrow or request) which is an admission of dependence and is somewhat shameful.

This traditional concept does indeed relate most directly to a fundamental aspect of true economic development, seeking freedom from need and achieving self-sustaining independence. While the 'good life' means different things in the subsistence and cash sectors, there is an important common thread – to be *oinibai* or *inaomata*. A goal on Tamana is to have plenty of fish and a house that is 'alive' – the possession of coconut lands and the ability to work hard. This ensures prestige and in this sense work does not imply drudgery. But in recent times, Tarawa has entered the pattern of expectations. To have children going to Tarawa for their education (with the prospect of salaried employment to follow) is to achieve freedom. The whole situation is now altered: seen in this context, subsistence work becomes 'drudgery', and 'cash' and 'freedom' become almost identical. It would appear that these ideas are fundamental in affecting economic change on the outer islands, creating a situation of 'pre-urbanisation' and influencing migration to South Tarawa.

North Tabiteuea

On North Tabiteuea, cash has been fitted into the economy as another resource: basically the economy here is still subsistence-based with very little cash appended. Cash is not necessary except for some capital items (bicycles, nets etc.) and most households have limited targets for income. The island is well known for its individualism and competitiveness, with jealousy and the ideal of equality enforcing conformity through various levelling mechanisms. The desire for individual enterprise is there but must take the form of group effort through *mronrons* (indigenous cooperative enterprise) to escape social sanctions. Innovation from within is very difficult because of these social pressures and competitiveness, for someone will always point out why a new development cannot work. All innovation therefore comes from government and from the outside, and in this way the external nature of the new impetus is most important in breaking the impasse. Things that people cannot do for themselves become very definitely a government responsibility. In spite of a strong interest in economic enterprise, therefore, people seek money mainly through employment off the island, remittances are often expected through the system of *bubuti* and in view of local constraints they seek development on the island to only a limited extent. One of the main goals is more free time, and people look for opportunities to cut down the time spent working in *babai* pits.

In view of the few money-earning opportunities that exist on most islands, it is scarcely surprising that the local people's preference for leisure is quite pronounced. However, this also illustrates the high value placed on *kakakibotu* (resting) and other forms of leisure, emphasised in the North Tabiteuea Report.

Butaritari

On Butaritari, the concepts of being rich in subsistence or rich in money are completely intertwined. For although the traditional concept is still uppermost – that real wealth comes from the possession of lands – it is quickly acknowledged that the number of bearing palms on a piece of land is of critical importance. And prestige and respectability are very closely associated with the capacity to 'live well'. To 'live well' means 'to eat well', as the Butaritari Report illustrates, and the complementary relationship between the cash and subsistence sectors is indicated in the equally high status accorded to *babai* and store foods. It is inconceivable that a feast would be held now without supplies of both types of food and it is an interesting commentary on social change that the importance of one is often explained in terms of the other.

The idea of development is not only closely associated with the concept of 'living well', stressing consumption, but also with 'keeping up'. Here again, people conform to an ideal minimum acceptable standard of receiving (or earning) 'enough' money. Apart from 'living well' and enabling one to 'keep up', money has limited use on Butaritari, for goods other than food have no prestige but are valued purely for their utility. Three categories of goods are recognised: necessary items (soap, kerosene, matches and tobacco); food; and 'big things' (utensils, cloth, and large capital items such as bicycles, etc.). Apart from these three kinds of purchases, money is needed for one other kind of general purpose – the payment of taxes, school fees and donations.

Conformity may be either a positive advantage or disadvantage in development, for an innovation such as banana growing has been widely accepted by most households in three villages on Butaritari but is still uncommon elsewhere. The importance of 'target income' or the 'drudgery of labour' where excessive amounts of time and energy must be spent to earn extra income should be noted, for people will only seek more than 'enough' in money income where it can be earned easily and with comparatively little effort.

Abemama

The ideal of economic development on Abemama closely parallels the findings on Butaritari, but here higher incomes, access to more land and a wide range in levels of sophistication in understanding European approaches affect attitudes. Although it is widely believed that Gilbertese live unto the day and do not understand the need for planning for the future, the reports point out that most families are aware, with the growth of their children, of likely future requirements. The planting of *babai*, which takes seven years to mature, is one indicator of planning for the future, and parents are conscious of the value of education gained now to qualify children to secure paid employment in the years ahead. But most notions are vague and thrust responsibility wholly on the government, which should (as informants told us) "find us an island", "get more lands for the people" and permit migration. The frequency with which many Abemamans visit Tarawa makes them keenly aware of the large volume of aid moneys that have been spent in recent years. It is felt that almost all this money has been spent on Tarawa and little in the outer islands. There are signs that a feeling of relative deprivation might be beginning and this relatively sophisticated outer island is highly active in lobbying government for a decentralisation of government activities and for more official projects on the island.

There are some on Abemama who are beginning to see cash as a definite substitute for subsistence production and are replacing traditional items of diet with purchased foods. There appears to be a disturbing trend among some people receiving regular remittances to be less concerned with maintaining coconut plantings or *babai* pits. There are indications, therefore, of a state of tension as development takes hold and the people's own priorities change and shift in response to new goals, new sources of wealth and perceived inequalities that become institutionalised.

Development and Development Planning

The Costs and Benefits of Development

In an attempt to summarise as objectively as possible the benefits and costs that Europeans have brought to Abemama (and indeed to the Gilbert Islands generally), the following balance sheet was drawn up:

Positive advantages introduced by Europeans	Disadvantages resulting from Europeans
1. Air service, shipping	1. Decay of *babai*, traditional skills, failure to conserve resources
2. Hospitals and medical service	2. Decline of the authority of the old men
3. Iron and steel, e.g. bush knives	3. Nutritional deficiencies and danger of dietary deterioration

4.	Utensils, implements, cloth, cooking utensils	4.	Colonial mentality and 'missionisation' – an apathetic, dependent society
5.	Some education	5.	Inappropriate education
6.	Roads, bicycles, motor cycles, trucks	6.	A partially inappropriate political structure
7.	Peace and order	7.	Economic dualism and wage dualism represented in gross over-development, over-centralisation, over-urbanisation of Tarawa and of modern services, coupled with the neglect of the outer islands, the subsistence economy, the traditional social and political structure and small-scale appropriate technology
8.	Impartial system of justice		

Inevitably, this reflects my own bias, although all the advantages and the first three disadvantages were identified by local informants; the other disadvantages (e.g. 4, 5, 6 and 7) were characterised in their responses. But 'development' becomes meaningful only when considered by the people themselves, in *their* own terms.

Development: Internal and External Views

During fieldwork, a shrewd observation was made that it is important for Europeans to have a development plan. This often is more important than the actual physical and cultural context to which the plan is supposed to apply. In general, the *imatang* (Europeans) did not appreciate the geographic difference between the Gilbert and Ellice Islands and other countries. It was believed rather cynically (and with some accuracy) that development plans often tend to be somewhat alike, irrespective of the country. The Development Plan had become something of a new gospel, the mark of legitimacy for some of the European officers in government, justifying their presence. But this cynicism did not lead the old men to reject totally the idea of planning. It was important for families to plan for the future, and especially to plant more coconut palms and limit the size of their families. People were very conscious in 1972 of the Family Planning Campaign which had been largely successful up to that date.

When they were asked to write an essay in 1972 on life in ten years' time, the senior pupils at the Island Council School projected a future of hardship, insecurity, land shortage and over-population, exorbitant store prices and lack of wage employment. At that time when phosphates would be exhausted, "people will not live well". Since few would be able to obtain jobs, how would they be able to "support the family"? "Coconut, *babai* and fish are not enough for the people." Pessimism was expressed as to the likely future copra price, yet "copra is our only means of existence". Sombrely, it was declared that in the years ahead, "it is not ... known whether the Europeans will continue to care for the Gilbertese and Ellice people".

In the late 1960s and 1970s, there were signs of some modification in European views on development and on the future of both island groups: with political and constitutional development, the impending end of phosphates and the failure of efforts to discover new sources of income, new objectives in development began to appear while past failures in policy were frankly admitted.

In part, this might result from the role of some European planners in the Gilbert and Ellice Islands[9] who were more indigenously-orientated than most of their forebears; in part from the changing climate of opinion in developing countries generally that was becoming more skeptical of the usual kind of indicative development plan.[10] Increasingly, these are seen to be technocratic documents produced largely by European officials working in a political vacuum. In the absence of political will and finesse, the government lacks real power to control the economy effectively and the forces governing it. In such a situation, a lot of faith is often placed in a development plan to achieve major goals; without political power, commitment and machinery, these hopes will be illusory. Yet development has become something of a cult in itself and development planning a very modish or fashionable method of ostensibly achieving targets. As Hughes (1973) and others have noted, development planning is usually characterised by many illusions and delusions: the people, politicians and even the planners themselves are often deluded or carried away by the propaganda or euphoria of the planning process. The cult aspect of development and many of the illusions and delusions of planners are nourished by the booming aid industry. Plans, of course, are often window-dressing to justify a government's policies and are produced for political purposes to gain more foreign aid, or represent little more than a set of estimates or shopping lists designed to take to overseas donors.

The other extreme (from the technocratic plan passed off with the aid of much quantification by sophisticated expatriates on unsuspecting locals) is the plan which spuriously attempts to involve 'the people' in the planning process. This approach, which involves what Hughes calls the "grassroots mirage",[11] may become populist or demagogic unless a sound and representative system of local government exists to enable genuine in-depth discussions to occur between central government and outer islands. Illusions that may be produced by quantification both dazzle and bemuse local readers and appear to lend truth or authenticity to the analysis of the economy or the argument that is presented, even though no national income accounts might exist or their accuracy is highly suspect.

Yet shorn of its all-too-common illusions and delusions, development planning remains a most important exercise. If it can be attained by planners and politicians, a sober hard-headed and clear-eyed view of any local situation can lead to serious analysis of economy, society and culture, and closer understanding of the benefits and costs of different objectives and of the conflicts between goals that will have to be faced in the future. Planning, being simply a "technique of arranging activities towards objectives",[12] cannot be objected to since it is not an end in itself but a means of demystifying the process, even though choosing between conflicting, alternative goals may be an unpalatable task. At its best, development planning involves "a collection of ideas, techniques of measurement and analysis, habits of logical and rigorous argument, and systems of operational research and control, which together should be of the greatest value to the public and private sectors in Pacific countries".[13]

Undoubtedly, with political and constitutional development leading to self-government and independence, development planning might lead to some coming together of the divergent viewpoints of Europeans and islanders. But clearly some serious differences do remain and the prospect of a neo-colonial situation emerging means that Eurocentric views of and solutions to local problems are likely to continue to be held by some Gilbertese and Tuvaluan leaders.[14]

In 1970, the first sentence of the Development Plan 1970-72 bluntly warned that a major if unwanted transformation of the economy of the Gilbert and Ellice Islands would occur later in the decade when the phosphates were exhausted. Concern was expressed at the rapid rate of population growth likely to occur during the decade and the fact that heavy investment had occurred in the 1960s in social fields and other areas that were not income-producing.[15] Unease was expressed at the uneven pattern of development that had led to rapid expansion of social and infrastructural services on Tarawa which encouraged in-migration from outer islands, while agricultural development in the outer islands had languished.

The Development Plan of 1973-76 went even further in revising earlier goals of development and in emphasising local self-reliance:

The long-term aim is sufficient economic strength to support political self-reliance. Though regional alliances and continued access to international aid have an important part in the long-term plan, the development objective is to attain a degree of economic independence which will enable the government to make its decisions according to the needs of its own people, without undue foreign influence.[16]

How was this to be achieved?

Even a moderate level of self-sufficiency, after phosphates are exhausted, can only come from the fullest exploitation of the resources of the sea, the greatest possible development of agricultural production; extending the early gains of family planning into a lasting reduction in family size; and more determined efforts to control consumption, personal and national, so as to increase savings and investment.[17]

The standard of living expected by the people has to be held at (or brought up to) the minimum level for a reasonably healthy family life. At the same time, there was growing concern at the effects of economic disparities, in class or regional terms, that had become glaringly obvious:

> The distribution of incomes ... as well as their gross increase must be managed in accordance with national objectives. The continued enrichment of an urban elite, at the expense of the rural areas, is an obvious danger; but it will occur unless it is deliberately avoided.[18]

A number of policies were suggested to counter these undesirable trends.

By the time of the Third Development Plan in 1977, the government had to report that "progress towards strategic economic goals has been negligible", despite advance on particular projects. Island development plans were now included in the overall plan. In spite of solid progress on new coconut planting programmes and protection of rural incomes after phosphates expire, "no major new resource other than the sea has been identified nor is one likely to be". The situation was assessed in sombre terms:

> Overshadowing all Plan activity and achievement is the continued failure of the production sector to establish new sources of national income necessary to maintain living standards in the post-phosphate era. Despite a good deal of talk, planning, expense and hard (though too often uncoordinated) effort the fundamental problems facing the economy are no nearer solution today than they were in 1973. Nor are the inherent constraints on development in a small, scattered and isolated atoll territory any less severe.[19]

In the short term, the Gilbert Islands had 'never had it so good', with a doubling of per capita income since 1973 due to a dramatic boom in the price of phosphate and continued foreign aid. Reserves increased greatly but there was little conscious restraint in government or personal consumption and the range of imported goods increased. In spite of the earlier warnings, the concentration of investment and employment on South Tarawa continued and the urban-rural gap widened further: "No practicable solution to the increasing drift of population to South Tarawa has yet been found".[20]

Development in Context

Views from the Ellice Islands: Nanumea

Up to a point, the considerable similarity of the meaning of development in a different culture, that of the Ellice Islands as revealed in the *Nanumea Report*, reflects not only a similar missionised colonial legacy but also the importance of a situation influencing the perception of development by outer-islanders in a far-flung island archipelago. The Nanumean view of development is based on many of the distinctions and views described above for the Gilbertese. There is the same association between 'living well' and development, both in terms of individual consumption and in terms of community access to such services as education, health and communication. There is a valuing of both traditional and cash sources of wealth, a view that neither alone is yet sufficient to provide the 'good life' for a family, together with a wariness about becoming too dependent on imported items for subsistence.

The Nanumean term for development is *fakatuumea* (literally, to build things), and the development changes that Nanumeans advocate are primarily in this vein: the construction of metal roofs to catch water (and to eliminate thatch making), an airstrip which would make it possible for seamen and other overseas workers to return home for vacations and would generally increase outside contact and opportunities, and a wider reef passage which would allow the island's sheltered lagoon to serve as a base for a commercial fishing industry. Small-scale projects, those requiring only a couple of thousand dollars and local labour and skills to achieve, are seen as appropriate development projects for the community itself to undertake. Large-scale projects, such as the air services and an improved reef passage, are regarded as dependent on government assistance.

Most Nanumeans view employment, particularly overseas employment, as the normal source of cash and of manufactured goods. The fact that most men between 20 and 45 work overseas at some time, that they are employed on short-term contracts and return home periodically, and that they regularly remit money to family members on Nanumea have all made overseas employment an important part of the life cycle as well as a vital part of the economy. Nanumeans would like to have greater opportunities for wage employment locally. In the meantime, they also want easier access to the island so that those overseas can maintain close contact with their home.

One outstanding component of the Nanumean view of development is its corporate character. Community unity and competent local government enable local development planning to have the welfare of the whole community as an ostensible goal. When benefits to certain individuals are incompatible with benefits to the whole community, policy decisions usually favour the latter though efforts are always made to protect any individuals who seem likely to suffer disproportionate negative effects. There is little class, religious or family factionalism to contend with. As in the Gilberts, there is a strong norm of conformity and equality, but the difference is that this is seen as being achieved through *interdependence*: the sharing of goods and services through reciprocity, the rotation of leadership positions among many members of the community, the recruitment of skilled individuals to fill service positions and the contribution of money to the island development fund by those employed. Perhaps it is this corporate orientation that leads Nanumeans to see the national government and themselves as partners in development and to expect that the benefits and opportunities that are available will be distributed equally through the group so that all Ellice Islanders will benefit.

The first development plan of Tuvalu, which achieved independence in 1978, was issued in that year to cover 1978-80. It was largely the work of European technical assistance provided by the UN Development Programme (UNDP). The plan concentrated "on the special problems and issues arising from independence, in particular the need to forge a new nation out of part of a former colony ...".[21] The immediate objectives were:

- to attain full independence for Tuvalu within the British Commonwealth;
- to develop a sense of national identity and commonness of purpose amongst all the people of Tuvalu;
- to strengthen and diversify the Tuvaluan economy as a means towards achieving ultimate self-reliance.

To achieve these objectives, priority would be given to:

- improving both internal and external air and sea communications;
- expanding agricultural and fisheries production for the local and export markets;
- providing Island Councils a wider role in determining priorities and projects in the islands;
- achieving balanced development of all islands;
- completing the development of Funafuti as the administrative capital of Tuvalu;
- continuing to reduce the rate of population growth through a comprehensive family planning programme;
- expanding health and education services consistent with resource availability and the needs of the country and, in the case of education, the job opportunities available.

Tuvaluan views were included in the plan as a result of meetings held by the UN Planning Advisor with the people on every island in the group except for Niulakita. These discussions "formed the basis of Island Development Programmes which are in some ways sub-plans within the overall plan".[22]

Although the Plan was a practical attempt to institute planning and establish machinery for implementation, it remains largely the approach of outsiders, to which island development programmes have been tacked on. No coherent set of objectives representing the views of the Ellice Island people was presented, although the main goal was said to be the creation of a nation out of nine scattered islands.[23] Basically, it is purely an economic document or list of estimates and it ignores social and cultural realities or the likely human consequences of future policies.[24]

Views from the Gilbert Islands

Gilbertese attitudes to development are intimately bound up with their attitudes to government. Even when government provides the funds to build some community asset such as a medical dispensary, it remains a 'government' building and people think maintenance costs should be met by government. Although such an asset is welcomed, it is often felt that wages should be paid for work on government projects, whereas if it were seen as a community project it would rely on the use of voluntary labour. The apathy of the people to government plans and projects reflects a history of paternalism and non-involvement of islanders. Similarly, the purpose of taxes is widely misunderstood as contributing more to the wealth of government rather than significantly affecting the welfare of the island. There seems to be little conception of a sense of social good that has carried the traditional values of obligation and reciprocity into the contemporary setting.

Because of the huge gulf between government and the outer islands, there is an urgent need for islanders to consider in depth the role and need for modern services so that, as their commitment to them becomes more explicit, the purposes of taxation will be more fully understood and accepted. As Betsy Sewell points out, "the local concept of Government is frightening, Government is nothing less than an arbitrary, external and thoroughly dictatorial power whose purpose is to force the people into obeying its command".[25] The greatest weakness of all, she suggests, is a real lack of sophistication in understanding the feasibility of planning from a 'Western' point of view. Self-government and independence mean little at the national level if islanders do not participate in planning for their own island and are not involved fully in new projects. Such involvement is not only a moral right and practical proposition but is also, she suggests, a political necessity.

Universal Goals

There are, of course, certain basic goals that are indeed universal for all cultures around the world, including the Gilberts and Tuvalu. Tony Hughes who was a Development Planner and senior public servant in both the Gilbert and Ellice Islands and the Solomons suggested that the things that really matter to a people can be essentially reduced to four fundamental goals:

1 the future wealth and happiness of the family;
2 the earning power and hence the real standard of living of this generation and the next;
3 the preservation or disappearance of the comforting and well-known features of their childhood;
4 and the feeling of being reasonably free, reasonably uncowed by physical or economic dangers, and reasonably sure that you are your own boss.

A fifth goal can be added to this list:

5 the protection, maintenance and enhancement of the local environment and its resources (land, sea and air) by using them in self-sustaining ways.

Sadly, as most Westerners will have heard, it is already too late with respect to this fifth goal as far as the people of Tuvalu are concerned. As a result of global warming, which is at least partly due to carbon dioxide emissions from a large number of modern nations, the sea level in the Pacific Ocean is rising steadily and inexorably. It appears certain that within a few years time, most or all of the low atoll islands of Tuvalu will be under sea level at high tide and compulsory resettlement will be needed to save the people.

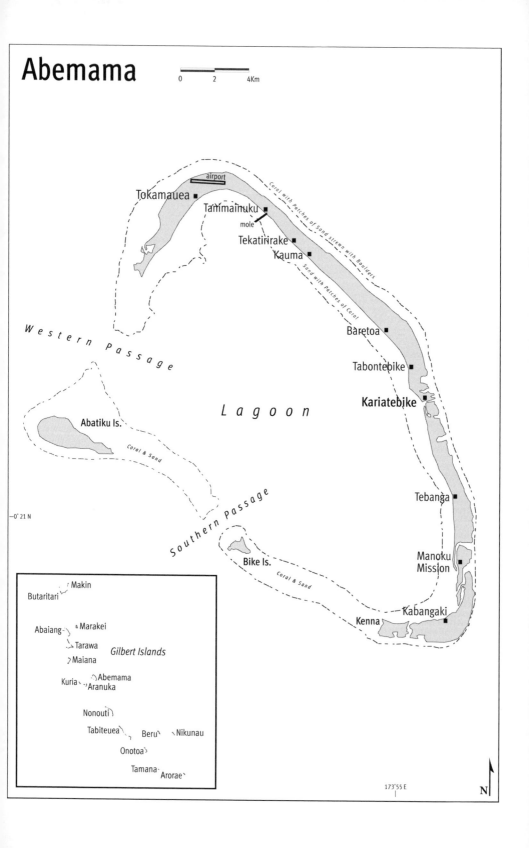

Abemama

0   2   4Km

airport
Tokamauea ■
Tammainuku ■
mole
Tekatinrake ■
Kauma ■

Coral with Patches of Sand strewn with Boulders

Sand with Patches of Coral

W e s t e r n   P a s s a g e

Baretoa ■

Tabontebike ■

Kariatebike ■

L a g o o n

Abatiku Is.

Coral & Sand

−0° 21 N

S o u t h e r n   P a s s a g e

Tebanga ■

Manoku
Mission ■

Bike Is.

Coral & Sand

Kabangaki ■

Kenna

Makin
Butaritari
Abaiang
Marakei
Tarawa
Maiana
Gilbert Islands
Kuria
Abemama
Aranuka
Nonouti
Tabiteuea
Beru
Nikunau
Onotoa
Tamana
Arorae

173°55 E

N

10

Abemama: An Atoll Economy in Kiribati

'Abemama: An Atoll Economy in Kiribati' is based on the Abemama Report (Watters and Banibati, 1984) and can be read in conjunction with my extended report that was the result of the Victoria University of Wellington Rural Socio-economic Survey of the Gilbert and Ellice Islands (see Watters and Banibati, 1984; and Geddes et al, 1982).

This essay presents Abemama as a case study of an island grappling with the twin issues of cultural and economic viability. A description of the island based on my fieldwork as well as on reading of its history and the literature on development generally is balanced by a discussion of the problems facing small islands. Abemama provides a microcosm of issues that both characterise and beset all small islands in the Pacific: the internal factors of tradition and developing viability, and the external factors of political and economic connectedness, counterbalanced by the wishes of the people for Western goods and future security. As a case study, therefore, it epitomises many of the great issues facing the whole of the Pacific region.

Consequently, this essay goes on to look especially at two main factors: the rapid urbanisation of Tarawa and its effects on Abemama and all the islands in the Gilberts group; and the increase in foreign influence and decolonisation from the late 1960s. While measures of consumerism may suggest modernisation, I argue that they represent dependency; and while projects and aid may seem the result of altruism and a wish to encourage advancement, they become instead superfluous edifices that do not always pay heed to local conditions or to local needs.

Abemama: The Island

Sir Arthur Grimble has eloquently described the "gem-like islets cast at random through ... the solitudes of the Central Pacific" that make up the Gilbert group. One of these is Abemama, which means "land of moonlight".[1] It lies some 150 kms south east of Tarawa in the Central Gilberts, almost on the equator and, as its name indicates, is a serene

175

and beautiful island.

Atolls are, however, amongst the most limited and difficult environments in the world for humans to live on. Abemama stretches in a semi-circular ribbon of coral sand and rocky outcrop for perhaps 30 kms, averaging about 300-600 metres in width (an area of 6,861 acres or 2,777 hectares). Its highest point is only about 4.5m above high tide level. On an island that entirely lacks rivers, the population of 2,381 in 1972 was totally dependent on a precarious geography. Primarily, the local people were reliant on the behaviour of the fresh water lens that floats on salt water (the 'Ghyben-Hertzberg lens') in wells and on the rich fish resources to be found in the lagoon and the surrounding ocean. They were at the mercy of the low water-holding capacity and severe nutrient deficiencies of the atoll's sandy coral soils, and the rather dry equatorial climate with its variable rainfall (mean of 1,346 mm) and not infrequent severe drought.

Two factors have enabled islanders in the Gilberts to achieve high population densities on some islands: the rich and varied marine resources (some 400 different species of reef and pelagic fishes have been identified)[2] and, in spite of the poor soils, the relatively uniform tropical climate which is favourable for high-yield horticulture. Moreover, although severe drought and occasional destructive hurricanes are major limiting factors, the Gilbertese have adapted well through distinguishing major different land types. For example, on the small southern reef island of Tamana, three main types have been distinguished: *aba ni mate* (the land of the dead) on the higher drought-prone shingle ridges; *aba ni maiu* (the land of the living) on lower and damper land; and *tetabo* (the place of staying alive), low-lying wet lands where the water lens is close to the surface or breaks the surface in wet periods.[3]

In 1972, the pressure of population on Abemama was marked. The island has only poor soils which result in the impoverished and very limited vegetation (only just over 60 flowering plant species); and only one or two large trees of some species still survived. Apart from the coconut palm and pandanus, very few fruit can grow under harsh atoll conditions – a native fig, breadfruit, papaya, pumpkin and *Morinda citrifolia*. Some flowering shrubs grew near villages, and in rare fertile spots such as old *babai* pits near the lagoon in the north, a few banana plants grew that bore diminutive fruit.

Historical Development and Social Structure

The impact of the West on the island was traumatic in the nineteenth century, though the full force was blunted somewhat by the able autocracies of Baiteke and Binoka. Tobacco and hoop iron had quickly become keenly desired items by the middle of the century. By the time of Robert Louis Stevenson's sojourn on the island in the 1890s, Abemama had become well known for its relative affluence and its polite, indolent and permissive society. Gunboat diplomacy taught Binoka the limits of independent action when he nourished ambitions to conquer the group, and British political and military power as well as Western economic power became the decisive factors. Spiritual conversion to Roman Catholicism and the stern unbending requirements of District Officers like George Murdoch accelerated the pace of social change, forcing society to readapt to new moral and legal codes of conduct.

Increasingly as the outside world impinged on Abemama, people began to play roles appropriate to the broader colonial social structure. In the traditional context, however, people continued to maximise their choice by gaining access to land from both lines (ambilineal descent). The main social unit above the household has continued to be the *utu* (clan), with members frequently cooperating.[4] With the imposition of new codes of sanitation and requirements of inspection under the colonial order, the *mwenga* or household seems to have been emphasised more as an accountable unit within the social structure. It remains the main residential and social unit and the main economic unit in the sense of sharing a common hearth. However, it is very varied in composition, three main types having been distinguished, and it remains a rather ephemeral or fluid social unit in which the actual members residing together frequently change.[5] Nor does it have much cohesion, for the head of the household rarely consciously directs its members.[6]

Abemama is a hierarchical island and the great authority of *te uea* (the high chief) and other *banuea* distinguishes it markedly from the more egalitarian Southern Gilberts. The role of the *unimane* supported the upper classes in this stratified society, but colonial policies have in general weakened the authority of the old men and the *maneaba* system in general. Although *maneaba* are still important places for social occasions, for ceremonial, dancing and decision-making, little of their former august aura or sanctity now remains. Modern trends have bypassed them, and they are, sadly, rather irrelevant.

Resources

Abemama is known as a 'rich' island in comparison with others in the Gilbert and Ellice Islands, and many people believe it to be 'lucky'. While 55 percent of the atoll is covered with coconut palms, only about 11 percent appears to be planted in rows,[7] and as much as 36.5 percent is under scrub, reflecting the relatively light population density (0.135

persons per hectare) compared with most islands. Very few people on Abemama are poor in the true Gilbertese sense (lacking in lands). We met only two genuinely poor people and they were poor because they had no *utu* members on Abemama whose lands they would have been able to use; their own lands lay on other islands. The 16 households studied intensively had a mean of 6.8 lands each, a liberal number containing abundant resources. Of these lands, an average of only 3.1 were used occasionally, with the more productive lands, or lands nearby, being preferred to distant lands over two miles away. The detailed counting of palms on sample lands revealed, however, the serious state of coconut resources – that old non-bearing palms exceed in number young, non-bearing palms, indicating the need for renewed coconut planting for the future. Households averaged 0.45 *ikaraoi* (cultivated *babai* varieties) pits each (an inadequate number for ceremonial purposes) and 2.1 *katutu* (uncultivated varieties of *babai*) pits.

Although the total number of *babai (Cyrtosperma chamissonis)* pits possessed was liberal, the failure often to replant on harvesting and the decline in *babai* cultivation and maintenance of pits marks a serious and probably irretrievable decline in an important component of the subsistence economy. This trend leads to some substitution of traditional staples and more frequent consumption of imported starches.[8] Only three households out of 16 spent more than three hours a week in *babai* work or harvesting, and only one household (significantly the one often assisting at weddings) consumed *babai* more often than in three meals during a six-day week.

The lagoon is one of the richest in fish resources in the group and it was extremely rare for a fisherman to return home empty-handed. Perhaps the subsistence affluence of Abemama, which in the earlier era of depopulation presented an abundance of resources to a small population, provided little incentive to plan for the future. Would it not be sufficient to trust nature to provide?

Increasingly, however, the economy of Abemama was being enmeshed more fully in the international economy as the copra trade grew, as circular migration for employment of at least some of the island's population became widespread[9] and as purchase of goods from the more numerous trade stores became part of the normal pattern of expectations. Traditional economic values[10] did indeed provide a solid basis in general for the guidance of modern Gilbertese: no respect was shown to men who were wasteful, or who foolishly sold their lands to obtain ready cash. A clear concept of laziness existed and true wealth could be gained only through the possession of lands. But a gap seems to have emerged between traditional attitudes and values and the behaviour required for the modern situation, caused perhaps by the markedly different requirements of modern times. Thus, while it was believed to be good to plant coconut palms for household requirements in the future, no great blame was levelled at people who failed to undertake this important task.

Subsistence Economy

The ease with which Abemamans can acquire food to meet household needs was illustrated in the time allocation data: as little as two hours per week are sufficient to feed a family at the most basic level. All forms of subsistence take on average about 24 hours per week or 22 percent of allocated time. The extent to which fishing, a popular activity, dominates the subsistence economy is illustrated by the figures on time spent per household: while only 1.5 to 2 hours is spent in fishing per consumption unit, the average figure per household per week is nearly 14 hours. While almost all households have nets or access to canoes to meet their needs, plus a moderate surplus of fish for drying and salting, only a handful of substantial entrepreneurial fishermen have emerged who plan to undertake fishing as a relatively large-scale commercial venture. To achieve that level of operation, aluminium boats, outboard motors, very large nets, and above all sustained motivation and organisation of *utu* members along the Frank Smith or H. Schutz model[11] would be necessary, or the cooperation of *mronron* partners. However, there are good sociological reasons for doubting the wisdom of official Western-style policies aimed at promoting the emergence of such individualistic entrepreneurs: such policies would be resented in an egalitarian society,[12] and be seen to be selective and divisive. More modest policies aiming at boosting production at the normal household level should result from better marketing, pick up, transport and wind-drying arrangements that should ensure a better return to the village producer. A deliberate policy of import-substitution would encourage production of salt fish on islands adjacent to Tarawa and save scarce overseas funds spent on imported meat and fish.

Production

Abemama copra production repeats the pattern of great variability over time in fishing activity. Household copra cutting is small-scale, episodic and discontinuous, but its very irregularity may well be a matter of routine. Thus households often sell small amounts of copra varying from four to five pounds (10 cents) up to 100-150 lb (or A$2-$3 worth) five or six times a month. Such a pattern probably reflects target production to earn small sums needed immediately, and the great irregularity in the availability of 'incentive goods' in the stores up until recent years. Production, then, is part of the cultural pattern of Abemamans and the underlying economic conditions that have led to the evolution of this sporadic pattern in which cash earning work is fitted in with many other highly desired social, ceremonial and household maintenance tasks that are part of the day's activities. This is not an immutable pattern, however, but merely a response to the situation villagers have grown accustomed to. Thus when, for example, an attractive new market suddenly appears (as in the case of handicrafts for the Suva festival), men showed they possessed the ability to respond quickly by greatly increasing the time spent on making items such as model canoes for sale.

Income

The income data[13] also confirmed this situation-determined interpretation of economic life. Except for the richest and poorest villagers, Abemamans depend on three, four or five sources of income that may vary markedly in amount throughout a year, or over several years. Villagers are not wholly 'peasant', although their interest in and 'commitment' to their lands and coconut resources may be considerable and peasant-like in years of good coconut prices. Nor are they wholly 'proletarian', although they are greatly attracted to full-time wage work and often regret that family circumstances or life crisis events have interrupted a formerly lucrative period of employment on Ocean Island, Nauru or Tarawa. Most households have engaged at some time or other in small-scale trading or *mronron* enterprises, while married women undertake bread or doughnut making, making sweets for sale or selling sour toddy. Two new more lucrative components of household income that have increased their potential contribution over recent years are remittances and government subsidy payments. If a son or daughter is fortunate enough to gain a full-time job off the island, the household can normally depend on some 'telmo' (telegraphic money order) remittances from time to time, perhaps to pay land or head tax, or school fees. While the evidence is not wholly conclusive, to the extent that it is predictable, it seems to act as a disincentive to other forms of production. In short, Abemamans do not depend on any one of these sources of income, but on all of them collectively. They are part-peasant, part-proletarian, part-time trader, partly dependent on unearned income, and partly subsistence gardeners and fishermen – in short, rational opportunists who seize new possibilities that a rapidly changing and unpredictable world presents.[14] Since the situation changes so greatly from year to year, it is entirely sensible for them to capitalise on the advantages of the moment. Such variability and fluctuations in prices provide little incentive either to plan or to save for the future.

The feedback effects of remittances on agriculture is a matter of grave concern, if the trends that have long been apparent in the societies of Niue, the Cook Islands and Western Samoa, which have become progressively more dependent on remittances from kinsmen in New Zealand, are any indication.[15] Local output is sometimes undermined, and a lethargic, Micawber-like attitude ('waiting for something to turn up') may be induced. Four of the six households which spent the low figure of less than 18 hours a week on all forms of subsistence received remittances or local salaries. Hence, the present day economy is made up of an accretion of separate, poorly articulated activities, and apart from a growing dependence on outside sources of employment, no clear pattern of economic evolution can be discerned over time. Adaptation is followed by readaptation. Abemamans may well be consigned economically to a state of limbo, becoming a 'permanently transitional' society. With the future so uncertain and the prospects of employment becoming bleak as the phosphate runs out, the vital importance of the subsistence economy and the limited security that it can give become readily apparent. Even if this is recognised, however, it may well be too late to revive some of the age-old skills of *babai* growing fully, and some of the finer skills of toddy cutting and specialised forms of fishing that are rapidly being lost. Already households spend less than two hours a week on *babai* work and harvesting. Nor is a sense of conservation present, for people have long become used to an abundance of local resources. For example, turtles are keenly hunted when they appear and on the two occasions on which I learnt that men had discovered a nest of turtle eggs, every egg was taken.

Activity Pattern

The diversity of time allocation patterns illustrates the considerable variability of circumstances affecting different households. Just as their needs vary markedly, depending on composition and the changing requirements of the life cycle, so can luck, the fortunes of family members in schooling and salaried employment, or success in *mronron* activities or fishing greatly affect economic strategy and the household activity pattern. Several household types are proposed, but these are by no means fixed categories, for household economic strategy may change greatly year by year depending on changed circumstances. Cash earning activities are usually supplementary to subsistence and do not usually compete with them, but in some instances (e.g. Households

14 and 16) cash earning acts as a substitute for some subsistence tasks. The diversity of household activity patterns emphasises the considerable autonomy of individuals; the weakness of any centralising function, allocative power, or overall direction or planning by the head of the household; and the lack of cohesion of the household as an economic unit. (If, on the contrary, these converse factors were strongly pronounced, Abemamans would approach peasant status.) The household is essentially a loose collection of individuals who contribute food or money to a common 'cooking pot' but largely go their own way and perform activities appropriate to their sex and age. While leisure is socially valued, visiting and various forms of social activity play an important part in life, which help to sustain or strengthen important social relationships. However, the model canoe-making activity suggested that resting or some social activity tended to fill a vacuum. Clearly, much disguised unemployment exists[16] and, if new markets were to appear, much currently unused labour in the villages could be mobilised. New opportunities should be planned to appeal to individuals, and it should be remembered that educational needs provide some of the most valued incentives. While people are committed to supporting their immediate family, a fundamental commitment also exists to their wider *utu*, as various fund-raising activities[17] and patterns of sharing on a day-to-day basis indicate.

Employment

The income and employment data illustrate vividly the degree to which Abemama, like other Gilbert Islands and indeed most parts of the South Pacific, is a dependent island, relying on the inflow of money earned elsewhere. In spite of an untapped potential that clearly exists to exploit subsistence resources more fully, the village on Abemama, as on other outer islands, is by now a subsidised entity that lacks real economic viability of its own. And while people appear in general to be content with living in such an externally sustained village society, they are in essence no longer purely 'villagers', although not yet 'townsmen'. Circular migration represents a compromise between the two worlds, and the large numbers of people and considerable periods spent in paid employment on Tarawa, Ocean Island, Nauru or elsewhere (Watters and Banibati, 1984, Chapter 9) illustrate the manner of their link to and accommodation with the outside world, a world which villagers are gradually recognising is necessary for their future survival.

Private Enterprise

There has been a long history of on-the-beach trading since the days of beachcombers and the local agents of European or Chinese trading companies. An extended period of monopoly in the import-export trade enjoyed by Europeans in the form of the Government Trade Scheme and the Colonial Wholesale Society has been followed by the recent monopoly of the Development Authority, and in the retail and copra trade by the government-sponsored Cooperative Federation. This official monopoly has not stifled or daunted small-scale enterprise, however, and the vitality of numerous attempts to operate *mronron* illustrates the continuing enthusiasm of villagers. The Tangitang Union reached a remarkable scale of activity and level of organisation that showed what could be achieved by indigenous enterprise. While projects harnessing group labour have not been very successful since Taburimai harnessed labour to dig some huge new *babai* pits in the early 1950s, the successful completion of the causeway at the government centre in 1972 illustrates the potential that does exist if local goals, enthusiasm and leadership can be combined with capital and skilled supervision provided by government.

Elements of enterprise are widespread and can be readily observed in household economic behaviour. But enterprise of a level that could be called 'entrepreneurship' seems to be predominantly associated with people of part-European or part-Chinese descent. The critical factor emerging from several case studies appeared to be the early upbringing that emphasised achievement-orientation, the acquisition of money and material goods, and a value system characterised by the 'Protestant Ethic'. A superior Western-style education was also believed to be important in giving greater skill in business practice and several had been influenced by the attitudes of the Seventh Day Adventist faith. Training in practical skills also played a significant role. Where these conditions did not occur, the chances of achieving entrepreneurship in productive, fishing or commercial fields appear much more remote due to a lack of sustained motivation, capacity for organisation and mobilising *utu*-based labour. However, in-migrants who were strangers on the island appeared to be less subjected to the 'levelling-down' tendency inherent in the requests of relations. The official approach to encouraging enterprise illustrated by the 'leader farmer approach' and in lending policies is based on the classic Western entrepreneurial model: at best, it is relevant to only 5 percent of the population. As it undermines the cohesion of the group, its wisdom (except for the rare few) could be doubted. An alternative extension strategy is a suggestion.[18]

Government Enterprise

Official attempts at enterprise usually have the advantages of careful organisation and planning, and close government supervision, and have often been characterised by the hard work and enthusiasm of government officers, both local and expatriate. These qualities brought a considerable measure of success to the Nonouti Agricultural Cooperatives, the most significant attempt at lifting production in the history of the Gilbert or Ellice Islands. A substantial area of land was pooled by the landowners, cleared and replanted. A combination of factors, however, ultimately prevented success from being achieved: the continuing drought, the drop in the copra price and wage dualism meant that absurdly high Tarawa wages provided a counter-attraction with which the project could not compete.

On Abemama, the history of the Manoku Agricultural Cooperative and the Coconut Replanting and Improvement Schemes illustrated many of the same deficiencies. The schemes were ethnocentric in many ways in that they were based on erroneous assumptions about Abemama and its social organisation, the meaning of land, how land and palms were viewed and used, and how work was performed. The basic data that led to projections of the copra output were faulty and it was not realised that the hardpan would provide a formidable obstacle in digging holes for replanting. Inadequate notice was taken of local views that it is wasteful to chop down coconut trees, and little appreciation was evident of the number of *utu* members who also share access to lands.

As the schemes remained essentially *government* rather than truly Abemaman schemes, they provided little real incentive to the people, and community education on the cooperative schemes appears to have been almost nil. Since the people did not become greatly involved in the schemes, they would spend much of their productive time working on their other lands. Yet some substantial results were achieved, due to the drive and determination of many officers, backed by a generally efficient and hard-working Department of Agriculture. The greatest success occurred at Manoku where atypical conditions exist: church organisation, discipline and leadership, and a desire to provide an example to the rest of the island. The fact that people joined the coconut subsidy schemes essentially to acquire money illustrates the importance of quick financial returns, but any renewed attempts at coconut replanting or improvement must be based on a more fundamental strategy that actually involves households in planning for their own future sustenance and income.

Education

Much of the Western-type education that has been introduced into the country in the last decade or two appears to be ill-fitted, inappropriate and often irrelevant to the needs of an atoll community. To some extent, dual education goals will always exist, for Gilbertese must understand more of the world of which they are an intrinsic part. However, in 1972 it seemed that only 10 to 12 percent of pupils at best will ever gain salaried employment, so there is a need both to equip students to fit happily and effectively into village life (if indeed this is still possible) and at the same time to provide training for the small numbers who will go on to secondary or tertiary education.

There seems to be a strong case for developing in tandem a type of education in which the best of traditional lore is combined with a modern school system. Great priority should be given to encouraging people to think through the purposes of education in an atoll environment and confronting the harsh reality that only a small minority of their children will acquire secondary schooling, the prelude to gaining a salaried position. This suggests that community or adult education should be greatly expanded to enable people to acquire new skills, revive valuable old ones, and attempt a reconciliation of the contradictory and potentially antagonistic values and trends bearing on their own lives. Such a community education system could stimulate the school to complement and *add to*, but not replace, the traditional educational system, which should itself be given direct and specific encouragement.

An important role in the future will clearly be played by teachers. It is to be hoped that their salaries do not become too high, and that they do not become elitist or alienated from society at large. It is noted that teachers combine a pride and love for their own culture and its past with knowledge of relevant parts of modern Western education. While the task of working out new syllabuses that combine the best of Western and Gilbertese elements may seem to have been largely accomplished, this is an ongoing process and much remains to be done in translating the syllabuses into actual teaching period topics. There is a need for more in-service 'refresher' courses and back-up services and resources to support outer island schools.

Attitudes to Government and Development

History has taught the Gilbertese to understand power. Ever since the early period of Binoka's rule, Abemamans have understood the basic reality: the 'commanding heights' of power are occupied by the British and are located outside Abemama – by the British on passing men-of-war, in the seat of government in Tarawa, at the High Commission for the Western Pacific, or ultimately at Whitehall or in Washington. Many older people argue for a system of government that will provide firm direction or even an authoritarian approach to the management of affairs. In part this reflects the legacy of missionisation and of colonialism, the passive, dependent qualities that unhappily seem likely to inhibit many Gilbertese from attempting initiatives at the household, village and community levels to improve their own conditions. The result is that many expect government to spoon-feed the people. Younger Abemamans favour a more liberal government role with more freedom being left to the individual. Although people are not slow to point to the deficiencies of government (such as taxation), they are appreciative of the benefits that it has brought: peace and order, education, the medical service, improved transport and communications, and a number of social and economic improvements. The very fact that Abemamans welcome so many external innovations which they now regard as right, proper and in fact indispensable, shows how fully the island is part of the international economy. The political implications of this situation are that Abemama's political system is now not purely island-based but is an integral part of a *national* system that has important links with other South Pacific states in an evolving regional bloc. Middle-aged and older people do not fully understand the necessity for taxation, though accepting the services it provides.

A major function of the member of the Legislative Council is believed to be his lobbying for government funds for Abemama; to some extent, his success as a member is judged in terms of his success in this role. At the same time, he is expected to listen to the complaints and requests of islanders and to bring them to the notice of the 'powers that be' in Tarawa. The Island Council is seen as not only the main organ of local government but also as mediating between the people and government in Tarawa. The Island Council in 1971-72 was generally efficient and competent in local government (partly because of the outstanding leadership of the Island Executive Officer, Teratabu Tira), and in energetically carrying out tasks that were deemed to be in the interests of the island as a whole. One of these roles was again an entrepreneurial one of attempting to lobby for government investment and a greater share of project moneys. A higher tax payment rate, however, remained a problem, with many defaulters escaping payment until the time that fieldwork ended. The other major problem was in the field of sanitation and hygiene, where the standard of wells and latrines falls well below that of most other South Pacific countries. The Island Council leaders often play a major part in organising the feasts, dancing and ceremonial held to welcome senior members of government and eminent visitors from overseas. In view of the warmth of the welcome and the small size of the island, it should be easy for visitors to engage in a genuine dialogue with islanders, a dialogue that should not encourage false hopes or unrealistic expectations but help to bridge the existing gap between government and the governed.

Attitudes toward development by older people were characterised by the view that life had been better and happier in the old days. While they saw money as a good thing, they recognised that it corrupts people, undermines the Gilbertese way of life and threatens the subsistence economy, as, for example, in maintaining *babai* pits. Few people recognised the need for planning in general terms, but people of all ages saw the value of plans to achieve specific purposes or to mitigate unfavourable trends, such as the need to limit the size of one's family or to plant more coconut palms. While memories of American technological prowess are still fresh, prompting people to call at times for the loan of a government bulldozer for land clearance or some sophisticated or dramatic approach to overcoming development hurdles, there is widespread recognition of the utility of many innovations at the 'intermediate technology' level – for outboard motors, aluminium boats for fishing, a second truck for the island and extra large fishing nets. Clearly, a government lending agency that is in close touch with actual conditions and needs on the outer islands would help people attain such worthwhile goals.

Attempts by government officers to obtain reliable information on social or economic conditions in outer islands often produce dubious results. However expert in their own fields they might be, it is most unlikely that they would obtain reliable information by formal questioning on flying visits. The employment of a specialist social scientist by government would meet this need. Abemama is relatively successful in obtaining project money and other benefits from central government. As the nearest outer island to Tarawa on the internal air service, there is a real danger that it will become a 'showpiece' outer island, to which many distinguished visitors are brought. There is a need for the island to think through a development plan of its own which fits in logically to the overall national development plan. One old man shrewdly expressed his cynicism of the whole business of development planning. *Imatang*, he said, do not appreciate that the Gilbert Islands are different from Fiji. Far from observing the most fundamental geographical principles of all – that countries differ in their environmental and socio-cultural characteristics – Europeans continue to persist in treating the islands as if they were either part of Western Europe or (if they are ex-Africanists) in trying to apply African models. Yet the old man sensed that it was important for the *imatang* to have a development plan. Whether the reasons are political, propagandist or psychological (to justify the presence and collective actions of white men in these remote islands in the twilight of empire), it is hard to say. Although the great merit of development planning cannot be doubted, he seemed to sense that it was also part of a ritualistic drama of decolonisation, the play of modernisation in which all the actors, European and Gilbertese, had to play out their parts.

Problems of the Outer Islands

While Abemama is in many ways more fortunate than several outer islands, it does suffer from many of the conditions that afflict all outer islands. The nature of government policies and external influences affecting Abemama, and more particularly the absence of policies that would encourage self-reliance, are critically important. While these issues lie mainly beyond the scope of this essay,[19] we will briefly consider two broad facets of this wider situation: the rapid urbanisation of Tarawa and the centralisation process affecting Abemama and the Gilbert Islands as a whole; and the increase in foreign influence and decolonisation in the late 1960s and early 1970s, which has led to the progressive dependence of the Gilbert Islands as a whole on the outside world.

Over-urbanisation and Over-centralisation

The growing primacy of Tarawa atoll, the seat of government and main link with the outside world, has been accentuated in recent years. Although Tarawa lay 500 miles north of the centre of gravity of population of the Gilbert and Ellice Islands in 1963, with 12 percent of the population living here, by 1973 this proportion had increased to 28 percent, with nearly 15,000 of the total 17,188 living in urban or peri-urban South Tarawa. In the whole of the South Pacific, only New Caledonia, Tonga and French Polynesia have a greater proportion of their population in urban areas.[20]

The growing centralisation of the country and lop-sided development is illustrated in the fact that in 1972 three-quarters of all cash incomes ($4.5 million) were earned in Tarawa and 80 percent of all government staff worked there.[21] With respect to purchasing power, the three largest cooperatives in South Tarawa together accounted for half of the country's $2.5 million cooperative turnover. Thus, while cooperative members in South Tarawa spent an average of $350 per head per year on cooperative store purchases in 1971, this was four-and-a-half times as much as the outer islands ($80 per head). The great employers of labour, government and the Development Authority paid out $3 million a year in wages and salaries on Tarawa, or 15 times as much as they paid in rural areas. Inevitably the spending on infrastructure and services was out of all proportion to the fact that only just over one quarter of the total population lived in Tarawa: 30 percent of the output of the Public Works Department was devoted to maintaining the living standards for the expatriate community.[22]

Although the population of South Tarawa produced very little, merely staffing the public service and providing other services, it came to depend increasingly on imported carbohydrates. In 1971, the Colony spent over $1,874,000 on imported food, beverages and tobacco (39 percent of all imports). The result is that what is often termed an advance in 'development' is really an advance in consumerism. Nutritionally sub-standard foods are becoming common in the diet; infant mortality is high; drunkenness and crime are causing local worries; and sanitation, pollution, and the problem of adequate and safe water supplies are issues of grave concern. It was estimated that a total of about $6 million would have to be spent in the five or six years after 1972 on public amenities for the town – a huge sum that would not be available for rural areas.

Although many people have recognised the inequities and potential danger of this process of over-urbanisation and over-centralisation, the country has slid gradually into an economic spiral, for the cost of relocating many services and government infrastructural stock would be exorbitant. In 1968, Riddell suggested that it would cost between $5 to $7 million, or more than the entire Colony Recurrent Revenue for 1966.[23] The consequences of these trends are not difficult to specify: a mounting stream of migration from outer islands to the already heavily populated Tarawa, a growing sense of deprivation in the outer islands in contrast to the conspicuous superiority of living standards and amenities on Tarawa, and a pronounced distortion of the whole economy due to the artificial escalation of incomes and prices on Tarawa that had an inevitable under-cutting effect on real rural incomes or wages. (We have noted above how workers refused to work for the Nonouti Agricultural Cooperatives for 40 cents a day.) The creation of an enormously expensive and over-developed (in relative terms) government centre with little real productive capacity of its own will impose a great strain on the country when the phosphate supplies run out.[24]

Not all these trends, of course, can be blamed on government or on the Development Authority – many unfortunate consequences have stemmed from the injection of large sums of British and other overseas aid money into a tiny atoll economy in an attempt to transform it into something it can probably never become. And Ocean Island contributed $850,000 in wages per year to 500-odd phosphate workers, income that filtered through the kinship network of redistribution to many outer islands. Growing dependence on foreign manpower exacted a high toll: the average local cost for the grossly expensive reliance on foreign skill was $7,000 per job in 1972 ($7,000 was paid overseas), although this was quite unrelated to the earning power of the country, and greatly distorted local expectations as to what was an acceptable or desirable living standard. The Financial Secretary complained in 1972 that there seemed to be a general feeling that money grew on trees cultivated by the government and that people had only to ask for $10,000 for each island.

Increase in Foreign Influence, and the Effects of 'Decolonisation' and Dependence

Associated with the over-centralisation and over-urbanisation of Tarawa has been the massive importation of all things foreign. From the late 1960s to the early 1970s, the rate of increase in the numbers of foreigners employed in the civil service was twice as fast as that of the public service as a whole. Since the new colonial service lacked the virtues of the old colonial service in that officers were not required to learn the Gilbertese language and culture and often stayed only for one or two tours of duty, they failed in the main to assist Gilbertese to work out an essentially *Gilbertese* development model in the economic, social and political spheres. Inevitably, perhaps, they have introduced foreign ideas, along with foreign money, foreign skills and foreign goods, all produced and priced according to factors that had nothing to do with the Gilbert and Ellice Islands.[25] Moreover, in this process of 'decolonisation' associated with the steps leading towards political development and self-government, almost all key decisions seem to have been taken by foreigners or to have been strongly influenced by them. Inevitably, the institutions, policies, methods of organisation and even the goals aimed at have been introduced from the outside, and as part of this process the norms of Western society have been transplanted into the local society. This process was probably inevitable given the reality of the modern world, and perhaps beneficial in many respects, but it has served to make the Gilbert Islands even more dependent on the outside world. Growing dependence undermines healthy self-reliance or confidence in charting an independent course of one's own. Thus, even as the Gilbertese are meant to be acquiring greater control over their own affairs, their dependence becomes ever more complete. Does decolonisation mean, paradoxically, growing dependence as a country 'advances' towards self-government and 'independence'?

A real tragedy is that many foreigners have come to work in the Gilbert Islands highly motivated to assist the Gilbertese and to work constructively in the great task of economic, social and political development. Yet, as in all colonial situations, there is little real communication between expatriates and Gilbertese. It is another case of the "working misunderstanding"[26] between Europeans and local people, for the two sides do not understand each other, listen to each other or take much notice of each other's wishes. Insulated by the barriers of language and culture, the expatriate obtains little more than a glimpse, and often a misleading glimpse at that, of what life is really like for the Gilbertese on an outer island.[27] When the expatriates state their assessments on local conditions, the response is often only a blank wall of polite non-communication, for Gilbertese are hesitant to correct their employers, people who could make or break their careers. Expatriates then often believe their assumptions to be correct and use them as the basis for formulating policies, but since the assumptions are often incorrect or merely half-truths, it is little wonder that inappropriate policies eventuate. And so both sides find it easier and less painful to avoid scrutinising their own assumptions, admitting that their own understanding is limited, their knowledge at best only fragmentary and often little more than a set of 'guestimates'. And so the stage play proceeds with local players performing ever more important roles as the day of self-government and then of independence draws closer, deluding themselves that they control their own destiny, even as their dependence becomes ever more complete. On the economic front, the set of policies and goals that together makes up a 'development plan' completes the illusion. The latest plan has been termed a 'Great Con', even though expatriates and Gilbertese are both at one and the same time unknowing tricksters and unwitting dupes of their own policies as they plunge in blind faith along the beguiling paths of 'modernisation'.

In the early seventies, it was apparent that only a few years remained if economic enterprises were to be established in two or three centres outside Tarawa. The acceptance of the 200-mile fishing zone, the hope that rich mineral or tuna fish resources would be found in the sea, and the prospect of a stronger regional South Pacific lobby for copra and other aid for the region have revived some hope. All the usual strategies of development – diversification, processing primary produce or greater priority for agriculture – are either impossible or ineffectual. Unless something rather miraculous 'turns up', the Gilberts are "stuck with an endless aid dependent non-productive, depressing and explosive urban/ rural imbalance".[28] The future is bleak indeed.

And yet perhaps one small crumb of comfort does exist. For after 80 years of British rule, in spite of mountains of paper penned in memoranda by many able men who laboured with drive and determination for years in lonely island stations,[29] little in the economic field has been achieved, outside the built-up areas of Tarawa and Ocean Island. New initiatives wither away in the white coral sand under the pitiless tropical sun, and the efforts of the *imatang* seem to have no more effect than the ceaseless waves breaking on the palm-fringed shores. Economic development, a peculiarly Western concept of large temperate land masses, seems at times to be a colossal, rather impertinent conceit of the Western mind which has been forced, almost irrelevantly, on the bemused Gilbertese. It is sadly ironic that on those islands such as Abemama in which the *imatang* has achieved the largest success in implanting a capitalist, commercial ethos, he has most seriously jeopardised the people's chances for the future. Elsewhere, where less 'success' has been achieved, a stronger ray of hope still exists that the subsistence economy and qualities of self-reliance will survive sufficiently intact, and that a sturdy independent Gilbertese culture and economy that incorporates many introduced elements will provide some security for the future. If not, the British government must accept the inescapable consequences of its own policies: to accept the Gilbert Islands as a permanent pensioner.

13. Erosion resulting from deforestation in the hilly interior of western Viti Levu, Fiji, 1983. (D. Leslie)

14. Somalani from the sea, showing typical overcrowding of small islands, Kove society, north coast of West New Britain, PNG. (Ann Chowning)

15. A relatively large, missionised village on the coast, Arawe, south-west West New Britain, PNG, 1982. (R.F. Watters)

16. A typical small hamlet in the great forest, Gimi Rauto, southern West New Britain, PNG, 1982. (R.F. Watters)

17. Taro growing in a new garden: shifting cultivation in Gimi Rauto. Note fence on left to keep out wild pigs. West New Britain, PNG, 1982. (R.F. Watters)

18. Men making holes to plant taro in a new garden, Dulago, Sengseng society of Passismanua, West New Britain, PNG. (Ann Chowning)

19. View from the gardens. Taro growing in an area of limestone, Seuk, Sengseng, Passismanua, West New Britain, PNG. (Ann Chowning)

20. Burning after felling. A garden of shifting cultivators. Gimi Rauto, near Kandrian, West New Britain, PNG, 1982. (R.F. Watters)

21. Girl playing bamboo flute, Dulago, Sengseng society, Passismanua, West New Britain, PNG. (Ann Chowning)

22. Trying to persuade man in the middle to accept pearl shells, Dulago, Sengseng society, Passismanua, West New Britain, PNG. (Ann Chowning)

23. Woman attending ceremony draped with wealth in shell money, Somalani, Kove society, north coast of West New Britain, PNG. (Ann Chowning)

24. Trader in full traditional regalia, Dulago, Sengseng society, Passismanua, West New Britain, PNG. (Ann Chowning)

11

Vicious Circle in Kandrian-Gloucester, Papua New Guinea: Report on a Development Options Project

'Vicious Circle in Kandrian-Gloucester, Papua New Guinea' is a summary of the Crown Agents and Land Resources Centre three-volume report on Kandrian-Gloucester published in 1982.

While marking exam papers in October 1981, the phone rang. It was a call from London asking if I would be willing to join The Crown Agents – Land Tenure Resource Centre (UK) team as leader to undertake a development options study on the remote area of Kandrian-Gloucester in the south and western areas of West New Britain Province (WNB), Papua New Guinea. I had received similar invitations before but, although I had worked in other hot wet tropical countries on tribal societies, had invariably declined. I had only visited Papua New Guinea briefly on two occasions and while I tried to keep abreast of some of the new nation's literature in teaching an Honours course on the South Pacific, I was hardly a specialist on the country. Such projects were invariably very brief – an intensive period of fieldwork for only a few weeks with a top-down approach that did not greatly involve the local people. However, this project seemed to have a team of highly competent participants, their proposal which won the tendered contract was well prepared, and with a government vessel laid on to enable us to visit villages and also a helicopter for visiting less accessible sites, I decided to accept. As the team consisted only of specialists competent in their respective disciplines but entirely lacking any experience of Papua New Guinea, I insisted that Ann Chowning, Professor of Anthropology in Wellington, be asked to read the report at draft stage and contribute her advice. She had undertaken fieldwork among three West New Britain societies: the Lakalai in the north, the Kove coastal people further west and the Sengseng in the remote rain forest of Passismanua in the south near Kandrian. After the fieldwork, the team would return to London for further discussions, reading and consultations.

The team comprised me as leader, and regional and rural planner, C.J. Tyrrell, Crown Agents, social planner and manager; C.G. Cox, Crown Agents, transport planner; P.S. Stutley, Crown Agents, agriculturist and marketing economist; A.B. King, Land Resources Development Centre, land use planner; E.Wyrley-Birch, Land Resources Development Centre, tree crops agronomist; M. Berry, Land Resources Development Centre, forestry; and K. Crean, Hull Fisheries Centre, fisheries.

This essay is a good example of the directive and prescriptive recommendations for development arrived at by a multi-disciplinary team invited by a national government (and funded by overseas aid) to suggest ways by which an area can become economically viable and even profitable. It suggests what can be produced and where it can be produced, and it also addresses local conditions and constraints and the importance of infrastructure.

Kandrian-Gloucester is portrayed principally as being caught in a vicious circle: the amount of goods that can be marketed (i.e. the surplus) is low because marketing facilities and transport are inadequate or non-existent, and marketing facilities and transport are inadequate because the volume of marketed surplus is too low to warrant expenditure and to support introduction of amenities or improvement of existing ones.

The Challenge of Development: Synthesis and Priorities

In studying the problems of development in the Kandrian and Gloucester area of West New Britain Province, the team became steadily aware that many of the conditions observed are widely repeated elsewhere in lowland Papua New Guinea. The terms "small, poor and remote"[1] aptly sum up the conditions of the project area and those of much of the South Pacific as a whole; taken together, they go a long way to explaining the economic stagnation and poverty (in a monetary sense) of the project area.

At the same time, the isolation of the area, its sparse population, and its lack of capital and skill make it difficult for it to respond in positive ways at a time when world market prospects are so bleak and macro-economic policy at the national level provides only partial assistance. Achieving development locally usually depends on a mix of these factors, but above all on the involvement of the provincial government and of the villages of the region.

The International Level

Papua New Guinea is above all an open, *export*-led economy. If it can increase substantially the income generated by expanding exports, such as coffee, cocoa, copper, oil palm, tea, copra and rubber, the export sector will 'tug along', as it were, the rest of the country in a manner that will ensure considerable benefits for the country as a whole. But equally, it is an export-*dependent* economy, and at the moment (and in all likelihood for a few years ahead) the receipts received for its exports are very depressed.

Given the structure of the country's economy, there is no escaping in the short term from the economic stagnation that is bound to occur. The internal market is far too small for local produce to compensate for the loss of external markets, and these external markets are themselves dependent on factors totally outside the control of the national government, such as whether or not frost may afflict the Brazilian coffee crop, the size of the annual Filipino copra harvest, the world copper price or the amount of oil palm produced in Malaysia.

The serious loss of export income, the steady rise in the cost of imported goods and the impact of inflation mean that there will be a substantial shortage of government funds and opportunities for public sector investment in development. The prospects for foreign investment and for 'bankable' aid projects are also, in general, not good. The adverse terms of trade are particularly serious for island economies like Papua New Guinea's, which are heavily dependent on fuels for transport, and the steady rise in the price of imported fuels during the 1970s has been a heavy burden. At the same time, the legacy of very substantial overseas aid from Australia in the recent past (in 1971-72, 53 percent of government expenditure was paid for by an Australian grant-in-aid) has led to many unfulfilled expectations among rural people who, unaware of the economic situation, not unreasonably expect the steady expansion of social services (including schools and aid posts) to continue at the rate of the good years. At the very least, they expect the status quo to be maintained.

The National Level

At the same time, the national government may wish to consider a range of policies that could in part ameliorate rural conditions. The legacy of colonial welfarism from the immediate pre-independence period has had unfortunate consequences with wages being unrealistically high. The indexing of wages to the consumer price index has meant that Papua New Guinea has become an exceedingly high-cost country

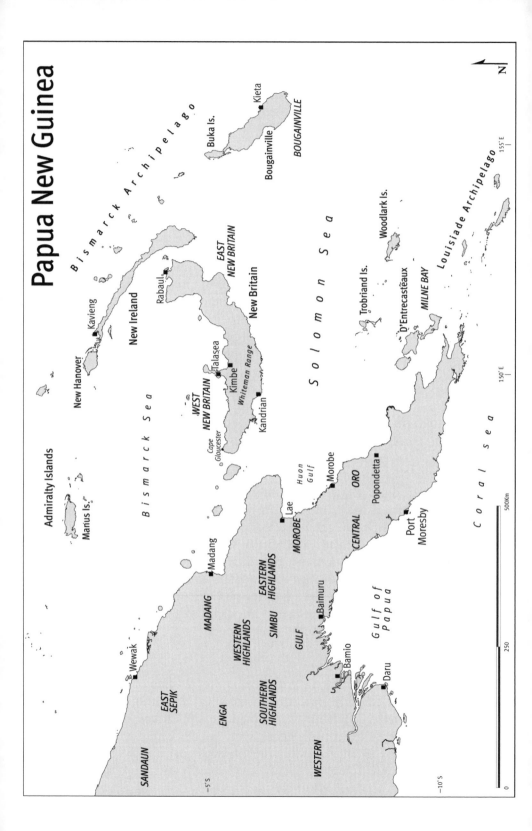

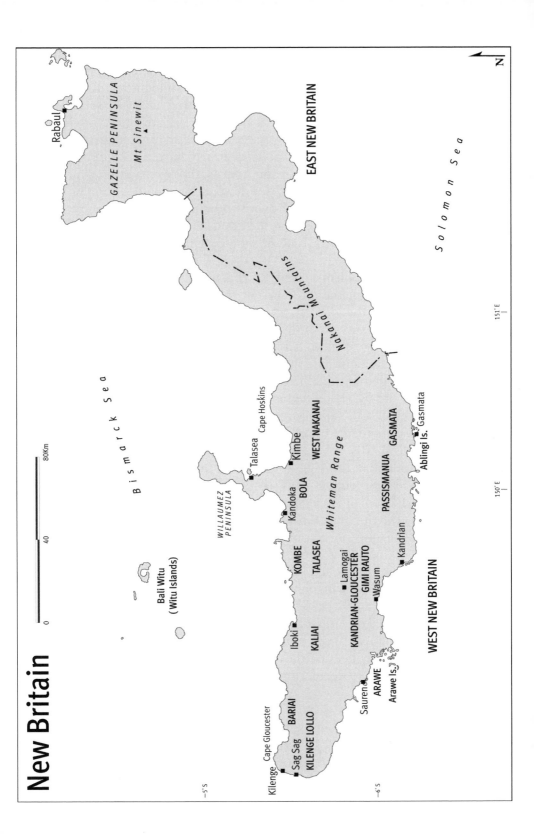

New Britain

Bismarck Sea

Solomon Sea

GAZELLE PENINSULA

Mt Sinewit ▲

Rabaul ■

EAST NEW BRITAIN

WEST NEW BRITAIN

Nakanai Mountains

Cape Hoskins

Talasea ■

Kimbe ■

WEST NAKANAI

BOLA

Kandoka ■

WILLAUMEZ PENINSULA

Whiteman Range

PASSISMANUA

GASMATA

Gasmata ■

Ablingi Is.

Kandrian ■

KOMBE

TALASEA

Lamogai ■

KANDRIAN-GLOUCESTER

GIMI RAUTO

Wasum ■

Bali Witu
(Witu Islands)

Iboki ■

KALIAI

BARIAI

Sauren ■

ARAWE ■

Arawe Is.

KILENGE LOLLO

Sag Sag ■

Kilenge ■

Cape Gloucester

0   40   80Km

150°E   151°E

-5°S

-6°S

N

in comparison with other developing countries which are often its competitors. Rural (as well as urban) wages are so high that a serious fall in the world market price, as has occurred recently, seriously threatens the survival of the oil palm and copra industries. It is obvious that government must not allow these important rural industries to collapse and price stabilisation policies clearly have a critical role to play. The exchange rate level of the *kina* is another issue that might concern the national government, for devaluation would enable higher prices to be paid to producers of export products. Another question is whether essential imports like capital goods and fuel for transport so critically needed by the rural sector should be favoured over imported consumer goods.

Many of the problems faced by the national economy in 1982 essentially arise from the structure of the economy and society that hardened during the 1960s, when the economy became severely distorted spatially and sectorally. Foreign domination of the economy, the rise of the great Bougainville copper mining industry, heavy infusions of Australian aid, the development of a public service that was uncoordinated and inefficient, growing dependence on expensive food imports and the rise of regional resentments that eventually forced the acceptance of provincial government, are all legacies of the period – legacies that contributed to or reflected the distortions.

In the early 1970s, a bold and imaginative attempt was made by a group of national and foreign advisers and politicians to correct these distortions, restore economic growth and bring its benefits to a much wider cross-section of society. Stimulated by the policies outlined by the Overseas Development Group (the Faber Report, 1973), the Central Planning Office (now the National Planning Office) produced *Strategies for Nationhood: Policies and Issues*, which introduced the celebrated Eight Aims. The new policies recognised the essentially rural nature of Papua New Guinea, the inappropriateness of capital-intensive economic growth, the failure of 'trickle down' development and the dangers of development based on large-scale foreign investment (all options for the 1980s which the team have reviewed). However, only limited success was achieved, partly because the distortions in the economy and society were very difficult to correct (many years' effort would be required) and partly because of the lack of wholehearted commitment to the new policies by the political leaders. The excesses of independence have helped to defeat these policies; thus the dismantling of the potentially valuable plantation system through the plantation acquisition scheme has seriously weakened the economy, just as the pace of devolution to provincial government is likely to place enormous new demands on taxpayers and threatens to dismember many valuable institutional structures needed for development (such as some local public services) that were patiently built up over the years. At least it can be said at the time of writing, seven years after the heady excitement of independence, that Papua New Guinea has now reached its 'morning-after' phase, when it can appraise its situation soberly in the cold light of a new day.

The National Public Expenditure Plan (NPEP) has wisely controlled the growth of government services and infrastructure. It helps to coordinate development expenditure and sensibly puts a brake on the expansion of services to a level that it is beyond the capacity of the economy to support: a growth in spending of 3 percent per year was fixed. However, the NPEP is only concerned with short-term planning horizons; as the team points out, planning effective rural development also requires medium and sometimes long-term planning and investment.

The Provincial Level

The West New Britain Provincial Government (WNBPG) will have to choose what kind of development is most appropriate for its province and the various regions within it, as well as the best strategy to employ to achieve it. In making these decisions, a large number of issues will have to be carefully weighed and technical matters closely studied; if the wrong development goals are chosen, or an inappropriate strategy is employed, it is likely that the situation of the people will actually be *worsened* rather than improved by 'development'.

The Meaning of Development: The Cruel Choice

Economic growth is an important objective pursued by all governments, for without it, resources will be lacking to carry out the government's other objectives. Moreover, redistribution, if it is desired, can best be achieved from the resources generated from growth. The rate of economic growth or of per capita income are also a measure of development, but it is not an adequate measure that is sufficient in itself. Thus, the distribution of incomes between different classes of people and between different regions and the creation of employment are also very important considerations for government. Moreover, although rapid economic growth might generate revenue, raise incomes and create some employment, it will increase the gap between the standard of living of different groups of people. It will also exact a heavy social cost in accelerating cultural change, undermining community cohesion and provoking feelings of deprivation among those who benefit least.

It might also on some land classes or soil types cause considerable environmental damage, and it is difficult always to foresee some of the consequences on the landscape and in society.

On the other hand, a slow rate of economic growth may ensure cultural stability and the retention of cherished tradition, but not be sufficient to generate enough personal income to induce young people to remain in local areas. Slow or zero economic growth does not always ensure social stability: in fact it may aggravate feelings of frustration and resentment at being neglected, and it is not likely to generate enough revenue to enable government to carry out its social policies, such as the provision of services, as well as implementing economic programmes. Thus, government is faced with a difficult and cruel choice as to which development objective to choose and which development strategy to employ in reaching that objective.

The problem of choice can perhaps be clarified by setting out the goals of development more explicitly (see Table 11.1):[2]

Table 11.1. Goals of Development of Ordinary People

1. The future wealth and happiness of the people.
2. The earning power and hence real standard of living of this generation and the next. (Note that 'income' includes both subsistence income and cash income.)
3. Preserving some of the comforting and well-known features of past life.
4. Feeling reasonably free, secure and sure you are your own boss.
5. Enhancing the position of women.
6. Preserving the environment and natural resources from destruction and enhancing sustainability.

Goals 1 and 2 can best be achieved by income-generating forms of economic growth, but if they are pursued too narrowly they can threaten goals 3 and/or 4. In practice, a government might well emphasise 1 and 2 primarily but pay considerable attention to ensuring that goals 3 and 4 are not lost sight of. Pursuit of 1 or 2 must not seriously impinge upon 5 or 6. And before a choice can properly be made, reliable information and data need to be gathered to enable decisions to be taken that are sound with respect to the technical issues that are involved. Thus, to illustrate, goal 4 can be achieved by promoting development of the village mixed subsistence-cash cropping economy with some *bisnis* activity of the usual small-scale sort. If, however, it is recognised that this traditional approach to development severely constrains the generation of substantial revenue for government, local councils and villages, then this factor must be taken into account.

Another very different development option would be large-scale resource development, which almost certainly for the project area would be timber milling. This would have the advantage of bringing in revenue to government and providing some infrastructure for the area, as well as meeting to a degree goals 1 and 2, but it would be at the expense of 3, 4 and 5. Large-scale milling would be a form of development that the government and people would, in all likelihood, be unable to control and it might do untold damage to the environment and destroy resources needed for future generations. Moreover, it might bring in much less revenue than that which could be gained in a few years by a stronger Forest Service. On the other hand, an intermediate solution such as the operation of small-scale portable timber mills – owned and operated by properly trained local people – might avoid some of the worst disadvantages, while bringing in some additional revenue and increased incomes.

It seems important, therefore, for governments to be fully aware of the likely consequences of their choice of development goals. Wide discussion and debate, careful planning and monitoring of current development projects can enable a government to gain a better idea of the likely consequences of the chosen development policy.

Kandrian-Gloucester: A Description

Human Resources

The population of the Kandrian-Gloucester study area in 1980 was 27,361, with over 94 percent living in villages and with very few non-citizens. The study area contains 32 percent of the rural population of West New Britain in 56 percent of the land area, and is very sparsely populated (an average of 2.4 persons/km^2 compared with 6.8/km^2 in the rest of West New Britain). Only one part, Kandrian Coastal, has a much higher population density, of 11.3/km^2 (still low in absolute terms).

Over 50 percent of the population are less than 18 years old, with nearly 20 percent in the 0-5 year age group. Crude population growth rates are very low (between 1.35-1.55 percent per annum from 1970/71 to 1978/79). There are 116 men to every 100 women in the villages, although the high rate of adult male absenteeism (36 percent) reduces the resident sex ratio to 104, slightly higher than elsewhere in West New Britain. Total absenteeism is 17.5 percent, a significant decrease over the past decade.

There are 208 villages with an average resident population of 124 persons, half the size of the average village in the rest of the province.

There are five major Austronesian language groups with 23 languages and dialects, and one small group of non-Austronesian language speakers.

The demographic picture, therefore, is of a sparsely populated area, linguistically diverse, with a predominantly young population living in small villages with low growth rates and high adult male absenteeism.

Physical Resources

Average annual rainfall varies spatially from 3,203 mm at Cape Gloucester to over 6,000 mm in the southeast, and temporally from 2,000 to 5,000 mm at Kandrian and 3,000 to 8,500 mm at Lindenhafen; but there are no inland rainfall records where rainfall is likely to be high.

Although East Arawe was hit by a small but intense cyclone in 1972, this is regarded as a freak occurrence. Within the study area, volcanic activity in the north-east Cape Gloucester coastal area is the major national hazard. The Cape Gloucester airstrip lies in the most likely path of any volcanic activity.

There are no sunshine records from within the study area.

There have been various mineral resource investigations in the study area, but none have so far proved successful. There should be sufficient limestone and gravel for building and road construction.

Land Suitability

Many of the soils are firm to very firm, preventing optimum growth of agricultural tree crops, particularly cocoa. Phosphorus deficiency is also likely. Teak and indigenous forest plantations do not seem affected.

About 20 percent of the study area contains significant land areas with slopes less than 10°, i.e. 2,000 kms²; while about a third of this land area, i.e. 650 km², slopes at less than 2°. Of the remaining 80 percent, another fifth consists of densely dissected plateaux, located mainly in Passismanua, east Kilenge-Lollo and east Kaliai, some of which is currently used for subsistence agriculture.

Currently, just over 2,600 kms² of the study area is not forested (grass, swamp, shifting cultivation etc.). Of the remaining forested area, some 2,200 km² is on very steep slopes and should remain under protection forest. The remaining area of some 6,600 km² is under loggable forest.

If the 2,000 km² of land on slopes less than 10° is considered to have some agricultural potential, then 4,600 km² could remain under permanent commercial forest. A comparison of current and potential land use maps shows there is plenty of unused land suitable for subsistence agriculture.

The following land units appear to offer the greatest overall agricultural potential:

- raised back reef plain (in Lamogai, Arawe East, Gimi Rauto, Eseli and Passismanua);
- recent volcanic plateaux, glaciers and piedmonts (in Gloucester-Airagilpua), with phosphorus deficiency a possible limitation;
- deltas and floodplains (in Arawe West, Kandrian Coastal, Bariai, Kaliai and Gasmata), with drainage and nutrient deficiencies, particularly phosphorus, as possible limitations.

The most extensive of the land units with a modal slope less than 10° is the raised back reef plain covering about 1,000 km². From a physical point of view, the most suitable crops for this land unit appear to be coffee, pepper and yam, and taro in the less well-drained parts. On purely physical criteria, rubber would be a suitable crop for the rest of the flat-to-moderately-sloping parts of the study area, while the only real limitations for pepper are a possible phosphorus deficiency.

Crop Suitability

Of the tree crops of most interest to the provincial Department of Primary Industry (DPI), *coffee* would appear to be the most suitable in the majority of the study area because it is more tolerant of soil compaction. It should grow reasonably well on the riverine units which are well drained and outside the very high rainfall areas.

Coconuts are suited to the beach ridges, low-lying but well-drained marine terraces and the well-drained riverine units outside the very high rainfall areas. They can be grown inside the very high rainfall areas if there is efficient and maintained drainage. Coconuts are also suited to the gentle lower slopes of Mounts Tangi and Talawe.

Optimal *cocoa* production will be limited in most of the study area by soil compaction, except possibly on the recent volcanic soils below Mounts Tangi and Talawe in Kilenge Lollo.

Taro is well suited to most of the riverine units (flood plain, backland and delta), although a serious taro blight since the 1950s has taken a heavy toll on this crop and led to the introduction of the new staples sweet potatoes and manioc (the latter is poor nutritionally). *Yams and cloves* are most suited to the marine units in the Cape Gloucester area. The rainfall appears to be too high for chillies. Bananas could be restricted by a possible nitrogen deficiency, and yam and cloves by heavy soil texture and phosphorus deficiencies.

Village Society and Economy

The most important social units in the study area are the household, the kinship group, the men's house and the village.

The critical factor for the team was to identify the socio-economic importance of each unit and the basic unit of cooperation:

- The household is important as the smallest and basic unit of production, procreation, socialisation and consumption. It has close ties with the patrilineal or cognatic kin group.
- The kinship segment or clan frequently controls the use and disposal of productive property, and thus acts as a political unit, but these segments are only local units. Competition for positions of authority occur between the major leaders, the 'Big Men', and nowadays the emerging rivalry of young, better educated men and the occasional entrepreneur.
- Chowning[3] agrees with Zelenitz and Grant (1980) that some anthropologists have represented some tribes (e.g. Kilenge) as more patrilineal than they actually are. She regards the fundamental feature of social organisation to be the small size of political units defined as groups within which organised warfare should not take place. These are no larger than a few hundred people who share co-residential ties and who are normally on friendly terms with one another. Other ties of descent are also important in reinforcing relationships based on shared wealth and cooperation.
- The village is a broader, more inclusive unit in which it is much more difficult to achieve cooperation since it may include several distinct and rival clans or lineages.
- Another serious obstacle to cooperation is the suspicion and low esteem that coastal people have for inland or bush people.

The primary principle of organisation in West New Britain is reciprocity. Reciprocal exchanges and reciprocal gift-giving are the most common way of distributing goods and services in these societies, and of increasing personal status and privilege. While there is a considerable difference in prestige between people, there is in practice a fairly even distribution of wealth. The principles of reciprocity and conspicuous distribution are quite contrary to such 'modern' economic principles as saving, investment and capital accumulation that are needed for development. But rivalry for wealth can impede generosity even between siblings.

There is some evidence that people find at times that the traditional customs are too onerous, expensive or no longer meet their needs, and that transitional economic strategies are beginning to emerge. However, in the dominant condition of economic stagnation, the study area has not proceeded far along the four theoretical stages of economic transition from subsistence to complete specialisation for the market:

- pure subsistence in isolation;
- subsistence with supplementary cash production;
- cash with supplementary subsistence;
- complete specialisation for the market.

Most communities in the study area lie between stage 1 and stage 2, with many coastal communities at stage 2, and the remoter inland communities of Passismanua close to stage 1. No communities had reached stage 3 (illustrated by the settlers in the Hoskins oil palm project).

For policy-making, the critical question is how to induce economic evolution from stage 1 to stage 3. It is apparent that production is not in general seriously limited by a shortage of the factors of production (land, labour and capital), but by a *demand* ceiling:

- the main developmental task is how to provide incentives to communities to induce them to combine land, labour and capital in ways that will produce additional production;
- the second main task is how to capitalise on a favourable response from villagers wishing to increase production.

The incentives emanating from the markets at Kimbe, Rabaul and Lae are not sufficiently persuasive because:

- the price of copra is so low as to discourage production;
- the stimulus provided by plantations to nearby communities has been removed, in their present abandoned or run-down state;
- transport in the area is poor and there is a lack of loads of sufficient size to induce ships to call.

West New Britain cannot expect a solution to the problem from improved price incentives to increase production which are unlikely due to poor medium-term export price forecasts for most commodities, and rapidly exhausting stabilisation funds.

While trade stores can encourage the development of a more commercial, cash-conscious rural producer, they can at the same time promote a socially undesirable form of consumerism. Much expenditure in stores goes on foods that are not very nutritious and do not need processing, on beer or on other wasteful forms of consumption. A continuing role for district administration and community education is to warn people about consumerism and poor nutrition from some imported foods.

Land Tenure

Land tenure in West New Britain reflects the general problem of subsistence gardening and the rights of social groups within cognatic group descent systems. The idea of land 'ownership' in a Western sense does not really exist. Problems inevitably arise:

- when non-traditional land uses are superimposed on customary ownership systems; and
- when large-scale ventures (such as foreign timber companies) require tracts of land.

It follows from the Eight Aims that land policy should be evolved from a customary tenure base, utilising land leased to the government for medium or long-term periods:

- Patient extension work by government patrol officers is required to change prevalent attitudes of suspicion, low esteem and rivalry between kin groups, and between villages in coastal and inland areas. Social and economic progress depends on harmony and cooperation between cultures and regions. Sadly, since independence, government officers have largely stopped patrolling. Missions do better at this than patrol officers, though they set up their own rivalries with each other.
- Response to incentive factors to increase village agricultural production should be encouraged by the WNBPG and Local Government Councils (LGCs) by providing support and advice on bookkeeping, management and business skills, and on agronomic and other matters to men of enterprise in the villages.
- Government support recommended above should be directed through any 'transitional' organisational channels (if they exist) that will lessen, if not completely avoid, the usual levelling mechanisms and constraints.
- The national government should regularly assess the forms of land-based security required for extension of credit facilities, to see whether they continue to meet the needs of both the lender and borrower.

At the village level, the concept of development may have particular and different meanings to those held at national or provincial levels because of certain traditional beliefs, practices and attitudes of Papua New Guinea society, including:

- a strong attachment to the land, whose permanent alienation is impossible, since ownership is regarded as collective and not transferable, and leasehold is the only compatible modern tenure concept;
- a disinclination to seek wealth for its own sake, but rather as a mark of status which is achieved only if wealth is shared;
- the importance of small group activity including *bisnis* groups;
- a strong attachment to close kin even though it militates against individual business activities;
- a greater interest in 'target income' than in a steady stream of income;
- a strong preference for leisure with periods of land work and ceremonial activities;
- the frequent return of those who obtain employment in urban areas to live in their villages, a feature almost unique to parts of Melanesia. This suggests that village life may hold out prospects as a counterbalance to urbanisation, and that agriculture is seen as a less inferior occupation in Papua New Guinea than in many other developing or MIRAB economies.

Nevertheless, there is ample evidence that villagers are prepared to adopt profitable new cash crop innovations.

Agricultural Production Systems

The village mode of production in the study area is similar to that in much of Papua New Guinea and consists of two distinct forms of land use: a grove of tree crops usually near the village, and food crop gardens which may be up to several hours walk away. Crops are grown and pigs raised for a mixture of goals:

- family consumption;
- reciprocity (gift exchanges), life crisis events and ceremonial feasts;
- redistribution to the Big Men, social group or church;
- insurance against natural hazards;
- market sale.

As the amount produced for market sale increases, competition and conflict may develop between the different goals of production.

Cropping is for about one year before bush fallowing, and there is frequent intercropping. Fallow sites are left for up to 11 years before reclearing. There is little prospect for some time of growing population pressure introducing changes to the agricultural system such as shortening the fallow length.

Official policy in the colonial period seriously undervalued or ignored shifting cultivation and other traditional root crop systems. At the low densities of population in the study area, it is an entirely rational and energy-efficient system of obtaining a livelihood, making liberal use of the resources in greatest supply (land and timber). Its one drawback is its low cash-earning potential. The extension policies practised by the DPI concentrate on promoting crops destined for sale, and neglect subsistence crops.

Improved productivity and a shorter fallow cycle will delay and possibly even prevent land shortages in the future. This may help to preserve the primary forest and concentrate the population (and thereby reduce the cost of infrastructure and services). Such changes should reduce the labour required for food production.

If villagers wish to earn cash incomes, then they can either:

• produce more traditional root crops to sell the surplus (but there is the lack of a sizeable urban market in the province or study area);
• grow traditional cash crops such as tobacco or betelnut; or:
• introduce new cash crops (for which considerable scope exists, particularly high value and easily transportable crops) into the inter-cropped gardens.

The 'social production' goal of subsistence production must be recognised in any attempt to commercialise the system. The DPI should be encouraged to carry out research on subsistence farming in the study area to improve productivity and shorten the fallow cycle.

Business Development

In West New Britain, as elsewhere in Melanesia, people widely believe that economic success can be achieved by imitating the forms of European economic organisation without mastering the skills involved. The most successful enterprises are those which are relatively divorced from the local socio-economic situation. The low level of economic surplus generated by resource development offers only restricted opportunities for trading. The general tendency has been for *bisnis* groups in the study area to survive only where there have been periodic replenishments of capital by the members, or through windfalls in the form of fish bait money, timber royalties or village development funds. They have not as a rule been economically viable, and do not always meet even their running costs. Inter-village rivalries contribute to the frequent division and sub-division of group membership. Business Development Division extension work is ineffective and wasteful of resources.

The WNBPG should examine the use of its existing agriculture and business development extension services to ensure that these resources are used more cost effectively and provide more appropriate advice. Business development officers should be equipped with simple 'pro-forma' project appraisal guidelines and handbooks for *bisnis* groups wishing to operate work boats, copra dryers and other common business ventures.

The team made the following conclusions after its field trip:

- Apart from subsistence cropping, there was a very low level of agricultural activity throughout the study area. The only commodity actually seen by the team being produced for export was copra. All other commodities such as vegetables, sago etc. were being produced for sale at local markets.
- The major reason for the low level of smallholder activity appeared to be the lack of marketing outlets for commodities such as cocoa, coffee and chillies. The production of birds-eye chillies declined to nothing because the DPI could not meet its obligation as 'buyer of last resort' to provide a satisfactory marketing system for chillies.
- Even if a satisfactory marketing system is provided, a sustained and high-level effort by the extension services will be required in maintenance, pruning, processing and other techniques to encourage smallholders to produce commodities such as coffee, cocoa and chillies.
- All the plantations seen by the team in the study area had either been abandoned or were on a care and maintenance basis and were in need of rehabilitation or replanting. The plantations were on some of the better and more accessible blocks of land along the coast of the study area. The national government's land redistribution policy was said to be partially responsible for the decline of the plantations. Owners were reluctant to invest in rehabilitation and replanting because of the uncertainty created by the policy. Another important factor was the current low price of cocoa and poor future prospects of copra.

Commercial Agriculture

The study therefore analysed the main modes of commercial agriculture which are worthy of consideration in accelerating production:

- the nucleus estate;
- cattle under coconuts;
- settler schemes;
- smallholders;
- plantations.

A combination of two or more is possible, and the most appropriate model may depend on the degree of vertical integration in the production process for each crop, the risk, the initial investment and other factors.

The Nucleus Estate Model

It should not be forgotten that most plantations occupy the best soils in the project area and often elsewhere: such valuable land cannot be allowed to lie idle or be overgrown by invading bush.

The nucleus estate model remains one of the most promising models of development and the team recommends government at both national and provincial levels to give close attention to forms of organisation. A nucleus estate enables smallholders occupying 'outgrower' positions relative to the central plantation to share in the benefits of a high level of management that an efficient plantation provides. The benefits of such economies will also extend to the outgrowers, as well as the infrastructure and services that the whole larger project will establish. However, the central plantation owners are only likely to be interested in the productivity of outgrowers if they need their output for the full utilisation of their central processing plant. An excellent example of this is provided in the province by the operation of the central oil palm crushing mills of Harrison and Crossfield which also serves the outgrowers on the settlement schemes. The applicability of the nucleus estate production model therefore depends on the nature of the crop; oil palm and tea are two that have been tried successfully in PNG, while the Cape Rodney scheme has also been promising for rubber. It would appear that cocoa does not lend itself so well to the nucleus estate model as there are fewer benefits accruing to scale from a larger central fermentary. However, it would be worthwhile to pursue the models – or variants of them – on a scheme currently contemplated in the Airagilpua River Itni area of Gloucester.

Cattle Under Coconuts

Some potential appears to exist for raising cattle under the shade of coconuts, especially in the north coast areas such as near Kimbe and in the west, near Gloucester, where a minimum of three months a year with rainfalls of not more than 100 mm enables sown grasses to compete with regenerating shrubs. Cattle were also seen under coconuts at the much wetter site of Ablingi plantation on the south coast, but in the time available the team was unable to investigate further whether such practices were ecologically feasible in this zone or to gain data on animal health, fattening rates and marketing.

An excellent example is, however, provided by the high quality management of Bob Wilson at Numundo, near Kimbe, an estate owned by Coconut Products Ltd, a subsidiary of Carpenters Ltd. He grazes 1,500 head of cattle (Santa Gertrudis and Brahmin), and sells 250 to 300 head per year. He achieves a 70 percent calving rate and sells at an average live weight of 195-200 kilos, after about 20 months. A barge operated by Coastal Shipping Ltd can take 100-150 head from Kimbe to Rabaul and he had perfected care of the animals on the barge to the extent that only one or two beasts at most were lost. Pasture under the coconut palms is mostly paspalum, with para grass being in-planted. The cattle are very healthy and there are few problems, as they are sprayed over a fortnight with DDT to combat screw worm fly. This estate was still operating successfully 20 years later.

There seems to be a real possibility of expanding cattle production on New Britain to the detriment of Australian imported cattle. However, the expensive government-owned abattoir is most inefficient, operating only for two hours a day and having a throughput of only about 750 head of cattle per year, although the local demand is estimated to be of the order of 2,000 per year. Moreover, the holding yards are inadequate and only larger companies like CPL are able to send beasts to be slaughtered, since they have other estates for holding cattle near Rabaul.

Settler Schemes

Settler schemes, comprising individualised holdings of a few hectares each, are historically attractive, not only in Papua New Guinea but also throughout the tropical world. Governments widely believe that settler schemes contribute significantly to production, general revenue and rural income by producing substantially higher output than normal; utilise unused land; and provide outlets for settlers from over-populated regions. Frequently, the administration in PNG has expressed the view that settlement schemes of individualised land tenure with secure title is greatly superior as a mode of production over customary forms of land holding, but it has been fully demonstrated only when planning and support for the schemes has been thorough rather than ad hoc, and when the total costs of the schemes have become very substantial. Moreover, the settler schemes which have been markedly successful in production and income terms – Cape Hoskins and Cape Rodney – are really nucleus estate ventures depending mostly on a larger central estate or processing and organisation nucleus. At the time of costing, the collapse of prices for both oil palm and rubber make the survival of even these schemes somewhat questionable: they are in desperate need of at least short-term government help.[4]

In general, expansion of settler schemes in PNG has not fully confirmed administration faith placed in them, although they have enjoyed some success. Settlers do not automatically switch from being subsistence farmers working 10 to 12 hours a week on their gardens to cash croppers who invest three or four times more man-hours a week on their holdings. The settlers themselves have also shared the unrealistically high expectations of government as to the levels of incomes that could be gained. Where government has not provided the basic infrastructure such as access roads, and there have been problems of collecting and marketing produce, output has been low. Often agencies have been slow to grant loans to settlers and few settlers have understood credit. Although settlers have often gone through a selection process, it appears that some who were chosen merely waited to gain the title to land with the possibility of future capital gain, or were interested in employing labour to do the actual productive work.[5]

The elaborate planning that led to the establishment of the Cape Hoskins Oil Palm Scheme has been heavily criticised[6] and by members of the WNB government on the grounds that local people were largely ignored and not involved or invited to participate in the scheme. This basic principle of involving local people in schemes should not be lost sight of, but at the same time it must not be forgotten that local people always seem to be the first to abandon their holdings at the onset of low prices or other difficulties (no persons of WNB origin purchased a settlement in the Hoskins Scheme from 1976-79), while the most successful settlers seem to be those drawn from groups whose home was some distance away,[7] perhaps because they had few alternative opportunities and the demands of their kin groups were less pressing. Where settlement schemes are sponsored by government, there should be regulations prohibiting the purchase of more than one smallholding by any one settler, and there should be provisions enabling settlers' children to inherit the property, but without any subdivision occurring. Where settler schemes are planned by government, there appears to be much merit in recommending two major cash crops rather than one (e.g. cocoa and hybrid coconut, or coffee and hybrid coconuts) to spread the risk. Moreover, a third of the holding should be devoted to food crops under a short rotation pattern.

The team is unable to recommend at present that government should sponsor any settlement scheme of this type. Nucleus estate ventures do, however, appear to be more promising, with the larger scale of output from a larger scheme likely to give a better return on investment. However, some success might accrue from grass-roots settler schemes of the 'get-on-with-it' type that require little government investment. Thus, once the Kandrian-Eseli road is improved, that route and the Gloucester-Sag Sag road should stimulate smallholder activity, so long as marketing outlets can be substantially improved. Such basic infrastructure is essential; having built the routes, it is government's job to see that these roads 'work' in stimulating production. Shipping, however, remains the most economic form of transport.

Smallholders

Looked at in the long view, smallholder planting of cocoa and coffee has been remarkably successful in Papua New Guinea over time. Thus, from 1956 to 1976, in both the lowlands and highlands, village areas bearing both crops increased from 4,000 ha to over 83,000 ha, with the combined output rising from 370 tonnes to almost 52,000 tonnes. This significant agricultural development was achieved with very low development costs and slight labour input. It has been estimated that coffee, cocoa and copra growers spend on average a maximum of less than 30 man-days per year on their smallholdings.[8] Thus, these crops as currently cultivated make limited demands on the time and resources of villagers, and this cash cropping at village level has absorbed directly only a very small amount of public capital. Apart from limited technical help – the assistance with planting materials at the early stages of development – only K1.6 million (or less than 11 percent of the aggregate value of village loans) was allocated by the PNG Development Bank over the period 1966-77 into copra, cocoa and coffee smallholders.[9] This form of rural development – the expansion of the area devoted to cash crops – rather than the intensification of production is the characteristic first stage of the economic development process. It is likely to remain the main feature of PNG involvement in commercial production for some time to come.

Models for coffee, oil palm and cocoa are discussed, derived from World Bank sources. The advantages of the Hoskins Oil Palm Scheme are seen as:

- a large increase in export earnings;
- large numbers of smallholders earning high incomes (when prices are high);
- significant tax revenues to national and provincial government (when prices are high);
- a focal point for local development in administration and trade;
- improved delivery of social services to a concentrated population.

Against these must be set the following disadvantages:

- a high requirement for imported capital assets and skills;
- social tensions arising from cultural differences and income disparities between settler groups and local people and between different settler groups;
- social problems of drunkenness, prostitution and malnutrition etc.;
- potential drain on government resources when prices fall below costs of production;
- danger of creating an elitist urban enclave attracting a disproportionate amount of WNBPG resources.

A clearer policy is required at national DPI level as to whether the individual family farm is a socially acceptable model of commercial production, and, if so, government resources should be more closely geared to its support.

The following strategy is recommended for promoting smallholder products:

- Wherever possible, crops should be recommended which are not only ecologically suitable but which are also likely to give the best price in the medium to long term.
- It is vital that buying points be sufficiently numerous to be reasonably accessible to most villagers.
- Buying points *must always* have sufficient cash to pay for crop purchases on the spot.
- Organisation of shipping services and advice (by radio etc.) as to shipping dates are important to improve regularity and maintain frequency.
- Money will have more utility if trade stores are reasonably common, well stocked, well run and contain a reasonable range of desired goods.
- Storage of perishable products at shipping points and advice on maintaining quality are necessary.

- Every effort should be made to strengthen motivation by improving incentive and linkage to the market. Extension officers can then come in to smooth the process, help with technical matters and provide storage advice.

The widespread introduction of new cash crops to the study area should not be considered until production levels and marketing arrangements are satisfactory for existing crops such as coffee, cocoa and chillies. This will involve setting up:

- an effective marketing system which can buy product for cash at any time; and
- an effective extension service to educate the farmers in maintenance and processing procedures and quality standards.

In particular, an attempt should be made to revive smallholder and shifting cultivator production of birds-eye chillies where rainfall is not too high. Attention should be focused on smallholders and shifting cultivators in all accessible areas (but initially in a limited area) along the coast and along inland roads such as the Kandrian to Eseli and Cape Gloucester to Sag Sag roads.

Trials should be initiated with crops such as rubber and pepper for possible introduction at a later stage.

Plantations

Every formal settlement scheme should include enforceable sanctions against serious under-utilisation of land. Stabilisation funds for all new cash crops should be considered at the beginning of major production promotion programmes. The climate of uncertainty created by the plantation acquisition scheme should be recognised by national government, and measures taken to reassure owners about future security and ownership so that they are encouraged to rehabilitate and replant their properties.

The economic viability of alternative methods of rehabilitating and replanting of moribund plantations should be investigated. Combinations of coconuts, coffee, cocoa and cattle are recommended. In particular, the Lindenhafen plantation near Gasmata is adjacent to an area of sparsely populated land which may be suitable for a nucleus plantation and associated outgrower smallholdings.

As a means of increasing the economic activity on the south coast of West New Britain, the possibility should be investigated of extending to the south coast the proposed development at Airagilpua of a nucleus cocoa estate (or plantation) with smallholders.

Marketing – A Vicious Circle

Very little information is available on the production, purchase or marketing of cash crops in West New Britain, and it is very difficult to identify the marketed output from the study area. The decline in plantation copra production seems, until recently, to have been largely offset by smallholder production.

The price and marketing problems of copra have the most important implications for the study area. As the copra plantations have, in the main, recently ceased operation, there is no longer the minimum load of local produce on offer (10 tonne loads) to attract coastal vessels to pick up. Only a small number of missions continue to handle locally produced copra.

West New Britain is caught in a vicious circle: marketing facilities and transport are inadequate because the volume of marketed surplus is low, but the marketed surplus is low because marketing facilities and transport are inadequate (and costly).

The DPI role to act as 'buyer of last resort' does not appear to be operating in the study area due to poor quality of certain crops (itself a reflection of lack of adequate extension) and insufficient funds available for purchase, as well as lack of transport. The combination of low produce prices and the costs of transport from the study area to Kimbe do not provide copra producers with an incentive to harvest. This is less true of higher value by weight commodities such as coffee, cocoa and chillies. The lack of information about, and understanding of, the DPI's role in quality control (grading standards), marketing and transport deductions leads producers in the study area to feel they are being cheated. Extension in the marketing field is as important as extension on crop production.

West New Britain does not appear to have a comparative advantage in any product where import substitution is desirable (beef, fish, poultry, eggs, pigs). The market itself is too restricted to justify production of more perishable produce including milk, fresh fruit and vegetables. The low value for weight of staple root crops means that it is very unlikely that West New Britain will be able to market them outside the island.

The provision of simple local market facilities is the most useful and cost-effective measure to promote increased consumption and import substitution in perishable foodstuffs. The trading and transportation of agricultural produce is more economic when combined with that of agricultural inputs and consumer goods, and there is in general little danger of the encouragement of cash crops at the expense of food crop production and nutritional levels. However, in Lakalai, oil palm cultivation is doing so well that many hamlets are now concentrating on this cash crop and neglecting subsistence crops.

In the absence of any significant cash outlet for cattle products, there is no substantial case for distributing improved genetic stock. The operation of the abattoir at Rabaul should be investigated as it is currently running at a fraction of its throughput capability.

For both coffee and cocoa, the aim of securing equality between provinces requires either provincial quotas, or a nationally-coordinated agreement about future expansion programmes over the next few years. The longer-term prospects for arabica and robusta coffee are reasonably good and may be further improved by the International Coffee Organisation campaign to promote consumption in the USA which has been declining slowly but consistently since the early 1960s. International collaboration is required to check any further short-term fall in cocoa prices and to reduce the severity of future cyclical trends. During most of the 1980s, little or no improvement in prices in real terms can be expected until the end of the decade unless a serious outbreak of disease or economic dislocation occurs in one of the main producing countries. There is a strong case, in a time of a rapidly declining Cocoa Industry Fund, for the government to promote a lower-cost industry based on increased smallholder production.

In real terms, there is little hope during the 1980s of any significant improvement in copra and coconut oil prices over the average level for 1981. For copra, there is a case for a subvention to the Copra Stabilisation Fund over the next two years to establish a more efficient industry; and despite a slight improvement in the first quarter of 1982 for oil palm products, the prospects of a return of palm oil prices in real terms to the average level of 1980 ($484) are remote. We concur with the Copra Marketing Board decision not to open a sub-depot at Kandrian, as it would mean meeting the costs out of already depressed returns to the copra producers in general. It could only be justified if it were substantially to increase the amount of copra on offer. A less costly alternative is to appoint an established trader in Kandrian as the Board's agent. Serious consideration should be given at national level to the replenishment of the Copra Stabilisation Fund through an annual subvention for the next two years in order to give time for a more efficient industry to be established.

The market prospects for high quality birds-eye chillies from Papua New Guinea generally appear good, provided that a reputation as a reliable supplier can be re-established. The initial success of the chilli programme in the study area demonstrated that farmers are prepared to innovate. A future programme should ensure that the DPI provide the necessary extension and marketing support, and that producers should be encouraged to bring produce to the buying points. This will be facilitated if production is concentrated – initially – in selected areas.

West New Britain should examine closely the economics of the production/storage/processing/marketing chain to identify those agricultural commodities for which it has a comparative advantage insofar as the wider market of Papua New Guinea is concerned. An initial examination suggested that smallholder production in the study area of beef cattle, fish, poultry, eggs, pigs, milk, root crops and fresh vegetables *cannot* be justified for this wider market alone.

The government should provide simple market facilities at growth centres in the study area as the most useful and cost effective measure to promote increased consumption and import substitution in perishable foodstuffs through market development. The DPI should use, on an agency basis, well-established trading enterprises as a more cost-effective method both to supply agricultural inputs and to purchase agricultural produce. A regular analysis should be made of the source of copra produced, in order to ascertain actual production in the study area and in order to calculate the West New Britain share of the export volume.

Transport

Shipping

The team concluded that:

- There is an excess of shipping capacity operating between Rabaul, Fulleborn and Kandrian.
- The setting up of the Provincial Shipping Authority appears to pre-empt or undercut the role of private shipping firms in transporting produce out of the region. Whether the province can continue to operate an efficient and regular service in view of the high operating cost of their vessels and their dual purpose nature (commercial and government patrolling) is a matter of some doubt. A complementary and cooperative relationship is needed between the Provincial Shipping Authority, coastal shipping companies and village work boats to ensure that costly overlaps of services do not occur for what are likely to be (at least initially) small cargoes.
- There are a number of excellent natural harbours on the south coast – Arawe, Kandrian, Ablingi, Lindenhafen, Gasmata, Fulleborn – most of which could be used by large ocean-going vessels.

- It is recommended that improvement work be carried out on the Kokopo wharf.

Roads

The team reached the following conclusions concerning roads within the study area, and the proposed Kandrian-Kimbe road link:

- Six large-scale road projects and eight lesser roads were evaluated by a standard cost-benefit methodology in the Department of Transport and Civil Aviation (DTCA) study; not one on this basis showed a positive nett present value, i.e. is worth undertaking. Roading is extremely expensive given the terrain and climate of the study area. The DTCA study concluded that, to be economically viable, a road is needed to serve 100 people per km on flat land or 200 per km in mountain terrain. On that basis, the Laiama-Eseli road needed a 'justifying' population of 2,000; in fact, it had about 1,500.
- The cost of a cross-island road is very great indeed. The estimated cost of a cross-island road from Eseli to the Via River (70 km) is about K3 million or about K43,000 per km. The annual maintenance cost on a cross-island road from Kimbe to Kandrian of 220 km is likely to be approximately K290,000, or an average of some K1,300 per km, which is higher than the K1,100 estimated by DTCA for existing provincial roads. Thus, it seems extremely unlikely that the construction and later maintenance of a transinsular road could be justified on economic grounds alone.
- The freight rate by road from Kandrian to Kimbe at K0.50 per tonne-km would be K110 compared to only K24 by sea, a figure quoted by Burns Philp for a round-island service. Even using a local work boat, it is unlikely to exceed K45 per tonne. Thus, sea transport is far cheaper than road transport on a cross-island road.
- Passenger fares should be cheaper for Kandrian-Kimbe on a hypothetical cross-island road compared to sea transport, and the time taken by the journey would be considerably less. However, the very small size of the population on the south coast makes this factor of little account.

The eastern cross-island route from Kandrian-Gasmata-Fulleborn to the Galai-Ubai road (with a 'non-forestry' length of 175-200 km) would probably cost an average of K20,000 per km, or K3.5-K4 million. The total distance from Kandrian to Kimbe by this route is estimated at about 350 km compared to 220 kms by the western route, with the Kandrian-Fulleborn section duplicating the cheaper sea route.

The construction of roads set out in the Five Year Plan would represent a very large capital commitment by the government. It would appear that the projected system of roading would total some 600 km, double the present provincial road network and involve an extra provision of the order of K700,000 per year for maintenance.

Transport Solutions in the Future

In view of the serious deficiencies experienced by the south coast with respect to the reliability and frequency of shipping services for exports and imports, there is a great merit in the alternative proposals of the DTCA study. These proposals are that the government should either:

- subsidise a regular shipping service from the south coast via Cape Gloucester and Bali Witu to Kimbe; or
- itself operate such a service using a work boat with dumb-barges.

The former is the most economically advantageous proposal and would operate for three years before the project became self-supporting.

The provincial government has already purchased three vessels. The operation of one, the MV *Tavur*, in its first monthly schedule allotted one week for transporting government officers on patrol, one week for visits to health centres, one week for buying agricultural produce and one week for transporting produce to Kimbe. This illustrates the problems that can arise with government becoming involved in commercial ventures: half the ship's time is spent on non-commercial, purely government matters. It is highly unlikely that this kind of service will meet the grower's needs, while its cost to the government (and the constant competition between two largely incompatible uses) is likely to be prohibitive.

The team has grave doubts as to the suitability of the vessels purchased for the provincial government. They are excessively expensive, costing about K52,000 instead of the price of more suitable wooden vessels of about K30,000. They have an unnecessarily high-powered engine (115 hp), which at cruising speed consumes 19 litres of fuel per hour instead of a more appropriate engine of 43 hp which consumes only 7.7 litres per hour. The additional speed of *Tavur*-type vessels would not appear to outweigh these disadvantages of much greater purchase and operating costs.

Major road projects, such as a Kandrian-Kimbe link or a coastal road from Kandrian to Fulleborn, are not justifiable on purely economic grounds and should not be proceeded with unless there are overwhelming social, political or administrative benefits.

The main roads which will revert to the government as a result of logging operations will be very valuable assets, but it must be appreciated that their proper maintenance will constitute a substantial financial commitment. If minor (feeder) roads are to be built, priority should be given to those leading inland rather than along the coast.

Construction and maintenance of the Kandrian-Eseli road, and of other roads in the Kandrian area, will mean that there will need to be a Works sub-depot in Kandrian. Local people should be mobilised to help maintain feeder roads.

Improvements to the marine transport system should take precedence over roads. The vessels of the Provincial Shipping Authority should operate on a commercial basis, and the other government agencies should pay commercial rates for their use of them.

If the provincial government wishes to encourage south-coast producers/consumers to use Kimbe as a main port, rather than the closer ports of Lae or Rabaul, then –

- maximum use should be made of any commercial service offering between Kandrian and Kimbe, by using Kandrian as a collection/ trans-shipment point;
- if no such service materialises and Shipping Authority vessels are used, competitive (and therefore sub-economic) rates would have to be charged for the Kandrian-Kimbe sector.

The Shipping Authority vessel to be stationed at Kandrian should offer a regular local coastal service, delivering export cargoes (e.g. copra) to Kandrian for trans-shipment. In this case, it is unlikely that the traffic would justify the purchase of any more work boats by local communities.

Any request for government assistance in financing work boats should be examined closely to see if the proposal is viable. The use of work boats should be confined to the local coasting trade, and in this case a 24-foot boat is likely to be more suitable than one of 32 feet. If government funds are involved, government should ensure that proper financial accounts are kept and should offer assistance and training to this end.

Kandrian should become the main buying/trans-shipment centre for the south coast, with adequate storage and handling facilities. Payments to producers must be made as quickly as possible. The provision of bulk fuel storage at Kandrian should be discussed with the fuel and shipping companies.

The extension of the Kandrian Vocational Training Centre to repair outboard motors on a commercial basis should be examined. The requisite tools and equipment, if not already there, would have to be provided, and a substantial initial investment in spare parts would be essential; but the existence of such a facility would be of very real benefit to the local owners. The Kilenge Mission should be approached to see if it would assist in the establishment of a similar facility at the mission.

Forestry

Probably the most important chapter in this report was on forestry, for the forest resources of the project area at the present state of knowledge represent the greatest single resource for the future. Moreover, since West New Britain has nearly 32 percent of the undeveloped commercial forests remaining in Papua New Guinea (with 5,000 sq. kms lying in the project area), and the country as a whole has nearly 26 percent of the timber resources of the entire Pacific Basin, its wise and efficient utilisation is the greatest development challenge of all. Over three-quarters of the study area is covered with relatively undisturbed tropical rain forest, the largest single forest type being lowland rain forest which, as in the rest of PNG, is unique in its species composition due to its geographical position on the Sahul shelf at its most easterly end.

PNG rain forests are related to those of Malaysia with its 500 species of valuable *Dipterocarps* (PNG has six such species). Standing as it does on the Sahul shelf, PNG has also acquired several Australian species such as *Eucalyptus deglupta*, and certain Antarctic species such as *Araucaria*, *Agathis* and *Nothofagus*. WNB forests are very varied in composition, but not so complex as the rest of PNG's forests which often carry some 100 economic species per hectare. In WNB, the bulk of the stand consists of relatively few commercial species. Taun (*Pometia pinnata*), Malas (*Homalium foetidum*), Erima (*Octomeles sumatrana*), *Calophyllum* species, *Terminalia* species and *Alstonia scholaris*, in varying proportions in different areas, make up some 50 percent of average forest stands. *Eucalyptus deglupta* occurs in pure stands on river alluvial gravels, and Kauri pine (*Agathis alba*) in valleys north of Fulleborn.[10]

Economic yields are generally lower in PNG, which average some 50m³/ha over 50 cms dbh (diameter breast height) as against Malaysian *Dipterocarp* forest with some 150m³/ha. Pure stands of Kamerere (*E. deglupta*) are an exception and can reach 290m³/ha.[11]

In studying forestry, the team was led inevitably to issues of national and provincial importance. In view of the great volume of the country's timber resources and its escalating value as long as its rapid, large-scale exploitation can be delayed, the nation and province have a short breathing space (for within a few years a number of timber species which at present have little marketable value will be in great demand). This period should be used for the substantial upgrading of staff by crash training programmes in Papua New Guinea and overseas, as well as expansion in numbers of staff.

The greatest need is to *control* wisely, and to *direct* and *regulate* the utilisation of timber resources. The first requirement for this is a much more efficient and strong Forest Service, possessing greater confidence that would come from greatly improved competence. (Withholding export permission for all or part of a log shipment is an effective way in securing the cooperation of a logging company that is not observing its contract.) Moreover, with West New Britain destined to become one of the great forest areas left in the Pacific Basin, the pressure and blandishments from foreign multinational companies desiring access to the province are likely to become intense.

The need for a strong, competent and *honest* public service (as well as a Forest Department within it) is obvious, and it will require close support and back up, especially in the provision of higher order services and sophisticated skills (such as the advice of company lawyers, marketing specialists and accountants) from central government to enable the provincial government to deal with transfer pricing and other complex business tactics employed by large-scale foreign firms. The provision of these skills, the establishment of the appropriate institutions, the large-scale training (both in-service and at institutions) involved, the proper organisation of marketing of timber products and the question of research are, in total, very significant issues, and in the view of the team they should be considered as a whole in relation to the future nature and capacity of the timber industry in all its aspects and the forest service at national and provincial levels. As such, its scope clearly calls for overseas aid for at least an eight-to-10-year period, with progressive devolution to national and provincial officers as they become trained and experienced in the many new functions.

The team recommends that Papua New Guinea make a genuine effort to move beyond the rudimentary pioneering stage in its forest industry and recognise the serious limitations of continuing to work on forest research data extrapolated from Indonesia and the Philippines. A reliable PNG database is essential to enable the Office of Forests to specify its requirements for future forest renewal and follow-up land use; to achieve this, a *lowland forest research institute should be founded*. Such an institute could install permanent and temporary sample plots, check forest inventories and carry out reforestation trials. The establishment of such an institution would demonstrate that the Papua New Guinea forest service was becoming a professional service worthy of overseas aid. In time, it would enable a genuine effort to be made to replace the volumes and values of timber removed.

Currently and in the immediate years ahead, enormous pressures are likely to bear on national and provincial politicians for early disposal of forest resources. Whatever the true facts of the matter might be, the Vanimo forestry controversy of 1981-82 illustrates the situation. Consideration and support by Cabinet at both national and provincial levels is necessary to enable politicians to withstand these pressures and to evaluate the issues in a proper manner. In the same way, great pressures are likely to bear on the Office of Forests and individual forest officers involved with effectively controlling exploitation, collecting revenue and monitoring the required programme of development. If they are not backed by a strong, honest and competent government, they will certainly not be able to withstand the pressures and temptations. At the same time, they need a substantial increase in staff numbers as well as a crash training programme. The WNB government staff in forestry of 19, with an annual forestry budget of K92,000 in 1981 (with no sum allocated to research or training), is quite inadequate for the large task involved.

As 80 percent of the project area was considered unsuited to permanent agriculture, and forestry is so important, the effects of intensive felling were examined by the team. Unacceptable damage to soils occurred in areas of North WNB Province as a result of intensive felling: organic matter and topsoil were severely disturbed, and the already compacted subsoil suffered further compaction as a result of drag and logging operations. It is suggested that soil examination be carried out in logged areas on sites of potential permanent agriculture.

Forest utilisation raised the question of follow-up land use, and the team endorses the proposals of Brightwell (1981) for better evaluation and execution of land use schemes. Foreign investment in log exporting should be restricted to more intensive logging operations when agricultural development, reforestation or the production of wood chips is a major consideration. It is suggested that where leasehold land is available in larger areas, the forests should be used for short rotation chipwood crops with some enrichment planting on less accessible land. Customary land would be used for enrichment planting, both by line-plantations and shade planting. Replanting should be done by the landowners under Forest Department supervision and the trees belong to the landowners.

Given the situation of WNB Province, considerable merit lies in small-scale mills, enabling local people to control and directly benefit from their own resources. The team suggests that if they are found by further investigation to be viable, up to five small-scale local mills could be established in the project area. While the appropriate locations of these are being determined and timber rights negotiated, potential employees of the new mills should be sent for training to the extended programme of the Timber Industries Training Centre at Lae. The team commends the quality of the training provided at the Centre but suggests that the programme be expanded to cover intermediate logging technology. It would be useful as part of their experience for trainees to work on actual milling operations.

The Provincial Forest Authority is unfortunately under heavy pressure for forest development to be pushed ahead, and in view of the shortage of revenue this option is tempting. However, the team believes this should be resisted as the schemes are often premature, conflict with national priorities and invariably encourage foreign-owned investment at the expense of small local development.

It is strongly recommended that the advice of the Office of Forests be followed with respect to the timing and disposition of all forest concessions under the existing Forestry Act 1973. Failure to do so will mean that the control needed by the Office of Forests will not be provided and the millers will have greater opportunities to take advantage of the landowners. The team also warns against a whole series of National Timber Authority agreements being negotiated in a way that would enable their gradual accumulation by possibly one company, so that collectively they could form one large block. The exploitation of one large virtually consolidated block would not be subject to the safeguards inherent in the conditions of a Timber Rights Purchase (TRP) permit. The team suggests that it is logical not to accept any large-scale forest development projects for the project area until existing concessions are properly controlled, all permit conditions are complied with, government machinery (at national and provincial levels) is examined and responsibility nationalised.

The team recommends that a commercial management group experienced in the forestry and timber industry should take a share in the management of the forests of the project area (and a share in the profits) for a period during which a devolution in management skills would take place. Furthermore, it is recommended that a nationally-owned marketing agency be set up, staffed initially partly by experienced expatriates together with nationals, to organise and plan the marketing of timber and timber products. A more aggressive policy of marketing home-grown products seems to be needed.

The team believes that a clear-sighted policy of import-substitution would greatly stimulate the local timber industry in Papua New Guinea, promoting the growth of 'down stream' industry. Thus, if the public service was required to use locally-made wooden furniture (office desks and chairs) rather than expensive, imported metal desks and chairs, the local timber and joinery industries would be assisted. If such a policy could be agreed upon in principle, the team would recommend a feasibility study in the project area on the establishment of a joinery factory (located perhaps at Kandrian or Gasmata). Further, the possibility of manufacture of low-cost housing modules, possibly at a later stage of development, should be closely considered (at present, such modules are imported from East New Britain). In the event of this manufacture being feasible, the south coast shipping route from Rabaul to Lae passing by the project area may become important.

Fishing

The first requirement of a programme to develop fisheries is to quantify the resource potential by gathering reliable data on the spectrum of marine resources which might be exploited, the level of sustainable exploitation of fish stocks and the potential of 'industrial' fishing. A dialogue is needed between the Provincial Fisheries Division and the national level on the costs and benefits of a marine resource assessment programme. Current indications are that the coastal waters ecosystem is fragile and, although supporting a diverse marine life, would be rapidly depleted by consistently heavy fishing pressure or under 'industrial' fishing. An experimental fishing programme should also be initiated to indicate the appropriate methods and gear needed to diversify the operations of the Kimbe Fisheries Development Project. It would also help to decide the location and specifications of further fisheries bases in the project area.

The team was disappointed to find that fishing forms merely a sporadic part of the subsistence livelihood of villages, and motivation towards developing fishing as a commercial venture is not high. Although Chowning[12] reports that interest is high among the Kove, it seemed that in comparison with a number of other South Pacific societies, the level of fishing skills and enthusiasm for fishing in the project area was not great. The task of fisheries extension officers in strengthening the motivation and arousing the interest of villagers in increasing a marketable surplus may therefore be difficult. It is clear that the requirement is for a team of competent, highly motivated and efficient extension workers. It is suggested that the problem areas that need the most attention are the logistics of marketing marine products; the development of appropriate technology for catching fish (and other marine products); storage, processing and preservation; the diversification of the artisanal fishing industry; business organisation; and upgrading of fishing vessels.

It is recommended that the first five-year programme concentrate on arousing the interests and imparting skills to fishermen in a small number of selected villages (including the Kove) with the aim of developing small, self-reliant, household industries producing high quality and, in some cases, high revenue-earning, marine products. It is suggested that emphasis be given to the following products:

- rock lobsters;
- bêche-de-mer and shells of commercial value;
- reef fish.

If some satisfactory development of self-reliance has occurred in the first five years, the five-10 year input should focus on increased business development, the expansion of product markets, upgrading of fishing vessels and consideration of the location of a commercial fisheries base at Kandrian. The main development alternatives at this point would be the development of a deep-sea line fishery and the localisation of baitfish catching.

The fishing project in many ways is an impressive innovation to the province, but it is currently heavily subsidised by government funds. The main reasons for its running at a loss are the high operating costs due to using sophisticated, energy-intensive vessels and processing/ preservation equipment; insufficient throughput of fish products; and competition from cheap frozen fish imports. A number of alternative strategies and marketing possibilities are possible that could help to make the project more efficient.

The provincial and national fisheries departments should realise that the dual goals of the project do in fact conflict:

- the need to establish the project as a viable commercial enterprise;
- reliance of the project on local fishermen to generate the catch throughput.

The project must be made commercially viable within the next five years, while the provision of an extension service for the subsistence sector is also improved. In the five-10-year development period, the province's commercial project should develop closer links with both the subsistence and national industrial fisheries sectors.

Rural Welfare

Resource Allocation

It is clear that at present there is no objective evaluation of the access to, distribution and impact of rural welfare services in West New Britain, nor is there the database and statistical monitoring that could enable such an evaluation to be regularly, accurately and easily carried out.

It is also clear that, with the exception of a few coastal communities, those areas which have not accepted the Local Government Council system have not received a fair share in the distribution of rural welfare facilities. These are, in the main, the smaller, most isolated villages, least linked into a cash economy.

The provincial government needs to identify appropriate economic indicators in order to distribute its share of each national sectoral programme budget within its districts. This study proposes certain provincial indicators which are compatible with national indicators, are easy to measure and can be disaggregated to a sufficiently low level to be able to be used for sub-district planning purposes. However, as a prerequisite to the use of these indicators, a provincial statistician should be appointed whose task will be to establish the database for the Provincial Data System.

The statistician could also complete, check and update the Rural Community Register, obtain all 1980 Census information including long- and short-form cross classifications, and advise each division on the establishment of its sectoral database. The statistician would then prepare a baseline set of indicators by census division, local government council and sub-district area, and work with each division on the regular monitoring of the level of its indicators and assist the provincial planner in analysing the areas of need in each sector, and in identifying projects and programmes to meet that need.

Education

The WNBPG's development strategy is to provide community education for all, with the emphasis on retaining young people within the village on completion of their studies. In the Kandrian-Gloucester area, there are 35 community schools with 17 staff and 3,095 pupils in the 7-12 age group. (This represents an enrolment of 60 percent of that age group compared with 78 percent in the rest of West New Britain and 82 percent as the national target for 1980.) Only two schools offer a complete range of classes from Grade 1 to 6, and only 19 schools have a Grade 6 class. The majority have two, three or four classes. Three-fifths of the schools are in isolated villages, where the teachers qualify for the disadvantaged school supplement.

The pupil-staff ratio is below the target national average, but reflects a low enrolment and small catchment rather than a positive attempt to improve standards.

There is a strong correlation between the percentage of the catchment school age group enrolled and the percentage whose village is within one hour's travelling time of the school. The percentage inside the threshold of access varies considerably within the study area, from 83 percent in Kandrian Coastal division to 29 percent and 15 percent in the adjacent Census Divisions of Passismanua and Gimi Rauto respectively. Enrolment likewise varies from 73 percent of the school-age group in Kandrian Coastal to 42 percent in Gimi Rauto respectively. The enrolment of girls is only two-thirds that of boys. An analysis of absolute progression rates suggests that while in West New Britain about 70 percent of children enrolled in Grades 1 and 2 are likely to progress to Grades 5 and 6, only 42 percent of children in the disadvantaged schools in the study area will do so, and only 33 percent of girls in such schools. Two in every three girls are likely to drop out before completing primary education.

As the Provincial Data System analysis of the access of villages to community schools was insufficiently complete, consistent, accurate and relevant, the team recalculated the access of each village and identified eight villages where a new community school was needed most. These eight schools, if built, will bring an average of 80 children each within the threshold of access and reduce the total of the school-age group outside the threshold from 41 percent to 28 percent, or by nearly one-third. Future community schools will become increasingly difficult to justify due to the successively smaller age-group catchment.

Educational achievement is measured, in both popular and political consciousness, by the result of the national Grade 6 examinations and selection for high school. Enrolment of the Grade 6 age group in the study area (43 percent) was only three-quarters that of the rest of the province, and particularly low for girls (28 percent) in the Kandrian district. The four educational division zones that constitute the study area were amongst the lowest in the province in terms of Grade 6 exam results, with an average of 38 percent compared with 59 percent for the rest of West New Britain. A mark in the range of 55-65 is the minimum required to stand a good chance of entry to high school on merit alone.

One contributory factor to the low achievement of primary school leavers in the study area must be the high turnover of staff. Nearly two-thirds of all staff were in acting posts in 1982 and 60 percent were in their first year at their school. There does not, however, appear to be much difference in this respect between disadvantaged schools and others.

Consideration should be given by the WNBPG to a 'continuity supplement' for all teachers eligible for the disadvantaged school salary supplement and payable for each year after the first that they work at their school; a fees subsidy to parents of pupils from the study area who are selected for high school; and utilising spare capacity at Kandrian High School to offer a remedial year to below standard Grade 6 school leavers to bring them up to Grade 7 entry standard.

Health

The provision of aid posts varies considerably within the Kandrian-Gloucester district, the Census Division of Bariai being best served and that of Passismanua nearly four times worse off.

The percentage of the population that is outside an acceptable threshold of access to aid posts or health sub-centres (taken as two hours' travelling time) varies from around 5 percent in Bariai and Kandrian Coastal to 24 percent in Arawe, with Passismanua being dramatically worse off with 61 percent of the 1980 population more than two hours away from the nearest treatment centre.

The team's analysis of the existing locations of aid posts and sub-centres suggests that the location of five new aid posts could be planned to bring a further 23 villages with a population of 1,800 people within the threshold of access. These new aid posts could be sited at Lindenhafen in Gasmata CD, Woro in Arawe, Hutkihyu and Maum in Passismanua, and Mokukli in the Lamogai area of Kaliai, and would reduce the percentage of the population of the study area further than two hours' away by one-third (from 21 percent to 14 percent). The most dramatic improvement would be in Passismanua, reducing the proportion by over a half, from 61 percent to 29 percent. The location of further aid posts would have progressively more limited impact as only the most isolated villages would remain outside the threshold.

The evaluation of the impact of health programmes is done through the monitoring of the incidence of special communicable diseases by the provincial surveillance officer. At present, each health centre, sub-centre and aid post should send a monthly report. There appeared to the team to be several areas where significant improvements should be made in monitoring and surveillance in order to achieve an accurate, updated, comprehensive and statistically significant flow of information that can be analysed quickly.

The special nutritional surveys carried out in the study area suggest that malnutrition amongst children in the 0-5 year age group is worst in the inland villages – in Passismanua over 50 percent of the children surveyed suffered from mild-moderate malnutrition, although only a tiny percentage were severely malnourished. The major cause is probably a poorly balanced diet with little protein and only one food group. It is clear that with its resources the Nutrition Section cannot do more than monitor the province's nutritional status, and educate and influence those government officials and community leaders who have direct contact with villages. The improvement of nutritional status cannot be achieved in isolation from wider improvements in health status and educational achievement, and in general economic wellbeing. Nutrition education by all government personnel should be increased in those areas indicated as having severe malnutrition problems. The DPI should start an extension programme with special reference to those foods with a high protein content, e.g. legumes.

Conclusion

This chapter has argued that development can take many forms and has many dimensions. The scale, manner and rate of resource development are all major issues. While the raising of cash incomes, the generation of revenue and widening the taxable base are important goals, so too are the establishment of schools or aid posts, the achievement of improved efficiency in the public service, and greater continuity, experience, or sense of commitment in teaching posts or public service appointments. Moreover, people who are only slightly involved in the cash economy also have a right to receive assistance; for aid in strengthening their food crop systems when endangered; and for the protection of their forests, hunting or fishing grounds from large-scale spoliation. Thus, 'development', like 'government', has many faces and embraces many functions: promoting and stimulating sound or specialist advice; establishing infrastructure; and at the same time guarding, conserving, protecting and acting as trustees for future generations.

The business development arm of the Commerce Division needs to be able to provide accurate information to villagers who wish to operate their own small work boats. This example illustrates indeed a good deal of what the whole problem of development is all about: people involved in development need to understand the *real costs* of production activities and acquire the technical knowledge and skills that will enable them to make the most appropriate decisions, innovations and investments that are most likely to pay off. If they make the wrong decisions or operate costly, inefficient boats, their ventures will probably be doomed to failure.

Nowhere is the need for increased efficiency more necessary than in the public service. Papua New Guinea has one of the largest public services on a per capita basis amongst developing countries. Moreover, this public service has a critically important role to play in the virtual absence of an indigenous private sector, promoting and guiding social and economic development and monitoring and regulating large-scale foreign development projects. It is clear that recruitment into the public service is the most desirable career open to the best secondary school graduates: salary levels are about four to five times higher than the average per capita income, and it is almost impossible to dismiss public servants for incompetence or idleness. These factors, of course, make it expensive to run.

Although the creation of provincial governments has delivered some real advantages in bringing government closer to the people, the pool of skilled manpower, already small, has been entirely drained by the need to staff 19 provincial public services in addition to the national service. In view of the complexity of planning and difficulty of introducing effective rural development, there will be major problems for provincial governments in effectively carrying through appropriate programmes.

Recently, a rural development specialist with 10-years' experience of Papua New Guinea commented on the public service in general in these terms:

> ... the bureaucracy, on whom fell the major task of carrying out the rural development programme, was incapable of its implementation. It proved to be entrenched, urban orientated and as inefficient, uncoordinated and as immune to political pressures as the colonial administration before it. Finally the attitudes of the rural people were either not taken into account or were misconstrued. With thirty years experience of broken promises and failed projects behind them, villagers transferred their mistrust of colonial officials to national government officials. The general breakdown in government services which followed independence confirmed their suspicions and deepened their cynicism and they began refusing to cooperate in projects unless frequently unrealistically high returns were guaranteed to them.[13]

This assessment of the public service may appear to be too harsh: members of the team were impressed by the ability, commitment and genuine concern for village conditions displayed by a number of government officers. And the very commissioning of this study of a depressed area demonstrates the concern of central government for rural conditions and a determination to improve them. However, the emergence of an urban elite (consisting to a considerable extent of public servants), which many observers would say already exists in Papua New Guinea (at least in Port Moresby and Lae), brings with it a number of very real dangers. At a time when the provinces of Papua New Guinea have a great need for government by a dynamic, committed class of energetic, innovative leaders who are sensitive to the needs of ordinary villagers, there is a real danger of the emergence in some provinces of an indolent, incompetent, urban-based class who are used to expecting, as of right, a relatively high standard of Western-style consumption, who are becoming more and more remote from the needs of villagers, and who are increasingly involved in self-enrichment, power-seeking and corruption. The quality of the public service, at both provincial and national levels, is clearly a topic of the highest importance. It is reported that there is plenty of corruption at the local level too.

Government must be aware of the possibility that any development innovation might have unforeseen consequences and unexpected implications. The 'journeys toward progress' that all development agencies, whether in developed or developing countries, have to make, is to learn to anticipate the likely impact and possible repercussions of new developments, as well as how to adjust to and deal with the unforeseen consequences. It is important that development really does ameliorate and not worsen the conditions of living of the people. One way of improving performance in development is to monitor closely the cost effectiveness of programmes. And a healthy scepticism for many apparently beneficial innovations is worth preserving until the full costs, including recurrent costs and implications, become apparent and can be evaluated.

There is no magic in any particular development policy or project, just as a road is not necessarily the solution for every backward area. Often, in the long run, the most effective policies are those that are the least spectacular or glamorous, but which lay the groundwork in many quiet, sensible ways for genuine social progress.

On the last day before we left WNB, we still had a helicopter available so I asked team members if anyone would like to accompany me to spend the night in a small hamlet on the top of the Whiteman Range (2,000 m) in the centre of the island. No one volunteered so the helicopter dropped me before nightfall. The people welcomed me and I inspected the meagre thatched houses on the bleak ridge top. Most of the men had worked on coastal plantations and spoke Pidgin, but some of the women had never seen a European before. As my Pidgin was very limited, I could not communicate properly with the people so I learnt very little. It was an interesting experience and I slept in one of their houses. I was, however, pleased when I heard the hum of the helicopter approaching through the misty morning.

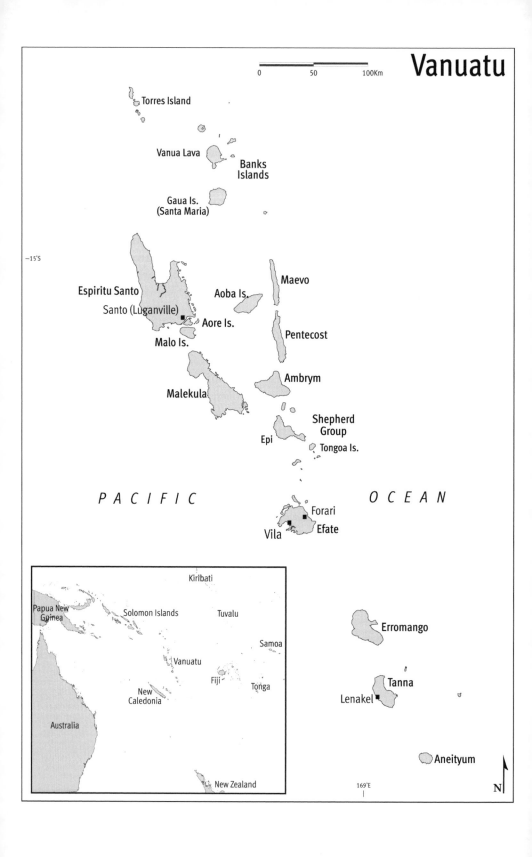

12

A Tale of Two Leaders: Independence, *Kastom* and Development in Vanuatu

'A Tale of Two Leaders' is partly based on 'Prophet in Paradise', an article I wrote under a pseudonym in New Zealand International Review, *September/October 1980. The essay arose from my two visits to Vanuatu, the first of which showed me why the British-French Condominium was often called the Pandemonium. When I was there in 1969, a French customs officer noticed that a visiting vessel had brought a load of New Zealand lamb, to which the British colonial staff was looking forward. However, he found something wrong with the import papers so the meat was dumped in the harbour. The next day was the turn of the British customs official and on that day some delectable chicken arrived from New Caledonia. Sadly too, the import documents were not quite correct so that cargo was also thrown overboard. Such tit-for-tat squabbles as well as different goals sought by the two European colonial powers added further complexities and obstacles to this extremely diverse mélange of cultures and languages. The country also exhibited a huge range of social groups, varying from the only slightly acculturated heathen Big Nambas of the remote mountains of central Malekula, to the sophisticated and highly missionised societies of Efate near Port Vila or the achievement-oriented Christians of Aoba.*

Late in 1977, following our successful surveys of the Gilbert and Ellice Islands and the Solomon Islands, the Ministry of Overseas Development, London, invited me to visit the New Hebrides. As independence was expected shortly, they hoped the local government would wish us to carry out a similar study and review the local economy and assess possibilities for future development. My colleague Roger Lawrence and I travelled to Vila and also to Espiritu Santo, Malekula and the southern island of Tanna. We had a meeting with Barak Sope, one of the leading politicians. He and the British officials were keen to initiate the survey but the French adhered to their common position of opposing British ideas: they turned the project down.

During the visit, I heard about the local leader Jimmy Stevens

*and his Nagriamel movement. I resolved to seek an interview
and our request was granted when we travelled to Espiritu Santo.
Talking to Jimmy Stevens, it became clear that the political
complexion of Vanuatu has for decades had a huge impact on
all aspects of life in the country. Somehow, a mix of extreme
political and religious movements and beliefs has led to a level
of volatility that is high even for Melanesia.*

*Later when I helped Tony Haas prepare Father Walter Lini's
autobiography from transcriptions of taped comments by him,
further light was shed on these issues. This new essay is an
attempt to understand a complex, multi-layered sectarianism
existing within a sense of nationalism that mostly coheres only
in the face of common and external threats.*

Introduction

Vanuatu is a Y-shaped group of 83 islands (12 large) totalling 12,200
sq. kms (see Figure 12.1). The two largest islands, Espiritu Santo (or
Santo) and Malekula, account for nearly one half of the total land area.
The large islands are volcanic with sharp mountain peaks, plateaux,
in some areas overlaid with limestone, and narrow coastal lowlands.
Dense tropical rainforests cover most areas, with some grasslands in
the south. Volcanic activity is common and earthquakes and tsunamis
are not infrequent.

Vanuatu, originally called the New Hebrides, has had a turbulent
past. Its sinister history is partly derived from its unhealthy humid
tropical climate and deadly diseases such as malaria and blackwater
fever, and the early reputation of its Melanesian people for their
ferocity, treachery and cannibalism. Undoubtedly, their hostility was
largely due to European traders making alliances with a certain tribe
only to find that there was an absence of powerful stabilising chiefs and
that their alliance incurred the jealousy of many competing tribes and
language groups.[1] Indeed, the most outstanding quality of Vanuatu is
the extraordinary diversity of cultures and languages. There are over
100 language groups, which is the greatest density of language forms
in the world. As Grace Molisa, the country's most outstanding woman
leader, has said, "every generalisation about Vanuatu is guaranteed to
be wrong".[2]

After the whalers of the early nineteenth century, explorer-traders
discovered rich forests of sandalwood on Erromango just as supplies
of this perfumed wood, so much desired by China, were exhausted

in Fiji. Later, sandalwood was found in quantity on Santo, Tanna and Anatom.[3] Missionaries followed, and although the Rev. John Williams of the London Missionary Society was killed disembarking at Erromango, Samoan Presbyterian teachers spread the mission through the southern islands.

As plantations developed in Queensland and Fiji to grow cotton and sugar cane during the American Civil War, the notorious trade of blackbirding began in order to recruit cheap labour. Although some Melanesians volunteered for the new experience, many were taken forcibly and treated much like slaves, and the traffickers were guilty of many inhumanities, leading at times to bloody reprisals by Melanesians. It is estimated that half the male population of the New Hebrides was involved at some stage in the notorious trade, with about 40,000 men taken to Queensland and another 16,000 to Fiji and New Caledonia.[4] This was a mere part of the labour reserve of over 360,000 workers in Melanesia (and Micronesia to a lesser extent) which between 1840 and 1915 provided workers for various forms of indenture.[5]

The failure of cotton and sugar was soon followed by the establishment of copra plantations around 1870, with many ruthless settler-traders arriving from Australia and New Caledonia. They were led by the Irish Catholic John Higginson who was determined to see the New Hebrides become a colony of France. In 1882, he founded the Compagnie Calédonienne des Nouvelles-Hébrides and bought over half a million acres of land from British merchants and indigenous tribes. This land was divided into lots and offered to French settlers on Efate, Malekula, Santo and Aoré. The era of copra plantations had begun.

With contact came disease and rapid depopulation, and the population plummeted to about 40,000 in the 1930s. The intermixture of competing French and British interests throughout the islands caused difficulties that were partly resolved in 1906 when France and Britain agreed to administer the islands jointly. The British-French Condominium was a unique form of joint government with separate government departments (French and British) as well as some mixed departments. Such a 'Gilbert and Sullivan-like' system was cumbersome and divisive, and often frustrated positive developments.

During World War II, the American military established major bases at Port Vila on Efate and Santo (Luganville) which became the two main towns in the country. Around half a million armed services personnel passed through, inducing far-reaching changes. Cargo cults and nativistic movements aimed at both reviving or perpetuating selected aspects of culture and involving prophetic myths arose or spread, such as the John Frum movement of Tanna and the Naked Cult of Espirito Santo. The local people were amazed by the technological and military might of the American war machine, the generosity of the GIs and the unbelievable array of Western consumer goods. Surely such wondrous 'cargo' must have been sent to earth by their dead ancestors and could not belong only to Americans. Was such cargo destined for them but intercepted by the white man?[6]

After World War II, there was a gradual weakening of the grade rituals whereby, on islands where the Big Man leadership existed, ambitious men could pass from one grade to a higher grade by making a gift of pigs, as well as woven mats, taro and yams. All pigs had to be killed on the one day, and to reach the highest grades sometimes over 100 pigs would be slaughtered.

Development in Vanuatu has had to contend with the sorts of social institutions that are inevitably part of a politico-religious system that relies for its survival and salience on traditional structures and cultural conservatism; for example, the sacrifice of boars with artificially curved tusks that were regarded as guaranteeing the cyclic renewal of life and the perpetuation of the cosmic order and which also supported the prevailing system of inequality.

Indigenous Politics: Party or Cult?

When I met the leader of the Nagriamel movement, Jimmy Stevens, he told me that the movement began in 1963 when he first started to oppose French planters. At about the same time, Chief Buluk and some bush people moved down the island close to Santo town and in 1966 he was joined by Stevens. This was the real beginning of Nagriamel.

Stevens described the movement as being a response to the forced transfer of all natives and planters out of the lowlands of east Espiritu Santo by the Americans during the Second World War. The land was required for military purposes, and the Americans promised that land belonging to New Hebrideans and expatriates would be returned to its owners at the end of the war. However, the expatriate planters moved in more quickly, taking advantage of the new roads and clearing land to put up fences. Paul Buluk spent several months in jail after a violent protest against the fencing and clearing of land just north of Luganville (later Santo town). Buluk and Stevens then prepared a proclamation, the 'Act of Dark Bush', forbidding settlers from extending their properties into the higher, cooler areas of *dak bus* (dark bush) which were held in *kastom* ownership.[7]

The name Nagriamel was described by Stevens as being a cross between the names of two plants – *nangaria*, meaning to stand up in honour, representing also the male sex organ and a fine lady, and *namele*, a plant that was always planted to mark ownership or a boundary, and also represented female sexuality. In addition, *namele* symbolised the return to peace and order after World War II. The two plants together (male and female) symbolised unity.

In a statement in December 1977, Jimmy Stevens described the aims of Nagriamel as fivefold:

- Working together to develop a better economic future.
- Regarding the land as the basis and essence of everything. By *kastom*, most of the land belonged to New Hebridean people and expatriates had no right to it. But at the same time, Nagriamel did not claim the land of all expatriates. Stevens said he wanted to live in peace.
- Working together in peace and friendliness. Stevens said that Europeans could stay in the New Hebrides after independence if they changed and respected the New Hebrides.
- Nationalism, self-sufficiency and independence were the main goals for the New Hebrides.
- The restoration of *kastom*.

Nagriamel was based at Vanafo, some 24 kms north of Santo, a village established by Chief Buluk and some bush people on land belonging to the big French company, Société Français des Nouvelles-Hébrides, which acquired the assets of the New Caledonian speculator John Higginson around the turn of the century. Stevens and Buluk were both imprisoned for six months for trespassing, but their incarceration led to a surge of popular support for them. Jimmy Stevens encouraged supporters of his movement to come and live at Vanafo and allotted each household 1 or 2 hectares each. If they worked well for five years, the committee promised to give them ownership of their land.

In 1967, Vanafo had a population of only 27 but it grew to over 200 in 1969 and over 500 in the 1970s. It was a neatly laid out village, with gardens, flagpole, sentry boxes and council meeting houses. Over the years, Nagriamel erected numerous signs on European-owned land claiming ownership of all 'dark bush land' outside the boundaries of known European plantations.

The community had 200 to 300 cattle as well as up to '1,000 cattle' on Chief Buluk's land. They grew dry rice, root crops, coffee and bananas. Although they could not grow coconuts well, cocoa appeared to be a promising crop. The movement was said to have a community chest containing funds, and from the mid-1960s agents travelled through the northern islands recruiting members and subscriptions. By

1969, $50,000 was said to have been paid to Nagriamel funds.

Undoubtedly, the guiding spirit of the conservative Nagriamel movement was its leader, Jimmy Stevens (also spelt Stephens). He reportedly had 23 wives and fathered four dozen children. While being of part-English, part-Tongan and part-New Hebridean extraction, Stevens was wholly New Hebridean in character, and possessed an ability to tap outside influences and to use them for his own ends. A patriarchal figure with an imposing air of authority, many of his basic ideas and the secret of his power appeared to have derived from the American influences of World War II. He dug up and sold caches of American equipment, drove a bulldozer, and worked as caretaker of a church and skipper of an inter-island steamer.

In 1968, the Nagriamel flag showing a white hand grasping a black hand was raised at Vanafo and about this time Stevens was given the title of 'Chief President Moses', apparently because he was seen to be leading his followers in the wilderness. In a country of so many cultures and sub-cultures, overlaid by both British and French colonial influences and many levels of development and social change, circumstances moulded the evolution of a movement that was partly political; partly a self-declared independent United Church;[8] partly a grass-roots nationalistic movement appealing for land and a return to *kastom*; and partly a cult with ritual, symbolism, and prophetic or millenarian touches. In short, it was a movement that appealed to a variety of cultural 'ecological niches' at different levels within the complex whole that was the New Hebrides of the day. This was represented in his organisation at three different levels: the *kastom* committee, the main council committee and the sophisticated upper council committee which met twice a week.

Some of the ideas of the movement were illustrated in Stevens' recognition that European education is of little use in the islands. He wanted a more technical education which taught the people how to use tools and how to use the land. He recognised and opposed the alienation inherent in Western education and saw that it was important to retain and strengthen *kastom*, the source of cultural identity and pride. Yet he rejected the myth-dream element of the true cargo cult, contrasting Nagriamel with the John Frum people of Tanna who depended on 'dreams' and on 'waiting' for the ship to come from the ancestors to deliver the cargo they so much desired. Instead, Stevens believed people must work to achieve what they wanted.

The secret of Stevens' success lay partly in his personality and partly in the movement's unique fusion of land grievances, tradition, nationalism and self-help development, presented in a parcel that included cult, ritual and strong indigenous elements. A pragmatic wheeler and dealer,

Stevens operated often in a traditional mould. Meetings took place under a giant banyan tree along the lines of the traditional *nakamal* – debate continued until compromise and consensus finally emerged.

Stevens also had a role as a modern leader who offered his followers a sure road to the future, for his experience and sophistication were seen as giving access to the knowledge necessary to produce European wealth. The link with Chief Buluk was also important as he was a traditional leader who possessed knowledge that enabled group resources to be increased.

In the early years, Nagriamel agents travelled to most of the northern islands of the group where Francophone interests and French planters were dominant, and then to Australia, New Caledonia and Fiji in search of 'advice'. A leading Fiji Indian lawyer and politician was engaged to appear for Stevens and Buluk when they were tried and sentenced to prison for illegal entry of European land. It has been suggested that these imprisonments strengthened the Nagriamel cause and made martyrs of them. Stevens was impressed by Fiji gaining independence in 1970, and petitioned the United Nations in 1971 for independence for the New Hebrides within a year.

Although Nagriamel was anti-foreign as far as land was concerned, in late 1977 there was evidence of considerable French influence at Vanafo – a fine French school, a new French dispensary, two tractors, several trucks and land rovers, and a well-equipped office with cane chairs and a pocket calculator. The French, fearing for the fate of their nationals, who mostly ran the plantations and some businesses, naturally supported regional movements that opposed independence. In the late 1960s, Eugene Peacock, an American land speculator, bought land in the Hog Harbour area of Espiritu Santo, and attempted to subdivide it for sale to expatriates. In the 1970s, the apparently sinister motives of the Phoenix Foundation, a champion of extreme monetarism, came to light. This foundation has been described as an extreme right-wing, fundamentalist group espousing ideas of "no government", "voluntary taxes" and unfettered free enterprise. One of its leaders, Harry Schultz, was well known internationally as an investment advisor, and included amongst readers of his newsletter was Margaret Thatcher.[9]

Father Walter Lini charged the Phoenix Foundation with smuggling radio equipment into Espiritu Santo in order to set up Nagriamel Radio, the planning since 1976 of operations to take over Santo and distract the government after independence, and the smuggling of weapons into Santo to supply Nagriamel, spending over US$250,000 in the process.[10] For Nagriamel to be engaged in such activities under the name of *kastom* was a perversion of its meaning and of the Melanesian way.

Such activities represent, of course, a classic form of penetration by large capitalist corporations – to back a sympathetic local party or movement which can become, perhaps unwittingly, the agent that assists acceptance and penetration. For his part, Stevens clearly acquired considerable local prestige from his alliance with such influential outsiders. In his determination to promote his movement at all costs, Stevens appears to have over-estimated his capacity to control powerful foreign interests; his alliance with them went so far that he jettisoned in effect some of his original nationalistic goals and became the tool of powerful foreign interests.

As a result of his growing links with French interests, at one point Stevens was taken to Paris and introduced to President Giscard d'Estaing. With the new National Party's strongly nationalist appeal gaining growing support, by the mid-1970s Nagriamel's following dwindled. When the British and French set up a constitutional framework for self-government and held elections in November 1975, Nagriamel in alliance with one of the Francophone parties gained only two seats in the new assembly, compared to 17 for the National Party. Stevens, supported by French and American business interests, claimed electoral irregularities and led a large protest rally in December 1975. He announced the imminent independence of Santo as the Nagriamel Federation. His alliance partnership dissolved immediately, and when the Condominium Government sent in the paramilitary police forces he was obliged to yield.

In the late 1970s, Stevens' mantle as the father of nationalism and the champion of indigenous rights against foreign interests was completely taken over by Father Walter Lini and the highly successful Vanuaku Party, which won 66 percent of the vote in the 1979 elections and became the first government of independent Vanuatu.

Stevens' second challenge on the national stage was more serious. After the Vanuaku Party triumphed in the elections of November 1979, Stevens refused to accept the validity of Nagriamel's electoral losses on Santo. He announced the formation of an independent state, the Republic of Vemerana, that was hailed by Harry Schultz in the New Zealand Herald as the "Switzerland of the Pacific",[11] and some of his militant followers occupied the British administration's offices. French officials assisted Nagriamel in blocking the police who were attempting to restore order. In 1980, the new independent government of Vanuatu, however, refused any concessions and accepted the help of the Papua New Guinea government which sent 450 troops to restore control. The Santo rebellion led to many injuries and arrests, and one death, one of Jimmy Stevens' sons. Hundreds of expatriate supporters of Nagriamel were expelled, which weakened the credibility of both some *kastom* and various Francophone opposition groups. There was a significant setback to economic development on Espirito Santo.

Jimmy Stevens above all appeared to be a shrewd, pragmatic, calculating man, a very articulate and charismatic orator in Bislama and an adroit politician. His alliance with and appeal to *kastom*, his acceptance of a church presence at Vanafo (he began with none) and his ever-changing alliances with powerful outside interests illustrate his readiness to adopt any expediency that would strengthen his cause. Although his movement claimed members from 15 islands in the northern New Hebrides and 20 percent of the country's population, the great bulk came from Espiritu Santo. At its peak, Nagriamel appears to have had a following of about 15,000 people. Lacking the sophistication of the overseas-educated Vanuaku Party leaders and the support the party received from the Presbyterian and Anglican missions (31 percent and 13 percent respectively), Jimmy Stevens and his lieutenants achieved little success in the legislature at Vila. (The French were supported largely by the 13 percent of the population who were Catholic.) Hence the movement seemed destined to remain a regional rather than a national one and its appeal was greatest to those at intermediate levels of social change.

But his proven record of stubbornness and capacity to resist cannot be doubted: Jimmy Stevens thrived on confrontations and publicity. While the very weakness of any widespread sense of nationhood and the strength of particularism (*manblong ples*) in the New Hebridean cultural kaleidoscope called for some kind of federation (a solution which obviously has great appeal), there was no possibility in such a small country that a drastic decentralisation of modern services implicit in his kind of solution would have been feasible. Whatever accommodation may ultimately have been arrived at, it is clear that with their launching of the canoe of independence Lini's party would not be able to tolerate this challenge to its unity.

Modern Political Development

Modern political development of a rather more mainstream style began some years earlier and co-existed with the politics and radicalism of Nagriamel. Walter Lini, a product of the Anglican missionised island of Pentecost, stood out in his early schooling and in 1968 attended St John's Theological College in Auckland. Feeling lost in the impersonal cities of New Zealand, the Vanuatu students at St John's joined with Solomon Islands and Gilbert and Ellice students to form an association for Pacific islanders. They had lively discussions and soon founded *Wontok*, a magazine which began to consider political issues from a Pacific islands viewpoint. Although he worked hard and performed creditably in his study, Lini became very dissatisfied and frustrated when in his second year he began to realise that all the teaching materials (books, theologies and philosophies) were foreign.[12]

At the end of 1968, he graduated and became Father Walter Lini. On his way back to Vanuatu, he spent some months in the Solomons. There he met his wife-to-be and also young members of the Anglican Church. Their discussions in a new social and sports club led to interesting enquiries into the kinds of future societies they hoped would emerge. These were reflected in the *Kakamora Reporter*, a lively anti-colonial magazine exploring new options for the future.

In 1971, Lini, Donald Kalpokas and Peter Taurakoto formed the New Hebridean Cultural Association which was a revival of the group they had established in Auckland, and they began *New Hebridean Viewpoints*. The response was great throughout the country; a year later the Association became the pro-independence National Party. Like Jimmy Stevens' movement, one of the National Party's main priorities was to fight the increasing alienation of *kastom* land to land speculators who descended on the New Hebrides in the 1970s.

Wealthy American speculators bought huge tracts of land for extremely profitable subdivision sales to retired businessmen and Vietnam War veterans. At this time, I heard of various Wairarapa farmers in New Zealand who were interested in the possibility of quick profits in the New Hebrides as well. By 1971, about 36 percent of Vanuatu's land was alienated, including about half of all cultivated land. The key policy platform of the new party was restoration of this land to its *kastom* owners, and land occupations became a key political strategy in the struggle for independence. A little later, villagers from Mele, near Vila, occupied land owned by the Catholic Church and 10 expatriate-owned plantations.

After the first three numbers of *New Hebridean Viewpoints* were published, Lini and the other leaders of the new nationalist movement had attracted attention from other South Pacific countries. The South Pacific Conference of Churches held a meeting in Fiji which Lini attended and his proposal for a further conference in Vila in 1973 – the SPADES (South Pacific Action for Development and Economic Strategies) – was accepted. That conference endorsed the policy of the National Party in opposing all land alienation and subdivision, and immediately the Presbyterian Assembly on Tanna passed a resolution in support of independence for the New Hebrides. In January 1974, Lini was elected

National President of the National Party, a full-time position, so he was granted leave of absence from the Anglican Church and travelled widely throughout his country explaining the goals of the party. The momentum increased as news of the anti-colonial movement in the New Hebrides spread internationally. In May 1974, through the help of a conference in Tanzania (whose sincere leader Julius Nyrere and *ujamaa* policy were widely admired by Western liberals), a representative was invited to address the UN Committee on Decolonisation and Lini was selected for this task. In order to pressurise the British and French to prepare the country for independence, he declared at the UN that the country wanted independence by 1977.

By 1975, the party had decided that the country should have a new name and the party's name should also change. It became the Vanuaku ('our land') Pati. They decided not to go to the Paris talks in 1977 as they believed the Condominium (and especially the French) was determined to slow down the progress towards independence. In the same year, Lini led his party's boycott of the New Hebrides Representation Elections for the same reasons. They decided to set up the People's Provisional Government and then the Government of National Unity. Finally, in the elections of 1979, the Vanuaku Party won an outright majority in the Assembly (26 out of 39 seats) which was to become the first parliament of the Republic of Vanuatu in July 1980.

Challenges to Lini and the Vanuaku Party

Walter Lini, clergyman, party leader, prime minister, is rightly regarded as the father of independence. As a Christian leader, his honesty, integrity and sincerity were widely admired. At times of crisis, he was determined and unwavering, even expelling the French Ambassador for a time, but often he could be conciliatory. He was single-minded and dedicated and had performed with distinction in the Western world. Fortunately, the motives of his backers, the Presbyterian Church and the Pacific Conference of Churches, were impeccable and he gained an international profile after appearing at the UN Committee on Decolonisation.

Lini and the other Vanuaku Party leaders strove hard to form a single meaningful administration from the three that existed up to 1980. And they attempted to build the country on its own authentic basis and achieve economic self-reliance. Many ni-Vanuatu agreed with the director of Vanuatu's Cultural Centre, Ralph Regenvanu, who argued that "Christianity and Western development are the two biggest things working against us", since both have a "you were lost but now you have been found philosophy which is blocking the country's development".[13]

Lini achieved stable government during much of his time as prime minister. In 1982, Vanuatu banned the visit of nuclear-armed warships (two years before New Zealand), making it South Pacific's first nuclear-free country. Its other claim to fame is as the originator of bungy-jumping.

Lini had to prove his genuine leadership the hard way, surviving a serious challenge to his authority from Barak Sope who in the late 1980s was often considered the most powerful man in the country. He was clearly ambitious and often opportunistic. After working in the long struggle for independence in comradeship with Lini, he became Vanuatu's outspoken roving ambassador afterwards and scourge of French colonial policies in Oceania. Then he expanded his business interests to include tourism and stevedoring. Several of his militants from Ifira (an island near Vila) were sent to Libya for training in 'journalism'; later they acted as his bodyguards.

When the Vanuaku Party lost ground in the 1987 election, Sope challenged Lini, now suffering from ill health, for the position of prime minister. He was beaten soundly but pressured Lini to be included in the cabinet. He was made a late addition, being granted two portfolios but not the one he most wanted. Later, the new Lands Minister abolished the Vila Urban Land Corporation (VULCAN) and its sister company in Santo. Sope had been a board director of VULCAN and the corporation's investments were seen to be the cornerstone of Sope's power-base, with widespread allegations of misappropriation of funds of up to 750 million vatu (NZ$10 million). Sope denied these accusations.

Sope launched a counter-attack over the abolition of VULCAN, involving not only Ifira but also the other villages having customary land in the capital – Erakor and Pango. The 3,000 protesters marched on the Prime Minister's office, denouncing Lini as both a "communist" and a "fascist", and attacked Vietnamese-owned businesses and a police truck with iron bars. Most of Vila's population of 20,000 felt threatened and soldiers had to be called in to use tear gas to quell the rioters. This Ifira challenge in support of Barak Sope did not succeed and Lini lamented that the rioters failed to respect their chiefs and customs, abusing *namele* leaves, the traditional symbol of peace.[14] But it was a forerunner to the ongoing challenge not only over land rights but also to leadership of the young, new nation.

Tradition versus Modernity: The Case of North Ambrym

The tension between tradition and modernity is illustrated by Mary Patterson's analysis of the varying roles of three leaders contending for power in North Ambrym. The interplay of status and precedence in an apparently fixed and competitive hierarchy related to place of origin and achievement requiring great organisational skill, political discernment and forceful personality was indeed a delicate matter. It required a judicious combination of "virtue" (membership of a great kindred) and "virtuosity" (demonstration that a great leader could arise "from nowhere" due to memorable deeds alone).[15]

Traditionally, demonstration of efficacy that displayed *helan* or power involved success in the spheres of the *mage* (graded society ritual), warfare, sorcery and horticulture, especially cultivation of long yams; the raising, acquisition and exchange of spiral tusked boars locally and overseas; and the creation and maintenance of alliances through arranged marriages and the attraction of women. Success in these fields was the result of access to ancestral funds of power and the manipulation of "secret and dangerous technologies".[16]

While the *mage* in northern Vanuatu was usually connected with peace (frequently mentioned in post-colonial valuations of *kastom*), in North Ambrym at least it is connected with secret societies and sorcery. As the drive for independence gained momentum in the 1970s, the national discourse of *kastom* rapidly intensified, and while this was often caught up with concern over land, it also involved local participation in development. The varied penetration of global market forces, the importation of novel national political institutions and the interaction of desires, fantasies and values affected the local region. The crushing defeat of Nagriamel's attempt at secession was followed by the Vanuatu Mobile Unit arriving in North Ambrym to interrogate and arrest local leaders of Nagriamel. Among those rounded up, beaten and publicly humiliated was Wilfred Koran, one of the three main leaders of the area. He was taken to Vila, gaoled and removed from his position as village chief.

Such an outcome was perhaps inevitable through the process that Walter Lini, as leader of the Vanuaku Pati, initiated by earlier building up a nationalistic fervour aiming at achieving independence. The movement was also based on the preservation of *kastom* conceived as adaptive to change and inclusive of Christianity. Such a view of *kastom* was the death knell to old *kastom* leaders, and Presbyterian supporters of the new independent government were also promoted to new positions of influence.[17] A new Council of Chiefs was appointed and given the delicate task in 1983 of distinguishing between acceptable *kastom* and those practices like sorcery that were "rubbish *kastom*".

In the pre-colonial era, the intense fragmentation of the local polity was mitigated by certain shared precepts, but in the modern period the

British-French, Christian-pagan, Vanuaku Pati-Nagriamel rivalry and variable access to cash earning opportunities compounded the local situation even further so that leadership positions were bitterly contested, becoming connected to various internal and then external divisions that local leaders were powerless to transcend. The most notorious of these leaders was Tofor, dominant in the 1970s. He was expert in the use of sorcery and his exploits included murder by both occult and overt means. In the seventies, he said he "cooked his enemies like copra".[18] However, his rival Willy Bongmatur, a man whose genealogy ascribed him with high status and whose maternal ancestors from Malekula were of the highest rank, was backed by the Presbyterians. In a vote of supporters of Tofor and Willy, the latter won by 17 votes to 10. Although Willy never gained overall support in North Ambrym due partly to Nagriamel and Francophone opposition and some doubts on his ancestry, he was elected to a new body of *kastom* advisors to the Assembly. This Council of Chiefs was extended to 24 members, and in 1977 when it changed its name to Malvatumauri he was elected to be first President of the organisation. His entry on to the national arena had begun and on Independence Day he stood at the right hand of Walter Lini, the father of independence.

His defeated rival Tofor, who earlier had been paramount in North Ambrym, increased his excessive consumption of liquor to the point that his behaviour became so erratic that his brother took over as village chief. Tofor, however, determined to act in the violent transgressive way that only a truly great chief would entertain: he tried to form an incestuous relationship with his eldest daughter. Fortunately he was thwarted by some men who gave him a severe beating. He was arrested and gaoled for several months. The day after Independence Day, Tofor arose very early, saying he was going to shoot birds. He lay in wait for the ringleader of the men who had beaten him up, shooting him as he came out of his house. Reportedly he also lay in wait for his two great rivals, Wilfrid Koran and Willy Bongmatur, but fortunately they did not emerge from their houses. Tofor was arrested and spent the next two years in the small asylum, *haus blong kranky*. The decline of the 'last great sorcerer of the Pacific' was slowed perhaps by his claim that God would punish his enemies: proof of this prophecy came when Walter Lini, then prime minister, suffered a stroke and the first of a series of hurricanes hit Vanuatu.

Sadly, the intense factionalism, hatred and violence of North Ambrym which led to the island gaining a reputation as 'the Mother of Darkness' in the late nineteenth century extended to the northern area up to the end of the twentieth century. Rather than seeing the disputes as symptoms of a deep malaise in the whole of North Ambrym that had its roots in the colonial period, a UN-funded project gave a preliminary diagnosis of the problem as a "breakdown in human interaction" and linked a "lack of community" to the land disputes.[19] Certainly, conditions reached a low with intense rivalry between Francophone and Nagriamel groups and the pro-British Presbyterian groups before 1980: rival groups blocked access to water supplies, competed with each other over the site for an airfield for many years and forced members of one community to travel to the only clinic by boat rather than by the road that ran through their domain. Even many North Ambrymese perceive themselves as 'backward', seeing their failure to improve their basic living standards as resulting from the fear, distrust and animosity inspired by sorcery and the lack of consensus that would enable leaders to transcend both ancient and recent divisions.

As Patterson explains, sorcery encompasses the moral economy of success, worth and virtue, so that "only envy, fear and conflict appear as their product. Victims of their own and others' publicity in recent years, North Ambrym's reputation as the Mother of Darkness is unhelpful at best in the efforts of her people to move beyond the acrimony of a sorry colonial history into what they desire and imagine as the light of a modernity that seems continually out of reach".[20] Fortunately, few regions in Vanuatu appear to have such a Conradian 'Heart of Darkness' reputation as the hapless area of North Ambrym. But as we explain below, that does not mean their prospects for transformative development are bright.

The Tree and the Canoe[21]

In an uncertain world, as Brookfield (1977) has argued, islanders minimise risk and maximise benefits by retaining residence, land and membership of their social group in their village, and participating from time to time in short- or medium-term employment on plantations or in town by means of a system of circular migration. Bedford (1973 and 1974) has analysed this process which seems likely to continue for a long time in Vanuatu, although over time the length of the period spent outside the village has increased, and the number of ni-Vanuatu living permanently in town has also steadily grown. He applied Ward's comments on Papua New Guinea to Vanuatu, that "evidence suggests that to talk of temporary urban dwellers is largely wishful thinking".[22]

While basically concurring with Bedford's detailed analysis as a geographer on Vanuatu mobility, Bonnemaison has added a valuable cultural perspective to our understanding.[23] By using a dual metaphor, the tree (symbol of rootedness and stability) and the canoe (symbol of journeying and unrestricted wandering), he explains how Melanesian civilisation defines its traditional identity. Traditional mobility was also territorial, linking places through alliances and reciprocity, and routes followed over land or sea were appropriated by social groups as if they were extensions of their own territories. There were three main kinds of traditional journeys: initiation journeys (a complex ritual for young men akin to a pilgrimage to the island of a mythical hero), exchange journeys of ritual social intercourse and gift exchange, and refuge journeys to places of asylum in times of danger.

The impact of European society was traumatic, for the Melanesians' own society and beliefs, adapted to a territorial micro-environment, were revealed to be without any real answer to the sudden intrusion of European society and the new space – physical and social – of which it was the expression. Once the initial period of forced labour recruiting and violence was over, Bonnemaison (1989) argues that the traditional pattern of journeying resumed, but now on a different scale. The voyage of initiation was reproduced but within a more global context which included elements of adventure; the acquisition of the tools, goods and gadgetry of whites (their 'cargo'); and the goal of satisfying the extraordinary cultural curiosity of the Melanesians. And when at the end of their overseas journey they failed to find the generosity or welcome they expected, they learnt a harsh lesson about the impersonality of the West and its relentless pursuit of material acquisition and the dominance that it sought to impose on their world. At the very least, it led them to the position where they could destroy the myth that Europeans embodied a higher spiritual power.

The two main agents of change in the colonial era were, of course, the missionary and the planter. The first tried to reconstruct Melanesian society to create a religious identity: to destroy the traditional order which they saw as pagan, and to substitute a Christian one. As the Iberian missionaries had done earlier in Latin America, the pastors encouraged people to abandon places of identity and dwelling sites that were loaded with meaning and symbols. This involved moving from the 'dark bush' (the world of darkness and paganism) and shifting to the coast, an area of light and brightness where the missionaries stationed themselves (served by mission ships) to experience the *niu laef* of the converts. In attempting to build the *niu laef*, the pastors tried to anchor their converts in a new village society (a model of pastoral and Christian harmony that they had failed to build in Europe) and to limit mobility as much as possible to protect Christians from outside influences.

The goals of the planters were diametrically opposed to those of the missionaries. Planters championed the cause of economic development and rejected the mission opposition to methods of labour recruitment. They espoused ideas of personal liberty and, since they wanted workers for their plantations, they supported a mobile and flexible Melanesian society that would be inserted into the circuits of capitalist production, marketing and consumption that they controlled. Both contending Western interests justified their actions by the belief that there was no longer any real custom or any authentic Melanesian society that had survived; rather, they saw a 'cultural void', a *tabula rasa* on which they could erect the new social system they desired. However, as Bonnemaison notes, neither of the two contending sides won – they could only cancel each other out. An uneasy compromise resulted, varying from island to island.

The European planters would never obtain the mobile labour force they desired, getting only small numbers of workers for short periods, and in the 1920s they turned instead to imported labour from Asia. However, this new labour, mainly Vietnamese, demanded a higher wage than the planters could afford and the smallest plantations were bankrupted. Indeed, the plantation economy has been in slow decline since the 1920s.

Nor did the missionaries achieve more than quasi-failure. There were rejections of the attempt to transform local social structures into Christian villages, as the island of Tanna illustrates in its unique and long-lasting John Frum movement which still survives. As Bonnemaison notes, "the lines of force of traditional society lay dormant beneath the surface waiting to re-emerge".[24] The only partial realisation of the missionary dream and the dubious faltering outcome of the planters' model were inevitable since both were based on false premises. A cultural void did not exist, for Melanesian society was far less destroyed than it had appeared to be: "Even more important, it retained in its heart of hearts a memory of its identity and ability to reconstruct itself according to its own standards".[25] This outcome was revealed in the nationalist movement and the return to *kastom*, led not only by Lini and the Vanuaku Pati, but also by Jimmy Stevens and Nagriamel. The independence of Vanuatu was indeed a veritable cultural revelation.

Since World War II, Melanesian societies have been much more integrated into the international economic system and the flow and mobility of people have greatly increased, becoming one of the distinctive characteristics of the region. But Bonnemaison argues that all these modern changes do not mean a change of identity or the death of traditional culture. Rather, he argues, "behind the outward appearance stands a society that is astonishingly true to itself".[26] The characteristics of the pattern of circular migration show the continuity with a remembered past, and the strength of the territorial bond is demonstrated by the frequency and regularity of return visits to the home village, news from home constantly flowing to the destination place, and migrants staying in places defined by territorial and ethnic links. As in the old days, 'companies' exist partly to control residential organisation, and the labour market and discerning modern sector employers should recognise and build on such knowledge in dealing with employees who "reproduce in an alien milieu the structure of the canoe and the area of alliance".[27] Thus Melanesians alternate between town, plantation and village as long as they have 'roads' and 'companies' to which to attach themselves: they reproduce within a modern economic space the circular pathways peculiar to their culture and their traditional world view.

Of course, at times, and especially when an economic boom occurs, mobility can overflow from its customary channels as movement becomes uncontrolled and some migrants can lose contact with their kin or village. But in difficult times, the reverse happens and migrants find renewed security from village and community values.

The independence of Vanuatu was achieved in the name of *kastom*. It was both a banner and a rallying cry of all the political parties, the government and even Christian leaders who earlier had tried to uproot it. While it means all things to all men, and in the villages *kastom* and land are closely associated, its deep concern with cultural identity lies at the heart of the new national identity. Many people believed that when colonial power ended, men would not only claim political sovereignty but would also reclaim and return to their traditional places of origin. Government encouraged such sentiments soon after independence by writing in the twelfth chapter of the constitution that the land of Vanuatu would "come back to Custom" – to the *man ples*, the rightful occupants as defined in terms of custom and genealogical affiliation. This land reform was aimed first at land alienated to Europeans through colonisation, and then in islands where land tenure problems were most acute it attempted to redistribute rights to Melanesian land according to the doctrine of first appearance. However, as Bonnemaison has noted (1984), after a century and a half of colonial impact, disruption and population movements, the ancient distribution of clans and territories has been upset. On some islands, almost half the population has lived for several generations on land where, following strict customary filiation, they have no right to be.

The Minister of Lands in the first independent government described the relationship between the land and the ni-Vanuatu as being like that between a mother and her child, and through this land the people retained their spiritual strength. This means that if land is the mother of identity, access is available to all who share that identity. The reactivation of ancient land rights might encourage a movement back into the 'dark bush' towards the interior of islands and lessen population pressure on the coastal areas. While this might encourage more balanced regional development, it would be expensive since building of roads to the interior would be required. Thus the clarion call of 'return land to *kastom*' has an economic dimension as well as a cultural one, a sense of regaining identity through the process of rediscovering places significant in the collective memory.

In recent decades, social change has had the effect of "widening horizons and multiplying roads", as Bonnemaison has noted:[28] new solidarities have emerged – regional, economic, religious, national – so that island societies are far less grounded on clans articulated around microterritories, and village-based societies are increasingly penetrated by the international economy and organised over larger areas. There is also an evolution of land rights that are more clearly individual in character.

Melanesians in general and ni-Vanuatu in particular need more than ever the tree, symbol of rootedness, as a sure anchor against the cruel buffets of the outside world. But even more, they need to rediscover canoes that re-establish the connection with venturing on the high seas and undertaking new journeys of discovery – to recreate, in other words, social units capable of adapting to the modern world while also preserving their own special values of identity.

If we put aside for a moment Bonnemaison's insightful metaphor of the tree and canoe and return to the conventional terminology of development literature, we can see that in the Vanuatu case, he is seeing economic dualism as a positive rather than a negative feature which, it is hoped, will be eliminated with further economic growth. This is so because Melanesian identity will be kept alive as long as mobility remains predominantly circular: if "one day their movement should become the rural exodus found in many Third World societies, the originality and identity of traditional Melanesian society will have joined the legion of dead cultures".[29] Thus, in contrast to Fiji where economic dualism ultimately should disappear, in Vanuatu and probably other Melanesian regions it needs to be preserved, so that journeying can continue, involving encounters, discovery, freedom, experience, creativity and earning money from wage employment. In this way, journeying, circulation and two-way movement can reconcile the tree and the canoe.

13

The MIRAB Economy in South Pacific Microstates

with I.G. Bertram

This essay is a version of three pieces of work that I co-authored with Geoff Bertram from Victoria University of Wellington; the theoretical model derived from this work has perhaps had the greatest impact of my career. The approach continues to have salience, and the acronym we developed (MIRAB: migration, remittances, aid and bureaucracy) is still used in scholarship today, with the model having its supporters and also critics. A report entitled New Zealand and its Small Island Neighbours, 1984, *and two articles on MIRAB which were published in* Pacific Viewpoint *(1985 and 1986) form the main body of this work.*

In 1983, as part of moves to make university research more relevant to the public and private sectors, Victoria University, based in the capital city of Wellington, established the Institute of Policy Studies. New Zealand had also reached a turning point as it moved from the astringent and personality-ridden National government of Robert Muldoon to the revisionist and politically ambiguous Labour government of David Lange and Roger Douglas: new policies needed to be worked out in a considerable number of economic, social and fiscal areas. This also extended to New Zealand's external relations in the South Pacific, and Southeast and East Asia, and to its defence arrangements. Soon I heard that the first project to be implemented by the new Institute of Policy Studies was to be a review of a number of Pacific microstates – the Cook Islands, Niue, Tokelau, Kiribati and Tuvalu – at the request of the Department of External Affairs and Trade.

For the first time, the Department was to make available all its records, including confidential correspondence of New Zealand prime ministers and other ministers to their island country counterparts, providing the information was treated sensitively. Although the Department was not in a position to fund the project, it arranged for free flights to the islands on board the airforce plane used for government purposes, and gave every assistance and back up through its high commissions in the respective countries.

I was invited to lead and select the team to carry out the research, and decided to recruit one of our finest graduates, Geoff Bertram, who had moved from geography to economics. In view of the enormous number of files, both in Wellington and the islands, that had to be read in addition to a voluminous literature, we also scoured the country for able graduate students. We recruited a good team from promising students of economics, geography and political studies from the Universities of Auckland and Canterbury as well as Victoria University in Wellington: Perry Bayer, Michael Bodensteiner, David Booth, Matthew Everitt and Carolyn Kelly.

Geoff Bertram and I visited the Cook Islands (Rarotonga and Aitutaki), Niue, Tonga and Western Samoa (the Tokelau Islands Government centre) to undertake fieldwork and to have wide-ranging discussions with government ministers and officials and to read files. I also visited Kiribati (Tarawa and Abemama) and Tuvalu (Funafuti).

The MIRAB Process – The Context

This paper presents the outline of a model of the MIRAB economy, which could usefully be applied to the South Pacific to help explain how some of the microstates of the region function and how the transition from the former colonial export economies occurred. The model as a whole and its elements (Mi – migration, R – remittances, A – aid, B – bureaucracy) direct attention to what is a relatively new and largely exogenous set of factors, which do not merely supplement on-shore commodity production in the islands, but also increasingly and decisively dominate the respective island economies and largely determine their evolution.

There are numerous references in Pacific literature to the changing economic behaviour of islanders and the breakdown of the colonial export economy. As Figure 13.1 shows,[1] the transition from the former colonial export economies to the new MIRAB order occurred mainly after 1950, and the fully evolved system was in existence for only a decade and a half even in Niue (the first of our case studies to reach a MIRAB steady state).

Models of Social Change

Of immediate interest is the theory of social change propounded by Firth on the basis of his Tikopia studies.[2] Firth's approach was based on his view of societies as self-regulating systems, and he gave relatively little attention to issues of power and conflict. Social change in his view arises largely in response to changes in external circumstances, leading to 'organisational change' within the local society. Such change can only proceed a certain distance before it reaches a point where it has structural effects – the original structure (e.g. of an institution) cannot be maintained, and structural change then occurs with the changing of established social roles and the emergence of new roles. This involves an alteration of the principles on which the society operates.

Firth's theory is valuable because it provides a dynamic view of society, recognises the importance of external forces, and traces the ramifying influences of choice following a change in the pattern of expectations and the expansion of society's subjectively-perceived wants. He was aware also of the limited flexibility of such societies and the risk that their integration into wider systems may result in breakdown. But change is not forced from without; rather, it involves choices among options by social actors within the small society.

A 1965 study by Finney traced such adjustment by comparing an outer-island of 'peasant' copra producers in the Society Islands and a peri-urban 'proletarian' community on Tahiti. Finney showed that rural decline was well underway and that there was a distinct preference for wage labour. 'Fast money' in the town was more appealing than 'slow money' earned from productive activity in the 'countryside', since the former gave an immediate, regular and sustained return. Finney's analysis clearly captures a 'MIRAB' transition occurring in French Polynesia: as military spending consequent upon French nuclear testing mounted, the old colonial economy ceased to exist, and society responded to new rent-type infusions of income coupled with the rise of tourism.

In research on rural social change in Eastern Fiji, Brookfield recognised the consequences of the incorporation of formerly autarkic systems into larger, world-wide systems. Brookfield criticised approaches to agrarian change (or lack of it) which tried to understand the agricultural sector in isolation from the wider context, on the assumption that farmers respond only to agricultural or rural incentives. Such analysis, Brookfield suggested, involved –

... asking why farmers do not, or cannot, respond to incentive or do not have incentive, but we are doing so in a context of thinking that assumes that they are only and inevitably farmers, and can be nothing else.[3]

In fact, Fijian farmers had at least two alternatives: to find wage employment locally, and to search for work and opportunity in Suva. Brookfield saw substantial out-migration from the "low productivity rural slums" to the more "developed" parts of Melanesia as a logical response to those external incentives.[4]

Similar results were found independently at about the same time by Wellington geographers and anthropologists working in the 1972 Rural Socio-economic Survey of the Gilbert and Ellice Islands.[5] Villagers proved remarkably responsive to non-agricultural, non-rural incentives and often depended on three, four or five sources of income. In general, their economic behaviour was highly situation-bound, and they showed a keen awareness of the new opportunities that were becoming available for the first time. In the 1960s, the public service on Tarawa was small and job opportunities accordingly few, but with the rapid expansion of British aid the bureaucracy expanded greatly in the 1970s so that a considerable proportion of families on the outer islands could formulate a strategy to secure government employment for at least one family member.

A significant step forward in understanding the contemporary Pacific and the MIRAB society was Marcus' 1981 paper on 'Power in the Extreme Periphery'. Although Marcus' argument was essentially based on elite strategies, he adopted a Wallerstein world-systems perspective that discounted the significance of nation-states as analytical units in peripheral areas, and concentrated instead on social classes and their geographical distribution. Tongans had for some time appreciated the offshore opportunities that existed for employment or business operations in New Zealand, Hawaii, California and Salt Lake City (the Mormon Church connection), as well as onshore wage work in the local bureaucracy and the church. Emulating their King Tupou IV, the commoner and elite families became truly multinational in their scope, achieving success in "the mixing and playing of options internationally".[6]

The view of an evolving Tonga that Marcus presented is clearly very different from the classic colonial export economy based on onshore resource development. In particular, the widespread multinational diaspora of members of interacting Tongan families made nonsense of the traditional European concept of a unitary nation-state which was so influential during the era of decolonisation.

The Example of the Cook Islands

Loomis (1984a and b) explored the evidence of declining homogeneity between Cook Islanders in New Zealand and those in the islands (as well as the division evident within the New Zealand-resident community between those born in the islands and those born in New Zealand).[7] He saw Pacific islander migration, remittances and return migration in the light of wider developments in the regional political economy, following Marcus in viewing the kindred or *kopu tangata* as a "family estate", dealing not merely with remittances between the mainland and islands but also with a wide array of two-way exchanges which can be conceived of more generally as "investments". His research on the Cook Island community in New Zealand explored the issues of why *kopu tangata* maintain the flow of 'investments' back to the islands, the extent and durability of the kin corporations, and the dynamics of rank and decision-making in resource allocation.

A significant step in the economic history of the Cook Islands was the Makatea migrant scheme which marked the beginning of the rise of the migration/remittance sector. Between 1942 and 1955, 2,906 Cook Islanders were recruited by a French company to work the guano deposits of Makatea in the Society Islands. With a minimum yearly wage of about $592 (a small fortune by Cook Islands standards) and a requirement that married men must remit at least two-thirds of their wages to their families, the Makatea scheme laid the foundations for the remittance economy in the Cook Islands.[8] Twenty percent or more of the male population aged 18-30 worked on Makatea at some stage, and many of these men migrated to New Zealand in the late 1950s. Curson interpreted the Makatea experience as a "dislodging" factor, initiating a process of step-wise migration and in the process "proletarianising" an important segment of the Cook Islands labour force.[9]

In the Cook Islands, a local observer of the expanding welfarist bureaucracy remarked as early as 1947 that –

> The parent country, in her eagerness to do her best for this dependency, has sapped the native's initiative by 'spoon-feeding' methods. Kava-mani, the Government, is now the thing to look to for any utilities and improvements.[10]

Similar points were made eight years later in the Belshaw-Stace Report (1955), which expressed worry at the risk that the obvious financial benefits of a closer relationship with New Zealand would sap the self-reliance of the local people. The report therefore argued for a determined *political* stance of decolonisation coupled with encouragement for local moves towards economic self-reliance, which they took as synonymous with onshore production of tradeable commodities – particularly agricultural products. Both Belshaw-Stace and Aikman (1956) recognised that self-reliant affluence was probably unattainable in the Cook Islands situation, so that New Zealand aid would continue to play a role; but both reports took it for granted that productive self-reliance should nevertheless be the guiding principle for economic policy, and both hoped that ultimately the level of dependence on aid to maintain local government services might be reduced or even possibly eliminated. Both recognised explicitly that so long as aid dependence remained a central plank of the economy, full sovereign political independence would be unattainable even if formal moves in that direction were made.

At about the same time, Cumberland (1954) was writing of the Cook Islanders' "neglect of their gardens" as people increasingly took up wage employment in the government, on the wharves, in the new knitwear and slipper factories established to serve the New Zealand market, and overseas.[11] Cumberland noted that over 2,000 Cook Islanders had taken passage to Auckland; that the export trade had diminished; and that, with the neglect of food crops, diet, health and housing had suffered.

In 1962, R.G. Crocombe documented what he called the "economic regression"[12] of the Cook Islands. He estimated that in the late 1950s the volume of export production of copra was 22 percent lower than in 1924-28, citrus was down 55 percent and bananas 10 percent. Crocombe attributed these long-run trends to paternalist colonial policies, which he felt had failed to promote economic development. He criticised the creation by New Zealand of a "disproportionately large administrative superstructure",[13] which had not contributed to increasing output. He suggested also that the system of land tenure had inhibited productivity growth, and that since World War II there had taken place a marked change in islanders' aspirations and values so that they now aspired to mainland consumption levels and social services. If transport were available at lower cost, Crocombe felt, "there is little doubt that the majority of islanders would shift to New Zealand".[14]

With hindsight, it is evident that Crocombe correctly identified many of the emerging characteristics of the new order, and pointed to several contributory factors in agricultural stagnation, but that his analysis was cast within a set of assumptions which diverted attention from the MIRAB effect. By treating the Cook Islands as though they were (or should be) an autonomous economic unit, rather than an increasingly integrated annex to the New Zealand mainland economy, Crocombe was naturally led to emphasise the negative side of the MIRAB process (especially the decline of local productive activity), and hence to present as "economic regression" a process which was in fact more of a restructuring of the village economy as households diversified their activities in order to benefit from aid and remittances.

A similar focus on local productive activity, but with more tendency to downplay the roles of migration and the government sector, is evident in the economic analysis by Kolff (1965a, 1965b). At about the same time, however, Johnston's (1967) study of village agriculture on Aitutaki was dealing more directly with these elements.

Johnston drew attention to the cumulative effect on agriculture of irregular shipping, insecure markets and consequent high wastage, all of which meant that cash cropping was perceived to be a high-risk, insecure activity. In addition, income from agricultural sources was low compared to that which could be gained from wage employment and the latter was greatly preferred.

Government policy gave precedence to social development and infrastructure (health, education, roads and the like) over agricultural development except in citrus growing, where the administration had intervened to promote export production. As a result, citrus growing had become "an enclave of administration commercialisation", resulting in a dual agricultural economy.[15] Growers had little participation in citrus growing because of the scale of input by the government sector; and the main success stories in citrus were administration employees or commercial entrepreneurs moving in to take advantage of the government-subsidised programme.

Johnston correctly emphasised that village agricultural producers operated in a wider framework which was "none of their making".[16] He viewed the problem of agricultural development in terms of a Myrdalian backwash situation created by the existence of the modern New Zealand metropolis. Social and economic opportunities within New Zealand were attracting youth and initiative away from the village in a tide of migration. Moreover, the provision of the New Zealand subsidy to government services had resulted in the erection of a structure of social amenities on a scale quite divorced from local productive capacity, so that a dependent society was created on the one hand, and a paternalistic administration on the other. Johnston contrasted this with the situation in British colonies where the level of social services was more closely tied to locally-generated revenue – a contrast which, as already noted, was more apparent than real in the case of the Gilbert and Ellice Islands Colony.

In keeping with the Myrdal model, Johnston focused upon the

prospect of a widening gap between the disadvantaged Cook Islands "periphery" on the one hand, and the mainland "core" of the New Zealand economy on the other. The only alternative to growing disparity between the two seemed to Johnston to be a situation in which "the islands became an integral part of this larger, richer economy and able to share in its growth".[17]

The irony of Johnston's position is that, having conceded the possible benefits flowing from increased economic integration with New Zealand, he did not question the logic of the 1965 move to self-government as the culmination of a process of decolonisation. In common with Kolff at the same time,[18] Johnston tended to see autonomous economic development as a desirable underpinning for a self-governing constitution, and thus to argue for an attempt to turn back the clock on the MIRAB process, rather than to analyse that process and attempt to come to terms with it. Like Crocombe, Johnston was strongly influenced by the prevailing mood of anti-colonialism in the 1960s, and tended to suppose that the blame for agricultural regression and the general stagnation of village production could be laid at the door of New Zealand paternalism and neglect. Because too much emphasis was thus placed on administration attitudes and policy, and too little on market forces and macro-economic trends, neither Crocombe nor Johnston achieved a satisfactory explanation for the developmental 'crisis' which they believed they had uncovered.

Referring back to Figure 13.1 and to the data from which it was drawn,[19] we find that in real terms the New Zealand budgetary grant to the Cook Islands more than doubled in 1951-55 compared to 1946-50. In response to this rising inflow of aid, many new public service jobs were created: non-private employment increased from 430 (a considerable number of whom would have been expatriates rather than Cook Islanders) in 1951 to 638 in 1956, 813 in 1961 and 1,464 in 1966.[20] The result was access to secure, regular incomes from paid employment for several hundred Cook Islands households; this in turn translated into the steep rise in consumption reflected in Figure 13.1, at a time of falling copra output and prices.[21]

The effects of the trends in aid and remittances sketched above were studied on the outer island of Atiu by Bollard (1979). In 1930, wages formed only 16 percent of money incomes on the island, the balance being provided by cash cropping. By 1950, a dramatic reversal had occurred: remittances now provided 48 percent of all cash incomes, wages and salaries an additional 26 percent, and cash cropping only 26 percent.[22] By 1974, wages and salaries (largely from government employment) had moved into the lead, with 65 percent; remittances were 32 percent and cash cropping 3 percent. The Atui transition to a MIRAB structure was more dramatic than the average for the Cook Islands, but by no means atypical.

The Example of Western Samoa

Although Western Samoa was not included in our data survey, it bulks large in social science work in the Pacific, and has been affected by the emergence of MIRAB features since at least the 1950s (the last decade of New Zealand colonial rule). As early as 1954, Stace noted the falling productivity of labour in export production.[23] His index of export volume per capita on base 1910-14 = 100 peaked at 120 in the period 1925-29, had fallen to 110 by 1945-49, and was back to 100 again by 1950-53. Pirie and Barrett (1962), using 1955 data, also showed copra production falling in total volume and volume per capita. They noted lagging development, evidence of emigration, malaise in the village economy and low status, even contempt, accorded to agriculture. Between 1926 and 1956, values fell by 26 percent. This underlying trend in production was masked by unusually high prices for export commodities in the early 1950s, and up until independence in 1962 the colonial administration, and most observers, continued to regard the country as a whole, including the export economy, as being in a sound condition.[24] In retrospect, however, it is clear that the 1950s brought to Western Samoa the same sharp increase in migration to New Zealand, together with the same increased inflow of government budgetary support, expansion of government employment and diversion of resources from local export production, that we have already encountered above for other New Zealand territories.[25]

In the 1960s, two major studies of the Samoan village economy virtually ignored the external dimension and the new structure of incentives,[26] but subsequent work by Shankman (1976) gave full weight to migration, remittances and other external factors in explaining the trends in the village economy.[27] In particular, dramatic declines both in the land area under crops, and in average agricultural productivity, were documented in the 1970s.[28] The trend in this direction had begun at least eight years before the end of New Zealand colonial rule.

Urbanisation and Social Change

The externally-driven MIRAB process, moving the islands from resource-based to rent-based economies and skewing the occupational structure towards bureaucracy and non-agricultural activities, has been mediated through the main town or island in each country: hence the transition to a MIRAB system was closely associated with urbanisation, involving the growth of what could be termed 'colonial-bureaucratic towns'. In all our cases, the rise of overseas aid and the expansion of the bureaucracy were sudden and substantial, though occurring at different times (about 1950 in the Cook Islands; after 1970 in Kiribati). Since overseas aid generally has a heavy Western and urban bias, and has to be mediated through the government structure, it was only to be expected that aid expenditure would primarily benefit the main island, and that outer islands would then seek to participate in the increased income flows by settling family members on the main island to seek jobs or run commercial operations, with the aim of channelling resources and opportunities back to their kin on the home island.

Lawrence has described this process in Kiribati as the growth of a "straddled economy".[29] Rather than describing an outer island such as Tamana in isolation, he pointed to the need to take account simultaneously of developments in the government centre on Tarawa, and among the Tamana community on that island. The Tamana household operated in a wider environment, in which the old resources of land, coconut palms, *babai* pits and ocean were supplemented and indeed partly replaced by the new rent-based employment and market opportunities of Tarawa. If the change was radical in an economic sense, it was equally revolutionary with respect to the perceptions and expectations of islanders. While important traditional concepts such as *tibanga* persist among Tamana people, and their desire to be *oinibai* is still essential in their lives (see Chapter 9), they see themselves operating under a different system of fate in Tarawa and achieving independence in a new way by an alternative livelihood that did not exist before. Work such as that of Lawrence on expectations and perceptions is unfortunately rare in the literature.[30]

The process of urbanisation in the South Pacific attracted a good deal of scholarly attention during the 1960s and 1970s, but most of the discussion was focused on the process of population movement itself, with port towns or main islands (usually described as the 'core') being seen to grow rapidly at the expense of the outer islands 'periphery'. Only a few studies went on to analyse the process of internal migration as a response to a wider process of social change[31] as the islands became more closely integrated into the regional labour market,[32] especially with the New Zealand mainland economy.

Culturally, the rise of towns and migration was seen to be associated with the spread of individualism, the adaptation of kinship principles to suit new situations; and the growth of new institutions such as trade unions, political parties and voluntary associations. Incipient class formation was beginning, though it was usually not recognised locally.

Villagers began to feel part of a larger society that they were 'in' but not altogether 'of', as 'pre-urban' values began to spread to outer islands.

Some scholars, including myself in the 1960s, have suggested that the urbanisation process involved social evolution of the islander from "tribesman" through "peasant" to "townsman".[33] Such evolutionary schemas, however, are over-simple. The Pacific islander living in Auckland is a townsperson, but one who is not detribalised despite having left his or her home island. Linkages with the home kin group remain strong even though the migrant's commitment to the new lifestyle in the *papa'a* city is definite and unquestionable.

* * *

The MIRAB Economy in South Pacific Microstates

Recent discussion in the pages of *Pacific Viewpoint* has addressed the problems of agricultural production and development in small Pacific island economies.[34] Watters has suggested that the stagnation or decline of village agriculture in the region must be understood in terms of two key elements: the village mode of production, and the wider economic environment which conditions decision-making within the village. In this essay, we develop these themes at greater length, focusing on aggregate economic indicators rather than detailed fieldwork, but obtaining results which we believe to be consistent with the field-research record, and helpful in interpreting it.

Conventional models of economic and social development (which have provided the basis of most writing on South Pacific agricultural development) incorporate labour migration, remittances, overseas aid and the government sector, but assume that these form part of the development process without dominating it. Our concern here is with a class of economies and societies in which the combined effect of migration, remittances, aid and bureaucracy (hereafter abbreviated to MIRAB) now *determines* the evolution of the system.

This essay describes the emergence of the MIRAB system in five very small Pacific island countries, considers some policy implications, and suggests that MIRAB systems are likely to prove more durable and sustainable than some observers expect.[35] Our concern here is to outline the argument.[36]

The Elements

In this section, we set out some of the conceptual bases for our MIRAB framework, and the combination of these elements in the MIRAB system.

Migration

In the literature on less developed economies, migration has been discussed extensively, but usually in terms of models which treat inter-regional or inter-sectoral labour movement by *individual workers* as a single-valued response to relative price signals.[37] There is also a considerable body of literature on 'circular migration', particularly in Africa, focusing again on the life-cycle decisions of individual workers.[38]

In recent years, two alternative formulations have gained appeal. Models of so-called "articulation of modes of production"[39] suggest a symbiotic interrelationship between subsistence agriculture and 'modern sector' firms, with the former providing cheap labour for the latter by ensuring the reproduction of labour and thus permitting a reduction in the modern-sector wage. Where the modern sector is geographically separate from the subsistence sector (as is the case with the growth poles of the South Pacific region), the relationship between the two halves of the dual economy involves processes of migration and remittances, and mutual adjustment by both poles to the imperatives of the modern sector's development. Discussion of such adjustments has on occasion been cast in terms of the useful conceptual apparatus of "cumulative causation" and "backwash effects" drawn from Myrdal.[40] To the extent that the analysis focuses on the dynamics of adjustment in the 'subsistence' or 'traditional' sector rather than upon the processes of capitalist development and accumulation in the modern growth pole, it points the way towards the model[41] to be presented here.

A second recent development has been a reappraisal of the balance of costs and benefits of out-migration from the point of view of the sending community. In contrast to the common approach of treating out-migration as a straightforward developmental loss to the community of origin, the new writings emphasise the extent to which migration, if viewed as a *collective* decision by migrants' family units rather than an *individual* decision by migrants themselves, can be seen as a 'profitable' allocation of household resources, potentially of long-run benefit to the growth of living standards in the sending community. For example, Griffin (1976) suggests that migration is a rational allocation of labour units by the peasant household, in order to raise that household's *collective* consumption and investment possibilities. Figueroa (1984), in his study of Peruvian highland peasant communities, finds that on average half of total household income arises from off-farm employment, much of it at a considerable distance from the village.

Migration from the small Pacific island societies appears to correspond quite well to this last group of models. [42] The movement of individuals takes place without severing the links binding them in their kin group of origin; and post-migration behaviour – the sending of remittances, and reciprocal visiting between the parts of geographically-extended kin groups – suggests the idea of an emerging new institution, the 'transnational corporation of kin', allowing kin groups to colonise and exploit economic opportunities across a wide range of economic environments.

Aid

The second element in the MIRAB system is aid. A long tradition in development economics treats aid as a supplement to domestic savings and/or foreign exchange earning capacity, with domestic resources providing the mainstay of economic growth and aid in a subsidiary role. [43] There has, however, been much discussion since 1970 of the question as to whether international aid flows should be viewed as supplements to the recipients' domestic *consumption* rather than *savings*. [44] To the extent that aid inflows are viewed as additional income, rather than additional investment, it follows that both savings and consumption in the recipient economy will be affected by changes in aid flows, but numerous writers have resisted the possibility that aid may 'crowd out' domestic savings and investment in an absolute sense. We shall argue below that in the MIRAB setting, the role of aid differs substantially from textbook stereotypes.

'Aid' to these communities, although usually described as 'development aid', has in fact tended to have the character of a straightforward supplement to local incomes and consumption, and accounts for a larger proportion of both. Up to half the budget of local governments is financed from offshore donors, and the share of government employment in total cash employment on the islands ranges from about half to over 90 percent. In balance-of-payments terms, aid inflows finance between 40 percent and over 100 percent of imports. Aid is, clearly, crucial rather than peripheral in the determination of incomes and consumption levels.

The other side of the aid coin is that these economies exhibit low capital-absorptive capacity – that is, profitable investment opportunities are few and far between, so that the possibility of utilising present aid flows for productive investment purposes does not exist. We argue below that in addition to the obvious resource limitations of small island environments, these economies exhibit the symptoms of so-called 'Dutch disease' – real exchange rates held up by large rent inflows, and effectively discouraging the expansion of tradeable-goods production.[45] Rents are income flows which are dissociated from any directly productive activity on the part of the recipient. Grant aid is effectively a rent, comparable to oil export revenues. Several other key sources of cash income in MIRAB systems are also best treated as rents – remittances from relatives overseas and philatelic revenue are good examples.

Bureaucracy

It is clear from the sketchy data available that the government sector is now the dominant cash employer in the five economies analysed below. With the exception of a few old-established trading firms, capitalist enterprises in the modern sector are few, relatively small, and usually based upon the employment of part-time or female labour which is available relatively cheaply from the village sector labour force. The government sector accounts for about 52 percent of total cash employment in the Cook Islands,[46] over 90 percent in Tokelau, over 85 percent in Niue (on the basis of unpublished preliminary results from the 1981 census), 80 percent in Kiribati[47] and over 60 percent in Tuvalu.[48] The remaining cash employment, apart from that in the Rarotonga tourist industry, is in small trading and manufacturing establishments, such as clothing 'factories' of Rarotonga, a coconut-cream and lime-juice plant on Niue, and the missions and cooperative stores of Tokelau, Kiribati and Tuvalu.

With percentages such as the above, it is clear that a large proportion of the kin groups in the islands are likely to have members working in the local government service at some level, so that wages and salaries paid out by government constitute a widely-dispersed source of cash income for households in the village sector. Because government activities (especially white-collar jobs) tend to concentrate on one island, or in one village, the process of placing household members into government employment often involves a process of internal migration, with subsequent remittances back to the home island or village.

MIRAB Systems

A number of the very small island societies of the South Pacific have developed economic and social structures of the sort outlined above. A large proportion of their labour force – in several cases, half – is resident overseas on a long-term basis, without severing their economic, social and cultural links with the home community. Remittances in cash and kind from those workers are distributed through kin-group channels to provide a major source of disposable income in the island economy. The migration is neither on a clear life-cycle basis, nor in the form of a severing of the ties between the migrant and his/her home community and household. Rather, the process appears to involve the internationalisation of the economic activities of island kin groups or households, acting to allocate their labour resources internationally to take advantage of niches of economic opportunity. The resulting economic units, which can be described as "transnational corporations of kin",[49] resemble the familiar transnational corporations of the global modern sector in their allocation of resources and transfers of income between units within the group. Where, for example, disposable incomes in the home community exceed desired absorption of resources by those resident there, net transfers will flow out of, rather than into, the island economy.

These patterns of migration and aid flow directly from the history of colonialism and decolonisation. This essay suggests, first, that the processes of social and economic change in the small island societies have to be understood in terms of local adjustment to external forces, rather than as endogenously-driven development; and second, that both the transnational corporation of kin and the large-scale flows of unrequited aid appear capable of continuous reproduction at least until the turn of the century. In many of the new states of the Pacific, establishing the conditions for 'modernisation' has meant an increase in 'dependence';[50] the two go hand in hand and are not alternatives.

The South Pacific Case

This section illustrates the emergence and dimensions of the MIRAB structure, using long-run statistical material for five small South Pacific communities: Cook Islands, Niue, Tokelau, Tuvalu and Kiribati.[51]

Migration

Migration is not, of course, a new phenomenon for Pacific island peoples. At the beginning of the 1950s, most small island societies in the South Pacific had a fair number of individuals with experience of travel and employment in the wider region. The notion of migrating to cash employment, as an alternative to working in petty commodity production at home, was well-established, and opportunities to do so were readily taken up as they became available.

Beginning in the 1950s, and to a dramatic extent in the 1960s and 1970s, the New Zealand labour market became open to migrants from those island societies which had been included within New Zealand's sphere of colonial administration or influence: Western Samoa, the Cook Islands, Niue, Tokelau and Tonga. The 'pull factor' was the emergence in New Zealand of a tight labour market as industrialisation proceeded. The 'push factor' was provided by increased population pressure in the islands, as population levels recovered from the demographic disasters of the nineteenth century. A facilitating element was improved communication. Links between the islands and New Zealand grew stronger as air travel extended through the region in the 1960s and 1970s.

Table 13.I. Islands-born Population by Place of Residence: New Zealand-linked Societies

	Cook Islands-born			Niue-born			Tokelau-born		
Year	In Cook Is	In NZ (%)	Total Niue (%)	In NZ lau	In Toke- (%)	Total NZ	In	In	Total
1936	11,943	157 (1)	12,100	4,105	54 (1)	4,159	1,170	0 (0)	1,170
1945	13,574	393 (3)	13,967	4,253	222 (5)	4,475	1,388	0 (0)	1,388
1951	14,757	999 (6)	15,756	4,553	330 (7)	4,883	1,571	10 (0.6)	1,581
1956	17,054	1,992 (10)	19,046	4,707	753 (14)	5,460	1,619	7 (0.4)	1,626
1961	18,378	3,374 (16)	21,752	4,868	1,414 (23)	6,282	1,860	23 (1)	1,883
1966	19,251	5,838 (23)	25,089	5,194	2,014 (28)	7,208	1,900	248 (12)	2,148
1971	21,317	7,389 (26)	28,706	4,990	2,912 (37)	7,902	1,655	950 (36)	2,605
1976	18,112	12,156 (40)	30,268	3,843	4,379 (53)	8,222	1,575	1212 (43)	2,787
1981	17,695	13,848 (44)	31,543	3,278	5,091 (61)	8,369	1,572	1281 (45)	2,853

Source: Data assembled from New Zealand and island census reports for years shown.

Table 13.I shows the impact of migration from three New Zealand-linked small territories to the metropolitan growth pole, on the basis of island and New Zealand census data. In 1951, of the estimated total population of island-born people, those living in New Zealand comprised only 6 percent of Cook Islanders, 7 percent of Niueans and less than 1 percent of Tokelauans. By 1981, these proportions had increased to 44 percent of island-born Cook Islanders, 61 percent of Niueans and 45 percent of Tokelauans. This radical reallocation of population, taking place within the space of a generation, produced dual but not separate communities. Kin and cultural ties between migrants and their home communities remain important, and the size of the migrant communities is dwarfed by the figures for gross travel flows between the islands and New Zealand.[52] Visiting between the two halves of each community remains at a high level, as does the flow of remittances in cash and kind from migrants in New Zealand back to home communities in the Cook Islands and Tokelau – or, in the case of Niue, from home communities in Niue to relatives in New Zealand.

It will be noted that as migration to New Zealand picked up sharply in the 1950s, the level of resident population in the Cook Islands and Tokelau stabilised. The *de facto* populations of these territories were virtually the same in 1981 as they had been in 1951. That of Niue, where special factors induced exceptionally strong out-migration in the 1970s, was down 28 percent. The main impact of out-migration has been to drain off net population increase. The extent to which migration was age- and sex-specific was probably greatest in the early phase and less in the more recent phase, as family dependants moved to join breadwinners established in New Zealand.[53]

The Cook Islands, Niuean and Tokelauan ethnic communities therefore now span two geographically-separate entities: the home islands and the New Zealand metropole. The New Zealand industrial labour market constitutes the 'modern sector' of the island economies, while the island-resident portion of each community operates the 'non-capitalist' or 'traditional' sector, together with the local government apparatus.

Given this new reality, which has been emerging steadily for four decades, it is inappropriate to analyse development prospects for either half of the islander population in isolation. The symbiotic links between the parts of this internationalised dual economy remain strong. The South Pacific (New Zealand included) is an integrated 'interaction area' – a continuous socio-economic field.

Kiribati and Tuvalu present a rather different picture. As successor states of a former British colony (the Gilbert and Ellice Islands), with no access to any metropolitan labour market, these two countries display much lower levels of *overseas* migration than do the New Zealand-linked territories. As Table 13.2 shows, only 4 percent of I-Kiribati and 15 percent of Tuvaluans were resident overseas in 1979, mainly on the phosphate islands of Nauru and Banaba (Ocean) and as seamen on international shipping lines. These countries have nevertheless been deeply affected by the migration-remittance process – but at the intra-national level of island-to-island movement. In Kiribati, the key internal growth poles have been Banaba (until phosphates ran out in

1979) and the government centre, Tarawa. Both have attracted migrants and generated flows of remittance incomes to outer islands. The 1978 census found that 45.9 percent of I-Kiribati aged 15 and over were not resident on their home island; and 69 percent of the total population of Tarawa were in-migrants from outer islands.[54]

In Tuvalu, the internal growth pole is again the seat of government, Funafuti, where aid-financed employment in government service is available for migrants from other islands. The 1979 census[55] found 45 percent of the total population (and 50 percent of males) were resident on islands other than their islands of birth. No less than 67 percent of the total population of Funafuti (and 70 percent of its male population) consisted of in-migrants.

Table 13.2. Kiribati- and Tuvalu-born Populations by Place of Residence

Year	Kiribati-born			Tuvalu-born		
	In Kiribati	Overseas (%)	Total	In Tuvalu	Overseas (%)	Total
1931				3,994	95 (2)	4,089
1947	31,513			4,487	579 (11)	5,066
1963	43,336			5,444	1,319 (20)	6,763
1968	47,682	1,404 (3)	49,086	5,782	1,683 (23)	7,465
1973	51,784	1,765 (3)	53,549	5,887	1,807 (23)	7,694
1979	56,213	2,299 (4)	58,512	7,349	1,303 (15)	8,652

Sources: Annual Reports of the GEIC, and census publications for the two countries.

Remittances

The flow of remittances from overseas-resident members of island households is a major source both of cash incomes in the village economy, and of import capacity in the balance of payments for each of our five case studies except Niue. Table 13.3 shows our estimates of the balance of payments position for the five economies in the last decade and a half, expressed in 1982 dollars. Taken as a percentage of total imports, gross remittance inflows amounted to 14 percent for the Cook Islands 1970-83, 4 percent for Niue over the same period, 8 percent for Kiribati 1975-83 (but rising to 13 percent in the 1980s following the exhaustion of phosphates), 14 percent for Tokelau 1975-83 and 20 percent for Tuvalu 1979-82. Expressed in 1982 dollars, and related to the figures for overseas-resident islanders in Tables 13.1 and 13.2, these remittance flows in the early 1980s were equivalent to NZ$288 per Cook Islands migrant, NZ$59 per Niuean migrant, A$870 per Kiribati migrant, NZ$78 per Tokelauan and A$460 per Tuvaluan.

Table 13.3. Some Balance-of-payments Estimates: Annual Averages $000 at 1982 Prices

	Com- modity exports	– Com- modity imports	+ Philatelic & tourism	+ Aid +	Remit- tances	= Residual balance
Cook Islands						
1970-74	8,638	20,524	-	12,694	3,371	+4,179
1975-79	5,413	32,345	6,000	12,798	3,923	- 4,211
1980-83	5,199	27,346	8,530	10,295	4,000	+678
Niue						
1970-74	608	3,172	-	4,700	50 ?	+2,186
1975-79	483	4,302	150	6,106	100?	+2,537
1980-83	568	3,984	300	5,353	300	+2,537
Kiribati						
1970-74	31,213	15,739	n.a.	n.a.	n.a.	n.a.
1975-79	35,581	18,712	1,000 ?	4,000	1,000	+22,069
1980-83	3,446	14,879	1,000	11,000	2,000	+2,567
Tokelau						
1970-74	85	363[a]		270[b]	8	[c]
1975-79	104	410[a]	40	236[b]	30 ?	[c]
1980-83	63	490[a]	100 +	227[b]	100 ??	[c]
Tuvalu						
1979-82	124	3,021	1,500	3,500 +	600	+2,703

Store goods only. [b] *Calculated as a residual.* [c] *See note b.*
Source: Bertram and Watters, 1984, p. 104.

Average remittance 'effort' thus measured varies quite widely. The highest rates are encountered in the case of Kiribati and Tuvalu. There are at least two reasons. First, overseas migration from these two countries is still mainly temporary, very specific to particular age and sex groups, and comprised almost entirely of productive workers. This means that the per-migrant remittance rate is very close to the per-worker rate, whereas for the New Zealand-linked cases the denominator includes many unproductive dependants. Secondly, Kiribati and Tuvalu have very limited migration outlets, so that a high value is placed on overseas employment opportunities. The best workers get these jobs, and the pressures on them to bring or send wage earnings home are much greater.

Viewed from the receiving end, gross remittance inflows accounted for NZ$226 per Cook Island resident, NZ$92 per Niuean, A$36 per I-Kiribati, NZ$64 per Tokelauan and A$82 per Tuvaluan. Cash income per *household* from this source would, of course, be higher. In absolute terms, the average impact on per-capita incomes from remittances appears relatively small. However, it is important to recall that remittances provide an important source of cash income in societies where most basic needs are met directly by household production within the village; and also that remittances are not evenly spread among households or through time. On some individual islands, thus, remittances are the largest single source of cash incomes; on others, they may be only a minor element.

The pattern revealed in Table 13.3 is typical also of several other, larger, South Pacific island economies. Tongan data[56] show that in 1976 export earnings were equivalent to 36 percent of imports, while overseas remittances, donations and gifts accounted for 52 percent. In 1980, following an apparent sharp increase in aid inflows, exports were down to 23 percent of imports, and remittances, donations and gifts to 34 percent. For Western Samoa, data for the early 1980s suggest that money-order remittances alone financed around 15 percent of imports on average.[57]

Aid

Returning to Table 13.3, it will be seen that aid inflows are now the dominant credit item in the balance of payments for each of the five island groups. In the first four years of the 1980s, aid has been equivalent to 38 percent of recorded imports in the Cook Islands, 134 percent in Niue, 74 percent in Kiribati, 46 percent in Tokelau and 116 percent in Tuvalu. In all cases, these aid inflows are current-account rather than capital account flows; that is, the funds arrive in the form of grants, not loans, and no 'overhang' of accumulating overseas indebtedness results. Aid in these societies, thus, is a form of rent income arising as a return on an asset which we might describe as 'aid entitlement'.[58] It needs to be distinguished sharply from other more familiar types of aid which take the form of drawing-down a community's international credit (that is, supplementing its present purchasing power at the expense of its future disposable income). The distinction is important when addressing the question of whether 'aid', as a dominant source of external cash income for very small societies, is reproducible over the long run.

The central role of external aid in the five cases in Table 13.3 is not untypical. Overseas aid to the whole South Pacific had grown to over $1 billion by 1980 – a per-capita average of A$213, or A$402 if Papua

New Guinea is excluded.[59] The degree of aid dependence varies widely, with several countries receiving in 1980 over A$500 of aid per capita: Cook Islands $520, Tuvalu $573, Wallis and Futuna $676, Guam $791, French Polynesia $944, Niue $970, Tokelau $1,063, American Samoa $1,091, Trust Territory of the Pacific Islands $1,101 and New Caledonia $1,234. By 1983, largely because of inflation in the intervening period, the Cook Islands figure had risen to about $726 per capita, Tuvalu to A$1,000, Niue to about $2,009 and Tokelau about $1,800. Kiribati, in contrast, was receiving only A$99 per capita in 1983.

Fisk (1978) has described the consequences of very large per capita aid flows for the case of Niue. On the one hand, aid has permitted the attainment of high living standards; on the other hand, it has resulted in an economic system which could not conceivably become self-sufficient without sacrificing those standards. Aid officials in the mid-1970s were hoping that Niue would in due course replace its budgetary support aid by internally generated revenue; in 1978, this would have required an additional $1.8 million of revenue, equivalent to about $450 per head of population. Since an average Niuean family of six people would not have a cash income, let alone taxpaying capacity, of $2,700 (six times $450), economic independence was clearly a long way off. Fisk could see little prospect of exports rising from the existing level of $150,000 p.a. to the required $2 million over the seven years then being canvassed as the period of aid phase-out.[60] (As Figure 13.1 shows, the average growth rate of Niuean export earnings in real terms has in fact been zero over the past 80 years.)

Bureaucracy and the Government Sector

The bulk of the aid inflow to our case study economies takes the form of budgetary support for local governments. The right-hand side of Figure 13.1 traces the expansion of government spending in real terms and the growing gap between local revenue and local expenditure (which, of course, corresponds to the availability of aid finance). Comparison with the commodity trade data on the left-hand side of the figure shows a close relationship between rising government expenditure (with much of the increase externally financed except in phosphate-rich Kiribati) and the surge of commodity imports, mainly of consumer goods, which has occurred over the past four or five decades in the case study economies.

Imports provide a good indicator of changes in material living standards, despite evidence that some imported goods have crowded out traditional locally-produced staples. In each of our five economies, the rent-driven 'takeoff' of imports occurred prior to decolonisation, not afterwards. The colonial powers, as an act of policy, set target living standards which they felt to be appropriate for South Pacific island populations, with high priority given to public goods such as health, education and communications. Expanding government sectors were the natural result – a process which can be described as 'welfare-state colonialism'.

The MIRAB Transition

The emergence of a MIRAB economy involves the appearance of new sources of cash income besides the production of export staples; as these alternatives are taken up, resources are diverted away from the production of staples. Quite apart from the very limited resource base in the islands, it is therefore no surprise to find both anecdotal and statistical evidence of stagnation or decline of village agriculture during the period of transition to the MIRAB system.

The growing separation between domestic production and disposable incomes in these small open economies is best reflected in the relative movements of commodity exports and imports, respectively. The historical trading performance of our five economies is summarised on the left-hand side of Figure 13.1. Despite variations of detail from case to case, the general pattern is consistent across all five. Imports have steadily diverged from commodity exports, creating what might be termed a 'jaws effect'. The Cook Islands, Niue, Tokelau and Tuvalu all exhibit low long-run trend growth of exports through both the colonial and the post-colonial eras, with only a temporary exception provided by the period of the citrus boom in the Cook Islands in the late 1950s and early 1960s, under the stimulus of a new government-promoted cannery.[61] In Kiribati, the pattern is obscured by the high level of export earnings associated with phosphates until the exhaustion of the Banaba deposits in 1979, but the relationship between export earnings and import demand during the early 1980s reveals an underlying economic structure closely resembling that of the other four cases.

Cook Islands citrus and Kiribati phosphates appear as exceptions to prove the rule that living standards have been driven up by rent incomes rather than by expanding productive incomes. By rent income, we mean the combination of remittances, budgetary aid, philatelic revenue and dividend incomes to governments – income flows, in other words, which accrue to the island communities by virtue of their identity and location rather than as a result of the sale of local products. In the mid-1980s, it is inescapably true that the real disposable incomes of the resident populations of all five economies are sustainable only if

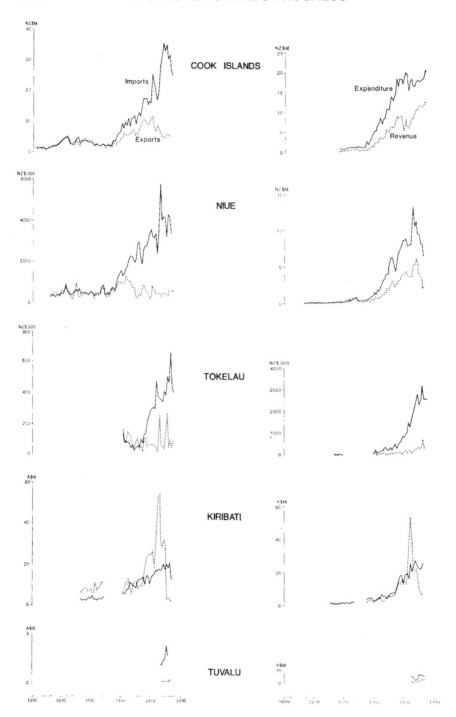

Figure 13.1. Exports and Imports, Government Expenditure and Revenue for Five Pacific Microstates

their current-account rent entitlements are in their turn sustainable. The question of what level export production might have attained had there been no MIRAB process – hence, what standard of living would have been attainable on the basis of local resource endowments alone – can only be answered speculatively. Our view is that our case study economies could not have attained comparable living standards on their own.[62]

Some Implications

The evolved MIRAB structure which was described in the preceding section may be summarised as follows for small Pacific island societies.

'Subsistence Affluence'

The land and sea resources available to the village mode of production are sufficient to guarantee the basic needs of the population. In this sense, subsistence remains attainable. The village economy retains control over most of those productive resources, and that control is not threatened by any competing mode of production. Thus the non-capitalist production sector provides the 'floor' below which real incomes in the islands will not fall unless the village mode is destroyed. The subsistence economy does not, of course, exist in isolation from the remainder of the economy. On the contrary, one of the features of Pacific island economies is the high degree of overlap and interpenetration between modern and subsistence sectors. Public servants and other participants in the cash economy live in the village, retain access to land and participate in village activities. Specialisation and division of labour, in other words, are incomplete.

Transnational Corporations of Kin

Family or kin units in the small Pacific societies act and calculate on a transnational scale, especially via the regional labour market. Their commitment of resources to activity in the islands therefore reflects their weighing-up of alternatives which include wage employment and offshore financial investment. The great majority of households are able to judge the relative merits of wage employment (locally and offshore) and household productive activity on the land or sea. Islanders have thus become proletarianised without, in the process, becoming a proletariat. Because they retain control over means of production, they enjoy considerable managerial autonomy and are not dependent upon wage labour for their survival.

'Dutch Disease'

The rapid increase in rent incomes of small-island communities over the past three decades has radically changed both the economic incentives and the constraints facing island households. This is especially true of sources of cash income. The investment of kin-group labour in the production of an agricultural surplus for sale on uncertain markets is only one of a number of alternative economic strategies. Kin can be expected to evaluate the return on such investment relative to the alternatives. On this basis, it would be expected that as the alternatives to commercially-oriented agriculture improve, so a reallocation of household effort away from agriculture would take place. Only under quite special conditions would this relative restructuring of kindred resource allocation be consistent with an absolute increase in agricultural productive activity.[63] An important feature of a MIRAB structure is thus the crowding-out of marginal productive activities by new opportunities to earn cash incomes in government employment and overseas.

From the point of view of local kin groups, the separation of local disposable income from domestic product means that there is no automatic link between increased local production and increased economic welfare. The constraint upon GDP growth in a MIRAB setting is not scarce resources *per se*, but rather the fact that the 'normal' incentives to expand local productive activities are rendered inoperative. Development planning, and development aid, therefore have very limited scope. Additional cash made available to village households is more likely to be allocated to increased consumption and capital outflow (e.g. to bank accounts in the metropolitan economies) than to increased local production. Similarly, additional resources made available in kind to raise agricultural productivity are as likely to lead to a reduction in the area cultivated as to increases in aggregate output, unless the external incentives faced by households are changed at the same time. This implies no lack of entrepreneurship, flexibility or diligence on the part of islanders – on the contrary, the 'MIRAB effect', like its close relative 'Dutch disease', arises precisely because of the economic responsiveness and flexibility of island household units in their open-economy situation.

The Sustainability of a MIRAB Economic Order

Confronted with evidence of agricultural decline, growing aid and remittances, large unproductive bureaucracies and continuing out-migration, many observers of the small Pacific economies have been inclined to assume that the MIRAB system is inherently a transitional and unsustainable social and economic formation, and thus not potentially a steady-state or permanent condition. From this perspective, the familiar conventional model of internally-sustained economic 'development' is claimed to hold the key for the long run, and is thus retained at the heart of both analyses of, and prescriptions for, the future prospects of these societies.[64]

While not wishing to discount such a view altogether, we think that the MIRAB system is likely to prove durable and persistent over a considerable period of time. In advancing this hypothesis, we are suggesting that the regional MIRAB system is capable of self-reproduction through time – that is, that the international kin corporation, the flow of remittances, and the availability of grant aid are all 'sustainable' so that present levels of consumption, together with present structures of the balance of payments and of government finance, are all likely to persist.

We begin with the question of the sustainability of the present type and level of aid. In comparison with other so-called developing areas, the South Pacific has been conspicuously successful in obtaining overseas aid, and since most of this aid has been grants rather than loans, the region is not saddled with an accumulating debt burden. The volume and type of aid reflect partly donor recognition of the 'special problems' of being small, isolated economies with limited internal markets; but more importantly show the realities of the decolonisation process and subsequent geopolitical calculations by the major regional powers.

The entitlement to ongoing grant aid arises from the 'obligations' of former colonial powers established during the colonial era and continued after decolonisation. Budgetary grants were unavoidable if the colonial powers' aspirations for their dependent territories (or, equally important, for their own international reputations) were to be realised; and they remain unavoidable in the post-colonial era unless New Zealand and/or the United Kingdom are prepared to see living standards slide in their former or actual dependencies; or unless they are prepared to be supplanted by other, competing, aid donors.

The key to the long-run aid entitlement of the case study communities lies thus in two characteristics of post-colonial politics. First is the ethical notion, widely held by both electorates and governments in the metropolitan states, that they have an obligation to underwrite the maintenance of the gains achieved by welfare-state colonialism. The second is the geopolitical reality that neither power is yet willing to relinquish its sphere of influence in the region, particularly if the competing potential aid donor by whom they might be supplanted is the Soviet Union.

We would therefore expect current-account aid flows to continue during the next couple of decades. Dramatic growth of real incomes from this source is not likely, but neither is any sharp collapse, despite dire forebodings in the 1983 Kiribati Development Plan.[65] There will, of course, have to be some adjustment of the rhetorical justification for aid flows as the last decade's commitment to self-supporting economic growth in the islands is supplanted by more explicit recognition of the MIRAB process. But the central point about aid is that it is easy to start, but hard to stop.

Turning to remittances, a familiar hypothesis advanced by Stark[66] is that migrants will tend to send back high levels of remittances in the first few years after migration, but thereafter the level of remittances is predicted to tail off as ties to the home community weaken. On this basis, it might be suggested that the present high levels of remittance incomes to small island economies will not be sustained for long. Such a view seems to us to overlook two important characteristics of the migration process in the Pacific: firstly, the maintenance of links between the migrant and the home community through the agency of the 'kin corporation'; and secondly, the continuing flow of new migrants, which in a sense makes up for any 'depreciation' in the island community's existing stock of migrant 'human capital' in the regional growth poles.

The balance-of-payments figures show a steep upward trend in overseas remittances to Kiribati, Tuvalu and Tokelau over recent years. In the first two cases, this reflects partly the switch from internal to external migration in the past decade (so that a greater proportion of total remitted labour earnings appear in the balance of international payments). In the case of Tokelau, the figures (which should be treated with some caution) probably reflect the facts that large-scale migration has been a relatively recent phenomenon and that the demand for cash goods in the islands has only recently begun to catch up with that in the other territories. In the case of Niue, the dominance of the local economy by the government is so great that even remittances have been 'crowded out'. Net private cash remittances flow from Niue to New Zealand, both to purchase financial assets in New Zealand and to contribute to the living standards of relatives there.

It is to the Cook Islands that we must turn for a case of a society where the main migration process dates back several decades, where the incentives to remit are fairly strong, and where we have consistent data available for analysis. Table 13.4 shows that, insofar as the Cook Islands are typical of MIRAB systems, the aggregate flow of remittances exhibits a great deal of stability over quite long time periods, and shows no sign as yet of tapering off.

**Table 13.4. Remittances Received in Cook Islands
Annual Averages, 1982 $000**

Period	Money orders	Other forms	Total
1942-46	476.3	n.a.	n.a.
1947-54	1,303.7	n.a.	n.a.
1955-59	2,134.3	n.a.	n.a.
1960-65	n.a.	n.a.	n.a.
1966-70	1,883.4	1,124.6	3,008.0
1971-75	2,202.4	1,322.0	3.524.4
1976-80	2,224.8	1,638.0	3,862.8
1981-83	2,626.7	1,576.0	4,202.7

*Sources: 1942-59 from Kelly, 1985, p. 105, based on Annual Reports of the Cook Islands
administration; 1966-80 from Hayes, 1982, Table 8.10, p. 364; 1981-83 from Bertram
and Watters, 1984, Table 6.12, p. 168, on the basis of data supplied by the Post Office in
Rarotonga.*

In per capita terms, money-order remittance inflows per resident
Cook Islander were $88 in the early 1950s, about $125 in the late
1950s, about $100 in the late 1960s, about $130 in the late 1970s
and $160 in the early 1980s. This does not give the appearance of any
tapering-off of incomes at the receiving end, which is what matters from
the point of view of reproducing the MIRAB system. Obviously, as the
number of migrants overseas rose, the amount remitted on average per
migrant has shown some downward trend, from about $700 in the late
1950s to about $200 in the late 1960s, and $120 in the late 1970s – all
figures based on money orders only, in 1982 dollars. Taking account
of other forms of remittances in cash and kind, the per-migrant figure
for the late 1960s was about $300, and for the late 1970s $200. A fair
amount of this trend is attributable to the changing age-sex structure
of the migrant community as dependent members of kin groups moved
to join economically-active migrants.

Conclusion

This essay has outlined some of the characteristics of, and forces at
work in, the emergence of MIRAB economies in some of the smaller
South Pacific nations. The transition process is by no means steady
or irreversible; it can be checked by the denial of migration outlets to
island labour (as occurred in New Zealand in the 'overstayer crisis'
of 1976); or by pressure from aid donors for recipient governments to
raise the proportion of their spending funded from local revenues; or
by occasional episodes of success with onshore productive activity in
the islands.

The transition, furthermore, tends to be self-limiting beyond a certain point, leaving societies which in conventional terms may appear 'permanently transitional' with mixed modes of production. Given the uncertainties of the wider world, and the value of traditional food staples in dietary and health terms, the maintenance of the subsistence base provided by the village mode is rational not only from the point of view of the kin group but also from that of society. It could be argued, in fact, that there is a case for aid donors to move towards greater direct subsidisation of agricultural production (including subsistence) and to lower the priority given to maintenance of large bureaucracies whose existence and size have tended to be justified by a quest for autonomous economic development which can now be seen to be misconceived.

The social, cultural and political consequences of the survival of the mixed modes of production in a MIRAB system are a sometimes incongruous mélange of neo-traditional, bureaucratic and commercial patterns of life. The resulting system, however, is highly flexible and adaptable, which is its great strength. Given the diversity and ambiguity in the forces of change, it is not surprising that islanders become adroit at "wearing the right hat" for the occasion[67] – at slipping easily from 'traditional' to 'modern' behaviour, at invoking 'traditional' or 'modern' precedents as the occasion requires, and at refusing to behave in what an outsider would see as a consistent and logical way.

Flexibility and ambiguity are likely to continue to characterise island governments' responses to metropolitan governments, increasing the latters' frustrations. In the era of decolonisation, the drive for self-government or independence provided an overall sense of direction, despite the contradictions between political and economic trends. In the present MIRAB era, this sense of direction is fading, to be replaced by an atmosphere of 'islands for sale', of political and diplomatic adventurism by some island leaders who attempt to 'touch' all their options without foreclosing any, in order to increase their room for manoeuvre. Metropolitan governments are only beginning to come to grips with the MIRAB phenomenon, and island governments have no reason to outpace them.

Indeed, there are diplomatic advantages to be gained by island governments persisting with the rhetoric of autonomous 'development' and insisting on their right, as self-governing entities, to determine their own goals. They may thus for some time find it advantageous to refuse to recognise the MIRAB model and its implications. An era of uncertainty and frustration for both sides of the aid relationship appears likely to ensue.

14

Has Progress Been Achieved?

Roads to Development

As I end this book in September 2007, the journeys of the individual countries of the Pacific towards progress look fraught with difficulties and dangers both from within and without. While there is little doubt that overwhelmingly Pacific peoples will choose some route that appears to lead to 'development', the notion of development may prove to be something of a chimera with many meanings.

As Murray Bathgate pointed out in his work on the Ndi-Nggai tribe who live in Guadalcanal, Solomon Islands, development even in the relatively rich and 'advanced' village of Taboko really only means 'change' and nothing more, since 'development' has involved the breaking down of one system (subsistence) and replacing it with another (cash cropping). This change in the means of sustenance has meant that ancillary services such as stores and transport services to market have been aligned to support and maintain a growing dependence on purchased foods. Moreover, in Bathgate's example, villagers are still spending most of their money on the same basic array of items introduced in the early days of trade – axes, bush-knives, calico and pots, then rice, biscuits, tinned meat, tea, sugar and tobacco. As incomes have risen, increased outlay on these items has been much more than any widening of the demand for other goods. Another relevant factor is that in the period after 1980 most coconut palms have matured and with high population growth there was a growing shortage of land available for gardening.

In short, the Ndi-Nggai around 1980 seemed to Bathgate to be moving into that phase that Diana Howlett, referring to the Goroka Valley of Highland Papua New Guinea, aptly termed an "infinite pause",[1] with the long-term prospects of each household obtaining a continuously rising per capita income and increased spending power becoming more and more elusive.[2] As Maev O'Collins (2005) has noted in relation to Papua New Guinea, development "has many faces", with continuity and change remaining strong factors in tribal life.

The Countries

Fiji

In December 1971, I returned to Fiji with my family, en route for Kiribati to begin our team's rural socio-economic project of that country and Tuvalu. We went to Nalotawa, partly to visit old friends and partly so my family could to see this village where I had earlier worked. As a crude road now existed as far as Nalotawa, we were taken there by taxi. We were welcomed warmly and presented *yaqona* to the villagers. I thanked Ratu Jone Lotawa and the people of Nalotawa for the privilege of being able to live there on my earlier visits and to study their situation. They were pleased to have been part of the study and did me the honour of presenting me with a ceremonial *tabua*.

The villagers said they were happy with their lot – some of the houses had been at least partly rebuilt in European materials. But when walking around the village it was apparent that there was much less space available, and several graves now occupied land that had previously been free.

Around 1960, I was not optimistic for the prospects of economic development in the dry zone hill country surrounding Nalotawa. The rolling country had mostly poor latosolic soils that were considerably eroded, droughts were a problem, and the *gasau* reeds and mission grass were almost unpalatable to livestock. The Agriculture Department saw little potential for the area. An investigation by the Food and Agriculture Organisation in 1971, however, changed this outlook: they recommended a large-scale afforestation project in north-west Viti Levu and Vanua Levu. The scheme proposed 53,600 ha. be planted in pine, of which 20,000 ha. were to be planted by 1978. In 1971, 4,000 ha. were planted near Nalotawa and about 2,280 ha. of land were planted each year between 1971 and 1978. There were considerable expenses on labour and road construction costs of about F$1 million a year (indeed, the road on which we had travelled to Nalotawa had been built for this project).

Lasaqa (1984) reported that the project planned to borrow F$12m by 1980, with $10m committed by the Commonwealth Development Corporation and other assistance from New Zealand and Fiji government grants. Major earnings from the timber were expected from 1982 when logging would begin and a chipping industry established; it was hoped that all debt would be cleared by 1989.

There were various benefits for the people of Nalotawa and the other villagers of the area whose lands had been taken up: rental for a 60-

year lease based on $1.25 per ha. per annum on planted land and 25 cents per ha. on unplanted land; and a premium of $3.12 per ha. paid to landowners when land was taken up. Fijian landowners were also to be paid 3 percent of the value of the standing crop at felling time, with a minimum payment of $50 per ha., whichever was the greater, at a rotation of 20 years and pro rata for longer or shorter periods. Lease conditions were to be reviewed every 10 years.

What was commendable about the scheme was the partnership between the Pine Commission (the statutory body set up by the government) and the village landowners. In the earlier period, the official majority had the main say in management, but as the commission's indebtedness was reduced, the landowners' representatives would grow in numbers and eventually have a controlling position when they had acquired sufficient experience as well as training in every aspect of the industry.[3]

Each year at Christmas, I exchanged greetings with my old friend the chief Ratu Jone Lotawa and invariably he wrote with glowing enthusiasm of the progress of the pine project. While I remained unaware of many details of the project and whether Nalotawa or other village landowners invested their rent income to obtain equipment or further training in operations and management, this enthusiasm seems to have been sustained.

One day in the mid-1980s, I literally bumped into Ratu Jone in a Wellington street. He was in New Zealand as a senior member of the Pine Commission board attending a conference on the timber industry and New Zealand aid. I was delighted and astonished and Bethlyn and I were fortunate enough to be able to invite him to dinner at our home. Shortly thereafter, I lost contact with Ratu Jone and with it news of Nalotawa; perhaps he fell ill and passed away.

In December 1980, rumours abounded in Fiji that the Phoenix Foundation (see Chapter 12) was behind an American pine forest exploitation deal that by-passed government channels and negotiated directly with landowners through a Fijian middleman. Fiji's *South Pacific Islands Business News* commented: "The situation that exists with Fiji's pine is made to order for the untrammelled free enterprise and the elimination of all government interference in business realised through the persuasion of breakaway local groups such as that on Santo", Vanuatu. The fact that the deal involved a shadowy concern called United Marketing Corporation based in Phoenix, Arizona, only added to the speculation.[4] The very low international prices for pine which affected New Zealand production in the 1990s are likely to have affected Fiji and this project. However, as I write (April 2006), the Chinese Premier has visited Fiji and signed a comprehensive trade agreement. Of course, in recent years other forestry developments in interior Viti Levu were noteworthy. A very valuable mahogany forest was ready for milling and it was alleged that this was to be sold illegally to American interests (possibly the Phoenix Foundation) by the traitor George Speight, leader of the mutiny of 2000, with the proceeds presumably going to the mutineers and their backers.

The Coups[5]

The paramount issue for Fiji over the last 60 years has been ethno-nationalism. When *Koro* was written in the 1950s and 1960s, I was surprised how few serious books on the country recognised the significance of this factor. (The Burns Report, 1960; Belshaw, 1964b; and Fisk, 1970, were notable exceptions.) Thus, it was no comfort to me at all that my dire predictions came true when Sitiveni Rabuka carried out a military coup in 1987.

Rabuka was hailed as the saviour of the 'Fijian Race' and was given life-long membership of the Great Council of Chiefs. Although David Lange's Labour government in New Zealand strongly opposed the coup, the Australasian international media felt the coup leaders were justified for what Naidu called "the 'rape' of Fiji's peculiar democracy".[6] They saw an indigenous people rising against the "migrant Indian race" to defend their right to self-determination, and this action was supported by the other Melanesian nations.

The appeals of the prime minister, Dr Bavadra, to the Queen, the British government and the governments of Australia and New Zealand largely fell on deaf ears. The US government appeared to welcome the coup as Bavadra's government had recently banned nuclear-powered and -armed ships from Fiji waters.

However, the Fiji Labour Party (FLP) and National Federation Party (NFP) coalition government led by Bavadra was not 'Indian' dominated. Although it had a majority of Indo-Fijian supporters, its cabinet comprised equal numbers of the two major ethnic groups and included representatives of general electors. It was Fiji's first genuinely multi-ethnic government, but without a strong representation of Fijian chiefs.

Strong protests against Rabuka's coup continued, culminating in a multi-ethnic 'Back to Early May Movement' which presented a petition of thousands of signatures to the Governor-General seeking a return to the Constitution. Efforts by the Governor-General and advisors led to meetings between Bavadra and Ratu Mara and to an agreement on some form of a government of national unity. As Rabuka and the extreme nationalists were not part of these negotiations, they acted decisively against further compromises and in September the second coup was carried out, detaining the FLP and NFP leaders again and violating their human rights. This second coup abrogated the 1970 constitution, the Queen ceased to be head of state and the military sought to rule itself with the assistance of extreme Fijian ethno-nationalists. Fiji lost its membership of the British Commonwealth.

Eventually, power was once again returned to the paramount chiefs of eastern Fiji. Rabuka and his allies, who included for some time Ratu Mara and Ratu Sir Penaia Ganilau (governor-general and then president), decreed a new constitution in 1990. This was heavily weighted towards Fijians who were to have most senior public positions, an absolute ethnic majority in parliament and no less than 50 percent of all public service posts.

Rabuka twice ran for elections under the 1990 constitution and ruled Fiji until May 1999. In the years 1987-1999, Fiji lost 10 percent of its population (and a great deal of skill) to emigration, mainly Indo-Fijians but also non-ethnic Fijians and some well-educated ethnic Fijians.

Leading up to the third coup, in the period 1997-99, it became clear that Fiji had changed considerably over the decade since the first coup. There were numerous disputes over chiefly titles, especially where they provided access to sizeable rental income from leases and royalties. A new generation of aristocrats had emerged expecting the perks of public office without the mana or cooperative tendencies of their fathers. Provincial and confederacy rivalries became more overt, and Rabuka openly opposed some of Ratu Mara's views and maintained that the latter had known about and approved the 1987 coup. There was an assertive new ethnic Fijian middle class that had benefited from affirmative action.

In this period, poverty had also increased and socio-economic differentiation advanced. Taxation and labour market reforms had adversely affected the poor. VAT (GST) was a heavy blow to smallholders and workers. Sugar cane leases began to expire and greater insecurity threatened the future of small farmers. Many people believed there had been poor governance, widespread corruption and mismanagement of public funds that had enriched elements of the aspiring Fijian middle class and not the people at large.

In this situation, Rabuka's Soqosoqo Vakavulewa ni Taukei (SVT) Party and the NFP that campaigned on its successful multi-ethnic cooperation platform were heavy losers in the 1999 election. The FLPs 'bread and butter' campaign appealed to the voters and the party led by Mahendra Chaudhry swept to power. In the year they ruled the country, several reforms were instituted. Among the casualties were George Speight, Chairman of Fiji Hardwood Corporation and a protége of Jim Ah Koy, the former SVT Minister of Finance; and Maika Qarikau, CEO of the Native Land Trust Board who was sacked from his board membership of the Fiji Development Bank.

In his 12 months in office, Chaudhry succeeded in alienating many people, and his leadership gave a pretext for the revival of the Taukei Movement. Subsequently, Fijian youths looted, burnt and trashed shops belonging to Indo-Fijians and others; harassed rural Indian communities; committed home invasions; and stole possessions, farm implements, produce and animals over a long period of time[7] without effective police response. On the same day, 19 May 2000, George Speight and seven members of the Counter Revolutionary Warfare Unit of the Royal Fijian Military Forces (RFMF) entered parliament and took Chaudhry and the coalition government hostage for 56 days.

Naidu (2007) claims that Ratu Mara had earlier managed to orchestrate the controversial resignation of the coalition government. The military commander, Voreqe Bainimarama, took over the reins of government on 29 May, deposing the president and declaring that he had abrogated the constitution. George Speight then sought to put in place a government of his own choosing. However, this did not happen. Following an accord by the military and hostage-takers under which the latter were granted immunity if they released the hostages and returned all arms, the hostages were released. Ratu Josefa Iloilo was appointed as the new president as well as a military-appointed interim government, led by the banker Laisenia Qarase as prime minister and comprising mostly ethnic Fijian professionals as ministers. The military later arrested George Speight and other coup leaders for their failure to return all arms and violently suppressed his supporters in five provinces.

In November 2000, a mutiny at Queen Elizabeth Barracks led to the killing of three loyal soldiers and Bainimarama only survived by fleeing for his life. The mutiny was put down and five suspected mutineers arrested and beaten to death. In sum, eight soldiers, two policemen and two rebels were killed in the coup and mutiny of 2000.

Bainimarama believed that in appointing Qarase, he was installing a man who would work in the interests of all communities. But from the beginning Qarase sought to please ethno-nationalists. An affirmative action policy for indigenous Fijians and Rotumans was proposed that the Great Council of Chiefs endorsed. The legal challenge to the attempted abrogation of the 1997 constitution was strongly opposed. Several supporters of George Speight's coup were rewarded with attractive appointments. Qarase converted his group of ministers into the Soqosoqo Duavata Lewe Ni Vanua (SDL) Party to fight the 2001 elections. He patronised the Methodist Church and worked to secure the support of other Christian churches with public funds siphoned off to a group of denominations to help post-coup reconciliation.

At the same time, desecration of Hindu places of worship went on with ineffectual police response. Home invasions, muggings, violent robberies and other street-level crimes and intimidation of Indo-Fijians and non-ethnic Fijians were common occurrences.

The SDL Party of Qarase won the 2001 general election although there were allegations of vote rigging and vote buying against the SDL.[8] In this period, the economy grew at a moderate rate but unemployment was high. Emigration continued, and Fiji became to some extent a remittance economy as a result of earnings of security workers in the Middle East and caregivers in metropolitan countries. Financial mismanagement and allegations of corruption were often reported.

The government blamed the instability of 2000 and the coup on Chaudhry. Several people implicated in the coup served as ministers, while others, such as the vice president, having been convicted for coup-related offences, were released after serving a fraction of their sentence under 'compulsory supervision orders'. The government was reluctant to support investigation and prosecution of those implicated in the coup and mutiny. It also blocked the renewal of the contract of Australian prosecutor, Peter Ridgeway, who had been successful in obtaining convictions of several coup supporters, and sought, unsuccessfully, the removal of Bainimarama as Commander of the RFMF as he was not prepared to 'forgive and forget'. Bainimarama persisted in opposing any dilution in the process of bringing to justice those involved in the coup and mutiny of 2000.

The relationship between the SDL/Matanitu Vanua Party (CMV) government and the military deteriorated in 2006 so that by the time of the election in August, the military was seen to be openly campaigning against it. With his electoral victory, Qarase was able to cultivate the business community and advocate public sector reforms involving his affirmative action policies. He invited the FLP to form the multi-party government in accordance with the constitution. But with a clear majority and support of some elements of FLP, the SDL confidently pushed its ethno-nationalist agenda supported by a majority of ethnic Fijian voters – a most undesirable trend if the wounds of the 2000 coup (let alone those of 1987) were to be at least partially healed. The military challenged this orientation of the government, seeing itself as the final protector of national interest as was clearly stipulated in the 1990 constitution. The government held that no such provision existed in the 1997 constitution, referring this matter to the president and then the Supreme Court.

The divide between the two sides deepened when the government proposed three bills that were strongly opposed by the Commodore. They were the Promotion of Reconciliation, Tolerance and Unity Bill; the I Qoliqoli Bill; and the Land Tribunal Bill. The first proposed to end the investigation and prosecution of those behind the coup and mutiny of 2000;[9] the second was to return the ownership of customary fishing grounds to their indigenous owners; and the third continued from the policy of the SDL/CMV government of allocating F$500,000 for customary land owners to buy back freehold land they felt had been taken without due recompense.

Over the last six months of 2006, the threat of military intervention grew louder. The tense game of brinkmanship between Qarase and Bainimarama was added to by the Commissioner of the Fiji Police, the Australian Andrew Hughes, who thought he could investigate the Commander for sedition and other officers for removing a container of arms from the Suva wharf without police approval. Bainimarama was in the Middle East for several weeks, but the armed forces remained totally loyal to his command.

The New Zealand government made a worthy last minute effort to stave off the coup, trying to mediate the dispute in Wellington, but after watching the Sukuna Bowl rugby, the Commander overthrew the Qarase government on 5 December 2006. This action led once again to Fiji's expulsion from the Commonwealth and to widespread international condemnation.

The Economy

Fiji grew at the rate of 3.4 percent in 2006 on the back of agriculture (especially sugar), forestry, fisheries, and an expansion in construction and services, stimulated especially by demand growth in the electricity and water sectors. There were signs, however, of problems to come, with a steep decline in the clothing industry by 25 percent with the loss of preferential access to export markets because of Chinese competition. Imports grew by 12 percent in US dollar terms while exports fell by 1.8 percent.

In March 2007, the Fiji economy was expected to contract by 2 percent. Moreover, on year-to-year figures, a fall in tourism became apparent at the close of 2006. In view of the Fourth Coup, the imposition of sanctions by overseas countries and continuing political uncertainty, it seems likely that foreign investment in the Fijian economy will be deterred for some time.

The one bright feature of the Fijian economy is the growth of the remittance sector which brought in US$183m in 2005. By June 2006, over 2,000 Fijians were serving with the British Army (many gained British citizenship) and another 1,000, mostly ex-Fiji army soldiers, were working in Iraq as mercenaries for security firms. At that stage, remittance money sent home made up 7 percent of GDP and exceeded NZ$272m a year; according to the Reserve Bank, it is second only to tourism and now surpasses sugar earnings. If informal transfers are added to formal ones, the total is estimated to be between NZ$374m and NZ$416m.

It is interesting to view Fiji today from the perspective of its overall economic evolution. The central question is the impact of capitalist development on Fiji primarily during its colonial period, which essentially involved Australian capital and enterprise. A study of this by Bruce Knapman (1987) found considerable achievements were made, especially in the sugar industry when the industry was in decline in other sugar-producing countries. Yet, in reviewing Knapman's book just after Rabuka's coup, Brookfield (1987) noted "this was wealth for foreigners who did business there, not for the Indian labourers who earned only 11 percent of the wage of a navvy in Sydney, and only partly for the Fijians whose initially-enforced participation in the cash economy remained selective right up to the time of the second world war".[10]

Fundamentally, Knapman argues that while Fiji's development path under colonialism was not ideal, "it was more fundamentally constrained by the low monetary productivity of tropical agriculture, and it would have been much worse without the striking efficiency achieved by the sugar industry under capitalist control".[11]

Knapman casts doubts on the view that Australian companies were able to sustain excessive profits during the Great Depression. He attacked the model of "dependent colonial economy" leading to underdevelopment, pointing out that capitalist development created opportunities as well as constraints. Brookfield notes, however, that Fiji might have got more from the opportunities if the colonial government had tried – or been allowed – to capture a larger share of sugar revenues, to devalue its currency as much as that of Australia in the 1930s and to make more use of its resources to strengthen social infrastructure.[12]

Certainly, the management of the sugar industry was not particularly efficient after 1970 and this appears to have been another fateful turning point in the history of Fiji. Knapman's analysis warrants reconsideration from 1987 in the light of the role of Fiji's traditional chiefly class in overturning a democracy that failed its first real test at a time when a significant number of 'individualistic' Fijians voted against the party of the chiefly class and their allies. The nub of Fiji's problem is aptly summed up by Brookfield:

> The paradox of the power of traditionalism in the Pacific's most mod-ernized and diversified economy arises directly from colonialism's failure to resolve the contradiction between support for increasingly corporate capitalism and entrenchment of a sort of stasis in the devel-opment of the indigenous people.[13]

This was the juxtaposition I first confronted in my fieldwork.

Kiribati

In 1984, I was able to make a brief return visit to Abemama, 12 years after my family's earlier residence on the atoll. I managed to borrow a motorbike and to visit all 16 households on which I had focused my earlier study or to meet a son or daughter of the original household head.

There had been considerable improvements in buildings. Two new schools had been built and another enlarged that was said to be run by Josefa Lameko, reputed to be an agent of the infamous American entrepreneur in Vanuatu, Sidney Gross. A fine new church had appeared in Tekatirirake. I noticed that many coconut palms had been cut down by the road and there was a considerable thinning of palms in general. At the same time, a great deal of saltbush (*Scaevola frutescens*) was evident.

Change was especially conspicuous at the Government Station, Kariatebike. The *maneaba* now had a horrible new iron roof (which would, however, collect valuable water), and the tiniest police station in the country was now three times larger. The pathetic thatched huts that comprised the 'hospital' of 1972 had been replaced by two new wards, and a resident doctor had superceded the dresser. A police officer, fisheries officer and carpenter now resided in the centre, and the Council Administrative Office had been extended. The greatest change was the existence of the relatively elaborate RLS (Robert Louis Stevenson) Hotel with the old US plane wreck from the north relocated nearby. Causeway Traders was a big, impressive private general store.

At the Catholic Mission in Manoku, Swiss Catholics had made improvements. A very efficient solar energy plant had replaced the old generator that frequently broke down. There was a fine new two-storey concrete school and other new buildings. However, Manoku now only taught catechists and no longer trained primary teachers. The Tutu *mronron*, a thriving business in 1972, had failed and been bought by Hong Kumkee, the part-Chinese trader who now owned two large stores. The airfield was in much worse condition than in 1972: its surface was rough and invaded by weeds.

It was a pleasure to meet Bauro Tokatake again, Te Uea or king of Abemama. In 1972, he had been the proud possessor of the only flush toilet on the island. He was President of the Island Council from 1968-77 and his uncle had become Island Executive Officer at the same time. Each month the Council funds were found to be short and his uncle asked Bauro to make up the difference. This situation could not be sustained and after a while his uncle was sacked and Bauro resigned as president. This represents a sharp decline from the efficient standards and leadership of the able and honest former Island Executive Officer, Teratabu Tira, now retired.

It was a moving experience to revisit the 16 households after the passing of 12 years. Two household heads had died and another, Nanotake, had been tragically lost at sea when his outrigger canoe was blown away in a storm as he fished outside the reef. In general, a household's socio-economic circumstances reflected demographic factors such as numbers in paid work, aging and numbers of children; and its motivation and luck. The fact that some government positions had been established on the island had provided an economic impetus and created some new opportunities for local wage work. Seven of the households had a member involved in this paid employment, while another four occasionally received telmo money orders. Seven relatives (three from one family) worked in Tarawa, two in Nauru and one in Kuria. Six households had no member in wage work or in employment on another island, and depended purely on subsistence, the sale of dried fish and other minor sources of income. Itaake of household 16 had got very fat, reportedly through eating a lot of doughnuts, and died. Kiarure of household 2, one of the largest copra producers in 1972, still cut a lot of copra and still helped the Catholic church in its fund raising. A major incentive for him was the necessity of paying school fees – $80 a term for four children plus the head tax ($10 for himself and wife) and land tax totalling $14.90 ($1 per acre for his 14.9 acres). However, he said he knew that "the government needs money".

When I asked people whether life was easier or harder than in 1972, most said it was about the same; a few said life was slightly better. Most noted that health had improved with the arrival of a doctor. (They did not yet seem to be aware of the massive government cuts in health spending.) One man, Tebao, made a clear distinction between what is good for a family and what is good for the country as a whole: "running out of phosphate doesn't affect our lives – only copra price does". They were, however, very fortunate in 1984 for copra reached the high price of 10 cents a pound compared to only 2 cents a pound in 1972, and the local wage work rate had gone up from $4 a week in 1972 to $16 a week (a relativity of four times higher compared to five times higher in copra prices). Four households even possessed a motorbike, though mostly they were infrequently used. Overall, however, most households still appeared to be consumption-oriented rational opportunists, very much situation-bound, responding in pragmatic ways to unpredictable changes that impinged upon them from year to year. They depended mostly on two, three or four sources of income. They were part-peasant, part-proletarian, part-time traders, partly dependent on remittances from relatives and partly on subsistence gardening, gathering and fishing. While relying on a substantial subsistence economy, they remained extremely poor in monetary terms.

The spread of saltbush may have reflected higher incomes from the high copra prices, the absence of labour in the form of wage earners on other islands and perhaps less interest now in the Coconut Replanting Scheme. The deterioration of the airfield may also have indicated a decline in efficiency and increased slackness in administration (in 1972, Abemama was well known as having the most efficient Island Executive Officer, Teratabu, in the country). It is also noteworthy that in 1984 only about half of the head taxes and land taxes had actually been paid. It was very hard to round up debtors and make them pay.

The Economy

It has become abundantly clear in modern Kiribati that changes in the national income are determined far more by earnings from abroad than by on-shore production of goods and services. Investment earnings in the Revenue Equalisation Reserve Fund (RERF) built up from the earlier sale of phosphate, exclusive economic zone (EEZ) access fees for foreign fishing vessels and other resource rents, sales of passports to foreigners, and remittances of Kiribati seamen and fishers on overseas ships, which in turn provide domestic tax revenues, make up the total of overseas earnings. GNP in current prices is estimated at about K$175m and GDP at about K$98m, a difference of $77m being income from abroad. Overseas aid in the years of 2000–2005 amounted to K$105m, or about 30 percent of the annual budget expenditure and over one-third of GDP.

GNP per head in 2002 was about K$1,987 or US$1,092, one of the lowest in Oceania. The effect of the oceanic weather cycle on fish catches led to a considerable drop in access fees and hence a fall in government revenue in 2003 and 2004. The considerable volatility of the economy is, however, cushioned by the only 'jewel in the crown' of Kiribati's economy, the RERF which had increased to about K$576m at the end of 2002. Public external debt was then about $11m or 6 percent of estimated GNP. At the end of 2002, official external reserves were 3.3 times GNP and eight times annual imports of goods and services. The drawdown in RERF interest earnings to pay the budget deficit was only K$15M in 2006. By April 2007, the RERF had increased to about K$660m – a very tidy sum. Government revenue totalled about K$64m in 2006, of which $30m came from taxes ($20m in import duties) and $31m from fishing licence fees.

The monetary economy, almost entirely based on Tarawa, is dominated by the public sector, which provides two out of every three formal jobs (and indirectly a good deal of the income that supports the informal sector) and four out of every five dollars of pay. Most government outlays, equivalent to over 100 percent of GDP, are quickly re-spent by the recipients on imported consumption goods. Imports thus cost about K$70m, whereas exports of copra from most rural areas and marine products (seaweed, aquarium fish) from a few islands contribute only about $7m-$24m, a ratio of about 5-10 to 1.

The decade of the 1990s was kind to Kiribati as it saw extraordinary increases in the value of the overseas financial reserves in the RERF, buoyant global economic conditions, rapid growth in EEZ access fees, a boom in passport sales and generally prudent fiscal management. This enabled a relatively large programme of government projects (seaport, schools, parliament, water and sewerage) which boosted construction activity. In the last two years, however, there has been concern about the soundness of such expansionary fiscal policy, related partly to the volatility of fishing licence revenues, continued pressure for support of public enterprises and even the fact that there have been reverses in the financial markets in which the RERF is invested.

The dominant issue remains the export of labour. Over the years, the 1,000 or so i-Kiribati young men who have worked for overseas (mostly German) shipping lines have brought substantial remittance income into the country. The employment of Kiribati seafarers almost doubled between 1989 and 1999, from 788 to 1,368. This explained the steady increase and almost doubling of the amount of remittances from A$5.6m in 1990 to A$9.7m in 1999, or almost A$12m if money gained at end of contract is added, not counting commodities brought back home.[14] Borovnik (2004) showed that although remittances do not decline over time, they are rather steady in the amount sent to families, while at the same time the amount sent to individual accounts is increasing. Furthermore, the *bubuti* (redistribution) system in Kiribati ensures that a share of remittances goes not only to all family members, but also to churches and communities. Thus, a number of non-migrant households are likely to benefit in many different ways.

Unfortunately, the substantial income hoped for from American tourists and fishermen visiting Kiritimati (Christmas Island), the largest atoll in the world, has not been realised. Although the fishing is good and cruise ships from Hawaii stop there, the recently built hotel is only mediocre and few people stay there. The Americans visiting do a bit of fishing, look around, perhaps buy a coke and soon reboard their cruise ship. It appears that an opportunity to tap a profitable and promising market has been lost.

The Kiribati Census, 2005

Calculations by South Pacific Commission (SPC) demographers based on the 2000 Census and UN estimates of fertility and life expectancy suggest that, by 2025, Kiribati could have a total population of 140-145,000. There might then be around 70,000 people in Tarawa (double that of 2000), 20,000 in Kiritimati and 50-53,000 spread among the rest of the Gilbert, Line and Phoenix groups.

The rate of population growth remains a worrying concern. In the 2000-2003 period, growth was 1.7 percent annually, ahead of the GDP growth rate of 1.4 percent. During 2000-2003, the population is estimated to have increased by 6,000, with two-thirds of that increase taking place in South Tarawa where almost half the total population lives, and much of the remainder in Kiritimati, the fastest-growing population centre. The population in mid-2007 is estimated to be about 98,000.

People are now moving into north Tarawa beyond the airport and the government is contemplating a growth centre in this area of the atoll but there are fears that this might interfere with the water supply for South Tarawa.

One of the few outer islands that was not already highly populated was Abemama which had about 2,300 people in 1972 when I lived on the atoll. By 2005, its total had reached 3,404, a medium growth of 48 percent since 1973, or an average of 1.55 percent per year (compared to an increase of 78 percent or a high average of 2.4 percent a year throughout Kiribati).[15] In scanning the populations of the eight villages in the 2005 census running from north to south on the island, I discovered the existence of a new village which certainly did not exist in 1972. It was Bangotantekabaia, located between Kariatebike (the Government Station) and the village of Tebanga. This area was near where the Te Uea or 'King' lived and held many of his lands. It appears that Te Uea, Bauro Tokatake, may have died and been succeeded by his son, and he may have acceded to requests of Abemamans and their relatives from other islands to rent some of his domains, perhaps cutting copra for him and fishing in the neighbouring lagoon. Certainly a substantial village now exists of 330 people.

This factor is entirely consistent with the flexible social organisation of i-Kiribati. In my census of all households on the island, I identified as many as 14 variations in relationships of members to the head of the household, which reflects the close links between the *mwenga* and other kin. Moreover, the frequency of kin visiting and staying for a few weeks, or months, during which they fitted into the normal household activity pattern before returning to their normal home or moving to another relative's household, was a feature that showed how society could quickly respond to perceptions of new opportunities.

There is, however, little doubt that Kiribati is rapidly running out of land. Kiritimati has been the last substantial island available to absorb considerable numbers of new settlers. A review (AEAS, 1992) of settlement on the Northern Line Islands of Tabuaeran (Fanning) and Teraina (Washington) in 1992 found that while about 1,000 settlers had been established on each island, the free-for-all access of settlers to government-owned land might prove to be unsustainable. One possible option was to increase the average landholding per settler household from one to five acres. However, further infrastructural developments are needed and there are worries about environmental impact. While the main goal was for the islands to supply the subsistence needs of the settlers, the two islands' economic potential may prove to be very limited; they are extremely isolated, and have poor water supplies and very small markets.

Kiribati has had two successful campaigns of family planning that achieved notable success, the first in 1971 and another in the 1980s. Unfortunately, between these campaigns, the population got away again and the current population growth rate is unacceptably high. It is clear that it is absolutely urgent that a new campaign, designed on the successful ones of the past, be introduced and, once success has been achieved in reducing the rate of growth, the authorities remain vigilant and perhaps even draconian in efforts to keep it at that level. The population already far exceeds the carrying capacity of the natural resource base, as Neemia and Thaman concluded in 1993.

The installation of two new sewerage outfalls several years ago lessened the danger of cholera or typhoid disease, but with further increase in population density dysentery is still common and in 2006 eight babies died of diarrhoea. Environmental problems are becoming acute and putting more pressure on government and society at large. The immediate dangers, which are most apparent in the urban areas, are groundwater depletion and pollution; the percolation of sewerage, human waste or effluent from domestic animals; the build-up and inefficient disposal of garbage and sewerage; contamination of shellfish and lagoon waters; over-fishing of reefs and lagoons; coastal erosion and sedimentation; shortage of firewood for cooking; and the breakdown of subsistence production systems and knowledge. These dangers all contribute to increased economic dependency and the incidence of ill health or malnutrition. As recently as April 2007, President Anote Tong appealed publicly to people not to take material from the beaches of Tarawa for sale for building materials. In the longer term, perhaps over 100 years, it is likely that the whole population will have to be resettled because, as a result of global warming, the atolls will be subjected to salination and later be submerged by the rising sea level.[16]

In view of these trends, the urban bias that has long existed in aid policies towards spending more on South Tarawa than on the outer islands, where the majority of the population lives, has been accentuated (although as south Tarawa approaches 50 percent of total population, it can be argued that this is no longer 'urban bias'). New Zealand aid, for example, is focused on urban development as well as basic education, human resource development and improving the public sector.[17]

To conclude, it is clear that Kiribati, a MIRAB-type economy, has moved ever further down the path of the MIRAB process – on-shore commodity production for export by perhaps 70 percent of the nation's labour force contributes only 10-20 percent of GDP, while external earnings now totally drive the economy. The logical next step, it would seem, is the further expansion of labour export in temporary immigrant labour schemes in metropolitan countries such as Australia and New Zealand.

Papua New Guinea[18]

The Economy

Over time, economic dualism has become even more pronounced in Papua New Guinea than in the other countries of Oceania. Indeed, the economy rests almost entirely on the large-scale export industries of minerals (copper and gold), petroleum, timber, fish and tree crops, which support a small urban formal sector. This is in contrast to the widespread subsistence or semi-subsistence rural economy based on the village mode of production which sustains over 80 percent of the population.

During the 1990s and up to 2002, the country experienced instability and even negative growth, with low prices for its exports, a contracting economy and a decline in the government's capacity to provide its people with access to markets and basic social services.

In addition to the unacceptably high population growth rate of 2.3 percent a year, there are several other formidable constraints to development: the country's imposing geography, natural disasters, enormous ethnic diversity, limited infrastructure, very poor social indicators (including a potentially serious HIV/AIDs epidemic), high crime rates, widespread rascalism, law-and-order problems, the failure to sustain broad-based economic growth and job creation in the 1990s, an under-sourced public sector with capacity limitations, ongoing governance difficulties, and widespread and deep corruption. Although an unfavourable external environment is partly to blame, there are many local problems that urgently need to be addressed. The result is that per capita GDP in 2004 was about 10 percent lower than at the time of independence in 1978.[19]

Although poverty analysis is constrained by weak and dated data,[20] in 1999 41.3 percent of the population were classed as being below the poverty line (with 93 percent from rural areas); by 2003 this had increased to 54 percent. The most disadvantaged provinces are the remote districts of Sandaun, East Sepik, Madang and Enga.

For GDP per capita, PNG ranks 120th in the world with US$2,543, but in the UN Human Development Index (HDI) it ranks at 139th out of 177 countries. It has very low life expectancy at birth (average only 57 years); a poor combined primary, secondary and tertiary education gross enrolment ratio; and pronounced gender inequality (less than 1 percent of seats in parliament are held by women). Since in many areas the services provided by government are virtually non-existent, it is fortunate that 40 percent of basic services for health and education are delivered by NGOs and churches.

During the first decade or so after independence, economic performance was satisfactory; though increases in GDP were small (averaging 1.4 percent over 1976-85), there was a gradual decline of dependence on aid and economic management was sound. However, the rate of growth of GDP fell each year from 1987, with negative results for 1989 and 1990 after a rebellion by dissatisfied landowners in the Panguna area forced the closure of the Bougainville mine, one of the largest gold and copper mines in the world. In spite of this, government spending continued to rise although now deprived of a major source of government revenue and export earnings.

From at least the mid-1980s, in many rural areas there was a visible deterioration of roads, schools, aid posts and other capital. The effects of this were often increased by the destruction of assets as a result of tribal fighting, 'payback' for non-payment of demanded compensation or vandalism. In the 1970s, problems of maintaining law and order had emerged but reached new levels in the 1980s, and the first of several states of emergency was declared in the capital Port Moresby with the PNG Defence Force (PNGDF) called in to assist.

There was a change of government in 1985 when the highlander Paias Wingti became prime minister. The passing of a new act emasculated the quasi-independent Public Services Commission and led to an increasing politicisation of the public service. It partially collapsed in areas such as WNB, with many of its former services lapsing. Little patrolling by extension officers occurred because the villagers would not listen to them and had no respect for them.[21]

The Bougainville crisis and war not only cut off revenue but also led to huge spending on defence, which rose from K40m in 1988 to K92m in 1991, and from 4.3 to 7.7 percent of total government expenditure. In spite of this, the defence budget was overspent by a massive 81 percent in 1991. Even so, PNGDF aircraft and boats could not be used in 1993-94 because they could not pay for fuel and maintenance.

Government borrowing expanded to cover the rising deficits. By 1994, debt repayment and servicing represented about one-third of government spending and the government was facing a fiscal crisis. A mini-budget was introduced and a loan of US$102m negotiated from a group of private lenders in the Cayman Islands. In August 1994, a new government came in headed by Sir Julius Chan; he devalued and then floated the kina but the government was forced to negotiate an emergency loan through the World Bank.

In view of its fortunate resource endowment, its generally sound beginning and its early bright aspirations, why has Papua New Guinea's economic performance been so poor?

Although commodity prices generally improved in the early 1980s after we completed the Kandrian-Gloucester project, low levels of growth in GDP, a steady decline in the real value of Australian development assistance, a high population growth rate and high unrealistic expectations on the part of PNG citizens placed great pressure on government finances. To many people, it seemed that the country was enjoying a mining boom as the second large gold and copper mine at OK Tedi came into production in 1982, but as tax concessions had earlier been granted and it did not contribute to public revenue until 1987, this was largely illusory. Soon afterwards, the Bougainville crisis ended the revenue from that mine and huge new costs of internal security were imposed; when OK Tedi and other mines came on stream in the early 1990s, they merely filled the gap.

It can be argued, however, that the fiscal crisis reflected more fundamental deficiencies in the country's political economy. In the period of accelerated late colonial development from 1945 to 1975, government had played a major role in development. Buoyed by substantial Australian aid, it promoted agriculture (especially smallholder development), marketing and small-scale indigenous business, and financed education and health services as well as the provision of basic infrastructure.

Prior to independence, smallholder agriculture continued to expand although its fortunes varied across the country. Plantation agriculture, however, had mixed success; oil palm production on plantations and nucleus estates flourished, but traditional plantation crops – copra, cocoa and rubber – stagnated. Many foreign-owned plantations were run down in expectation of land claims by Papua New Guineans leading to expropriation or forced sale; many were sold or sub-divided, and with the low prices of the late 1970s and often inexperienced managers, many plantations performed poorly.[22] Moreover, for partly cultural reasons, small business ventures achieved only limited success and manufacturing grew at only a modest rate.[23]

At a time when the demand for cash was increasing, partly for education or transport, only those with salaried employment or a few types of self-employment were prospering, while in many areas infrastructure was deteriorating and access to government services declining. In this situation, the appeal of substantial revenue and infrastructure development from large-scale mining and petroleum prospects and then from logging was great for a national government with a weak tax base, declining real levels of development assistance and heavy demands on public expenditure. For some communities that had minerals or millable logging projects, the prospect also looked bright to cash in on these resources, but for others that lacked these, the future looked increasingly gloomy when government failed to meet their development demands. They became increasingly frustrated and anti-government in attitude.

Political Instability and Weakness of the State

At independence, Papua New Guinea adopted a Westminster-type of parliamentary system, and the heady nationalism and euphoria of the late 1960s and early 1970s associated with the establishment of the University of Papua New Guinea in 1966 seemed to provide a good basis for a growing sense of national identity. The catalytic leadership of Ulli Beier in literature and culture, the launching of the literary journal *Kovave* in 1969, the publication of Albert Maori Kiki's stunning autobiography, *Kiki, Ten Thousand Years in a Lifetime* in 1968,[24] and the appearance of the country's first novel, Vincent Eri's *Crocodile* in 1970,[25] are outstanding features of this period. Nevertheless, expectations were not fulfilled for the emergence of a sense of national identity or the development of a proper party system.

Only three parties have been a significant force for over two decades – Pangu, the People's Progress Party and the Melanesian Alliance; others have proved to be transient. The major parties have never been sharply differentiated ideologically, have not developed a substantial mass base, have revolved around a few key individuals and displayed strong regional loyalties. Party discipline has been weak and membership fluid. Given this unstable, frequently changing or fluid nature of politics, governments are always made up of coalitions and 'party hopping' is frequent. Over time, there has been a tendency of candidates at elections either *not* to align themselves to a party, or to align themselves loosely to more than one. Their aim is to maximise their bargaining power in the post-election horse-trading that occurs when attempts are made to put together a successful coalition. When this tendency is also combined with the high level of turnover of MPs, with 50-55 percent of members failing to win re-election, we can see that the political environment is conducive to short-term advantages and not to rational long-term and consistent policy making.

To explain the behaviour of politicians and the forms of corruption they practised, Ron May (2004) quotes the Nigerian scholar Peter Ekeh who suggests that the colonial experience in Africa produced a historical configuration involving two public realms in post-colonial Africa: a "primordial" public realm government by "primordial groupings, ties and sentiments", and a colonially-derived "civic" public realm. He argues that most educated Africans are members of both these public realms:

> ... they belong to a civic public from which they gain materially but to which they give only grudgingly [and] ... they belong to a primordial public from which they derive little or no material benefits but to which they are expected to give generously and do give materially ... their relationship to the primordial public is moral, while that to the civic public is amoral. The dialectical tensions and confrontations between these two publics constitute the uniqueness of modern African politics ... The unwritten law of the dialectic is that it is legitimate to rob the civic public in order to strengthen the primordial public.[26]

The effects of this confrontation, according to Ekeh, included "tribalism" and corruption.[27]

Ron May quotes a speech of former finance secretary and central bank governor, Mekere Morauta (who became prime minister in 1999):

> '... the most corrosive and intractable problem we face now is corruption'. Morauta went on to talk about 'the institutionalisation of short-term ad hoc decision-making and the catastrophic decline in the power, status, morale and productivity of the bureaucracy', a development which he dated to the mid 1980s ....[28]

In recent years, AusAID and other international institutions have worked very hard to solve this "corrosive and intractable" problem and indeed convert Papua New Guineans from their fluid, inconsistent, anarchic and policy-weak style of 'Big Man Politics', and substitute modern, efficient and well-tested methods of government, management and administration. Michael Somare, the Father of Independence, has been an outstanding leader in many ways over the last 30 years, but now is the time for new leaders committed to root-and-branch reform and to strong but open and responsible government. Morauta and some others offered perhaps the best hope for Papua New Guineans to get the leaders they deserved in the 2007 election. Sadly, this has not happened, with the return of Somare to head the new government; the people have voted for continuity rather than change.

Vanuatu

Economy, Culture and the Future

In the neighbouring country of Vanuatu, we have seen, following Bonnemaison, that the buffeting of the outside world has meant that ni-Vanuatu need more than ever the tree, the symbol of rootedness. At the same time, social change has also widened horizons and so 'multiplied the roads' leading to development. New solidarities have emerged – regional, economic, religious, national – so island societies are no longer based on clans and their micro-territories. But at the same time, to be able to utilise these new roads they need to rediscover canoes that re-establish connections with venturing on the high seas so they can undertake new journeys of discovery.[29] It is too early to say whether they have done this yet (in the form of social units capable of adapting to the modern world while also preserving their own special values of identity). The first seasonal workers in the vineyards and fruit orchards of New Zealand in 2007 are the pioneers and explorers of this new journey. Whether they will succeed and initiate a promising new road that larger numbers of ni-Vanuatu can follow remains to be seen.

The plantation economy which was strong in colonial times in a situation of open resources was weakened as ni-Vanuatu repossessed some of this land. The labour force for plantations also dropped as many Vietnamese were repatriated to Vietnam after the ending of the war there. The fall in copra prices was a further blow, in addition to mounting transport costs. Beef cattle introduced much earlier as 'lawn mowers' beneath coconut palms have become much more important as copra declined. Beef is a useful export. Thus, the plantation as an institution can only be understood within the environment in which it exists, as I have already argued for Fiji (see Chapter 8 above). This illustrates Thompson's 1957 thesis that the plantation is a transient institution involved in a cycle of change.[30] In a situation of increasingly closed resources, with labour and transport costs that are too high, it is heading towards its own destruction.

Subsistence agriculture[31] is still the main base of the economy in Vanuatu, with 75-80 percent of the population engaged in the village mode of production or smallholder production of coconuts in 2003. When the GDP is calculated in constant prices, the agricultural sector produces on average 3,304 million vatu, and of this subsistence agriculture contributes 1,776 million vatu or 54 percent. The main exports today are copra and coconut oil, beef, kava and timber. Economic development is hindered by dependence on relatively few commodity exports; vulnerability to natural disasters (cyclones, volcanic activity and earthquakes); long distances from main markets and between constituent islands; political instability, especially in the 1990s; and various incidents of political adventurism or scams of the 'banana republic' type that we have described in Chapter 12.[32] However, with a climate and soils conducive to growth and the relative scarcity of many pests and diseases, some high-value organic niche markets are being accessed, for example, cocoa, vanilla and canarium nuts (*mangai*). Together, agricultural products account for 60 percent of total exports and about 20 percent of GDP.

Tourism was Vanuatu's fastest growing sector (40 percent GDP) in 2000 and the growing numbers of tour ships is encouraging; 50,000 visitors travelled to Vanuatu in 2004. The maintenance of Vanuatu's status as a tax haven and international offshore banking and financial and other services centre (about 2,000 registered institutions) helps to offset the serious current account deficit, in which imports exceed exports often by a ratio of about 4 to 1. Total commodity exports are stagnant or declining on a per capita basis. Industry as a percentage of GDP declined from 15 percent to only 10 percent from 1990 to 2000.

The economic future of Vanuatu remains extremely precarious, with an estimated labour reserve of tens of thousands of probably increasingly frustrated people seeking employment outside the village sector, since formal sector employment growth is very limited.[33] The resources of the country are few unless the exclusive economic zone of 680,000 sq. kms reveals undiscovered wealth. Agricultural products fluctuate widely in price and the current population growth of 2.6 percent per year is about the same as current economic growth. The population of 213,000 in 2004 had a per capita GNI of US$1,130 (2003).[34] Malaria still exists in the country and education remains very underdeveloped. Adult literacy is about 70 percent for women and 63 percent for men. Only 20-25 percent of students reach junior high school, and three-quarters of candidates fail an exam in Year 10. The school of Ranwadi with some of the lowest fees in the country receives about 25 percent of its funding from the government and 15 percent from the church; the remaining 60 percent comes from the students' families.[35] In 1985, there were only three BSc graduates in the country. Although desperately needed in education, most of them would be lost to senior administration positions.[36]

Squatter settlements such as Blacksands comprise about 30-40 percent of Port Vila's rapidly growing population of about 30,000. Here poverty occurs amongst the population which has escaped from the village sector and the city's modern sector; only one-third of 5-15 year-olds attend school and unemployment runs at 55 percent.

The prospects of Vanuatu did not look bright in 1990, 10 years after independence, when the Pacific Forum met in Vila. As the 1990s progressed, the leaders of the Vanuaku Party were seen to have lost much of their earlier lustre. On the morning after independence, the mirage began to disappear and the grand hopes of the leaders who had struggled bravely for nearly 25 years seemed gradually to drift away. Of course, many of the leaders were much older now and tired, and Lini, the father of independence, was a sick man. After his stroke, ill health increasingly hampered him and he died in 1999.

It is clear that the parlous political and business state of the country occurred as Lini became too old and ill to retain his former predominance. By the late 1990s, observers declared the Vanuaku Party to be broken; politics had become a mêlée between a whole range of minor factions, mostly dominated by personal interests. Corruption clearly was no longer absent.

A model of self-reliance for the economy may appear to be admirable but it is paradoxical that, in effect, a dual economy supported by overseas aid has to operate to keep the country afloat. Thus, the 75 percent of the population who are still village dwellers dependent mainly on the village mode of production rely also on this particular pattern of circular or pendular migration that links their home village to a place of employment. And, ironically, while ni-Vanuatu hope tourists visiting their shores will appreciate and admire their attempts to rebuild their colonised culture on *kastom*, the spectacle of the slaughter of scores of pigs, sometimes by ceremonial clubbing in a re-enactment of a traditional grade ritual pig ceremony,[37] is hardly appealing to visiting tourists, even if they are not animal rights activists. Tourism, the tax haven and, above all, overseas aid enable the current account deficit to be balanced (Australia, the European Union, France and New Zealand are the major donors).

Since independence in 1980, Vanuatu has received more than NZ$2.3 billion in assistance and in the last 10 years more than V$29 billion in overseas aid (bilateral and multi-lateral assistance). Undoubtedly, the precarious economic situation and political instability of Vanuatu in the late 1990s rang alarm bells, but Vanuatu has itself been extraordinarily successful in extracting large sums of overseas aid from donors. When the American Millennium Challenge Corporation created a set of criteria on which to base aid, they tried to select developing countries that "rule justly, invest in people, and promote economic freedom". In its search for candidates, Vanuatu was very lucky to be judged the winner and was awarded US$65 million over a period of five years. In the mid-1990s, a Comprehensive Reform Programme (CRP) had been worked out by the ADB and Australia and large volumes of aid funds were applied to improve governance, capacity building in central government agencies, and education and health.

The flow of aid continues to mitigate the balance of payments problem in Vanuatu and therefore assists in maintaining macro-economic stability. When aid is removed from the balance of payments, it translates into a large deficit in the current account balance.

The Development Fund budget in 2006 totalled V$81.8 million, of which donors provided as much as V$50.9 million or over 62 percent of the total.

It is somewhat refreshing to note that in 2001 Vanuatu backed out of a commitment to join the World Trade Organisation. A former Director of Trade saw free trade as having to do with "neo-colonialism in disguise" – a "shark-eat-sardines model of business"[38] that Vanuatu would be wise to avoid. By 2006, however, it was reported that Vanuatu was reconsidering whether it should follow Tonga's disastrous decision to join the WTO. And even more serious is the sale on Efate and Aoré near Santo of registered leasehold land for 75 years with a right of renewal following the setting up of the Vanuatu Investment Promotion Authority (VIPA) in 1998. This has led recently to a mini land boom, with many New Zealanders attracted to the prospect of buying good blocks of land with access to the sea or good sea views for NZ$70,000-120,000. It seems that Vanuatu may be returning to a situation like that of the 1970s when clans submitted to the enticements of cash and sold large areas of land. A New Zealand real estate agent states, "Vanuatu is as safe as houses. I can't imagine anything dreadful happening. I can't see the *kastom* owners taking their land back". Is she correct or will a new Walter Lini or another Jimmy Stevens emerge to take land back again for their people as part of a renewed attempt to restore *kastom*?[39]

Although Jimmy Stevens died in 1994, Nagriamel still exists. Frankie Stevens, one of Jimmy's sons, is one of several leaders of the movement. In 2004, Nagriamel supported West Papua's movement for political independence from Indonesia, and in April 2006, six out of nine councillors of the Union of Moderate Parties (UMP) joined Nagriamel. In May 2006, the Head of State visited Vanafo on the four-hundredth anniversary of Fernandez de Quiros' landing in Santo to urge acceptance of the National Reconciliation Process (NCP) by Nagriamel with the nation's government.[40]

In a country in which only one tenth of the population is formally employed and the formal sector can absorb only small numbers of new employees each year, the danger of trouble, caused by disaffected, frustrated youth, is obvious. Violent rioting by restless 'Master Lui' youth in Honiara, Solomon Islands, sends a powerful warning that all efforts should be made to prevent similar conditions developing in towns like Vila or Luganville in Vanuatu. Huge urban drift seems to be occurring, squatter settlements are growing steadily and, although I have been unable to find precise demographic or income figures, about 40 percent of people are said to be living below the poverty line. Some observers claim that social instability and crime are increasingly evident in Port Vila,[41] and without more jobs created the situation is likely to deteriorate further.

Balancing the Formal Sector and the Traditional Sector

The formal sector in 2000 provided employment for 14,272 people.[42] Around 3,500 school leavers enter the workforce each year.[43] For the formal sector to be able to absorb all new entrants, employment would have to grow over 10 percent a year, whereas it is only growing slightly and many newly-trained teachers and nurses are currently unemployed due to government's financial constraints.

A survey in 2001 showed that women comprised 37 percent of employees in the formal sector, working especially in the wholesale and retail trade and hotels and restaurants. Increased female employment will enhance their status and self-confidence and improve their position in society, as women's pioneer Grace Molisa so dearly wished.

The growth of tourism offers the best prospects for the expansion of formal employment in the medium term. Vanuatu has comparative advantages in international tourism, possessing pristine tropical ecosystems, beautiful scenery, and interesting and friendly cultures, although these are to be found well beyond Port Vila where the industry is currently centred. The number of tourists has grown from 49,000 in 2002 to over 62,000 in 2006, and the number of cruise ship tourists from just under 49,000 in 2002 to over 65,500 in 2003.

Increasing numbers of cruise ships visit remote locations and inject relatively large amounts of cash into provincial economies (estimates of US$40,000 per day per ship), though on an irregular basis. While this is a windfall gain, severe distortions are caused to local economies by the availability of 'easy money'. This combined with the unreliability or infrequency of visits and preference for specific locations that favour individual communities rather than others have resulted in social unrest and severe disruption of traditional lifestyles.[44]

The real 'binding restraints' on the production sectors in Vanuatu are geography and scale – both obvious and immovable. But sustained productivity, though at sub-optimum levels, has occurred from agriculture and tourism. The problem appears to be multiple inefficiencies throughout existing value chains, with economic inefficiencies defined as activities where waste, friction or other undesirable economic factors are present which could be changed so that everyone gains, or someone gains while no-one else loses.[45]

The traditional sector based on the village mode of production is often regarded as backward and unproductive, but it should not be underestimated and also needs support. This largely non-monetised rural economy has successfully supported a 90 percent increase in the rural population since independence (from about 95,000 in 1980 to an estimated 180,000 now), indicating that a subsistence affluence factor did exist.

The MIRAB Economies in the Twenty-first Century

The Meaning of MIRAB

Further east lie the micro states of Polynesia: Tonga, Samoa, Niue, the Cook Islands and French Polynesia. The great voyaging people who first settled the far-flung islands of the vast ocean were Peter Buck's 'Vikings of the Sunrise'. From the Second World War, they began the first stages of a new migration which expanded from journeys to the phosphate islands of French Polynesia to journeys to New Zealand in search of employment. The mobility of labour and the readiness of islanders to migrate to the metropolis have, of course, been crucial factors in the evolution of this new mode of production (the MI factor), just as have the remittances back to the 'caretaker' kindred in the home islands (R), the availability of larger sums of aid funds (A), and the major importance of bureaucracies (B) in managing and directing the whole process. Although it is true that the sound growth of MIRAB economies like Samoa and the Cook Islands is mainly derivative, relying on continued economic growth in the metropolitan country (the 1980s period of restructuring, unemployment and low economic growth in New Zealand perhaps increased poverty in the mini-states), the impressive growth of recent years has been relayed on to the island economies. And there are already signs that some MIRAB economies like the Cook Islands might be on the way to becoming successful SITEs (Small Island Tourist Economies)[46] although in Oceania, apart from French Polynesia, there is no sign yet of the emergence of any PROFIT economies (P – People considerations – citizenship, residence and employment; R – Resource management and intra-national recognition; O – Overseas engagement; F – Finance; and T – transportation),[47] like Jersey, Bahamas or the Isle of Man.

In the 20-odd years since the publication of the MIRAB model (Bertram and Watters, 1984), a rather substantial international literature has appeared on this topic. In February 2004, a conference was held in Wellington, 30 to 40 years after the end of colonialism in Oceania, to discuss the current state of research into the political economy of small islands in the world system, and in that light, the future of the MIRAB model. It was clear at the conference that there was widespread support that, as a *descriptive* device, the rather ugly acronym MIRAB captured the four main elements of the late colonial and post-colonial economies in Niue, Tokelau, the Cook Islands, Kiribati and Tuvalu; and as an *analytical* tool it had also gone a good way to explaining the real dynamics sustaining and shaping the economies of these very small nations. Thus, it was argued that the MIRAB approach was far more revealing than the later and largely unhelpful neo-classical economics of the Asian Development Bank (1995) which underpinned economic reforms in the mid-to-late 1990s.[48] Moreover, by 2004 there was wide acceptance that internationally 23 countries could be identified as MIRAB, 31 as newly-termed SITEs (which overlaps with MIRABs), and 14 as PROFITs (which overlaps with SITES, see Figure 14.1).

In his summing up of the conference and a new generation of research on small islands, Bertram (2006) suggests that the MIRAB model is still well and truly alive and kicking, but that a new, more comprehensive taxonomy can be outlined (see Figure 14.1) and that it is perhaps appropriate now to see MIRAB in this wider context. Along with MIRAB, the PROFIT and SITE economic structures constitute temporary equilibria in a field where other possible equilibria exist,

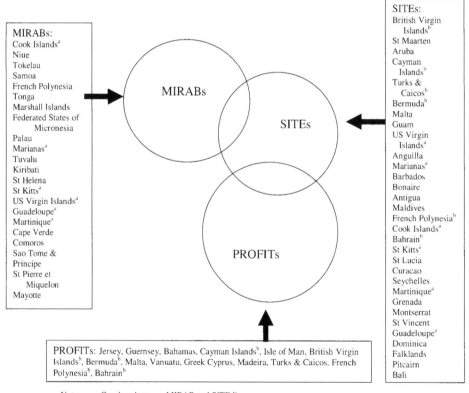

MIRABs:
Cook Islands[a]
Niue
Tokelau
Samoa
French Polynesia
Tonga
Marshall Islands
Federated States of
    Micronesia
Palau
Marianas[a]
Tuvalu
Kiribati
St Helena
St Kitts[a]
US Virgin Islands[a]
Guadeloupe[a]
Martinique[a]
Cape Verde
Comoros
Sao Tome &
Principe
St Pierre et
    Miquelon
Mayotte

SITEs:
British Virgin
    Islands[b]
St Maarten
Aruba
Cayman
    Islands[b]
Turks &
    Caicos[b]
Bermuda[b]
Malta
Guam
US Virgin
    Islands[a]
Anguilla
Marianas[a]
Barbados
Bonaire
Antigua
Maldives
French Polynesia[b]
Cook Islands[a]
Bahrain[b]
St Kitts[a]
St Lucia
Curacao
Seychelles
Martinique[a]
Grenada
Montserrat
St Vincent
Guadeloupe[a]
Dominica
Falklands
Pitcairn
Bali

PROFITs: Jersey, Guernsey, Bahamas, Cayman Islands[b], Isle of Man, British Virgin Islands[b], Bermuda[b], Malta, Vanuatu, Greek Cyprus, Madeira, Turks & Caicos, French Polynesia[b], Bahrain[b].

Notes: a. Overlaps between MIRAB and SITE lists.
          b. Overlaps between SITE and PROFIT lists.

Figure 14.1. A Taxonomy of Small-island Political Economies

and where movement from one equilibrium to another (or to a new one) takes place when for any reason positive feedback shocks overcome the stabilising negative feedback that sustains each state of equilibrium.

Government can be either a reinforcer of the built-in stabilisers which sustain actual structures – or may trigger a switch to another mode of articulation with the global system. External forces and circumstances dictate the set of opportunities open in the short and long run, but islanders and their institutions choose the actual trajectory. Social scientists can document this 'from within' the process itself, or stand back and attempt to model it from outside, but we do not have a reliable crystal ball.

Island researchers should therefore cultivate (i) openness to the new and unexpected; (ii) demystification of the concept of sustainability, whose opposite is not the bogey of 'unsustainability', but simply transition to a new and different equilibrium; and (iii) awareness that change within a given steady state is seldom dramatic or extreme – but that once positive feedback operates and cumulative network externalities start to drive the transition to a new pole, some islands may make quite sharp transitions.

The economist readily assumes that the collective and individual choices made by islander communities represent an optimising response to the external field of threats and opportunities – which is really the only basis on which one can evaluate the old and the new steady states as "better" or "worse".[49]

Bertram goes on to utilise the analogy of a child's toy, the kaleidoscope. When held up to the light, a person looking through can see an orderly, stable pattern. When the external situation is changed by rotating the instrument, a shift takes place to a new stable pattern which does not shift if the tube is held still:

> Turn again, and yet another new pattern appears. Each successive pattern is stable in the short run, and each is path-dependent in the sense that it is formed by rearranging the same elements as were present in the previously observed pattern. But it is not possible to retrace the path – change is irreversible. Turning the tube backwards does not restore the previous pattern; instead, yet another new pattern appears. The kaleidoscope moves inexorably to a new pattern each time it is disturbed. There is no mathematical limit to the number of orderly patterns that can be produced by even a simple kaleidoscope; yet there is a finite sequence of actual patterns produced by any given kaleidoscope through time as it is turned repeatedly ... Only the likely fact of its appearance can be predicted, not its substantive character.[50]

Thus, Bertram argues that the "evolution of island economies and societies is in many respects a kaleidoscopic process. One can observe stability in the present and one can tell the story of the past sequence of temporarily stable patterns. One can predict that a new stable temporary equilibrium will emerge from the next change in external circumstances, and that the new pattern will incorporate all the elements of its predecessor, but what the new pattern will be cannot be predicted. It can be described only once it has appeared."[51] In conclusion, Bertram sees from this standpoint the MIRAB model as a "taxonomic description of a state of island political economy which has been, and is, but has no deterministic guarantee of continued existence".[52]

Bertram's kaleidoscope analogy is indeed apt and generates some worthwhile hypotheses. We need a lot more research into each of the four 'pillars', 'drivers' or 'locomotives' of these small-islands economies. But in the kaleidoscope model, there is no relationship or feedback between elements in each new pattern; and perhaps with other factors the relationship is entirely haphazard or fortuitous. In reality, however, in MIRAB economies there is considerable interaction between the four factors. Take, for example, the drastic restructuring and refinancing programme in the Cook Islands in the mid-1990s carried out by the Asian Development Bank (the Cooks' primary creditor) and New Zealand, the former imperial master. The public service was halved in 1996, from 2,905 to 1,461. In this context, as Marsters, Lewis and Friesen (2006) argue, "one might have imagined the 'R' to have taken on much greater significance as the 'A' and 'B' fell away. In fact it was the 'MI' that provided the necessary adjustment within the MIRAB structure along with a decline in cash incomes for many. The Cook Islands experienced a mass out-migration, particularly from the outer islands. From a resident population of 18,071 in 1996, there was a 25 percent loss to 13,400 in 2001".[53]

My own view is that this ADB-New Zealand-driven policy based on the neo-liberal thinking of the Washington Consensus such as 'one policy fits all' was bound to fail when applied to a largely MIRAB economy. Indeed, it would have been a reasonable prediction in a broad way that migration would flow outwards to New Zealand in search of employment in the case of sacked public servants as there seems to be at least a semi-functionalist relationship between some of the major factors in the economy.

In general terms, *structures, systems* and *processes* exist in each country or region, with *links* between microstates or satellites and the neighbouring metropole. Conventional categories or legal statuses embodied in terms such as 'nationality', 'nationalism', 'state', 'sovereignty' and 'independence' are too limiting, since it is abundantly clear that for some decades these small island entities have each existed not in a bounded, discrete way, but in numerous ways internationally linked by networks to people, careers, jobs, institutions, firms and cultures in the larger metropolitan countries. In this phase of globalisation, the Pacific Ocean has been an open field of interaction. Political choices or options available, such as 'self-government' compared to 'independence', have, however, been of major importance, since self-government meant unhindered access to migration for people from the Cook Islands, Niue or Tokelau (since they were New Zealand citizens), whereas Samoans and Tongans did not have the same access as they were from independent countries. The microstates with the highest GDP per capita in US dollars and higher indices of human development are those with ease of migration or closer integration with their metropole (Palau, Cook Islands, Niue), while politically independent countries (Tonga, Samoa and Tuvalu) are markedly poorer in terms of these criteria. It is also significant that larger countries, including those with much more abundant resources, such as Papua New Guinea, the Solomons and Vanuatu, have only one half or one quarter of real GDP per capita than do Palau and the Cook Islands.

We should note that Bertram and I originally applied the MIRAB model to only five micro states; by 2006, however, 22 island states have been termed MIRAB (see Figure 14.1). The rent-dependent model applies to a greater or lesser degree to many South Pacific countries, many of whom have moved "from subsistence to subsidy", as Connell notes (1991). Indeed, as this book shows, this applies to a considerable extent to much larger countries such as Vanuatu, and even Papua New Guinea, although the latter also has large mineral and forestry resources.

The MIRAB Economy and Political Linkage to Metropolitan States

There have been a number of studies such as Bertram (2004) that have shown that the per capita GDP of small island economies and their growth through time are explained to a large extent by two variables: the closeness of the political linkages tying each island to a corresponding metropolitan patron in the core of the world system, and the level of per capita GDP in the metropolitan patron economy. Thus, Bertram (1999a and b) found that for a sample of 22 Pacific island economies, sovereign independent microstates had an average per capita GDP of only US$1,220 compared to US$2,187 for territories 'in free association' with the United States and New Zealand; and US$22,615 (or $14,423 excluding Hawaii) for territories that were politically integrated with France, the United States and New Zealand. He did regression analysis of 22 Pacific island economies and of 60 small islands worldwide which provided support for the hypothesis, at least over the last three decades of the twentieth century.

With respect to the countries we have been concerned with in this book, there is still a substantial difference in the per capita income between sovereign independent countries and countries in 'free association', i.e. having self-government but retaining free migration entry of labour into the metropolitan country. For example, in 1999 the Cook Islands, an 'associated' or 'free association' country, had a GDP per capita about 60 percent higher than that of Samoa; and in 2004, the gap had widened considerably, with the Cook Islands showing much closer integration or linkage with New Zealand and having a GDP per capita over three times higher than the independent sovereign state of Samoa.

The historian Professor Jim Davidson, who was a key constitutional advisor to both Samoa and the Cook Islands in the period leading up to independence or self-government, was a passionate and sympathetic friend of Pacific islanders (and especially Samoans), but he did worry a lot about the health of the Samoan economy and would not have been troubled to differ from the current academic fashion at the time of downplaying or ignoring 'economic viability' (to use the terminology of the day) as "criteria for independence".[54] Davidson believed the weaknesses of the Samoan economy posed a threat to the orderly progress of the independent state, but he may not have pointed out these weaknesses and greater isolation resulting from independence (and the contrasting advantage of the route to the future that the Cook Islands was to choose in 1965). However, it appears that at the eleventh hour a very senior official of the New Zealand External Affairs Department was responsible for gaining the trust of Tupua Tamasese Meo'ole (one of the two 'royal sons' or *Fautua*) towards New Zealand's good intentions and for persuading the Samoans to opt for full independence rather than self-government.[55] Such advice has clearly condemned Samoa over the last 40 years to a mean per capita income well below that of the Cook Islands. I also recall the comment made at a conference by Jock McEwen, former head of the Department of Island Territories, who referred to meeting the Samoan Prime Minister a few years after independence at the Samoan airport. The latter said to him, "In choosing independence we made the wrong decision. The choice the Cook Islands made would have been better for us". It was indeed a fateful decision, for over the last 40 years the difference in income between the two countries has been substantial.

Afterword

My Journey Towards Progress

My own journey towards progress has involved lessons that have informed my whole life as a geographer, including some lessons that emerged very early out of my first forays into fieldwork. When I arrived in Suva to begin my research in 1958, I met a geographer, Gerry Ward of the University of Auckland. Over a beer we compared research plans and as he had been there a week he pointed out he had prior claims to studying the issues of population and resources. I had to defer to him in these subjects of classic geographic enquiry, and perhaps because of this, but also because of my anthropological and historical bent, I directed my attention to the areas of Fijian culture, social structure, political economy and social change.

At about the same time, Professor O.H.K. Spate of the Australian National University began his enquiry for the Fiji government into the economic problems and prospects of the Fijian people. This resulted in the Spate Report, a most valuable study which was planned as the forerunner to the more wide-ranging Burns Commission on population and resources and the readiness of the country to stand alone in a few years time when it achieved political independence.[1] The argument about the future of Fiji had begun and I wanted to be part of it.

After reading reports in the Department of Agriculture and other government departments, a friendly conservation officer, Colin Whitehead, took me, Bethlyn and baby Jane on a reconnaissance tour of Viti Levu. We visited numerous villages, inspected subsistence and cash-cropping gardens and fields, talked to many villagers and governing chiefs, and looked at erosion. We observed the changing vegetation as we moved from the higher rainfall of the wet zone to the less humid dry zone dominated by reeds and wild grasses.

Even more important than the fundamental differences in rainfall, vegetation, and related soil types and crops between wet and dry zones was the contrast between the two main forms of land use: the relatively advanced capitalistic development of sugar growing on the fertile alluvial (*bila*) soils that ran in a strip near the sea in the dry zone of Viti

Levu, and the much more traditional Fijian village agriculture in the wet zone and on grassy and reed-covered hills of the dry zone.

This geographic or ecological dualism appeared to coincide rather neatly with the ideas of J.H. Boeke (1953), the Dutch economist with whose theory of economic dualism I was already familiar. This theory distinguishes between the traditional peasant or tribal sector and the modern/capitalist sector, and whereas he believed pessimistically that traditional peasant economies are so vastly different from capitalist ones that economic theory cannot be applied to them, I soon arrived at the conclusion that there is considerable interaction between the two. Moreover, the differences between the two are not between maximisation and non-maximisation, but between different kinds of maximisation.[2]

As I became more and more engrossed in my fieldwork, I thought again of the concept developed by the English social and political historian, J.S. Furnivall (1939), of *plural society* which is preferable to Boeke's view. A plural society is one in which the values held by the several component populations are such that they lack a central political loyalty which overrules sectional interests, and hence they lack socio-cultural homogeneity or even understanding. The separate populations have differing modes of organisation that are reflected in the economy, and also have differing roles to play in the economy. The country as a whole may be held together by the imposition of colonial law. Furnivall used his notion of plural society to reveal the weaknesses of colonial capitalism which did little to advance the interests of the traditional sector (which was all too evident in Fiji in the 1950s and 1960s – other approaches were needed to open the door to new policies).

It was easy, in the 1950s, to look positively on the economic dualism model, for two-sector models were widely favoured in Third World economic debates, with Arthur Lewis (1955), for example, arguing that economic growth could be initiated by attracting low-cost labour from the large pool that existed in the backward village sector to the towns and cities where new industries could be established cheaply. Of course, Fiji was a very small country in which industry was virtually non-existent, but there seemed to be some potential for small manufacturing or processing factories to be set up that would capitalise on new cheap, un-unionised labour.

In the late 1950s, roughly 80 percent of the Fijian population lived in about 1,000 villages scattered throughout the colony. Although no two villages were exactly alike in environmental conditions, sub-culture, social structure, leadership and response to opportunities for participating in the cash economy, a certain number of major types could be distinguished. A basic distinction arose between villages in average per capita income and between villages where socio-cultural features and local forms of organisation were more than usually favourable for economic development. These differences, and the qualities which underlay them, distinguished the four villages I chose to study. Environmental and agronomic differences were also important: the amount of land per capita, the fertility of local soils, transport costs to the market, and location in the dry or wet zone were factors that differentiated villages from one another.

As fieldwork proceeded, it became apparent that a number of criteria indicated the rate of economic development or social change occurring in the four villages. These nine factors were: cash crop production, land and population density, attitudes to land use and tenure, use of European foodstuffs, wage labour and traditional forms of group work, external wage labour, urbanisation, wage labour as a proportion of total income, and leadership.

Thus, my observation and participation in the villages where I carried out fieldwork focused not only on some of the usual areas of study of the discipline of geography (crop production and land use, for example), but also on more anthropological and sociological factors (attitudes towards land use and leadership, for example). It occurred in the context of the Burns Commission's study of natural resources and population trends in Fiji which, while very useful, was very much based on a conventional development model (i.e. more produce = more wealth = more savings and investment = a higher standard of living = development). Such studies were typical of the Western colonial/capitalist approach which sat like a template over local conditions and was used as a guide, measure and goal.

My study of Fiji, although very much a product of its time, differed in that it was also based on the responses of local people to questions about life style, satisfaction, the wage economy and 'the good life'. I was aware too of the 'pluralism' of Fijian society, between Fijians and Indo-Fijians, and also between those with money in the cash economy and those who occupied the largely subsistence end of the spectrum.

At the time of my research on Fiji, I was partly influenced by the Talcott Parsons school of sociology with respect to the modernisation process. This both over-emphasised the American model of modern capitalist development and believed that it would inevitably extend to and become normative in all parts of the world. The pattern-variable approach of Parsons, Shils and others is too simplistic and mechanistic in implying that modernisation involves a movement over time from one pole ('traditional') to the opposite ('modern'). A preferable approach is to study the emergence of new roles being played by people in society as it changes from one stage to the next.

I was not sufficiently aware then of taking into account a people's own ideas of development. Fieldwork did not address this intrinsic point of view or all parts of the population, especially in terms of gender. I did not adequately include women in my gathering of data and largely overlooked their role in development. This major deficit was, to some extent at least, a result of the contemporary context and current theory. As a fieldworker, I acted largely as an outside observer, following the current ethnographic methodologies of participant observation with more emphasis on observation, relatively short-lived as it necessarily was, and less on participation. For all the limitations, temporal as well as methodological, of my fieldwork, I nevertheless became aware of the complexities of dealing with people in their dynamic contexts, and notably of issues of racial tension existing between the Fijian and Indian communities in Fiji.

Along with a number of other social scientists, I used the word 'peasant' although often in inverted commas to identify a non-village agricultural smallholder. It was a useful part of a tentative typology of 'tribesmen', 'peasants', 'farmers', 'proletarians' and 'townsmen'. Of course, there were virtually no 'farmers' in Fiji in the early 1960s in the thoroughly capitalistic, commercial sense, and the people who were called 'peasants' were *galala* or 'independent farmers'. However, when I later studied peasants in Peru and southern Mexico I realised that this intermediate category which is useful in a *relative* sense is not satisfactory in any general, comparative way. Fiji and other Oceanic countries were *tribal* in nature and they had not possessed money as a medium of exchange, markets or market places, cities, elites and a class structure; nor had they been part of an empire or state that extracted rent and other services (see Watters, 1994).

The thesis that developed out of this fieldwork and was argued in *Koro* was that the rate of economic development in Fiji was largely determined by the process of social change. This growing perspective forced me, the geographer, to grapple with cultural and social factors normally dealt with by anthropologists. Equally, of course, it could be argued the opposite way, that social change is also greatly affected by the rate of economic development. Thus, I have no apology to make for offering what appears to be a circular argument. Such processes were, of course, also powerful factors in making the relatively 'modern' sugar zone of the 1950s and 1960s more successful by attracting new investment and labour, and the traditional sector as represented by largely subsistence 'traditional' villages like Nalotawa less successful. I agree with C.S. Belshaw that 'economy' and 'society' are better thought of not as separate concrete referents but as abstract models which use different but complementary principles for the analysis of the *same* phenomena.[3] Thus, *Koro* is not really a geographic study; rather, it is an inter-disciplinary study. In a purely personal way, the brief friendly meeting with Gerry Ward over a beer in Suva in 1958 was an important turning point on my own journey to progress.

This journey continued after *Koro* was published in 1969, when a review of it appeared in the *Journal of Administration Overseas*. The reviewer turned out to be a senior economist at the Ministry of Overseas Development in London. He wrote to me on behalf of the Ministry enquiring whether I would be interested in undertaking a similar, wide-ranging study of the village sector in the British Solomon Islands Protectorate, which was likely to become an independent nation in about a decade. I accepted on the basis of forming a small team of carefully selected and prepared graduate students, geographers and anthropologists who would undertake the fieldwork study and report to both the Solomon Islands government and the MOD; at the same time, the members of the team would also undertake PhD theses on socio-economic change and development in the islands.

Late in 1969, Bethlyn and I flew up to Guadalcanal to discuss the project in the capital. As we flew across the lagoon to land, we saw the great quantities of trucks, jeeps, office equipment and other items that the Americans had dumped into the sea after defeating the Japanese on Guadalcanal during World War II. In Honiara, I had detailed discussions with senior government officials and a number of heads of government departments. One senior expatriate administrator later queried the value of the project. He said that if he wanted to know how villagers grew cash crops and so on, he would call "a boy" who worked in the department to come to his room and explain how things were done! This was just the sort of response that confirmed the project's validity. If planning was to be rational and realistic, government needed to acquire a detailed knowledge and understanding of population, resources, land utilisation, cropping systems, labour availability and mobility, social and cultural effects on production and trading, and many other aspects of the village situation. Moreover, it was usually quite inadequate to plan aid, interventions and innovations purely on what economists in London (or jaded expatriate administrators) might deduce villagers' motivations and aspirations to be.

This was illustrated by the coconut-planting scheme that was introduced into the Solomons from 1969. At first, villagers were required to plant an area of 5 acres before receiving the subsidy payment – an area that was too big and required a large amount of labour to clear the land. It was later reduced to 3 acres or more (between 180 and 270 palms) but took no account of how coconuts fitted into the rotational bush fallow system; the palms had to be planted in a contiguous block within 9 months. While this scheme contributed to an increase in acreage of palms in West Guadalcanal, it was clear that many households were growing at a considerable rate, and land would have been planted in palms to meet their needs even if no subsidy was paid. In this case, the team was able to recommend that the subsidy scheme be confined to areas which had a low planting rate under the existing system.

In the initial discussions, it was made clear to me that in such a diverse country, three regions were of critical and over-riding importance and their characteristics had to be studied and their needs balanced: the Western District, where most of the coconut plantations were located, as well as substantial areas of forestry and significant village copra production; Malaita, a very populous poor island which was rather traditional in socio-cultural terms and lacked substantial development opportunities; and Guadalcanal, the main island in the group in which the capital, Honiara, was located and which also possessed various resources and the only substantial plains of considerable agricultural potential.

To gain a brief introduction to the village scene and to discuss the project with the villagers and invite their comments on its objectives, I was driven in a Land Rover to Verahue in west Guadalcanal, accompanied by Bethlyn and an interpreter. We met the Headman and villagers and there were smiles and handshakes all round. Then an awkward silence followed – Bethlyn broke the ice by walking down to the beach to look for seashells, whereupon all the children within sight joined her, laughing, to collect shells. I was unable to visit the Western District, but I flew to north Malaita where I had talks with J.L.O. Tedder, the very experienced District Commissioner. He drove me round the northern area and I had useful discussions there with villagers.

We returned to New Zealand by flying the long way home – the spectacular route over the Roviana lagoon (perhaps the most stunningly beautiful scenery in the whole South Pacific), New Georgia, Bougainville, and the Buka passage to Rabaul, Lae and Port Moresby.

After advertising the project and considering a range of graduates in New Zealand and Australia, I selected John M. McKinnon, a geographer to work in Vella Lavella of the Western District; Ian Frazer, an anthropologist to study north Malaita; and the geographer, Murray Bathgate, to study north-western Guadalcanal. With myself as director we made a team of four. The first year was involved in training and reading the literature[4] in Wellington. The second year was spent in the villages and the Western Pacific Archives. The final year was involved in completing the three island reports and combined Team Report.

As in my earlier case study of Fiji, the method of inquiry adopted incorporated perspectives from social and economic anthropology, development anthropology, economic and human geography, history and economics. Our interdisciplinary method was premised on the understanding that the processes of economic development and social change cannot be examined independently of each other: one must raise questions concerning the objectives of economic development in a traditional society undergoing pronounced change and moving from a colonial status to political independence.

The ODA, pleased with the Solomons project, invited us to undertake an even larger socio-economic team survey in the Gilbert and Ellice Islands. Our approach became more multi-layered when I undertook leadership of this survey in 1971-72. Again, I worked in a team which meant that the strengths and methodologies of several academic disciplines underpinned the planning and application of our involvement. By this time, I was committed to the notion that development projects imposed from the outside seldom do little more than create words on paper and dis-ease in local administrations. The varying efficacy, usefulness and applicability of the Solomon Islands project, as well as other development projects, had made clear the fact that development which has no endemic resonance will not do any good. Our aim in the Gilbert and Ellice Islands, therefore, was to try to arrive at an inside-out approach to the culture; to see what the goals and aspirations of the people were; what worked and did not work; what would be useful and able to be embraced by them; and what would be simply irrelevant and prescriptive. Our task was to carry out a stock-take of actual resources and analyse how production occurred, how labour was utilised, how income was gained and assess prospects for the future.

The same sort of approach was adopted in 1981 when I was asked to lead the Kandrian-Gloucester project in Papua New Guinea which was designed to review development options. However, looking back on that project today, I realise that my first misgivings about it were correct: I suspected it would be a top-down project as it did not involve local officers working as equal partners with us and it was not structured in a way that would enable extensive discussion of the options and their respective advantages and disadvantages. Inevitably, this would have required different organisation and planning and more time to hold extensive discussions with villagers, WNB officials and government ministers. Community education and a whole series of meetings down to village level would have been required to explain why it is so important, for example, to choose the right size and powered work boat if copra marketing is to remain economic, or the pros and cons of small-scale logging enterprises compared to large-scale ones.

The fault was not with the team, which was very competent and dealt with the various development issues in thorough and appropriate ways. The main deficiency was in the vision and underlying assumptions about development upon which the project was based. The addition of an anthropologist, Professor Ann Chowning, to the team as an advisor was essential and made a great difference to the analysis, but there was nevertheless a lack of expertise or understanding of West New Britain cultures, societies and value-orientations. Deductive, a priori reasoning is not enough when proposing innovations – they must become empirically based, and be appropriate and meaningful to local societies. And in the end, they have to be the innovations of the local people.

It was the stated intention of the Central Planning Office to use the project as a model to be followed by other provinces as they set out their various development options to make choices for the future. The team produced a thorough (three-volume) report which could be broken up, simplified and rewritten in numerous short sections on different topics in Pidgin for widespread public discussion and community education, down to and including school journals.

My fieldwork experience and knowledge over these 25 years or so in the Pacific became the model for all my future work, some of which I carried out on my own and some of which I undertook as part of a team. I do not regret that decision to embark on a much broader and more demanding analysis. As academics we have an obligation not only to discover or collect new facts; we also have an obligation to examine their meanings. As I said in 1972, "....social science must do more than merely record facts: it must attempt to explain them". To do this we must, at times, tentatively enter new domains. After working in Fiji, my research in other countries in the Pacific, in Latin America (Peru, Venezuela and Mexico) and in China has followed the inter-disciplinary path for the same reasons.

Development: Reflections on a Future Agenda

Most people in the islands of Oceania still live in the neo-traditional or village sector and suffer from the typical problems of development: inadequate housing and services; minimal access to education, health and welfare; low incomes; problems with transport, markets and ways to improve productivity; and reliance on migration and remittances.

We have noted above that neo-traditional forms of shifting cultivation or fallow systems will be coming under growing stress as population increases in the countryside. As the fallow period shortens, there will be inadequate time for full restoration of soil fertility and nutrient status and there will be invasion of poorer quality plants and weeds. The structure and aeration of the soil may also deteriorate, leading to soil compaction. As shrubs and weeds replace larger forest trees, the quality of leaf litter will reduce and so the organic matter (and nitrogen level) will also drop. Higher value crops such as taro or yams may not grow well under these conditions, leading to substitution by inferior crops like cassava. The solution is to enrich the fallow by planting fast-growing species that provide good leaf litter that will enable the soil fertility to be restored in a shorter time. A traditional tree used throughout the tropics to enrich the fallow is *Leucania glauca*, and *Inga* from South America has produced remarkable results in trials over many years in Honduras. Both of these can be considered for Oceania, and could probably enable farmers to move from shifting agriculture to permanent cultivation. Of course, careful quarantine procedures and ecological impact studies are required before introducing any new species, as well as consideration of life-cycle, disease resistance, co-cropping and other factors.

Soil conservation may also need to be practised if over-cropping occurs, especially in hilly ground. We have noted the important study by Leslie and Ratukalou on the serious effects of this in Vanua Levu when sugar cane was planted on poor soils (including *talasiga*, humic latosols and steep-land stony clays) as part of the ill-fated Seaqaqa Cane Scheme, one of the largest and most expensive projects in Fiji that was designed to increase sugar cane production. The natural geological erosion rate is high in Fiji because of the youthful landscape, lithologies and uneven topography. By world standards, lands with slopes greater than 8° would be considered incapable of growing sugar without unacceptable damage.[5] Yet the Fiji Sugar Corporation allowed cane growing on land up to 10° slope, and NLTB staff would classify any land then growing cane as 'arable', irrespective of slope.[6] In spite of the emotional attachment, loyalty and protection that Fijians are meant to hold towards their land (the *vanua*) from which they came, Fijians themselves have been culprits for accelerating soil erosion on sloping land along with all the agencies of government. After a two-and-a-half-year delay, endorsement of the first rural land policy in the Pacific by the Qarase government in 2005 was a major step forward, but implementation still requires political will as well as financial and bureaucratic commitments that have never before been demonstrated by any government.[7] The buoyant agriculture sector led to an expansion of agriculture on to unimproved land, but at the end of the 1970s this expansion had reached its limits. R.G. Ward pointed out that policies:

> ... which depended on subsistence farming absorbing (at a satisfactory level of living) those who cannot find work in the urban or fully commercial sectors, will become increasingly difficult to maintain. At the same time, several of the processes of change in agriculture and land use have the effect of undercutting the foundations of Fijian social structure and so are at odds with the other policy of supporting that structure.[8]

A sad but logical consequence of these trends can be seen today, 20 years later, in the recourse of Fijians to a remittance economy by seeking dangerous jobs in the Middle East as a major source of income. Ward also pointed out that if the government had implemented existing regulations pertaining to soil conservation, there would be no problem.

When I first began fieldwork in the Dry Zone of Viti Levu in 1958-59, *vetiver* grass was occasionally planted on sloping land along the contour line. Nearly 40 years later, when working in the sub-tropical uplands of southern China, I found *vetiver* to be a remarkably successful solution for minimising erosion and soil loss on sloping ground. When looking further at the role of *vetiver* which is often regarded as almost a miracle anti-erosion plant, it was frequently noted that its great effectiveness had been proven in Fiji. Yet sadly, for many years now, it appears that only a fraction of *vetiver* remains, and it is rare for conservationists to use it in Fiji![9]

The coconut palm is clearly the single most important plant in the subsistence economy of islanders on coral atolls and usually their only commercial crop. The importance of copra in the outer island economy varies considerably, reflecting in part differences in the relationship between population, resources and environmental factors (especially rainfall), but also differing levels of participation in the cash economy and access to alternative sources of income. All such factors must be taken into account in interpreting the various responses of different islands to external forces such as price changes and government-sponsored incentive programmes.

The coconut palm can be seen as acting somewhat like a 'bank', holding nuts that can be made into saleable copra when other sources of income (such as remittances, wage income or sales of dried fish) decline. It remains of vital importance on remote atolls where no other form of income exists, apart perhaps from sale of dried or salt fish and export of labour.

Over the years, there have been numerous projects implemented in the hot wet tropics of post-tribal Oceania that evolved in vastly different European and British contexts. Thus, regional planning techniques, especially when based on urban 'growth poles', and decentralisation have been even less effective in Fiji, for instance, than they have in Europe. As Overton (1987) has explained, the very costly attempts in Western Vanua Levu in the 1970s to initiate rapid economic growth by regional planning have failed. These projects, designed to create employment, give equal access to welfare services and provide the productive capacity to sustain long-term growth, have failed. Yet in every region in which I have worked, one can find examples of successful production schemes, of entrepreneurship and small businesses that succeed. Careful empirical description and analysis of these ventures and the conditions under which they succeed is a valuable task, useful for policy formulation, for they document what already exists and works.[10]

In 1978, the Director of External Aid Division of the Ministry of Foreign Affairs in New Zealand invited a large number of consultants and specialists from a considerable number of disciplines who had all worked in Western Samoa to meet and discuss what he considered to be a crisis in New Zealand's aid to that country. Over a number of years, the Aid Division had funded project after project to set up or improve agricultural production in the village sector but virtually all had failed. Every few years a new enthusiastic agronomist would emerge, believing he had the answer, only for his pet project to meet the same fate as all the rest. Each one successively tried to 'reinvent the wheel'. It was as if large sums of money had been poured into a bottomless pit – all of it had gone, with nothing to show for it. The day of detailed discussions and debates on this problem was fascinating and tantalising yet ultimately frustrating. There was a good deal of collective experience and knowledge about Samoa present, but we could not at that point identify what went wrong or recommend a solution.

Looking back, I believe we should have stressed the lack of

motivation on the part of Samoans to involve themselves fully in the various projects. The fundamental point about development, of course, is that a development project must be the people's own – they must really want it, be committed to it and must own it. A widespread reason for failure of projects is that they do not meet this simple but fundamental condition of being the people's own project. The biggest reason for failure, however, was that Samoans had for some years been increasingly committed to MIRAB-type behaviour – for seeking higher incomes that could be gained off-shore by migration to New Zealand. They already saw the poor prospects that agriculture in the village environment offered, in comparison to regular wage employment.[11]

Forty years ago, Harold Brookfield and Doreen Hart were "startled" by the huge differences in incomes from village cash cropping in different parts of Papua New Guinea. There was almost ten times of difference between per person incomes in the island provinces of East New Britain and New Ireland and the emerging coffee growing areas such as Eastern Highlands compared to the "almost pitiful incomes of the four westernmost provinces – East Sepik and West Sepik, Southern Highlands and Western".[12] Using 1966 data, Brookfield and Hart argued that development in the country was closely associated with the production of export cash crops and as a result was heavily influenced by the quality of the environment. The pattern of poverty revealed 30 years later by the 1996 World Bank poverty survey was evident in patterns of inequality that existed even before the arrival of colonialism or capitalism. Poor areas almost always reflect severe environmental constraints: very high altitude, high rainfall, steep slopes, flooding and poor soils.[13] Plantations were mostly established where better land was available, which influenced smallholder cash cropping for export and in addition access to domestic markets for sale of fresh food and betel nut. Thus, rather than poor places being poor because of involvement in unequal market relationships (as some development theories predict), they are poor because of environmental factors and because they cannot engage with the market.

Building roads is not a practical solution for the reduction of poverty. The majority of rural people already had access to a road as a result of a vigorous road-building programme in which rural people built thousands of kilometres of road by hand. But many of these roads have long since fallen into disrepair and are impassable when wet. Much of the 1975 rural road network in parts of PNG is now impassable, and over the last few years the government has spent on road maintenance only 40 percent of the amount required to maintain national highways. Since the late 1990s, it appears that people are responding to this situation by increasing rural-to-rural and rural to peri-urban population movement.[14]

Development is thus a dilemma. It may be imposed from the outside and thus not adopted by local people or adapted to local conditions; and it may be identifiably unsuccessful because of local conditions. Access, opportunity, capacity and poverty are the great determinants of development, cultural and social viability, and equity. By referring always to the local, we – the outsiders – can only hope to guard ourselves against paternalism and the imposition of foreign and irrelevant value systems and measures of success. We can perhaps hope to do little more than this, and to see from the inside out. To be a catalyst or facilitator assisting a community to identify its own problems or issues and to discuss how to deal with those which they can control is, however possible, leading them to choose their road to development, and to take responsibility for and ownership of it.[15]

Conclusion

Several perils face the small fledgling island nation states of Oceania, some of which are circumstantial and unassailable, such as location, climate, poor soils and distance, and some of which could embody some of their salvation.

The first of the latter is geopolitical strategy. It is interesting to note that in May 2007 US Secretary of State Condoleeza Rice addressed a visiting group of Pacific leaders and assured them of American interest in the Pacific. She said they were calling 2007 'the Year of the Pacific' (they would hardly call it the Year of the Middle East!) saying: "It encapsulates our efforts to expand our engagement with your countries and to reaffirm America's historic role in the Pacific".[16] Evidence that this is just not empty rhetoric exists in the construction of a new US$65m embassy in Suva. The staff of the embassy will include a 'public diplomacy officer' tasked with sharing information about American policies and values throughout the South Pacific. There is also an expectation there will be a build-up of American military bases in the Pacific. At the same time, the United States is competing diplomatically with its great and rapidly expanding partner, China.

The second is likely to be the mounting wave of resource extraction that is sweeping through the Pacific. The recent generous offer of the European Union to extend assistance of F$400m to the new military government in Fiji in return for the early restoration of democratic elections came as a surprise to many. In this case, the motive may well be the rich, partly untapped fishery resources in the Pacific[17] (the vast

Kiribati waters are believed to be very promising); access to these may be attractive as Europe's traditional fishing oceans have become largely exhausted. There are also rumours that the age of seabed and seafloor mineral exploration and extraction is about to begin. Poor, widely scattered archipelagic states that currently possess few resources could conceivably be transformed if their vast EE Zones are found to contain rich mineral deposits. Their independent sovereign status would then be of enormous value. Indeed, the alleged demise of sovereign states due to the globalisation process certainly would not occur.

As we contemplate the new 'pattern of islands' in its current situation, if I can employ Arthur Grimble's title to his classic memoir on the Gilbert and Ellice Islands Colony, we must view it in the context of the world as it is today. It is clear that in the future we will live in a world of disorder and will need to accept a multipolar world. The end of the old empires, the birth of scores of newly independent nations and their increasing realisation of the non-fulfilment of their goals, together with the effects of World War II, the revolution of rising expectations and rapid population growth ending the old stabilities opened a great new Pandora's Box. There was constant flux and the appearance of change, but in reality the kaleidoscope had moved a few times and the patterns were different but not fundamentally changed. The result has been widespread perceived deprivation and growing disorder. In 1989, Halliday noted that since the end of World War II there had been over 140 conflicts costing over 20 million lives, and almost all were in the Third World and linked to the Cold War between the USA and the USSR. I am sure this frequency of warfare has been just as great since 1989.[18] And along with the relative decline in the hegemony of the United States in the world (realisation of which also brings new dangers), we can expect the gradual climb of the emergent and increasingly confident China which might equal the US in GNP by about 2030, and the emergence of India, Brazil, a more balanced European Union, and a more democratic South America, India and APEC.

Within this context, the small Oceania states have to contend with increasing intensity of globalisation through the agency of outside powers: Japan, Korea, Malaysia, the Philippines and increasingly PR China and Taiwan, as well as the US, France, Canada, Australia and New Zealand. In the 1980s, the competition in logging and tuna fishing reached a much higher level, only to be exceeded again in the next two decades. Currently, the pressure to gain access to resources and efforts at dollar diplomacy appear to be greater than ever.

We have described the distinctive character of several Oceanic countries over the last 50 years and their situation today, including the severe challenges many face, including poverty, marginalisation, racism, growing inequality, land issues, economic stagnation, poor governance, lack of a civic culture and rapid resource depletion. More than ever, development often turns out to be merely extraction, repeating the early history of predatory exploitation by foreigners. Moreover, the region cannot count on a level playing field with respect to trade. Following on from the exclusion of many developing countries' sugar cane exports through widespread cultivation of subsidised sugar beet in European countries, the stalemate of WTO trade talks at Doha in 2005 has added to the worries of some of the poorest countries in the world that depend on exports to the EU. The fallout of failure to reform key rules of the WTO is now widely being felt, with millions of jobs and thousands of companies dependent on exports to the EU directly threatened.

As many as 76 former colonies of European countries (including a number in Oceania) benefited for more than 40 years from a system of preferential lower tariffs on their exports to the EU. When other developing countries lacking access to this system challenged it in the mid-1990s, the WTO ruled it discriminatory. A hunt began to replace it with a system that still benefited former colonies but did not land the EU in breach of WTO rules.[19] A deal was meant to be found by December 2007; failing this, the developing countries would be subject to tariffs on their exports.

The sting arising from the new system of Economic Partnership Agreements (EPAs) was that the WTO required reciprocity. What had started out as the EU doing some poor countries a favour became a trade deal in which the EU was given duty-free access to the markets of developing countries. In effect, the old trade liberalisation agenda that acquired notoriety in Seattle in 1999 is reappearing through the back door. For developing countries that have been lumped into six regional negotiating blocs, the EPAs have become a nightmare in view of the December 2007 deadline, with fears that economic disruption and chaos will ensue.

EPAs raise three major concerns:

- While every developing country has used tariff protection historically to develop infant industries, the EPAs restrict that; a surge of European imports could wipe out fledgling industries or agricultural sectors.
- Governments stand to lose a major portion of their revenue that comes from tariffs (while the EU assures them aid will increase, this only deepens their dependence).

- It is not known how EPAs will affect regional trade, an important new area.[20]

As promotion of EPAs is mainly done behind closed doors in bilateral negotiations, the bully-boy behaviour of the EU is mostly invisible. In 2007, both Australia and New Zealand have also been pushing strongly for trade liberalisation in the South Pacific through acceptance and implementation of the Pacific Agreement on Closer Economic Relations (PACER) trade agreements as part of the economic integration goals of the Pacific Plan. Fortunately, the October 2007 Pacific Forum did not back their moves and it is apparent that several Pacific countries have decided not to accept these moves that would commit them to free trade with Australia and New Zealand.

As near neighbours of the island countries and linked to them by extensive networks, Australia and New Zealand have demonstrated through the focus and apportionment of their aid programmes that they accept the need to assist these countries with their developmental and environmental problems. Indeed, the vital interests of both countries suggest they must continue to do so, and their dominance in the region and the progressive integration of the island countries with the metropolitan economies of Australia and New Zealand are shown clearly in the one-sided trade statistics. Over the seven-year period 2000-2006, Australia exported goods worth a mean of NZ$2,734.85 million dollars a year to the Pacific islands and imported in return a mean of NZ$2,280.113 million – a favourable balance of NZ$454.737 million. In the same period, New Zealand exported a mean of NZ$1013.77 million in goods per year and imported in return a mean of NZ$146.12 million, an excess of NZ$866.88 million. Thus, New Zealand exports exceeded imports from the Pacific region by almost 7 to 1. With respect to the Australian figures, it is worth noting that 81.9 percent of Australian imports from the Pacific islands comes from PNG, 11.4 percent from Fiji and 3 percent from New Caledonia; the remaining 21 countries of the Pacific including the relatively large countries of the Solomon Islands and Vanuatu contributed only 3.7 percent of Australian imports.[21]

In 2007-8, Australia provided overseas aid totalling A$747.66 million to the Pacific islands and New Zealand NZ$441 million (at the mean rate of exchange for 2007 of NZ$1 = A$0.8184, the New Zealand aid figure is equivalent to A$387.4 million).[22] In spite of the considerable benefits offered by this aid, as well as the commitments and responsibilities that New Zealand and Australia have towards their near neighbours in the region, I suspect that the vast majority of New

Zealanders (and perhaps Australians too) rarely spare a thought for the countries of Oceania and their inhabitants except as an attractive holiday destination to escape to in the depths of the southern winter. The island countries deserve much more than that.

To conclude, I must thank and pay tribute to many people who have assisted me in my research for the original books and research papers as well as for this particular book. They are thanked in the Acknowledgements. But above all I want to express my gratitude to the many villagers of the Pacific and especially those of Abemama and Fiji who allowed me to live among them for a while in an attempt to gain a little insight into their lives. It was indeed a great privilege for me, an outsider and a working journeyman, to have been accorded this experience. Kam bati n rabwa. Vinaka vaka levu sara.

Abbreviations

ACP	Africa, Caribbean and Pacific [states]
ADB	Asian Development Bank
ALTA	Agricultural Landlords and Tenants Act (F)
ANZUS	Australia, New Zealand, United States (military alliance)
APEC	Asia-Pacific Economic Cooperation
AUSAid	Australian government aid
CMV	Matanitu Vanua Party (political party, F)
CRP	Comprehensive Reform Programme (V)
CSA	Colonial Sugar Agreement
CSR	Colonial Sugar Refinery Company (F)
DPI	Department of Primary Industry (PNG)
DTCA	Department of Transport and Civil Aviation (PNG)
EEZ	exclusive economic zone
EPAs	Economic Partnership Agreements (EU)
EU	European Union
FAO	Food and Agriculture Organisation (UN)
FLP	Fiji Labour Party
FSC	Fiji Sugar Corporation
GATT	General Agreement on Tariffs and Trade
GDP	gross domestic product
GEIC	Gilbert and Ellice Islands Colony
GEIDA	Gilbert and Ellice Island Development Authority
GNI	gross national income
HDI	Human Development Index (UN)
IMF	International Monetary Fund
LGC	Local Government Council(s) (PNG)
LSE	London School of Economics
MIRAB	migration, remittances, aid, bureaucracy (type of economy)
MOD	Ministry of Overseas Development (GB)
NCP	National Reconciliation Process (V)
NFP	Indian National Federation Party (F)
NGO	non-governmental organisation
NLTA	Native Land Trust Act (F)

NLTB	Native Land Trust Board (F)
NPEP	National Public Expenditure Plan (PNG)
ODA	Official Development Assistance (GB)
PACER	Pacific Agreement on Closer Economic Relations
PIM	Pacific Islands Monthly
PNG	Papua New Guinea
PNGDF	Papua New Guinea Defence Force
PROFIT	People consideration – citizenship, residence and employment; resource management; overseas engagement; finance and transportation
RERF	Revenue Equalisation Reserve Fund (K)
RFMF	Royal Fijian Military Forces
SDL	Soqosoqo Duavata Lewe Ni Vanua (political party, F)
SITE	Small Island Tourist Economy
SPADES	South Pacific Action for Development and Economic Strategies
SPAS	South Pacific Agricultural Survey
SPC	South Pacific Commission
SVT	Soqosoqo Vakavulewa ni Taukei (political party, F)
TRP	Timber Rights Purchase (PNG)
UMP	Union of Moderate Parties (V)
UNDP	United Nations Development Programme
UNESCO	United Nations Educational, Scientific and Cultural Organisation
UNFPA	United Nations Fund for Population Activities
VIPA	Vanuatu Investment Promotion Authority
VULCAN	Vila Urban Land Corporation (V)
WESTEC	Western Samoa Trust Estates Corporation
WHO	World Health Organisation
WNB	West New Britain (PNG)
WNBPG	West New Britain Provincial Government (PNG)
WTO	World Trade Organisation

Glossary

aba ni maiu [K]	land of the living
aba ni mate [K]	land of the dead
ahia [Ta]	fruit (*Eugenia malaccensis*)
aiga [S]	bifurcated descent group, extended family
api [T]	area of agricultural land (3.2. ha.)
babai [K]	starchy root vegetable, type of taro (*cyrtosperma chamissonis*)
banuea [K]	nobility
bele [F]	vegetable
bila [F]	alluvial soil
bisnis [PNG]	business
bito [F]	sub-clan (Western Viti Levu), corresponding to *tokatoka*
boraoi [K]	conformity, equality
bose vaka turaga [F]	council of chiefs
bubuti [K]	reciprocity, giving of gifts that are commented on/ asked for
buli [F]	district chief
bure [F]	house
dak bus [V]	dark bush
dalo [F]	taro
fa'a Samoa [S]	the Samoan way
fa'alavelave [S]	ceremonial feast(s)
fakatuumea [Tu]	to build things
fale [S]	house
fautua [S]	royal son
galala [F]	independent farmer
gasau [F]	reed (*Miscanthus floridulus*)
haus blong kranky [V]	asylum
helan [V]	power
i-Kiribati [K]	person indigenous to Kiribati
i tokatoka [F]	sub-clan
ikaraoi [K]	cultivated varieties of *babai*
imatang [K]	European, non-local person
inaomata [K]	security, freedom

kabirongorongo [K]	money that you spend
kakakibotu [K]	resting, leisure
kanaka [Mel.]	'blackbird' labour
karinimane [K]	money that you keep
kastom [V]	form of indigenous ownership, custom
katutu [K]	uncultivated varieties of *babai*
kaubai [K]	rich in things
kaumane [K]	money
kawai [F]	yam
kina [PNG]	money, currency
kopu tangata [CI]	family/kindred estate
koro [F]	village
kumala [F]	sweet potato, kumara
mage [V]	graded society ritual
magiti [F]	feast
malaga [S]	ceremonial journey(s)
man ples [V]	rightful occupant/ owner
manblong ples [V]	strength of particularism
maneaba [K]	community meeting house
mangai [F]	canarium nut
mape [Ta]	chesnut (*Inocarpus edulis*)
masalai [PNG]	malevolent forest beings
matai [S]	chief
mataqali [F]	minimal clan structure
mau [F]	vegetable
meke [F]	dance
mronron [K]	small indigenous enterprise
mwenga [K]	household
nakamal [V]	debate that continues until agreement is reached
namele [V]	plant, used to mark ownership or boundary
nangaria [V]	plant, to honour, male sex organ, fine lady
niu laef [V]	new life
oinibai [K]	self-sufficient, free to control one's activities
papa'a [CI]	European, visitor
pule [S]	control over land, power
rara [F]	village green
roko [F]	provincial chief
roro [F]	leaves of *dalo*
tabua [F]	whale's tooth used in ceremony
talasiga [F]	poor stony clay soil, humic latosol
tama-a-aiga [S]	paramount chief

taulele'a [S]	untitled men
te uea [K]	high chief
teitei [F]	gardens
tetabo [K]	the place of staying alive
tibanga [K]	luck, fate
tikina [F]	administrative district
toises [S]	measurement (cf. yard or metre)
tokatoka [F]	sub-clan
tui [F]	chiefly title
unimane [K]	old men
utu [K]	clan
vaka vanua [F]	in accordance with custom
vanua [F]	land, confederation
vatu [V]	currency
veikau [F]	waste or village common lands
vi [Ta]	golden apple (*Spondias dulcis*)
vulagi [F]	stranger
yaqona [F]	plant used to make kava (*Piper methysticum*)
yavusa [F]	maximal clan structure

Key	
CI	Cook Islands
F	Fiji
K	Kiribati
Mel.	Melanesian
PNG	Papua New Guinea
S	Samoa
T	Tonga
Ta	Tahiti
Tu	Tuvalu
V	Vanuatu

References

Note: The various papers in *Asia Pacific Viewpoint*, 4 (1), April 2006, contain a large number of references on MIRAB economies and other variants.

AEAS (Appraisal, Evaluation and Analytical Support Unit), 1992, *Report of the Joint Review of the Tabuaeran and Teraina Settlement Project*, Wellington and Tarawa.

Aikman, C.C., 1956, *First Report on Constitutional Survey of the Cook Islands*, Wellington.

Ala'ilima, Vaiao J. and Fay C. Ala'ilima, 1964, 'Samoan Values and Economic Development', MS International Development Institute, Honolulu: East-West Center.

Alkiri, William, 1978, *Coral Islanders*, Arlington Heights, Illinois: Aim Publishing Company.

Allen, B.J. (Bryant), 1969, 'The Development of Commercial Agriculture on Mangaia: Social and Economic Change in a Polynesian Community', Palmerston North: Geography Department, Massey University.

____, 1983, 'Paradise Lost? Rural Development in an Export-led Economy: The Case of Papua New Guinea', chapter 8 in David A.M. Lea and D.P. Chaudri (eds), *Rural Development and the State: Contradictions and Dilemmas in Developing Countries*, London and New York: Methuen.

Allen, B., R.M. Bourke and J. Gibson, 2005, 'Poor Rural Places in Papua New Guinea', *Asia Pacific Viewpoint*, 46 (2), pp 201-17.

Allen, Michael R., 1964, *The Nduindui: A Study in the Social Structure of a New Hebridean Community*, PhD thesis, Canberra: Australian National University (ANU).

____, 1968, 'The Establishment of Christianity and Cash-Cropping in a New Hebridean Community', *Journal of Pacific History*, 3, pp 25-46.

Anon. (n.d., 1972), 'Background to Development', MS, Tarawa.

Apter, David E., 1965, *The Politics of Modernization*, Chicago: University of Chicago Press.

Asian Development Bank, 1983, *Economic Survey of Kiribati*, Manila.

____, 1995, *Cook Islands: Performance, Issues and Strategies*, Rarotonga: Office of Pacific.

Australian Government AusAid, 2004, *Pacific Regional Aid Strategy, 2004-09*, Canberra: Commonwealth of Australia.

Baddeley, J.G., 1978, *Rarotonga Society: the Creation of Tradition*, PhD thesis in Anthropology, University of Auckland.

Baldachino, G., 2006, 'Managing the Hinterland Beyond: Two Ideal-type Strategies of Economic Development for Small Island Territories', *Asia Pacific Viewpoint*, 47 (1), pp 45-60.

Barnes, J.A., 1962, 'African Models in the New Guinea Highlands', *Man*, 62, pp 5-9.

Barrau, J., 1955, *Subsistence Agriculture in Melanesia*, Noumea.

Barrington, J.H., 1968, *Education and National Development in Western Samoa*, PhD thesis, Wellington: Victoria University of Wellington.

Bassett, I.G. (ed.), 1969, *Pacific Peasantry: Case Studies of Rural Societies,* Palmerston North: New Zealand Geographical Society.

Bathgate, M.A., 1973, *West Guadalcanal Report*, Wellington: Victoria University of Wellington Socio-Economic Survey of the Solomons.

____, 1993, *Fight for the Dollar: Economic and Social Change in Western Guadalcanal, Solomon Islands*, 2 vols, Solomon Islands Reports, Monograph No. 1, ISBN 0-908901-05-4, Alexander Enterprise, 18A Amritsar St, Khandallah, Wellington.

____, I.C. Frazer and J.H. McKinnon, 1973, *Socio-Economic Change in Solomon Island Villages*, Wellington: Victoria University of Wellington Socio-Economic Survey of the Solomons.

Bayliss-Smith, T.P., 1982, *The Ecology of Agricultural Systems*, Cambridge: Cambridge University Press.

____ and R.G.A. Feachem (eds), 1977, *Subsistence and Survival: Rural Ecology in the Pacific*, London: Academic Press.

____, Richard Bedford, Harold Brookfield, Marc Latham, with Muriel Brookfield, 1988, *Islands, Islanders and the World: The Colonial and Post-colonial Experience of Eastern Fiji*, Cambridge: Cambridge University Press.

Bazeley, Peter and Ben Muller (Uniquest Pty Ltd), July 2006, *Vanuatu: Economic Opportunities Fact-finding Mission*, AUSAid and NZAid.

Bedford, Richard, 1973, 'A Transition to Circular Mobility', in H.C. Brookfield (ed.), *The Pacific in Transition*, London: Edward Arnold.

____, 1974, 'Models and Migration in a Melanesian Archipelago', *New Zealand Geographer*, 30 (2), pp 129-50.

____, 1984, 'The Polynesian Connection: Migration and Social Change in New Zealand and the South Pacific', in R.D. Bedford (ed.), *Essays on Urbanisation in Southeast Asia and the Pacific*, Christchurch: Department of Geography, University of Canterbury.

____, 1999, 'Mobility in Melanesia: Bigman Bilong Circulation', *Asia Pacific Viewpoint*, 40 (1), pp 3-17.

____ and John Overton, 1999, 'R. Gerard Ward: Quintessential Pacific Geographer', *Asia Pacific Viewpoint*, 40 (2), pp 111-35.

Beeby, C.E., 1968, 'Education for Change in the South-West Pacific', cyclostyled, Christchurch: 40th ANZAAS Conference.

Bellam, M.E.P., 1964, *The Melanesian in Town: A Preliminary Study of Adult Male Melanesians in Honiara, British Solomon Islands Protectorate*, MA thesis in Geography, Wellington: Victoria University of Wellington.

____, 1969, 'Walkabout Long Chinatown: Aspects of Urban and Regional Development in the British Solomon Islands', Seminar on Urbanisation and Resettlement in the South Pacific, Wellington: Victoria University of Wellington.

____, 1980, *A Question of Balance. New Zealand Trade in the South Pacific*, Wellington: New Zealand Coalition for Trade and Development.

____, 1981, *The Citrus Colony: New Zealand-Cook Islands Economic Relations*, Wellington: New Zealand Coalition for Trade and Development.

Belshaw, C.S., 1957, *The Great Village*, London: Routledge and Kegan Paul.

____, 1963, 'Pacific Island Towns and the Theory of Growth', in A. Spoehr, *Pacific Port Towns and Cities*, Honolulu: Bishop Museum Press, pp 17-24.

____, 1964a, 'Social Structure and Cultural Values as Related to Economic Growth', *International Journal of Social Science*, 16, pp 216-28.

____, 1964b, *Under the Ivi Tree: Society and Economic Growth in Rural Fiji*, London: Routledge and Kegan Paul.

____, 1965, *Traditional Exchange and Modern Markets*, Englewood Cliffs, New Jersey: Prentice Hall.

____, 1967, 'Comments on *Primitive and Peasant Economic Systems* by Manning Nash', *Current Anthropology*, 8 (3), pp 245-6.

Belshaw, H. and V.D. Stace, 1955, *A Programme for Economic Development in the Cook Islands*, Wellington (Belshaw-Stace Report).

Berg, E.J., 1961, 'Backward-Sloping Labor Supply Functions in Dual Economies – the African Case', *The Quarterly Journal of Economy*, 75 (3), pp 468-92.

Bertram, I.G., 1980, 'Economic Characteristics', in Government of Tuvalu, *A Report on the Results of the Census of Tuvalu 1979*, Funafuti.

____, 1999a, 'The MIRAB Model Twelve Years On', *The Contemporary Pacific*, 11 (1), pp 103-38.

____, 1999b, 'Economy', in M. Rappaport (ed.), *The Pacific Islands, Environment and Society*, Hawaii: Bess Press.

____, 2004, 'On the Convergence of Small Island Economies with their Metropolitan Patrons', *World Development*, 32 (3), pp 343-64.

_____, 2006, 'Introduction: The MIRAB Model in the Twenty-first Century', *Asia Pacific Viewpoint*, 47 (1), April, pp 1-13.

Bertram, I.G. and R.F. Watters, 1984, *New Zealand and its Small Island Neighbours: a Review of New Zealand Policy Toward the Cook Islands, Niue, Tokelau, Kiribati and Tuvalu*, draft report to Ministry of Foreign Affairs, Institute of Policy Studies, Wellington.

Bienefeld, M., 1984, *Work and Income for the People of Fiji. A strategy for more than just survival*. Final report to the Government of Fiji by the Fiji Employment and Development Mission. Parliamentary Paper No. 66, Suva, Government Print.

Boardman, D., 1969, 'From Atoll to City – The Migration of the Tokelau Islanders to New Zealand', Seminar on Urbanisation and Re-settlement in the South Pacific, Wellington: Victoria University of Wellington.

Boeke, J.H., 1953, *Economics and Economic Policy of Dual Societies*, New York.

Bogotu, F., 1968, 'The Impact of Western Culture on Solomon Islands Society: A Melanesian Reaction', BSIP Newssheet No. 10, 31 May, Honiara.

_____, 1971, 'Politics, Economics and Social Aspects of the Developing Solomons', *South Pacific Bulletin*, 21 (1), pp 33-35 and p. 42.

Bohannan, Paul, 1964, *African Outline*, Harmondsworth: Penguin.

Bole, Filipe, 1969, *The Life and Work of Ratu Sir Lala Sukuna*, MA thesis, Wellington: Victoria University of Wellington.

Bollard, A., 1979, *Agricultural Project Design and Evaluation in an Island Community*, Development Studies Monograph No. 15, Canberra: ANU.

Bonnemaison, Joel, 1977, 'The Impact of Population Patterns and Cash Cropping on Urban Migration in the New Hebrides', *Pacific Viewpoint*, 18 (2), pp 119-32.

_____, 1984, 'The Tree and the Canoe: Roots and Mobility in Vanuatu Societies', *Pacific Viewpoint*, 25 (2), pp 117-51.

Bonnemaison, Joel and Bernard Hermann, 1975, *New Hebrides*, Paris: Les Editions Du Pacifique, Publications Elysées.

Borovnik, Maria, 2004, 'Remittances: An Informal but Indispensable Form of Income for Seafarer Families in Kiribati', Paper presented at Workshop on Remittances Microfinance Technology, Brisbane: University of Queensland.

Boserup, Ester, 1965, *The Conditions of Agricultural Growth: The Economics of Agrarian Change under Population Pressure*, London: Allen and Unwin.

Boyd, Mary, 1968, 'Independent Western Samoa', *Pacific Viewpoint*, 9 (2), pp 154-72.

_____, 1969, 'The Record in Western Samoa from 1945', in Angus Ross, *New Zealand's Record in the Pacific Islands in the Twentieth Century*, Auckland.

Brightwell, N., 1981, *Draft Reforestation Policy for Papua New Guinea*, Hohola (PNG): Office of Forests Draft Report.

Brookfield, H.C., 1962, 'Local Study and Comparative Method, an Example from Central New Guinea', *Annals of Association of American Geographers*, 52, pp 242-54.

_____, 1972, *Colonialism, Development and Independence: The Case of the Melanesian Islands in the South Pacific*, Cambridge: Cambridge University Press.

_____, (ed.), 1973, *The Pacific in Transition*, London: Edward Arnold.

_____, 1977, 'Constraints to Agrarian Change', in John H. Winslow (ed.), *The Melanesian Environment*, Canberra: ANU, pp 133-8.

_____, 1987, 'Export or Perish: Commercial Agriculture in Fiji', Chapter 4, in Michael Taylor (ed.), *Fiji Future Imperfect*, Sydney: Allen & Unwin, pp 46-57.

Brookfield, H.C. and D. Hart, 1971, *Melanesia: A Geographical Interpretation of an Island World*, London: Methuen.

Bryant-Tokalau, Jenny and Ian Frazer, 2006, *Redefining the Pacific*, Aldershot: Ashgate.

Buchanan, Keith, 1970, *The Transformation of the Chinese Earth: Perspectives on Modern China*, London: G. Bell & Sons, New York: Praeger.

Buck, P., 1949, *The Coming of the Maori*, Wellington: Whitcombe and Tombs.

_____ 1959, *Vikings of the Sunrise*, Chicago: University of Chicago Press.

Burns, Sir A., T.Y. Watson and A.T. Peacock, 1960, *Report of the Commission of Enquiry into the Natural Resources and Population Trends of the Colony of Fiji, 1959* (Burns Report),

Suva: Legislative Council Paper 1/1960, Government of Fiji.

Burridge, K., 1960, *Mambu, A Melanesian Millennium*, London: Methuen.

Carswell, Sue, 2003, 'A Family Business: Women, Children and Smallholder Sugar Cane Farming in Fiji', *Asia Pacific Viewpoint*, 44.

Chambers, Anne, 1984, *Nanumea Atoll Economy. Social Change in Kiribati and Tuvalu*, Development Studies Centre Monograph No. 6, Canberra: ANU.

Chapman, M., 1995, 'Island Autobiographies of Movement: Alternative Ways of Knowing?', in P. Claval and Singaravelou (eds), *Ethnogeographies*, Paris: L'Hamatan, pp 247-59.

Chapman, T., 1976, *The Decolonisation of Niue*, Wellington: Victoria University Press.

Chenery, H.B. and A. Strout, 1966, 'Foreign Assistance and Economic Development', *American Economic Review*, 56 (4), pp 679-733.

Chowning, Ann, 1969, 'Recent Acculturation between Tribes in Papua-New Guinea', *Journal of Pacific History*, 4, pp 27-40.

----, 1977, *An Introduction to the Peoples and Cultures of Melanesia*, Manlo Park, Calif.: Cummings Pub. Co.

Clammer, J. (ed.) 1978, *The New Economic Anthropology*, London.

Clarke, W.C., 1971, *Place and People: An Ecology of a New Guinea Community*, Canberra: ANU Press.

----, 1973, 'The Dilemma of Development', in H.C. Brookfield (ed.), *The Pacific in Transition*, London: Edward Arnold, pp 275-98.

----, 1977, 'The Structure of Permanence: The Relevance of Self-subsistence Communities for World Ecosystems Management', in T.P Bayliss-Smith and R.G.A. Feathem (eds), *Subsistence and Survival: Rural Ecology in the Pacific*, London: Academic Press.

Connell, John, 1975, 'Pacific Urbanization: The Exceptional Case of Tarawa Atoll', *Geographic Review*, pp 402-4.

----, 1978, *Taim bilong mani. The Evolution of Agriculture in a Solomon Island Society*, Development Studies Centre Monograph No. 12, Canberra: ANU.

----, 1980, *Remittances and Rural Development: Migration, Dependency and Inequality in the South Pacific*, Development Studies Centre Occasional Paper No. 22, Canberra: ANU.

----, 1991, 'Island Microstates: The Mirage of Development', *The Contemporary Pacific*, 3 (2), pp 251-87.

Connew, Bruce and Brij V. Lal, 2007, *Stopover*, Wellington: Victoria University Press.

Corner, F.H., 1962, 'New Zealand and the South Pacific', in T. Larkin (ed.), *New Zealand's External Relations*, Wellington: New Zealand Institute of Public Administration, pp 130-52.

Crocombe, R.G., 1962, 'Development and Regression in New Zealand's Island Territories', *Pacific Viewpoint*, 3 (2), pp 17-32.

----, 1964, *Land Tenure in the Cook Islands*, Melbourne: Oxford University Press.

----, 1968-69, 'That Five Year Plan', *New Guinea and Australia the Pacific and Southeast Asia*, 3, pp 51-70.

----, 1969, 'Crocombe to his Critics', *New Guinea and Australia the Pacific and Southeast Asia*, 4, pp 49-71.

----, 1971a, *Land Tenure in the Pacific*, Melbourne: Oxford University Press.

----, 1971b, 'Review of R.F. Watters, *Koro*: Economic Development and Social Change in Fiji', *Journal of the Polynesian Society*, 80 (4), pp 505-20.

Crocombe, R.G. and Marjorie, 1968, *The Works of Ta'unga*, Canberra: ANU.

Crown Agents, in association with Land Resources Development Centre, 1982, *Kandrian-Gloucester Development Study, West New Britain*, 3 volumes, Port Moresby: National Planning Office.

Cumberland, K.B., 1954, *Southwest Pacific*, Christchurch: Whitcombe and Tombs.

Curson, P.H., 1973, 'The Migration of Cook Islanders to New Zealand', *South Pacific Commission Bulletin*, 23, Noumea.

Dalton, George, 1961, 'Economic Theory and Primitive Society', *American Anthropologist*, 63 (1), pp 1-25.

_____, 1969, 'Theoretical Issues in Economic Anthropology', *Current Anthropology*, 10 (1), pp 63-102.

Davidson, J.W., 1970, *Samoa mo Samoa: The Emergence of the Independent State of Western Samoa*, Melbourne and London: Oxford University Press.

Davis, T.R.A., 1947, 'Rarotonga Today', *Journal of the Polynesian Society*, 56 (2), pp 197-218.

Douglas, E.M.K., 1965, *A Migration Study of Cook Islanders*, MSc thesis in Geography, Wellington: Victoria University of Wellington.

Ekeh, P., 1975, 'Colonialism and the Two Publics in Africa: A Theoretical Statement', *Comparative Studies in Society and History*, 17 (1), pp 91-112.

Elkan, W., 1967, 'Circular Migration and the Growth of Towns in East Africa', in R. Jolly et al (eds), *Third World Employment*, London: Penguin.

Epstein, A.L., 1967, 'Urbanisation and Social Change in Africa', *Current Anthropology*, 8 (4), pp 275-95.

Epstein, Scarlett, 1968, *Capitalism, Primitive and Modern: Some Aspects of Tolai Economic Growth*, Manchester: Manchester University Press.

Erasmus, Charles, 1967, 'Upper Limits of Peasantry and Agrarian Reform, Bolivia, Venezuela and Mexico', *Ethnology*, 6 (4), pp 349-80.

Eri, Vincent, 1970, *The Crocodile*, Brisbane: Jacaranda Press.

Escobar, A., 1995, *Encountering Development: The Making and Unmaking of the Third World*, Princeton, New Jersey: Princeton University Press.

Faber Report, 1973, *see* Overseas Development Group.

Fairbairn, I., 1961, 'The Migration of Samoans to New Zealand', *The Journal of the Polynesian Society*, 70 (1), pp 54-70.

_____, 1970, 'Village Economies in Western Samoa', *The Journal of the Polynesian Society*, 71 (1), pp 18-30.

Farrell, Bryan H. and R. Gerard Ward, 1962, 'The Village and its Agriculture', in James W. Fox and Kenneth B. Cumberland, *Western Samoa: Land, Life and Agriculture in Tropical Polynesia*, Christchurch: Whitcombe & Tombs.

Field, Michael, March 2004, 'Fiji sugar turns sour', *Pacific Magazine*, Honolulu: Pacific Basin Communications.

_____, 22 April 2004, 'Mitterand dream dies with Fiji leader', *Dominion Post*, Wellington.

_____, 21 June 2006, 'Fiji pays for risky business', *Dominion Post*, Wellington.

Figueroa, A., 1984, *Capitalist Development and the Peasant Economy in Peru*, New York: Cambridge University Press.

Finney, Ben, 1965, 'Polynesian Peasants and Proletarians: Socio-Economic Change among the Tahitians of French Polynesia', *The Journal of the Polynesian Society*, 74 (3), pp 269-328.

_____, 1967, 'Money Work, Fast Money and Prize Money: Aspects of the Tahitian Labor Commitment', *Human Organization*, 26 (4), pp 195-9.

_____, 1968, 'Bigfellow Man Belong Business in New Guinea', *Ethnology*, 7 (4), pp 394-410.

Firth, Raymond, 1936, *We the Tikopia: A Sociological Study of Kinship in Primitive Polynesia*, London: Allen and Unwin.

_____, 1959a, *Economics of the New Zealand Maori*, Wellington: R.E. Owen.

_____, 1959b, *Social Change in Tikopia: A Re-study of a Polynesian Community after a Generation*, London: Allen and Unwin.

Fiscal Strategy Report, 2006, *Vanuatu Public Expenditure and Financial Accountability*, Rotterdam: ECORYS, Netherlands, for European Commission Delegation, Vanuatu.

Fisk, E.K., 1962, 'Planning in a Primitive Economy: Special Problems of Papua New Guinea', *Economic Record*, 38 (84), pp 462-78.

_____, 1964, 'Planning in a Primitive Economy, from Pure Subsistence to the Production of Market Surplus', *Economic Record*, 40 (90), pp 156-74.

_____, 1970, *The Political Economy of Independent Fiji*, Wellington and Auckland: A.H. & A.W. Reed.

_____, 1974, 'Rural Development', *New Guinea, and Australia, the Pacific and Southeast Asia*,

9 (1), pp 51-60.

____, 1978, *The Island of Niue: Development or Dependence for a Very Small Nation*, Development Studies Centre Occasional Paper No. 9, Canberra: ANU.

____, 1981, 'Economic, Social and Political Trends in the South Pacific in the 1980s', in *Papers of the Fifteenth Foreign Policy School*, Dunedin: University of Otago.

Fisk, E.K. and R.T. Shand, 1970, 'The Early Stages of Development in a Primitive Economy: the Evolution from Subsistence to Trade and Specialization', Chapter 9, in C.R. Wharton Jr (ed.), *Subsistence Agriculture and Economic Development*, Chicago: Aldine, pp 257-74.

Fisk, E.K. and D. Honeybone, 1972, 'Belshaw's "Emergent Fijian Enterprise" after Ten Years', in T. Scarlett Epstein and David H. Penny, *Opportunity and Response: Case Studies in Economic Development*, London: C. Hurst & Co., pp 173-92.

Fison, L., 1881, 'Land Tenure in Fiji', *Journal of the Royal Anthropological Institute*, 10, pp 332-52.

Foley, Roger, 19 September 2006, 'Landed in paradise', *Dominion Post*, E4.

Fortune, K.R., 2000, 'Nagriamel', in B.V. Lal and Kate Fortune (eds), *The Pacific Islands Encyclopaedia*, Honolulu: University of Hawaii Press.

Fraenkel, Jon, 2004, *The Manipulation of Custom*, Wellington: Victoria University Press.

France, P., 1968, 'The Founding of an Orthodoxy: Sir Arthur Gordon and the Doctrine of the Fijian Way of Life', *Journal of the Polynesian Society*, 77 (1), pp 6-32.

____, 1969, *The Charter of the Land*, Melbourne: Oxford University Press.

Frank, Andre Gunder, 1969, *The Sociology of Development and the Underdevelopment of Sociology*, Stockholm: Zenit.

Franklin, Harvey, 1969, *The European Peasantry: The Final Phase*, London: Methuen.

____, 1978, *Trade Growth and Anxiety: New Zealand. Beyond the Welfare State*, Wellington: Methuen.

Franklin, H. and D. Winchester, 1992, *A Casual History of the Teaching and Research of Victoria Geography from the Fifties to the Nineties*, Wellington: Victoria University of Wellington, Department of Geography.

Frazer, Roger, M., 1964, 'The Fijian Village and the Independent Farmer', in H.C. Brookfield (ed.), *The Pacific in Transition*, London: Edward Arnold.

____, 1969, *An Analysis of Interprovincial Migration of Fijians using a Technique of Age-Cohort Analysis*, MS.

Freeman, Derek, 1964, 'Some Observations on Kinship and Political Authority in Samoa', *American Anthropologist*, 66 (3, I), pp 553-68.

Furnivall, J.S., 1939, *Netherlands India: A Study of Plural Economy*, Cambridge: Cambridge University Press.

Geddes, W.R., 1959, 'Fijian Social Structure in a Period of Transition', in J.D. Freeman and W.R. Geddes (eds), *Anthropology in the South Seas*, New Plymouth: Avery, pp 201-20.

Geddes, W.H. et al., 1982, *Islands on the Line – Team Report, Atoll Economy: Social Change in Kiribati and Tuvalu*, Development Studies Centre Monograph No. 1, Canberra: ANU.

Geddes, W.H., 1983, *Tabiteuea North Atoll Economy: Social Change in Kiribati and Tuvalu*, Development Studies Centre Monograph No. 2, Canberra: ANU.

Geertz, Clifford, 1963, *Agricultural Involution in Indonesia*, Berkeley and Los Angeles: University of California Press.

____, 1965, *The Social History of an Indonesian Town*, Cambridge, Mass.

Gilson, R.P., 1952, *Administration of the Cook Islands*, MSc (Econ) thesis, London: University of London.

____, 1963, 'Samoan Descent Groups: A Structural Outline', *The Journal of the Polynesian Society*, 72 (4), pp 372-7.

Gordon, G.D.I., 1974, *Aspects of Maukean Population Migration*, MA thesis, Palmerston North: Massey University.

Gourou, P., 1948, 'Notes on China's Unused Uplands', *Pacific Affairs*, 21 (3), pp 227-38.

Government of Kiribati, 1983, *National Development Plan 1983-1986*, Tarawa.

____, 2005, *Census of the Republic of Kiribati*, Tarawa.

Government of Tuvalu, 1980, *A Report on the Results of the Census of the Population of*

Tuvalu 1979, Funafuti.

Grattan, C. Hartley, 1963, *The Southwest Pacific to 1900*, Michigan: Ann Arbor.

Griffin, K.B., 1970, 'Foreign Capital, Domestic Savings, and Economic Development', *Oxford Bulletin of Economics and Statistics*, 32, pp 99-112.

____, 1976, 'On the Emigration of the Peasantry', *World Development*, 4 (5), pp 353-61.

Griffin, K.B. and J. Enos, 1970, 'Foreign Assistance: Objectives and Consequences', *Economic Development and Cultural Change*, 32 (2), pp 99-112.

Grimble, Arthur, 1972, *Migrations, Myths and Magic from the Gilbert Islands*, arranged by Rosemary Grimble, London: Routledge and Kegan Paul.

Groves, M., 1963, 'The Nature of Fijian Society', *Journal of the Polynesian Society*, 72 (3), pp 272-91.

Gunson, W.N., 1960, *Evangelical Missionaries in the South Seas, 1797-1860*, PhD thesis, Canberra: ANU.

Haas, A., 1970, 'Independence Movements in the South Pacific', *Pacific Viewpoint*, 11 (1), pp 97-119.

Halliday, F., 1989, *Cold War, Third World*, London: Abacus.

Hardaker, J.B., E.M. Fleming and G.T. Harris, 1984, 'Smallholder Modes of Agricultural Production in the South Pacific: Prospects for Development', *Pacific Viewpoint*, 25 (2), pp 196-211 and 223-26.

Harré, John and Frances McGrath, 1970, 'An Interim Report on Raiwai Village', cyclostyled, Suva: University of South Pacific.

Harris, J.R. and Todaro, M.P., 1970, 'Migration, Unemployment and Development: A Two-Sector Analysis', *American Economic Review*, LX, pp 126-42.

Hart, K., 1974, 'A Model of Development to Avoid', *Yagl-Ambu, Papua and New Guinea Journal of the Social Sciences and Humanities*, 1 (1), pp. 8-15.

Harwood, L.J., 1950, 'Observations on Indigenous Systems of Agriculture', *Agricultural Journal*, 21, 1-2, Suva.

Hayes, G.R., 1982, *Migration, Population Change and Socioeconomic Development of the Cook Islands 1966-76*, PhD thesis, University of British Columbia.

____, 1983, *Population of the Cook Islands*, ESCAP/South Pacific Commission Country Monograph Series No. 7.3, New York and Noumea.

____, 1984, *International Migration in the Pacific Islands: A Brief History and a Review of Recent Patterns*, Working Paper presented to Conference on International Migration in the ESCAP Region, Manila, 6-12 November.

Hocart, A.M., 1952, *The Northern States of Fiji*, Occasional Publication No. 11, London: Royal Anthropological Institute of Great Britain and Ireland.

Hooper, Antony, 1961, 'The Migration of Cook Islanders to New Zealand', *The Journal of Polynesian Society*, 70 (1), pp 11-17.

Horne, J., 1887, *A Year in Fiji*, London.

Howlett, Diane, 1973, 'Terminal Development. From Tribalism to Peasantry', in H.C. Brookfield (ed.), *The Pacific in Transition*, London: Edward Arnold, pp 249-88.

Hughes, Tony, 1972, 'What is Development?', *Pacific Perspective*, Suva: South Pacific Social Sciences Association, pp 8-19.

____, 1973, 'All Done by Mirrors', *Pacific Perspective*, 1 (2), Suva, pp 18-25.

Jansen, A.A.J., n.d., *The Nutritional Status of Gilbertese Children*, MS, Tarawa.

Johnston, K.M., 1967, 'Village Agriculture in Aitutaki, Cook Islands', *Pacific Viewpoint*, Monograph No. 1, Victoria University of Wellington.

Kaplan, David, 1968, 'The Formal-Substantive Controversy in Economic Anthropology: Reflections on its Wider Implications', *Southwestern Journal of Anthropology*, 24, pp 228-51.

Kay, Paul, 1963, 'Urbanization in the Tahitian Household', in Alexander Spoehr, *Pacific Port Towns and Cities*, Honolulu: Bishop Museum Press, pp 63-73.

Keesing, Felix, 1942, *The South Seas in the Modern World*, London.

Keesing, Felix and Marie H. Keesing, 1956, *Elite Communication in Samoa: A Study of Leadership*, Stanford: Stanford University Press.

Keesing, Roger M., 1967, 'Christians and Pagans in Kwaio, Malaita', *The Journal of the Polynesian Society*, 76 (1), March, pp 82-100.

Keith-Reid, R., 2001, 'Fiji's Worst Political Dilemma. How to Solve the Expiring Land Lease Issue', *Pacific Magazine*, Honolulu.

____, 2005, 'Fiji seeks rescue of its neglected "vanua" ', *Pacific Islands Report*, Pacific Islands Development Program, East-West Center, University of Hawaii.

Kelly, C., 1985, *Aid, Development and a MIRAB Economy: New Zealand and the Cook Islands*, 1901-1984, MA thesis, University of Auckland.

Kenyatta, Jomo, 1938, *Facing Mt Kenya: The Traditional Life of the Kikuyu*, London: Heinemann.

Kiki, Albert Maori, 1968, *Kiki: Ten Thousand Years in a Lifetime. A New Guinea Autobiography*, Melbourne: Cheshire.

Kindon, S., 1999, 'Contesting Development', in R. Le Heron, L. Murphy, P. Forer and M. Goldstone (eds), *Explorations in Human Geography: Encountering Place*, Auckland: Oxford University Press, pp 173-202.

Knapman, Bruce, 1987, *Fiji's Economic History, 1874-1939: Studies of Capitalist Colonial Development*, Canberra: ANU, Centre for Development Studies.

Kolff, J., 1965a, *The National Income of the Cook Islands*, MA thesis, Victoria University of Wellington.

____, 1965b, 'The Economic Implications of Self-Government for the Cook Islands', *Journal of the Polynesian Society*, 74 (1), pp 114-24.

Kunkel, John M., 1961, 'Economic Autonomy and Social Change in Mexican Villages', *Economic Development and Cultural Change*, 10, 1, pp 51-63.

Lal, B.V. and K.R. Fortune (eds), 2000, *The Pacific Islands Encyclopaedia*, Honolulu: University of Hawaii Press.

Lam, N.V., 1982, 'A Short Note on the Nature and Extent of Subsistence Surplus in Papua New Guinea', unpublished paper.

Lasaqa, I.Q., 1968, *Melanesians' Choice: a Geographical Study of Tasimboko participation in the cash economy, Guadalcanal, British Solomon Islands*, PhD thesis, Canberra: ANU.

____, 1969, 'Honiara Market and the Suppliers from Tasimboko West', in H.C. Brookfield, *Pacific Market Places*, Canberra: ANU, pp 48-96.

____, 1973, 'Geography and Geographers in the Changing Pacific: An Islander's View', Chapter 12, in H.C. Brookfield (ed.), *The Pacific in Transition*, pp 299-311.

____, 1984, *The Fijian People Before and After Independence*, Canberra and New York: ANU Press.

Latukefu, S., 1967, *Church and State in Tonga: The Influence of the Wesleyan Methodist Missionaries on the Political Development of Tonga, 1826-1875*, PhD thesis, Canberra: ANU.

Lawrence, Peter, 1964, *Road Belong Cargo: A Study of the Cargo Movement in the Southern Madang District, New Guinea*, Manchester: Manchester University Press.

Lawrence, Roger, 1983, *Tamana. Atoll Economy: Social Change in Kiribati and Tuvalu*, Development Studies Centre Monograph No. 4, Canberra: ANU.

____, 1985, 'Views from the Centre and Periphery: Development Projects in Tamana, Southern Kiribati', *Pacific Viewpoint*, 26 (3), pp 547-62.

Lea, D.A.M., 1964, *Abelam Land and Sustenance*, Unpublished PhD thesis, Canberra: ANU.

Legge, J.D., 1958, *Britain in Fiji, 1858-80*, London.

Leslie, Davie and Inoke Ratukalou, 2002a, *Review of Rural Land Use in Fiji. Opportunities for the New Millennium*, Suva: Ministry of Agriculture, Fisheries and Forestry.

____, 2002b, *A Rural Land-use Policy for Fiji*, Suva: Ministry of Agriculture, Fisheries and Forestry.

Lewis, W.A., 1954, 'Economic Development with Unlimited Supplies of Labour', *The Manchester School of Economic and Social Studies*, 22 (2), May, pp 139-91.

____, 1955, *The Theory of Economic Growth*, London: George Allen and Unwin.

Lewthwaite, Gordon R., 1964, 'Man and Land in Early Tahiti: Polynesian Agriculture through European Eyes', *Pacific Viewpoint*, 5 (1), pp 11-34.

Lewthwaite, G.R. et al, 1973, ' "From Polynesia to California": Samoan Migration and its Sequel', *The Journal of Pacific History*, 8, pp 133-57

Lini, Father Walter, 1980, *Beyond Pandemonium: From the New Hebrides to Vanuatu*, Suva: University of South Pacific.

Lockwood, Brian, 1968, *A Comparative Study of Market Participation and Monetisation in Four Subsistence-Based Villages in Western Samoa*, PhD thesis, Canberra: ANU.

_____, 1971, *Samoan Village Economy*, Melbourne: Oxford University Press.

Long, Richard, 12 December 2006, 'Suffer the Fijian workers', *Dominion Post*, Wellington.

_____, 26 June 2007, 'Sanctions a side issue in Fiji', *Dominion Post*, Wellington.

Loomis, T., 1984a, 'The Cook Islands Community in New Zealand and its Influence on Cook Islands Development', unpublished research proposal, Auckland.

_____, 1984b, *The Counterfeit Savage: A Study of Cook Islands Society*, PhD thesis in Anthropology, University of Adelaide.

Lopreato, J., 1967, *Peasants No More*, San Francisco: Chandler.

Mara, Ratu K.K.T., 1997, *The Pacific Way: A Memoir*, Honolulu: Center for Pacific Studies, University of Hawaii.

Marcus, G., 1981, 'Power on the Extreme Periphery: The Perspective of Tongan Elites in the Modern World Systems', *Pacific Viewpoint*, 22 (1), pp 48-64.

Marsters, Evelyn, Nick Lewis and Wardlow Friesen, 2006, 'Pacific Flows: The Fluidity of Remittances in the Cook Islands', *Asian Pacific Viewpoint*, 41 (1), pp 31-44.

Maude, H.E., 1963, 'The Evolution of the Gilbertese Boti: An Ethnohistorical Interpretation', Wellington: Polynesian Society *Memoir*, No. 35.

May, Ron, 2004, *State and Society in Papua New Guinea: The First Twenty-five Years*, Adelaide: Crawford House Publishing.

McArthur, Norma and J.F. Yaxley, 1968, *Condominium of the New Hebrides: A Report on the First Census of the Population, 1967*.

McCreary, J.R., 1969, 'The Process of Polynesian Re-Settlement in Auckland', Seminar on Urbanization and Re-settlement in the South Pacific, Wellington: Victoria University of Wellington.

McElroy, Jerome, L., 2006, 'Small Island Tourist Economies Across the Life Cycle', *Asia Pacific Viewpoint*, 41 (1), pp 61-77.

McGee, Terry, 1967, *The Southeast Asian City*, London: G. Bell and Sons.

McKenzie, J., 1983, *Vulnerability or Viability? The Problem of Economic Development in Western Samoa 1962-82*, Research Essay for BA Hons in Geography, Wellington: Victoria University of Wellington.

McTaggart, W.D., 1963, *Noumea: A Study in Social Geography*, PhD thesis, Canberra: ANU.

Mead, Margaret, 1928, 'The Role of the Individual in Samoan Culture', *Journal of the Royal Anthropological Institute*, 58, pp 481-96.

Mercer, J.H. and Peter Scott, 1958, 'Changing Village Agriculture in Western Samoa', *Geographic Journal*, CXXIV (3), pp 347-60.

Mitchell, D.D., 1976, *Land and Agriculture in Nagovisi, Papua New Guinea*, Monograph 3, Boroko: IASER.

Mitchell, J.C., 1966, 'Theoretical Orientations in African Urban Studies', in M Banton (ed.), *The Social Anthropology of Complex Societies*, ASA Monographs 4, London: Tavistock.

Mohammed, Kahlil, 1962, *The Sugar Industry in Fiji*, unpublished MA thesis, Christchurch: University of Canterbury.

Montgomery, Charles, 2006, *The Shark God. Encounters with Myth and Magic in the South Pacific*, London: Fourth Estate.

Moore, Clive, 2004, *Happy Isles in Crisis: The Historical Causes for a Failing State in Solomon Islands, 1998-2004*, Canberra: Asian Pacific Press, Australian National University.

Morrell, W.P., 1960, *Britain in The Pacific Islands*, London: Clarendon.

Munro, Doug, 2006, 'Disentangling Samoan History: The Contributions of Gilson and Davidson', Chapter 18, in Doug Munro and Brij V. Lal (eds), *Texts and Contexts: Foundations of Pacific Historiography*, Honolulu: University of Hawaii Press.

Munro, Mike, 29 August 1990, 'Pomp and problems for Vanuatu', *The Dominion*, Wellington.

Myint, H., 1964, *The Economics of the Developing Countries*, London: Hutchinson.

Myrdal, Gunner, 1957, *Economic Theory and Underdeveloped Regions*, London: Duckworth.

____, 1968, *Asian Drama: An Inquiry into the Poverty of Nations*, Harmondsworth: Penguin.

Naidu, Vijay, 2007, 'Coups in Fiji. Seesawing Democratic Multiracialism and Ethno-nationalist Extremism', *Devforum*, Wellington: Council for International Development, pp 24-33.

Naipaul, V.S., 1979, *A Bend in the River*, New York: Alfred A. Knopf.

Nash, Manning, 1966, *Primitive and Peasant Economic Systems*, San Francisco: Chandler.

Nayacakalou, R., 1955a, 'The Fijian System of Kinship and Marriage', *Journal of the Polynesian Society*, 64 (1), pp 49-59.

____, 1955b, *Tradition, Choice and Change in the Fijian Economy*, Auckland: MA thesis, University of Auckland.

____, 1957, 'The Fijian System of Kinship and Marriage', *Journal of the Polynesian Society*, 66 (1), pp 49-59.

____, 1959, *Village Life in Fiji*, Wellington: School Publications Branch, Department of Education.

____, 1963, 'The Urban Fijians of Suva', in Alexander Spoehr, *Pacific Port Towns and Cities*, Honolulu: Bishop Museum Press, pp 33-41.

Neemia, Ibintabo and Randy Thaman, 1993, 'The Environment and Sustainable Development', Chapter 27, in Howard Van Trease (ed.), *Atoll Politics*, Macmillan Brown Centre for Pacific Studies, University of Canterbury, and Institute of Pacific Studies, University of the South Pacific, Suva.

NZAID, 2006, *Annual Review 2006/07*, Wellington: NZAID.

____, 2008, *The Aid Budget*, 1 February 2008, Wellington: NZAID.

Newlyn, W.T., 1977, *The Financing of Economic Development*, London.

O'Collins, Maev, 2005, 'Development Has Many Faces: Reflections on Continuity and Change in Papua New Guinea', in Claudia Gross et al (eds), *A Polymath Anthropologist. Essays in Honour of Ann Chowning*, Research in Anthropology & Linguistics, Monograph No. 6, Department of Anthropology, University of Auckland, pp 105-12.

Ogan, E., 1972, 'Business and Cargo: Socio-economic Change Among the Nasioi of Bougainville', *New Guinea Research Bulletin*, 44, Canberra: ANU.

Oliver, D., 1955, *A Solomon Island Society*, Cambridge, Mass.: Harvard University Press.

Overseas Development Group, 1973, *A Report on Development Strategies for Papua New Guinea*, for the World Bank and UNDP, University of East Anglia and Port Moresby (Faber Report).

Overton, John D., 1987, 'Roads, Rice and Cane. Regional Planning and Rural Development in Western Vanua Levu, Fiji', *Pacific Viewpoint*, 28 (1), pp 40-54.

Oxfam Briefing Paper, September 2005, 'The Fijian Sugar Industry', Online, 60 pp.

Paijmans, K., 1970, 'An Analysis of Four Tropical Rain Forest Sites in New Guinea', *Journal of Ecology*, 58.

Parsons, Talcott and Edward Shils (eds), 1954, *Towards a General Theory of Action*, Cambridge, Mass.: Harvard University Press.

Patterson, Mary, 2002, 'Leading Lights in the "Mother of Darkness": Perspectives on Leadership and Value in North Ambrym, Vanuatu', *Oceania*, December, Sydney.

Perrings, Charles, 1979, *Black Mineworkers in Central Africa: Industrial Strategies and the Evolution of an African Proletariat in the Copperbelt, 1911-41*, London: Heinemann.

PIMS, 1990, *Kandrian Gloucester Integrated Development Project*, Three volumes, Primary Industry Management Services, Sydney, in association with Tropical Rural Development Group (ANU) and CARE Australia, Canberra.

Pirie, Peter, 1976, 'The Demographic Effects of Local Socio-Economic Change on Small Populations: A Samoan Example', in A. Leszek, A. Kosinski and John W. Webb, *Population of Microscale*, Christchurch: New Zealand Geographical Society and Population Commission, IGU, pp 79-97.

Pirie, Peter and Ward Barrett, 1962, 'Western Samoa: Population, Production and Wealth', *Pacific Viewpoint*, 3 (1), pp 63-96.

Pitt, David, 1970, *Tradition and Economic Progress in Samoa*, Oxford: Clarendon.

Polanyi, Karl et al, 1957, *The Great Transformation*, Boston: Beacon Press.

Potter, Jack M., 1968, *Capitalism and the Chinese Peasant*, Berkeley and Los Angeles: University of California.

Powles, Michael (ed.), 2006, *Pacific Futures*, Research School of Pacific and Asian Studies, Canberra: ANU.

Quain, Buell, 1948, *Fijian Village: An Anthropologist's Account of Fijian Institutions, Ethics, and Personalities*, Chicago: University of Chicago Press.

Rahnema, Majid, 1992, 'Poverty', in W. Sachs (ed.), *The Development Dictionary: A Guide to Knowledge as Power*, London: Zed Books, pp 158-76.

Ranis, G. and J.C.H. Fei, 1961, 'A Theory of Economic Development', *American Economic Review*, 51, pp 533-65

Rappaport, R.A., 1967, *Pigs for the Ancestors. Ritual in the Ecology of a New Guinea People*, New Haven and London: Yale University Press.

Reddy, Mahendra, 2003, 'Farm Productivity, Efficiency and Profitability in Fiji's Sugar Industry', *Fijian Studies*, 1 (2), pp 225-40.

Republic of Kiribati, 1980, *Report on the 1978 Census of Population and Housing*, Tarawa.

Republic of Kiribati, n.d., *National Development Strategies, 2004-2007*, Tarawa.

Riddell, Robert, 1968, *A Capital Centre at Tarawa*, Report to the Resident Commissioner, mimeo., Tarawa.

Rist, G., 1997, *The History of Development: From Western Origins to Global Faith*, London: Zed Books.

Robie, David, 1988, 'The Ifira Challenge', *New Zealand Listener*, June 25, Wellington.

____, 2007, 'Handle with Care: The Pacific Forecast for the Year is Not Promising', *New Zealand Listener*, 13 January, Wellington.

Rose, Jeremy and David Gurr, 2002, 'Vanuatu', in T. Richards, J. Rose, Margot Schwass, *New Zealand Abroad. The Story of VSA in Africa, Asia and the Pacific*, Auckland: Bridget Williams Books.

Roth, G.K., 1953, *The Fijian Way of Life*, Oxford: Oxford University Press.

Rutherford, Noel, 1966, *Shirley Baker and the Kingdom of Tonga*, PhD thesis, Canberra: ANU.

Rutz, Henry J., 1978, 'Ceremonial Exchange and Economic Development in Fiji', *Economic Development and Cultural Change*, 26, pp 777-805.

Sahlins, M.D., 1962, *Moala: Culture and Nature on a Fijian Island*, Ann Arbor: University of Michigan Press.

____, 1962-63, 'Poor Man, Rich Man, Big-Man, Chief: Political Types in Melanesia and Polynesia', *Comparative Studies in Society and History*, 5, pp 285-303.

Salisbury, Richard F., 1970, *Vunamami: Economic Transformation in a Traditional Society*, Melbourne: Melbourne University Press.

Salter, M., 1970, 'The Economy of the South Pacific', *Pacific Viewpoint*, 11 (1), pp 1-26.

Sauer, Carl, 1952, *Agricultural Origins and Disposals*, New York: American Geographical Society.

Scarr, Deryck, 1967, *Fragments of Empire*, Canberra: ANU Press.

____, 1980, *Ratu Sir Lala Sukuna: Soldier, Statesman, Man of Two Worlds*, London: Macmillan Education Limited.

Schumacher, E.F., 1973, *Small is Beautiful. A Study of Economics as if People Mattered*, London: Blond and Briggs.

Scott, James C., 1998, *Seeing Like a State: How Certain Schemes to Improve the Human Condition Have Failed*, New Haven and London: Yale University Press.

Scott, John, 1994, *Poverty and Wealth: Citizenship, Deprivation and Privilege*, London: Longmans.

Seers, D., 1979, 'The Meaning of Development', in D. Lehmann (ed.), *Development Theory: Four Critical Studies*, London: Frank Cass.

Sen, A., 1966, 'Peasants and Dualism With and Without Surplus Labour', *Journal of Political Economy*, 74, pp 425-50.

____, 1981, *Poverty and Famines: an Essay on Entitlement*, Oxford: Oxford University Press.

____, 1983, 'Development: Which Way Now?', *Economic Journal*, 93, pp 745-62.

Sewell, Betsy, 1983, *Butaritari. Atoll Economy: Social Change in Kiribati and Tuvalu*, Development Studies Centre Monograph No. 3, Canberra: ANU.

Shankman, Paul, 1976, *Migration and Underdevelopment: The Case of Western Samoa*, Boulder, Colorado: Westview Press.

Shineberg, D., 1967, *They Came for Sandalwood: A Study of the Sandalwood Trade in the South-west Pacific, 1830-1865*, Melbourne: Melbourne University Press.

Skinner, T.M., 1968, *Report on Localisation of the Civil Service*, MS, Tarawa.

Sodhi, Gaurav, 2006, 'Island state gathers the aid', *Dominion Post*, Wellington, 5 April 2006.

Sofer, Michael, 1987, 'Progress through Transformation – a Fijian Village', *Pacific Viewpoint*, 28, 1, May, pp 1-19.

----, 2007, 'Yaqona and the Fijian Periphery Revisited', *Asia Pacific Viewpoint*, 48, 2, August, pp 235-49.

South Pacific Commission, 1984, *South Pacific Economies 1981: Statistical Summary*, Noumea.

Sparhawk, W.N., 1965, *Notes of Forests and Trees of the Central and Southeast Pacific Area*, Washington: US Department of Agriculture.

Spate, O.H.K., 1959, *The Fijian People: Economic Problems and Prospects*, Legislative Council Paper No. 13, Suva: Government of Fiji (Spate Report).

___, 1961, 'Under Two Laws: the Fijian Dilemma', *Meanjin*, 19 (2), University of Melbourne, pp 166-81.

Stace, V.D., 1954a, *Economic Survey of Western Samoa*, South Pacific Commission, Noumea.

____, 1954b, 'The Pacific Islands in Modern Commerce', South Pacific Commission Technical Paper, No. 54, Noumea.

Stanmore, Lord (Sir Arthur Gordon), 1897, *Fiji: Records of Private and Public Life 1875-80*, 4 volumes, Edinburgh.

Stark, O., *Economic-Demographic Interactions in Agricultural Development: The Case of Rural to Urban Migration*, David Horowitz Institute for the Research of Developing Countries, Research Report No. 2/78, Tel Aviv.

Steward, Julian, 1956, *Theory of Culture Change*, Illinois: University of Illinois Press.

____ (ed.), 1959, *Plantation Systems of the New World*, Washington: Panamerican Union.

____ (ed.), 1967, *Contemporary Change in Traditional Societies, Vol. III, Mexican and Peruvian Communities*, Urbana, Illinois: University of Illinois Press.

Stone, David, 1967, 'Self-government in the Cook Islands', *Journal of Pacific History*, 1, pp 168-78.

Strickland, Mana, 1968, *Colonialism and Self-Government Exemplified by Events in the Cook Islands*, unpublished paper presented to 40th Congress of ANZAAS, Christchurch.

Sumbak, J.H., 1980, 'Plantation Crops', in R. Gerard Ward and A. Proctor, *South Pacific Agriculture: Choices and Constraints*, Canberra: Asian Development Bank and ANU Press.

Thompson, E., 1957, 'The Plantation Cycle and Problems of Typology', *Caribbean Studies*, Kingston, Jamaica: Institute of Social and Tropical Research.

Tisdell, C. and Fairbairn, T.I.J., 1984, 'Subsistence Economies and Unsustainable Development and Trade: Some Simple Theory', *Journal of Development Studies*, 20 (2), pp 227-41.

Todaro, Michael, 1977, *Economic Development in the Third World*, London: Longman.

Truman, Harry S., 20 January 1949, *Inaugural Address*, Washington DC: Joint Congress Committee of the USA.

Turner, H.A., 1967, 'Report on the Wages, Incomes and Prices Policy', Legislative Council Paper No. 26, Suva (Turner Report).

Twyford, I.T. and A.C.S. Wright, 1965, *The Soil Resources of Fiji*, Suva: Government Printer.

Valentine, C.A., 1963, 'Social Status, Political Power and Native Responses to European Influence in Oceania', *Anthropolitical Forum*, 1 (1), pp 3-55.

Van Wijnbergen, S., 1984, 'The Dutch Disease: A Disease After All?', *Economic Journal*, 94, pp 41-55.

Walsh, A.C., 1964, *Nuku'alofa, Tonga: a Preliminary Study of Urbanization and In-Migration*, MA thesis in Geography, Wellington: Victoria University of Wellington.

____, 1967, 'Tonga's Development Plan', *Pacific Viewpoint*, 8 (1), pp 96-99.

____, 1970, 'Population Changes in Tonga: An Historical Overview and Modern Commentary', *Pacific Viewpoint*, 11 (1), pp 27-46.

____, 1982, *Migration, Urbanization and Development in South Pacific Countries*, ESCAP Comparative Study on Migration, Urbanization and Development in the Pacific Region, Country Report VI, New York.

____, 2006, *Fiji: An Encyclopaedic Atlas*, Suva: University of the South Pacific.

Walter, M.A.H.B. (ed.), 1981, 'What Do We Do About Plantations?', Monograph 15, Boroko: IASER.

Ward, Marion (ed.), 1972, *Change and Development in Rural Melanesia*, papers delivered at the fifth Waigini Seminar, Canberra: Research School of Pacific Studies, ANU.

Ward, R. Gerard, 1961a, 'A Note on Population Movements in the Cook Islands', *The Journal of the Polynesian Society*, 70 (1), pp 1-10.

____, 1961b, 'Internal Migration in Fiji', *The Journal of the Polynesian Society*, 70 (3), pp 257-71.

____, 1965, *Land Use and Population in Fiji*, Overseas Research Publication No. 9, Department of Technical Co-operation, London: HMSO.

___, 1971, 'Internal Migration and Urbanisation in Papua New Guinea', in M.W. Ward (ed.), *Population Growth and Socio-economic Change*, Boroko and Canberra: New Guinea Research Bulletin 42, pp 81-107.

____, 1984, 'Production or Management – Where is the Problem?', *Pacific Viewpoint*, 25 (2), pp 212-17.

____, 1985, 'Land, Land Use and Land Availability', in H.C. Brookfield, F. Ellis and R.G. Ward, *Land, Cane and Coconuts*, Papers on the Rural Economy of Fiji, Canberra: Department of Human Geography, ANU.

____, 1986, 'Reflections on Pacific Island Agriculture in the Late 20th Century', *Journal of Pacific History*.

____, 1987, 'Native Fijian Villages: A Questionable Future?', in M. Taylor (ed.), *Fiji: Future Imperfect*, Sydney: Allen and Unwin, pp 33-45.

Ward, R.G. and A. Proctor (eds), 1980, *South Pacific Agriculture – Choices and Constraints: South Pacific Agricultural Survey, 1979*, Canberra: Asian Development Bank with ANU Press.

Watson, W., 1958, *Tribal Cohesion and the Money Economy*, Manchester.

Watters, R.F., 1958, 'Cultivation in Old Samoa', *Economic Geography*, 34 (3), pp 338-51.

____, 1960, 'Fiji: Blueprint for Development', *Pacific Viewpoint*, 1 (2), pp 246-48.

____, 1963, 'Sugar Production and Culture Change in Fiji: A Comparison Between Peasant and Plantation Agriculture', *Pacific Viewpoint*, 4 (1), pp 25-52.

____, 1968, 'Urbanisation and Social Change in Fiji', unpublished paper, Seminar on Urbanisation and Re-settlement, Victoria University of Wellington.

____, 1969a, *Koro: Economic Development and Social Change in Fiji*, Oxford: Clarendon Press.

____, 1969b, 'Tribesmen or Peasant? The Evolution of Rural Society in Fiji', in I.G. Bassett (ed.), *Pacific Peasantry*, Palmerston North: New Zealand Geographical Society, pp 7-21.

____, 1972, 'Reply to R.G. Crocombe's Review of *Koro*: Economic Development and Social Change in Fiji', *Journal of the Polynesian Society*, 81 (1), pp 90-108.

____, 1984, 'The Village Mode of Production in MIRAB Economies', *Pacific Viewpoint*, 25 (2), pp 218-23.

____, 1987, 'MIRAB Societies and Bureaucratic Elites', in A. Hooper, S. Britton, R. Crocombe, J. Huntsman and C. Macpherson (eds), *Class and Culture in the South Pacific*, Chapter 3, 32-55, Suva. Centre for Pacific Studies, University of Auckland and Institute of Pacific Studies.

____, 1994, *Poverty and Peasantry in Peru's Southern Andes, 1963-90*, London: Macmillan.

____, 1998, 'The Geographer as Radical Humanist: An Appreciation of Keith Buchanan', *Asia*

Pacific Viewpoint, 39 (1), pp 1-28.

Watters, R.F. and K. Banibati, 1984, *Abemama. Atoll Economy: Social Change in Kiribati and Tuvalu*, Development Studies Centre Monograph No. 5, Canberra: ANU.

Weightman, Barry, 1989, *Agriculture in Vanuatu. A Historical Review*, British Friends of Vanuatu, Cheom, Surrey.

Whitelaw, J.S., 1966, *People, Land and Government in Suva, Fiji*, PhD thesis, Canberra: ANU.

Whitmore, T.C., 1975, *Tropical Rain Forests of the Far East*, Oxford: Clarendon Press.

Willis, R., 1985, 'Natural Gas, Energy and Resource Development: New Zealand and Western Europe, A Comparison', *Pacific Viewpoint*, 26 (3), pp 584-94.

Wilson, Kent R., 1972, 'A Review of Village Industries: The Urban-Rural Choice in Entrepreneurial Development', in Marion Ward (ed.), *Change and Development in Rural Melanesia*, papers delivered at the fifth Waigini Seminar, Canberra: Research School of Pacific Studies, ANU, pp 520-9.

Wolf, Eric, 1955, 'Types of Latin American Peasantry: A Preliminary Discussion', *American Anthropologist*, 57, pp 457-71.

Wolpe, H. (ed.), 1982, *Articulation of Modes of Production*, London.

World Bank, 2006, *At Home and Away. Expanding Job Opportunities for Pacific Islanders through Labour Mobility*, June, online.

Worsley, Peter, 1957, *The Trumpet Shall Sound: A Study of 'Cargo' Cults in Melanesia*, London: McGibbon and Kee.

Wright, A.C.S., 1963, *Soils and Land Use of Western Samoa*, Soil Bureau Bulletin 22, Wellington: Government Printer.

Zelenitz, M.C. and Jill Grant, 1980, '*Kilenge Narogo*: Ceremonies, Resources and Prestige in a West New Britain Society', *Oceania*, 51 (2), pp 98-117.

Notes

Foreword

1 Stone, 1967
2 Watters, 1998, p. 2.
3 McKinnon in Watters, 1998, p. 10.
4 Cros Walsh in Watters, 1998, p. 11.
5 Gourou, September 1948, p. 237.
6 Franklin and Winchester, 1991.
7 Walsh in Watters, 1998, p. 11.

1   Introduction

1 Personal communication from M.J. Ormsby, Second Secretary, NZ High Commission, Apia, Samoa, 1 April 1977.
2 Ibid.
3 Bedford, 1999, p. 10, citing Chapman, 1995, pp 257-8. Emphasis in original.
4 Escobar, 1995, p. 23.
5 Truman, 20 January 1949.
6 See Escobar, 1995.
7 Todaro, 1977, p. 51.
8 Nayacakalou, 1959, p. 39.
9 Watters, 1960.
10 Weightman, 1989, pp 63-63.

2   The Economic Response of South Pacific Societies

1 The terms are used to refer to abstract models of 'tribalism' and 'peasantry', a comparison of which points up some of the processes of change. Elsewhere, I have suggested such a model for Fiji (Watters, 1969a and 1969b). The empirical data against which the model can be tested are provided in Watters (1969a), cf. the models used in the analyses of change of Geertz (1963) and Finney (1965). It might, perhaps, be more appropriate to refer to Melanesian societies such as the Solomons as 'half tribal'.
2 Apter, 1965.
3 'Modernisation' thus includes the evolution of urban-industrialism and its effects, the establishment and growth of towns, the growing urbanisation of island populations, massive population growth, altered age structures and large-scale societies, changing land use systems, changing regional economic disparities and investment patterns, increased market participation, changes in occupational structure, increased specialisation of function and the development of new occupations and new roles, changing patterns of demand with new expectations and aspirations, and changing internal relationships in the economy.

Closely related to such economic trends are the set of processes underlying the weakening of traditional social relationships that lead to the emergence of new patterns of social relationships. These social changes involve the replacement of one social structure by another and involve both 'organisational' and 'structural' change (Firth, 1959b). Perhaps the most significant results of these changes in social organisation and increasing role differentiation are the evolution of a new incipient class structure, the rise of important new social units and the decline of the old ones, and the challenge of new elites.

Accompanying and underlying these structural and institutional changes in the economic and social fields are behavioural changes, involving changes in goals, the means to attain goals and the appearance of new incentives. Normative or ethical change provides the ideational and moral justification for the above sets of modernising processes.

4   Kaplan, 1968; Nash, 1966.

5   See, for example, Michael R. Allen, 1964; Walsh, 1970.

6   As early as 1883, planters claimed that at least £1,700,000 of Australian capital was invested in Fiji. Morrell, 1960, p. 393.

7   Although the impact of the West has been cataclysmic enough, especially in Melanesia, in much of Polynesia, it has been less traumatic than in parts of West Africa or Southeast Asia. Perhaps this is one reason why the more literate societies up to 1970 had not yet produced a great indigenous novelist like Chinua Achebe (*Things Fall Apart*) of Nigeria to portray the agony and ambivalence of a people caught up in the great process of social transformation. (However, after 1973 the work of the Samoan Albert Wendt describes the frustrations and pain of social change, of biculturalism, of identity, the shattered dreams of independence, of what has been lost and not attained.) I suspect that the theme of protest is more common in Melanesian writing for this reason. Although not a novel, *Kiki* (1968) is an interesting assertion of indigenous nationalism. See also Bogutu, 1968. A rare example of Polynesian protest is Mana Strickland (1968). Of course, Melanesia is also the area of cargo cults, nativistic movements and current nationalistic political movements such as the Mataungan Association of Rabaul, the Bougainville mining dispute, and the Nagriamel party in the New Hebrides (*Pacific Islands Monthly [PIM]*, July 1969) and others. After 1970, the Kanaka independence movement was important in New Caledonia and later independence movements built up in Tahiti and French Polynesia.

8   See the study by R.G. and M. Crocombe (1968) of the work of a Polynesian mission teacher. Studies which touch on missionisation include Gilson, 1952; Gunson, 1960; Latukefu, 1967; Rutherford, 1966; and *Journal de la Société des Océanistes*, 25, December 1969.

9   See Keesing, 1967, and Montgomery, 2006, on Malaita; and Michael R. Allen (1964 and 1968) on Vanuatu.

10 Gilson, 1952.

11 Gilson, 1952; Crocombe, 1964.

12 Wright, 1963.

13 Lockwood, personal communication.

14 Although many studies briefly describe plantations, few examine its role carefully as an agency of change. Chowning (1969) has also remarked on this point.

15 Geertz, 1963.

16 Fisk, 1962.

17 Some confirmation for this hypothesis can be found in the importance of unproductive entrepreneurs (compared to productive entrepreneurs) who do not increase the stock of capital or production but are picture-theatre operators (Johnston, 1967, pp 100-5), taxi-drivers, plumbers (Watters, 1969a, p. 207) or those engaged in tertiary occupations.

18 Michael R. Allen, 1964.

19 Op. cit., p. 12.

20 Finney, 1968; cf. Scarlett Epstein, 1968.

21 For example, Stace, 1954a.

22 Farrell and Ward, 1962, pp 232-6.

23 It is suggested that the concepts comprising the above crude models of 'Polynesian' and 'West Melanesian' social structures could be given an empirical interpretation (i.e. made substantive) by application, for example, to Samoa and the Solomon Islands. The model then acquires some explanatory power when dealing with economic problems insofar as these can be studied by means of a set of formal propositions about the logic of choice. Thus, for example, study of the social organisation (the 'structure' in action) of Samoa or the Solomons must include as one dimension the choices that individual actors make in allocating scarce means among alternative ends. Important choices or decisions that lead to 'economic' activities include the type and number of crops grown and goods consumed;

whether a harvest is partly sold or distributed in a gift exchange; decisions affecting saving, investment and innovation; and 'normative' or deviant behaviour concerned with these activities.

For a guide to the voluminous literature on Samoan social structure, including the important earlier work of Turner, Stair, Krämer, Mead and Keesing, see Freeman, 1964. Many major references to the west Melanesian type of social structure are given in Sahlins, 1962-63. For an interesting theoretical discussion on the issue applicable to this region, see Belshaw, 1964b.

24   Cf. Mercer and Scott, 1958; or Rutherford, 1966, p. 47, for Tonga.
25   See Berg, 1961; and Myint, 1964, Chapter 4. Income elasticities for various classes of purchased goods calculated from Lockwood's data in Western Samoa suggest that, except for a small number of luxury expenditures such as bus fares, consumption of purchased goods rapidly approaches a low saturation level: "There appears to be a high marginal propensity to service the high income villages, and these savings are used in the main, to finance emigrants to New Zealand and non-traditional housing" (Lockwood, personal communication).
26   Pitt, 1970.
27   Gilson, 1963.
28   Boyd, 1968, pp 159-60.
29   Lockwood, 1968, p. 167.
30   Op. cit., p. 53.
31   Finney, 1968, p. 407.
32   Watters, 1969a, Chapter 6.
33   J.C. Mitchell, 1966, pp 43-51.
34   Nayacakalou, 1963, p. 38.
35   Watson, 1958.
36   McArthur and Yaxley, 1968, p. 57.
37   Whitelaw, 1966, pp 207-12.
38   Kunkel, 1961.
39   See Bellam, 1964 and 1969, for the Solomons; Walsh, 1964, for Tonga; Fairbairn, 1961, for Western Samoa; Ward, 1961a, Hooper, 1961, and Douglas, 1965, for Cook Islanders' movement to New Zealand; Ward, 1961b, Belshaw, 1963, Nayacakalou, 1963, Roger Frazer, 1969, and Watters, 1969c, for Fiji; McArthur and Yaxley, 1968, for the New Hebrides.
40   Thus, although the Turner Report (1967) suggests that wage dualism has not yet developed in Fiji, the comparison is made between urban clerical salaries and sugar cane earnings, which are the highest rural incomes in the colony.
41   Barrington, 1968, p. 223; Pirie and Barrett, 1962.
42   Johnston, 1967.
43   Finney, 1967.
44   Cf. the comments of Fisk, 1964, on the utility of money.
45   Australia being excluded because of its immigration restrictions.
46   In 1959, I found one relatively 'traditional' Fijian village possessed only one imperfect radio. Another, more 'Westernised' village had eight radios and occasionally newspapers were brought back from town.
47   For example, see the interesting ideology of the millenarian cult of Daku, Fiji, in which the world was seen as divided into 'Continents' and 'Islands' (Spate, 1961).
48   Barrington, 1968; Beeby, 1968.
49   Islanders from the Cooks, Tokelau and Niue can enter New Zealand freely as New Zealand citizens, but Tongans are excluded. Walsh (1967) notes the growing numbers of a Western-type élite in Tonga and the increasing difficulty of providing employment for them. See also Haas, 1970.
50   Geertz, 1965, p. 13.
51   Thus, in west Aoba where fresh water is scarce, natives planted dense groves of coconut palms to remedy the deficiency; this gave the area an early advantage when modern trading

began (Michael R. Allen, 1964, p. 4).

52 For example, the Potlach timber agreement in Western Samoa which gives access to an American company to Savai'i, and the Hog Harbour land sales in the New Hebrides to Americans.

53 Bellam (1969, p. 85) calculates that about 70 percent of copra produced by Solomon Islanders delivered to Honiara is handled by Chinese middlemen.

54 Watters, 1969a, Chapter 6, cf. Erasmus, 1967.

55 Bellam, 1964 and 1969, pp 86-93.

3 Subsistence Affluence in the Pacific

1 Fisk, 1970.

2 Lockwood, 1971, p. 4.

3 Op. cit., citing La Perouse, pp 58-130, 117; and Keesing and Keesing, 1956, p. 17.

4 Watters, 1958, pp 350-1.

5 Lewthwaite, 1964, p. 23.

6 Op. cit., pp 11-34.

7 Lockwood, 1971, Chapter 7.

8 Fisk and Shand, 1970, p. 262.

9 Fisk, 1970, Table 10 and pp 39-40 citing the Fiji Census of 1966, Council Paper No. 9 of 1968, Suva.

10 Fisk, 1970, Table 11 and pp 40-1.

11 Op. cit., p. 42.

4 The Village Mode of Production and Agricultural Development in the South Pacific

1 Watters, 1969a.

2 Weightman, 1989, p. 60.

3 Op. cit., p. 63.

4 Cf. Bohannan, 1964, pp 167-71.

5 Ward, 1986, p. 220.

6 This ancient method of crop planting occurs because many crop plants have become seedless and asexual, depending on humans and their digging sticks for survival. See Sauer, 1952.

7 Watters and Banibati, 1984.

8 Regrettably, this problem was not dealt with by the new independent government and, compounded with other grievances, the situation exploded into the dangerous civil war of 1998-2003 (see Moore, 2004, and Fraenkel, 2004).

9 Ward, 1986, p. 220.

10 Op. cit., p. 221.

11 Watters and Banibati, 1984,

12 Ward, 1986, p. 221.

13 Lockwood, 1971, Chapter 7.

14 Sumbak, 1980, p. 238, in Ward and Proctor, 1980.

15 Ward, 1986, p. 222. Bellam, 1980, reviews the numerous difficulties of the Cook Island fruit trade to New Zealand.

16 Bertram and Watters, 1984, p. 160.

17 Ward, 1986, p. 223.

18 Brookfield, 1972; Ward, 1986, p. 224.

19 Crown Agents, 1982.

5 Fiji: The Development of Traditionalism

1 Gordon to Carnavon, 20 September 1875, Stanmore, 1897, vol. 1, pp 214-15. (Gordon was later given the title of Lord Stanmore.)

2   Legge, 1958, p. 168; Morrell, 1960, p. 374.
3   Stanmore, 1897, vol. 1, pp 197-9.
4   France, 1969, p. 174.
5   Account of discussions of Council of Chiefs, Wilkinson to Gordon, 8 January 1879, Stanmore, 1897, vol. 3, p. 499.
6   Morrell, 1960, p. 398.
7   Op. cit., p. 372.
8   Keesing (1942, pp 66-80) and Firth (1959b, Chapter 13) have proposed rather similar four-phased schemas of social change for different island societies experiencing Western penetration – firstly, initial impact and drastic testing of native institutions, followed by a stage of restabilisation in which elements of old and new are integrated in a "hyphenated native-trader-mission-official culture". Thirdly, a period of disintegration, restlessness and a search for a more satisfactory basis ensues before the final stage is reached of attaining new stability within the setting of modern civilisation. In this schema, the Fijian period of 1874-1900 would approximate to the second phase of reintegration, withdrawal and consolidation.
9   It is not clear whether Gordon envisaged a slow, assimilative evolution of the Fijians, as did J.B. Thurston. See Grattan, 1963, p. 479.
10   Scarr, 1980, Foreword, p. x
11   Op. cit., p. 19. On Sukuna, see also Bole, 1969.
12   Scarr, p. 23.
13   Op. cit., p. 47.
14   Op. cit., quoting Sukuna, 1980, p. 49.
15   Op. cit., pp 21, 47.

6   Nalotawa: A Late Colonial Village

1   Roth, 1953, pp 2-3, 52.
2   Geddes, 1959, pp 201-20. On social organisation, see also Nayacakalou, 1955a, pp 44-55 and 1957, pp 44-59; Sahlins, 1962; Roth, 1953; and Groves, 1963, pp 272-91.
3   Belshaw, personal communication to Spate, quoted in Spate Report, p. 10. Fison, in a classic account of social structure and land tenure, described the larger unit as a *mataqali* instead of a *yavusa*, with each *mataqali* comprising several *yavusa*. See Fison, 1881, pp 332-52.
4   Spate Report, p. 6.
5   Op. cit., p. 6.
6   This is typical of many villages in Fiji. About 0.2-0.3 acres is representative of hilly, rain forest areas in other parts of Melanesia. See Ward, 1965, p. 57, 199; Barrau, 1955; and Brookfield, 1962.
7   Twyford and Wright, 1965.
8   Harwood, 1950, p. 7.
9   Horne, 1887, p. 80.
10   A full analysis is given in Watters, 1960, pp 59-99.
11   The Chinese banana (*Musa paradisiaca*) is strictly speaking an exotic crop, but as a plantain (*Musa fehi*) was indigenous in Fiji, its adoption was more in the nature of the acceptance of a new variety rather than a new crop.
12   All monetary figures are estimates that can only be regarded as approximately correct. The total for each household was reached only after patient and protracted questioning of the head of the family. Incomes and expenditure were worked out separately and the total of each provided a check on the accuracy of the other figure.
13   Polanyi et al (1957), Dalton (1961), and others have stressed that Westerners commonly assume that in all societies production above subsistence level is motivated by the profit motive. But such production is only characteristic of market economies which exist in market societies. At least three other kinds of economies clearly exist – reciprocity economies, 'mobilisation exchange' and redistributive economies ('planned economies')

– and in these economies the motives for production and economic relations cannot be explained by classical Western economic theories which have evolved to explain market relations in a market economy. In a reciprocity economy, production beyond subsistence will be motivated by social, prestige and ceremonial ends, and economic activities will be affected by social institutions vastly different from those characteristic of a market society. With 'mobilisation exchange' which commonly occurs early in the contact situation before traditional structures weaken, traditional leaders capitalise on their position of authority and status to amass and redistribute wealth from new money-earning activities (e.g. Fiji in the 1890s, although examples are still not uncommon today), or social units such as descent groups utilise their corporate nature for investment, marketing or perhaps production (e.g. the Tolai of New Britain, studied by Scarlett Epstein, 1968). Of course, market, reciprocity and mobilisation exchange principles overlap, and economies in which they coexist are not uncommon, requiring new economic theories appropriate to such complex and distinctive structures. Nalotawa, along with other traditional Fijian communities, is transitional between a predominantly reciprocity economy and a market economy; the mobilisation exchange function is no longer significant. Thus, theories appropriate to explaining economic behaviour in market economies are only partially applicable at this stage of economic development.

14 Only two men in Nalotawa had bank accounts, with deposits of £11 and £8 respectively.

15 The requirement is that £100 be earned annually.

16 The men of Rara described the founding of their settlement as being entirely due to the settlement of 'exempted people' at Rara. Daku in the Rewa delta is also a good example of this form of settlement; see Spate, 1961, pp 166-81.

17 The Agriculture Department has been conducting experimental work into fertiliser response and pasture establishment in the Ba hills.

18 An excellent example of the effect of a new road linking an inland village to the market is provided by Naluwai in Naitasiri Province. When I visited, the new road had been open for only six months, but the change in the income and consumption levels of some people was quite pronounced. Whereas marketing cash crops had previously meant a journey of 15 miles downstream by bamboo raft to the roadhead, which would take a night in flood time or up to two days in dry weather, Suva could now be reached by bus in only an hour. Now nearly all men visited Suva each week and one man who marketed for six people spent two days each week in the city. The people claimed that their standard of living had increased and, as Suva shops were cheaper than those in nearby Vunidawa, they now bought more European foods. With lower transport costs, a truck from a large city firm now delivered goods to the village store each week.

19 Although in 1963 he reported that things "are still quiet here in the *koro*", Jone Lotawa had acquired a licence to utilise 180 acres of land near the Yaloku road to "start a cattle farm". The villagers were enthusiastic about the Roko Tui Ba's order to carry out the Forestry Department's tree-planting campaign, and some acres of Nalotawa land were being planted with seedlings supplied by the Department. The most successful of the new developments is likely to be Jone Lotawa's venture into cane-growing on 10 acres of land leased at Vokabuli, six miles away, and the acquisition by the *galala* of Rara of a small dairy herd to produce *ghee* for sale to nearby Indians (Personal communication, 12 January 1963).

7   Sorolevu: A Sugar-growing Village

1 Mohammed, 1962, p. 69, citing Legislative Council Debates, 1933, p. 161.

2 Spate Report, p. 18.

3 A discussion of Fijian and Indian cane growing in Ra Province is given in Frazer (1964) who also compares the yields of tenants and contractors.

4 Ratu K.K.T. Mara, 1997.

5 Since sugar cane is a relatively easy crop to grow in terms of the necessary field operations that should be performed, it was possible to check the efficiency of the grower by obtaining

data on the extent to which most of these operations were performed efficiently, or indeed performed at all.

6   Assistant Economic Development Officer (Western, 1959).
7   Spate Report, para. 17.
8   Ratu K.K.T. Mara, 1997.
9   The sole exception was the enterprising son of the *Tui*, who hoped eventually to purchase a tractor.
10   In 1959, this practice was still common in many Fijian villages in the cane zone.
11   These issues are discussed in Watters, 1969a, pp 164-74.

8   Fiji in Retrospect

1   Fisk, 1970, chapter 4.
2   Ward, 1986 and 1987.
3   Brookfield, 1987, p. 50.
4   Ibid.
5   Leslie and Ratukalou, 2002a, p. xiv.
6   Op. cit., p. 7.
7   Oxfam Briefing Paper, September 2005, p. 13.
8   Leslie and Ratukalou, 2002b, p. 3.
9   Op. cit., p. xvi.
10   Ibid.
11   Ibid.
12   Leslie and Ratukalou, 2002b.
13   Reddy, 2003, p. 227.
14   Oxfam Briefing Paper, September 2005, p. 10.
15   Reddy, 2003, pp 228-29.
16   Watters, 1963.
17   Oxfam Briefing Paper, September 2005, p. 10.
18   Reddy, 2003, Table 5, p. 232.
19   Op. cit., Table 7, pp 236-7.
20   Op. cit., Table 3, p. 231.
21   Op. cit., p. 231.
22   Op. cit., Table 6, p. 233.
23   Op. cit., Appendix 1, p. 240. Reddy compares the advantages and disadvantages of ALTA and NLTA for both tenants and landowners.
24   Keith-Reid, March 2001, p. 1.
25   Connew and Lal, 2007.
26   Reddy, 2003, p. 237; Oxfam Briefing Paper, September 2005. In 2003, the rejection by Japan of a shipment of Fiji sugar on grounds of poor quality was attributed by the FSC to burning cane. Academics, however, blamed the inability of the FSC to develop its milling capacity to mill the cane within 24 to 48 hours of its being burnt and harvested.
27   Reddy, 2003, p. 237.
28   Op. cit., Table 8, pp 237-38. The price/ton average paid to growers was F$51.14 with cost/acre of $38.00 ($25 farm production cost and $13 a ton harvesting and transportation costs), giving a net return of only $13.14 a tonne.
29   Carswell, 2003.
30   Oxfam Briefing Paper, September 2005, p. 10.
31   Op. cit., p. 14.
32   Bagasse is the remainder of the cane mass after the cane juice has been extracted in the crushing process. This fibrous, woody biomass, often burnt to provide steam to power machinery in cane mills, has a considerable potential when burnt to generate electricity.
33   Field, March 2004.
34   Field, 21 June 2006.
35   *Pacific Islands Monthly*, March 1961, p. 27.

36 The cane dispute and the Commission's findings are discussed in Watters, 1963, pp 46-51.

9   What is Economic Development? A Study of the Gilbert and Ellice Islands

1   The Ellice Islands became Tuvalu in 1978, and the Gilbert Islands became the Republic of Kiribati on independence in 1979.

2   Fisk, 1974, p. 52.

3   Ibid.

4   Ibid.

5   Op. cit., p. 53.

6   In Tarawa in 1972, the late Dr Joan Tully ran a conference on achieving increases in output through cultural change.

7   This criticism does not, of course, apply to all. A considerable number of District Officers admired the skills of local production and organisation. Under indirect rule, aspects of the *maneaba* (community meeting house) system and rule by the old men (*unimane*) were supported at least selectively or tacitly. But the loss of the magico-religious qualities of the *maneaba* struck a grievous blow at the traditional political-ceremonial system (Maude, 1963). All real power clearly lay with the European. And the main economic influences up to World War II were on-the-beach traders, small stores and trading companies. Government clearly favoured capitalistic enterprise, though after the war when the companies did not return it adopted a protective role, initiated the Colony Wholesale Society (later succeeded by the Development Authority or GEIDA) and strongly backed the cooperative movement. Very little was done to strengthen the subsistence economy.

8   Fisk, 1974, p. 53.

9   Hughes (1973) believes that the interplay of six main influences largely determine the nature of a plan in many South Pacific countries: 1. the preceding plan and collection of ongoing projects; 2. presumed attitudes of potential investors; 3. policies of major aid donors and lending institutions; 4. attitudes of planning staff; 5. character of political government (usually the plan is not highly politicised, reflecting a laissez-faire ideology); 6. the so-called elite or 'enclave clientele'.

10 Undoubtedly, a milestone in encouraging genuine indigenous economic planning in the South Pacific was R.G. Crocombe's trenchant criticism of the World Bank plan for Papua New Guinea as being ethnocentric, inappropriate, and developing a type of economy that would be substantially owned and controlled by Europeans and outsiders. Similar criticisms could be levelled at several other South Pacific development plans. See Crocombe and the ensuing debate (1968-69, 1969); and Hughes, 1972, and 1973, which are directly relevant to the Gilbert and Ellice Islands.

11 Hughes, 1973, p. 20.

12 Op. cit., p. 24.

13 Ibid.

14 It is interesting to read comments on the development plans and issues as indicated in reports of debates in the Legislative Council; for example, see *Atoll Pioneer*, No. 13, 30 November 1972 and No. 40, 7 June 1973.

15 Development Plan, para. 1.3.

16 Development Plan, 1973-76, Para. 10.12.

17 Op. cit., Para 10.13.

18 Op. cit., Para 10.16.

19 Development Plan, 1977,

20 Op. cit., p. 6, para 17.

21 Tuvalu Development Plan 1978-80, p. 1.

22 Op. cit., pp 145-53.

23 Of course, full participation of islanders in discussing the goals of development must be a two-way and educative process. Carried to an extreme, it can lead to an abdication of planning for a 'lolly scramble' – a preference for parochial and short-term goals at the

expense of strategy or less visible national and long-term goals. Islanders need to understand the price paid for neglecting the latter. As Hughes (1973) notes, the "grassroots mirage" of involving the people can lead to unrealistically long shopping lists of development goals for each island. This leads to government advising the people to be patient and wait. Then the people see through this tactic and demand 'bribes' for further support of the plan. It appears this situation might well occur in Tuvalu in 1980. The best way, of course, to involve the people is through an effective representation system of local government.

24 In terms of Anne Chambers' three alternative development options, it is a 'hodgepodge' though depending primarily on a Western model of development. For her thoughtful comments on development options, see Chambers, 1984, pp 160-1.

25 Sewell, 1983.

10   Abemama: An Atoll Economy in Kiribati

1   Grimble, 1972, p. 14.

2   Alkiri, 1978, p. 18. Bayliss-Smith (1982, p. 59) notes that coral reefs are "oases of high productivity in the midst of comparatively barren tropical seas". Like the tropical rain forest, the coral reef is an ecosystem that exists "in a climatically stable environment that has developed over a long period of evolution". Both are "rich in species, highly productive but depend upon an efficient and rapid recycling of a limited stock of mineral nutrients for their continued survival". Both these ecosystems are easy for humans to disrupt.

3   Roger Lawrence, 1983, p. 5.

4   Watters and Banibati, 1984, Chapter 2.

5   Ibid.

6   Op. cit., Chapter 8.

7   The actual planted area is likely to be somewhat higher. Figures based on aerial photograph analysis.

8   Op. cit., Tables 8.1 and 7.8.

9   Op. cit., Chapter 9.

10 Op. cit., Chapter 4.

11 Op. cit., pp 133, 148-51.

12 In spite of the hierarchical qualities of Abemama society, the spirit of egalitarianism, strong elsewhere in the Gilberts, is quite pronounced.

13 Watters and Banibati, 1984, Chapter 7.

14 This view is supported by the detailed income, expenditure and consumption data gathered as well as that on production. In 1972, a year of very low copra income, the mean income of 16 households in the stratified random sample was only A$8.16 per week, with estimated annual household income ranging very greatly from $1,218 to only about $85. Expenditure similarly varied markedly, with a mean of $4.09 per household per week, including annual tax payments and school fees. Overwhelmingly, income was spent at the local cooperative trading store, with the main purchases in order being flour, sugar, rice and tobacco. Small sums were spent on small capital items, feasts, gambling, debts and fines.

The consumption data which were also gathered over 10 weeks throughout the year showed that nearly 80 percent of the mean expenditure of the 16 sample households was on store goods (or 61 percent if spending on taxes and school fees is included), of which 45 percent was on imported foods, generally of very poor dietary value.

Local protein is important in most households' diets. Thus, 61 percent of all meals included local protein, and of this 87 percent was from fish foods. Local starches provided on average 63 percent of total starch eaten, and imported starches nearly 37 percent. Coconut foods dominate among local starches (nearly 73 percent), compared to 8.3 percent for pandanus fruit and 7.4 percent for *babai* foods.

Of the 11 households that had moderate to high per capita incomes of over $50, most ate imported starch frequently, and only one of this group was below the mean. Conversely, as might be expected, of the four households of relatively low incomes (below

$30 per capita), three ate imported starches infrequently, while the other was a little below the mean of 45 percent of meals. In general, consumption data indicate a definite tendency to consume more store foods (imported flour, rice and sugar in particular) as incomes increase (see Watters and Banibati, 1984, Chapter 7; and Team Report, 1984).

15   See Shankman, 1976; Gordon, 1974; and Chapter 4 above.
16   Watters and Banibati, 1984, Chapters 1 and 8.
17   Op. cit., Chapter 10.
18   Op. cit., pp 155-6, 168.
19   They are discussed in the Team Report, 1984.
20   Connell, 1975, p. 403.
21   Some of the following information is derived from an unpublished paper, Anon., 1972.
22   Skinner, 1968.
23   Riddell, 1968, p. 4.
24   Jansen (n.d.), p. 2. See also the remarks of the economist, M. Walsh and others, 1974, pp 22-28.
25   Anon., 1972.
26   Bohannan, 1964.
27   Anon., 1972.
28   Ibid.
29   Perhaps the most outstanding *imatang* who achieved much, especially in social fields, included H.E. Maude, Grimble, B.C. Cartland, Reid Cowell and D.G. Kennedy in the Ellice Islands.

11   Vicious Circle in Kandrian-Gloucester, Papua New Guinea: Report on a Development Options Project

1   This term was used by the Australian geographer, Diane Howlett (1973).
2   Developed partly from Seers, 1979, and Hughes, 1972.
3   Chowning, personal communication, March 2007.
4   D. Hulme, personal communication.
5   Hulme, in press, a.
6   See, for example, Valentine, 1979.
7   Hulme, in press, b.
8   Lam, 1982.
9   Ibid.
10   See Whitmore, 1975; Paijmans, 1970; and Sparhawk, 1965. An excellent summary is given in the ADB report, Ward and Proctor, 1980.
11   Whitmore 1975.
12   Chowning, personal communication.
13   Allen, 1983.

12   A Tale of Two Leaders: Independence, *Kastom* and Development in Vanuatu

1   Bonnemaison and Herman, 1975, p. 15.
2   Rose and Gurr, 2002, p. 233.
3   Shineberg, 1967.
4   Scarr, 1967.
5   Lal and Fortune, 2000.
6   Of the huge literature on cargo cults, three studies are perhaps notable for the quality of their analysis: Worsley, 1957; Burridge, 1960; and Peter Lawrence, 1964.
7   Fortune, 2000, p. 304.
8   Op. cit., p. 305.
9   *New Internationalist*, 101, July 1981.
10   Fortune, 2000, p. 305.
11   *New Internationalist, 101, July 1981.*

12   Lini, 1980, p. 15. The leader of the New Zealand Opposition Labour Party, David Lange, launched the book at a small function in Wellington, delivering a brilliant speech on Vanuatu without reference to any notes.
13   Rose and Gurr, 2002, p. 240.
14   Robie, 1988.
15   Patterson, 2002, p. 3.
16   Ibid.
17   Op. cit., p. 7.
18   Op. cit., p. 4,
19   Op. cit., p. 1.
20   Op. cit., p. 11.
21   This section is largely based on Bonnemaison, 1984.
22   Ward, 1971, p. 20.
23   Bonnemaison, 1984, p. 143.
24   Ibid.
25   Op. cit., p. 144.
26   Ibid.
27   Op. cit., p. 145.
28   Op. cit., p. 147.
29   Op. cit., p. 148.

13   The MIRAB Economy in South Pacific Microstates (with I.G. Bertram)

1   Op. cit., p. 509.
2   See especially Firth, 1959.
3   Brookfield, 1977, p. 125.
4   Ibid.
5   Watters and Banibati, 1984; Lawrence, 1983; Geddes et al, 1982; Sewell, 1983; Chambers, 1984.
6   Marcus, 1981, p. 62.
7   Loomis, 1984a, 1984b.
8   Hooper, 1961, p. 12; Curson, 1973, p. 16.
9   Curson, 1973, pp 17, 25.
10   Davis, 1947, p. 213.
11   Cumberland, 1954, p. 260.
12   Crocombe, 1962, p. 17.
13   Op. cit., p. 29.
14   Op. cit., p. 31.
15   Johnston, 1967, p. 110.
16   Op. cit., p. 111.
17   Ibid.
18   Kolff, 1965b, p. 124.
19   Bertram and Watters, 1984, Tables 6.15, 6.18.
20   Kelly, 1985, Table 2.24.
21   In 1952 and 1954-58, the copra price fell substantially below its long-run average – IMF *International Financial Statistics*, 1984 Yearbook.
22   Bollard, 1979, pp 54-57.
23   Stace, 1954a, p. 20.
24   For example, see Corner, 1962, p. 142.
25   See Shankman, 1976, Table 3.
26   Pitt, 1970; Lockwood, 1971.
27   Shankman, 1976. See also Lewthwaite et al, 1973, on Samoan migration to California.
28   Shankman, 1976; Pirie, 1976; and Ward and Proctor, 1980.
29   Lawrence, 1985, pp 547-62.
30   See, however, Douglas, 1965; Baddeley, 1978; and Loomis, 1984a and b on Cook Islander

perception.
31   Cf. Watters, 1968, based on Kunkel, 1961.
32   Recently a major research project has been undertaken by John Connell who has produced
      country reports on migration, employment and development in the South Pacific on behalf
      of the South Pacific Commission. The research project which covers 24 countries has been
      sponsored by the United Nations Fund for Population Activities (UNFPA). The reports are
      published by the South Pacific Commission, Noumea.
33   Bassett, 1969, which also includes Watters.
34   Hardaker, Fleming and Harris, 1984; Watters, 1984b.
35   Harold Brookfield, for example (personal communication, 1985), has suggested that these
      societies would be better classified under the heading MIRAGE, a reference to a belief in
      their non-sustainability.
36   Bertram and Watters, May 1984.
37   W.A. Lewis, 1954; Ranis and Fei, 1961; Harris and Todaro, 1970.
38   Elkan, 1967; Bedford, 1973; Bathgate, 1973.
39   Wolpe, 1982; Clammer, 1978; Perrings, 1979.
40   Myrdal, 1957, see pp 31-35 and 27-31 respectively.
41   Our MIRAB concept has much in common with the models of 'Dutch disease' (de-
      industrialisation) in the mainstream economics journals, e.g. Corden and Neary, 1982;
      Van Wijnbergen, 1984.
42   A useful recent survey of some of this literature is in Hayes, 1982, Chapter 2.
43   For example, Chenery and Strout, 1966.
44   Griffin and Enos, 1970; Griffin, 1970; Newlyn, 1977.
45   The concept of Dutch disease is also dealt with by Richard Willis in 'Development New
      Zealand'; see Willis, 1985.
46   Hayes, 1983, p. 193.
47   Asian Development Bank, 1983, p. 8.
48   Bertram, 1980.
49   Cf. Loomis, 1984b; Marcus, 1981.
50   Cf. Kelly, 1985, p. 13.
51   The data, and most of the analysis, are drawn from a recent study of these societies
      sponsored by the Institute of Policy Studies, Victoria University of Wellington; see Bertram
      and Watters, 1984.
52   Recently, Hayes (1984) and Bedford (1984) have shown that visiting between the Pacific
      islands and New Zealand is very frequent. In the 20-year period 1962-82, gross movement
      of people between the islands and New Zealand totalled 400,000. Net migration (as
      distinct from short-term visiting) represented only 9 percent of this figure, or 16 percent
      of arrivals. Hayes (1984) shows that a high proportion of the permanent Cook Islands
      migrants to New Zealand are skilled or semi-skilled; but this does not mean that unskilled
      people remain immobile in the islands. Interviews by the present authors with members
      of several households in Kakupu village in Niue suggested that people lacking the skills or
      confidence to settle permanently in New Zealand nevertheless visit relatives there and are
      familiar with conditions in the metropolis.
53   Curson, 1973, p. 19, Table 11.
54   Walsh, 1982, p. 169; Republic of Kiribati, 1980, Vol. 1, Table 9.
55   Government of Tuvalu, 1980, p. 52.
56   Ministry of Finance Report, 1980; Government of Tonga.
57   McKenzie, 1983, p. 19.
58   On the 'entitlement' concept, see Sen, 1983, pp 754-60; and 1981, p. l passim.
59   South Pacific Commission, 1984, Table 12.
60   Fisk, 1978, pp 6-8. The theme is developed further in Fisk, 1981.
61   Cf. Bellam, 1981, p. 29.
62   In this connection, it is interesting to note the discussion in the current Kiribati Development
      Plan of the impossibility of sustaining present living standards in a situation of aid-less
      autarky. See also Tisdell and Fairbairn, 1984.

63   See, Sen, 1966, for example.
64   Equally, it should be noted that some observers view the region as in a transition towards a condition of absolute dependence and social collapse – a view which we do not share.
65   Government of Kiribati, 1983.
66   Cited in Connell, 1980.
67   Baddeley, 1978, p. 457.

14   Has Progress Been Achieved?

1   Howlett, 1973, pp 249-88.
2   Bathgate, 1993, pp 961-4.
3   Lasaqa, 1984, pp 124-5, referring to the Native Land Trust Board File, Nabou Pine Scheme, 4/11/1737, 4/11, 4336.
4   'Phoenix: ashes to ashes', *New Internationalist*, 101, July 1981.
5   This account is heavily indebted to Naidu (2007), an excellent analysis of the four coups.
6   Naidu, 2007, p. 28.
7   Op. cit., p. 30.
8   Op. cit., p. 31.
9   The journalist Mike Field stated that the real issue is not the freeing of George Speight as a result of this bill but that a large number of ruling Alliance Party members would not be able to stand for parliament because of the many minor charges against them (Radio NZ, 17 June 2005).
10   Brookfield, 1987, p. 6.
11   Ibid.
12   Ibid.
13   Ibid.
14   Borovnik, 2004, p. 6.
15   Government of Kiribati Census, 2005.
16   TVONE News Report, April 2007.
17   Personal communication, NZAID, April 2007.
18   I am indebted to the excellent analysis of May (2004) for this section.
19   ADB Country Information: Papua New Guinea, 27 March 2007.
20   Based on analysis of Dr John Gibson, Waikato University, as part of World Bank poverty assessment in 1999.
21   Personal communication, Ann Chowning.
22   A conference was held on plantation agriculture in Port Moresby. See Walter, 1982, and Ward and Proctor, 1980. There does not appear to have been any substantial effort made by government to transform the plantation from its former colonial character and to save it for this new economic role.
23   Kent Wilson.
24   Cheshire paperback edition, 1970.
25   Jacaranda Publishing.
26   Ekeh, 1975, p. 108.
27   May, 2004, p. 319.
28   Op. cit., p. 67.
29   Bonnemaison, 1984. The literature on the early nefarious 'black birding' trade of forced labour, bringing many young men from Melanesia to work on the sugar plantations of Queensland, also included many volunteers who eagerly looked for new opportunities abroad.
30   Thompson, 1957.
31   Fiscal Strategy Report, 2006, p. 7.
32   Economic data are derived from online Vanuatu Government Statistics; Australian Government Department of Foreign Affairs and Trade, June 2006; US State Department, Bureau of East Asian and Pacific Affairs, October 2005; New Zealand Ministry of Foreign Affairs and Trade, Pacific Division, March 2006; and Fact Monster Country Profiles.

33 World Bank, 2006.

34 The exchange rate was A$1 – 82.6106 vatu in December 2005.

35 Chris Davidson, New Zealand Educational Adviser, personal communication.

36 Rose and Gurr, 2002, p. 238.

37 Fiscal Strategy Report, 2006, p. 34.

38 Rose and Gurr, 2002, p. 242.

39 Foley, 2006, E4.

40 *Vanuatu Daily Post*, Issue 1723, 11 May 2006.

41 Sodhi, 2006, p. 85.

42 Fiscal Strategy Report, 2006, Table 4.

43 Op. cit., p. 11.

44 Op. cit., p. 23.

45 Bazeley and Muller, 2006, pp 10, 15.

46 McElroy, 2006, pp 62 and 61-77.

47 Baldachino, 2006, pp 54 and 45-60.

48 Marsters et al, 2006, p. 31.

49 Bertram, 2006, pp 11-12.

50 Op. cit., p. 12.

51 Ibid.

52 Ibid.

53 Marsters et al, 2006, p. 34, citing UNDP country cooperation report on Cook Islands, 1998, retrieved from UNDP website.

54 Munro, 2006.

55 This was passed on to a thesis writer, Munro, 2006, Chapter 18. See also Boyd, 1968, pp 74-75. J.W. Davidson's *Samoa mo Samoa* is an extraordinarily interesting participant history of decolonisation. Although he was right that "the constitution had to reflect what the Samoans wanted, and not what New Zealand thought suitable for them", his close involvement with Samoan leadership did result in his writing "a high politics, or *matai* version" of Samoan society. He could not, publicly at least, admit that Samoan society had a dark side, as Derek Freeman once told Davidson. See Munro, 2006, Chapter 18.

Afterword

1   Spate, 1959; Burns et al, 1960.

2   Belshaw, 1965, p. 96.

3   Belshaw, 1967, pp 245-6.

4   For example, the methodologies and findings of recent studies on Fiji (Sahlins, 1962; Ward, 1965; Watters, 1969a; and Belshaw, 1964b); the Fisk model of transition from subsistence to market production (Fisk 1962 and 1964; and Fisk and Shand 1970); the comparative studies on Samoan social change (Pitt, 1970; and Lockwood, 1971); the similar analyses of Tolai development and change in East New Britain (Scarlett Epstein, 1968; and Salisbury, 1970); a range of Papua New Guinea studies on development and change (Finney, 1968; Brookfield and Hart, 1971; Brookfield, 1973; D.D. Mitchell, 1976; Ogan, 1972; Connell, 1978; W. Clarke, 1973; and Howlett, 1973); as well, of course, as the literature on the Solomons including the writing of Solomon Islanders themselves (e.g. Bogotu, 1968 and 1971) and other Pacific Islanders (Lasaqa, 1968, 1969, 1973).

5   Leslie and Ratukalou, 2002a, p. 3.

6   Bienefeld, 1984.

7   Keith-Reed, 2005.

8   Ward, 1985.

9   This is also confirmed by Leslie and Ratukalou, 2002a.

10 See the case studies of independent farmers, entrepreneurs, leaders, cooperative societies and community development in *Koro* and the case studies of enterprise in the Abemama report.

11 Pirie and Barrett, 1962, had already documented the 'malaise' of agriculture in Samoa

some 15 years earlier.

12   Brookfield and Hart, 1971, p. 301.

13   Allen, B., et al, 2005, p. 202.

14   In 2000, around 100,000 households, or 10 percent of all households in PNG, were resident in a province other than that in which the head of the household was born. Op. cit., p. 214.

15   A skilled and very experienced fieldworker can initiate wide-ranging discussions with villagers, inviting them to identify the various issues and/or problems confronting local or regional development, to prioritise them and to discuss how they can be dealt with. Over a period of weeks, the discussions can lead to broad agreements about the various problems, their relative importance and how to tackle them. Using a mobile computer and geographical information system, all relevant data, e.g., rainfall, soil fertility, crop harvests, prices, costs, income, transport costs, rate of deforestation, erosion data and land topography, can be recorded. Baseline fieldwork can also be carried out to be used in conjunction with the emerging plan, set of priorities and specific goals of the community. John McKinnon in Wellington has pioneered in recent years what he terms a MIGIS (mobile interactive geographical information system) approach and, supported by NZAID, has used it successfully in peasant communities in China, Cambodia, Vietnam and India. Robert Chambers of the Institute of Development Studies, University of Sussex, where I was a Visiting Fellow in 1979, has devised a similar facilitator approach.

16   'Pacific the stage for big powers' new rivalry', *The Dominion Post*, Wellington, 30 June 2007.

17   However, Japan's quota for southern bluefin tuna has been slashed in half for 2007 and the next four years. Japan admitted its fleet caught more than one-third more than its international quota. *Guardian Weekly*, 23 November 2007.

18   Conflicts in Africa since then and the Cold War have cost US$3 billion, equivalent to all the foreign aid over the same period, caused millions of deaths and shrunk economies experiencing conflict by 15 percent on average. *Guardian Weekly*, 26 October 2007.

19   *Guardian Weekly*, 23 November 2007.

20   Ibid.

21   Personal communication from M. Webb, Ministry of Foreign Affairs and Trade, 11 December 2007.

22   Although New Zealand made a substantial increase in aid in 2007-08, its official aid level for 2007-8 represents only 0.28 percent of gross national income, well below the 0.7 percent of GNP it is meant to reach in aid by 2015 to meet the goals of the 2000 Millennium Development Goals Agreement. The excess of NZ$866 million in trade figures for New Zealand's commerce with the Pacific islands is almost twice as large as total aid from New Zealand to all countries – a pattern which is unfortunately all too common for rich developed countries. In most years, a little over 50 percent of New Zealand's total ODA goes to the Pacific islands.

Australian overseas development assistance (ODA) to the Pacific (excluding PNG) doubled to A$383 million in 2004-05. Funding for PNG increased from A$334 million in 2003-04 to A$436 million in 2004-05, and Solomon Islands aid increased from A$38 million in 2003-04 to A$202 million in 2004-05 to strengthen governance and economic reform (about A$1 billion has been provided in aid to the Solomons by Australia from 2003-08). Vanuatu and Fiji programmes increased by more than 25 percent in 2004-05 (Australian Government AusAid, 2004, p. 24). Significant items in Australian ODA to the Pacific in 2007-08 are A$355.9 million to PNG, A$161.7 million in regional aid, A$95.4 million to the Solomon Islands, A$32 million to Vanuatu and A$28.7 million to Fiji. Australia, of course, has somewhat different geopolitical concerns to New Zealand and greater involvement with Asia: in 2007-08, total AusAid for Asia was A$1,119.2 million, of which A$458.8 million was for Indonesia and A$511.5 million for other countries in Southeast Asia. See Australian Government AusAid, 2004; NZAID, 2006 and 2008. The pattern of total ODA to the Pacific changes from year to year with new donors appearing, some increasing aid and others not doing so.

Index

Abemama, 18, 46, 52, 53, 88, 155, 163-4, 175-92, 255, 292, 331; cash economy on, 179-82; Chinese traders in, 182, 292-3; churches on, 18, 156, 177, 183, 184, 292, 293; economic development in, 162-3, 178-9, 180-2, 292-6; education in, 164, 183, 185; employment in, 178-9, 180, 181, 182, 185, 188-9, 292-3; geography of, 176-9; health issues in, 186, 293; household incomes on, 180-2; housing in, 292; incomes on, 180-2, 293-4; land issues in, 88, 163-4, 176, 177-8, 184, 297; leadership in, 183, 184; migration in, 164, 178, 182, 293; plantations on, 88; political organisation in, 177, 185-6; population issues in, 88, 176, 177-8, 188, 296; remittances in, 164, 180-1, 293; social change in, 189; social structure on, 177, 184; subsistence affluence in, 175, 178, 179, 180, 181-2, 187, 293-4; subsistence economy on, 179; trade in, 183; transport issues in, 179, 186, 292, 293-4; Western impact on, 164-5, 176-7, 182, 190-1; *see also, babai*; bananas; breadfruit; coconut palms; copra; fieldwork; fishing, commercial; food sources; natural disasters and hazards, impact of; papaya; poverty; Tangitang Union; taxation, issues of; water, availability of
Abemama Island Council, 18
Abemama, places, *see,* Bangotantekabaia; Kariatebike; Manoku; Tebanga; Tekatirirake
Abemama Report, 175
Ablingi, 211, 218
ACP countries, 145, 146
ACP Sugar Protocol, 145
Africa, 27, 28, 29, 66, 73, 145, 265, 302-3
agricultural development, 81-102, 130-8, 167, 217-18, 224, 256-7, 260-1, 264, 277, 278, 282; *see also,* Cook Islands; plantations
agricultural extension officers, 88, 123, 144, 215, 216
Agricultural Landlords and Tenants Act (ALTA) (Fiji), 148-9
agriculture: commercial, 79, 88, 89-90, 121, 278; traditional, 58, 59, 70, 73-74, 275; *see also,* cash crops; subsistence agriculture
Ah Koy, Jim, 288
aid, 28, 53, 72, 79, 88, 92, 190, 194, 195, 254, 255, 263, 264, 266-7, 268, 271, 272,

273-4, 275, 278-80, 281, 282, 303, 306, 309, 329; American, 306; Australian, 195, 198, 303, 306, 330; British, 190; New Zealand, 259, 261, 262, 298, 306, 325, 330; programmes, 43; *see also,* AusAID; Cook Islands; Fiji; Kiribati; New Zealand Aid; Niue; Overseas Development Administration; Papua New Guinea; Tokelau; Tonga; Tuvalu; Vanuatu
Aikman, C.C. (Colin), 259
air travel, 269, 293; *see also,* tourism; transport issues
Airagilpua, 203, 210, 215
Aitutaki, 59, 255, 260
Ala'ilima, Vaiao J. and Fay C., 83
alcohol, introduction of, 36, 55-56, 58, 69, 95, 206
Allen, B.J. (Bryant), 63, 83
Allen, Michael R., 57, 61, 63, 71
Alley, Rod, 20
Alliance for Progress, 28, 43
Ambae, 84
Ambrym, North, *see,* North Ambrym
American Civil War, 237
American Millennium Challenge Corporation, 306
American Samoa, 92
Anatom, 237
Anglican Church, 243-4, 245
Anguilla, 310
anthropologists, studies by, 74, 78, 257, 318, 319, 320, 322
anthropology, discipline of, 14, 24, 27, 32, 35, 37, 78, 318, 321, 322
anti-colonialism, 244, 245, 261
Antigua, 310
ANZUS, 43
Aoba, 57, 61, 63, 71, 235
Aoré, 237, 307
APEC, 328
Apia, 68, 82, 89
Apolosi Nawai, 50, 100
Apter, David E., 59
Arawe, 202, 203, 218, 230
Arizona, 285
Armstrong, Warwick, 32
Aruba, 310
Asia, 27, 28, 29, 32, 33, 48, 254; *see also,* Asians in the Pacific; China
Asia Pacific Viewpoint, 33; see also, Pacific Viewpoint